Traynham

60-15808

4-9-62

FRANCE, EUROPE AND THE TWO WORLD WARS

FRANCE, EUROPE
AND THE
TWO WORLD WARS

RENÉ ALBRECHT-CARRIÉ
Professor of History, Barnard College
Columbia University

HARPER & BROTHERS, PUBLISHERS
New York

TABLE OF CONTENTS

PART. III. THE FALLACIES REVEALED
Chapter V: LES ANNÉES TOURNANTES

Chapter VI: THE ABDICATION OF FRANCE

PART IV. EPILOGUE
ANOTHER TWENTY YEARS OF CRISIS

PREFACE

That ours is a troubled age few would deny, and the twentieth century is sometimes compared to such a period as the sixteenth—another great transitional passage. Almost fifty years after the breakdown of 1914, the contending forces unleashed, though not created, by the First World War are still struggling to achieve an elusive stability, making all the sharper the contrast with the far more settled conditions of the preceding century. But there are no real breaks in history, and our present uncertainties are but the fruit of earlier seed, of which the nineteenth century saw the gradual ripening.

That century, if stable, was certainly not static. The most important single aspect of it was the conjunction of economic and political developments, French and Industrial Revolutions—the combined effect of which was in turn the opening up of possibilities unprecedented for the great masses of mankind. Democracy, the rising of mass man, may thus be regarded as the peculiar nineteenth-century contribution to the unfolding of the course of history.

However, this phenomenon was largely confined to Europe and to some lands of European settlement. At the same time, the power that resided in Europe had the effect of making that small Eurasian peninsula virtual mistress of the earth outside the Western hemisphere. This great expansion of Europe, domestic and external, was the work of distinct units, increasingly national states, that carried it out under conditions of strenuous competition among themselves. It is a law of life that any existing organism seeks first of all to maintain its identity, and the sovereign state had come to be the fundamental unit within which society organized its existence. The anarchy that sovereignty implies was only mitigated by the tacit acceptance by all of the right of all to exist; the balance of power was the principle that made an ordered anarchy prevail among the powers. The very real consciousness of common heritage was insufficient to overcome the centrifugal one of separate identity.

As a token of their high level of civilization, the powers thought they had learned to accommodate their differences in peaceful fashion, a belief fostered by the occurrence of nearly half a century of peace among the great. They were mistaken, and the explosion of 1914 may be regarded as the result of too much power confined within too small a space. Power is often viewed as evil and corrupting, but the attempt to deny or ignore its existence usually has the effect of achieving results opposite to those intended by well-meaning ignorers of reality. Power, as Napoleon said, is never contemptible.

The purpose of the present discussion is an analysis of a particular instance of the operation of power. The First World War in this respect had such far-reaching consequences that its participants were incapable of appreciating their impact. Thinking of a return to interrupted normality, they failed to understand that an order had died, and the constraints they strove to impose on the infant developing made necessary another violent upheaval and the passing of a generation before acceptance could be gained for the view that, whatever the beclouded future might hold in store for mankind, it is irrevocably set upon a novel course. The two world wars and the intervening period thus constitute a single unit.

It is perhaps not surprising that the necessity of so wrenching a readjustment should not have been perceived in 1919; but the misunderstanding bedeviled the international scene during the uneasy twenty-year truce. Herein lies the reason for the title of this book. The First World War was only secondarily a Franco-German quarrel. But the conflict had the effect of showing the extent of German power, making the German bid for dominance in Europe its central issue; France, on the other side, was but one, and not the most powerful, member of a vast coalition. But circumstances made France the ultimate decisive battlefield, and her contribution to the common purpose in some respects the largest—conditions that insured her a correspondingly large voice in the peace. Conscious of her hurt and her weakness, France wanted above all to be ensured against the German danger.

The record of French power had been long and impressive, but its relative decline since Napoleon was clear. Moreover, of the two most powerful members of the victorious coalition, the United States was relatively insensitive to the power relationships of Europe; Britain, highly aware of these but blinded by tradition, looked upon the latest conflict in the same light as it had on earlier ones. Britain had fought the Kaiser, as she had fought Napoleon, because of a threat of continental hegemony, hence for the restoration of a suitable balance of power.

There was no question in 1919 that Germany's defeat was total, her power at the time nonexistent. But, to make matters worse, in addition two other great powers were eliminated: revolution in Russia had led to civil war and chaos in that country; the Habsburg state had simply ceased to exist. Add to this—again largely for reasons of power—the negative Italian contribution. The total result was to leave France the one effective and organized unit on the continent of Europe. France could not, even if she would, withdraw from Europe, and the distribution of power indicated above constituted for a long term a dangerously unbalanced and unsound situation. There were in Europe a number of states that shared the French desire to preserve the fruits of victory by maintaining the status quo; thus around the nucleus of French power there grew the French organization of Europe.

It is not very surprising that, in the circumstances, the French obsession with security and with the German danger should have appeared to Americans and Britains, and to some others as well, a pretext for hegemonic intent. America withdrew in disgust, soon to decide her intervention had been a mistake, while the Anglo-French alliance took on the color of a Franco-British duel. Yet all this was fundamentally the result of misunderstanding, for French policy was basically dictated by not wholly unreasonable fear. But there was irritation with France and futile half-hearted opposition to that nation instead of a positive contribution to a sound restoration of order. The Danubian situation called for solution, and at some future time both Germany and Russia would have to recover in the councils of nations places commensurate with their true power.

Twentieth-century France could not expect to, or be expected to, control Europe. In fact she lacked the will to do so, and the supreme irony lies in the fact that she failed to make use of even what power she had: asserting herself when there was no danger or risk, she abdicated as soon as a real threat reappeared. In this aspect of the situation lies a subsidiary theme of the present study, for the fundamental reason of the French surrender is to be found in the nature of the whole French complex. In other words, the fact that France is a democracy found reflection in the hesitancy and confusion of French policy, foreign no less than domestic. The French people in their overwhelming mass wanted security and peace, but they were unwilling to pay the price of peace based on the French organization of Europe; strange as it may seem, their shortcoming lay not in their aggressive will, but in the lack of it. The ultimate price was disaster, resulting from the fumbling of the thirties and the abject surrender to incompetent British leadership in 1936, which date is, for that reason, chosen as essentially the terminal date of the heart of this story. The events of 1940 came as a rude awakening to the French people no less than to outside observers. In this intimate interaction between domestic conditions and foreign policy in a democratic milieu lies a lesson for other democracies.

The pace of events in our time is such that 1939 seems far remote. Yet it is near, and the pitfalls of contemporaneity must be borne in mind. But there is also the compensating advantage that the immersion in one's own time makes possible an apprehension of its flavor denied remoter periods. It is hoped that familiarity with the French milieu may have contributed the asset of understanding rather than the shortcoming of bias.

In the preparation of this discussion, I am indebted to the Rockefeller Foundation, the generosity of which made possible a sojourn abroad, mainly in France, and to the Social Science Research Council of Columbia University and to Barnard College, which are to be credited with making time available for the writing of the results and for their final publication. Too numerous for individual acknowledgment are those persons who, in one form or another, have contributed their time and advice; but I must single out for mention Philip E. Mosely, Thomas P. Peardon, and Bertrand de Jouvenel. For the use while in Paris of the facilities of the *Institut des Sciences Politiques* and of the *Bibliothèque de Documentation*

Internationale Contemporaine I am also very grateful. Needless to say, institutions and individuals bear no responsibility other than that of assistance; for views and opinions expressed I alone am responsible. If this attempt succeeds in throwing some useful light on a piece of fast receding history, its purpose will have been accomplished.

R. ALBRECHT-CARRIÉ

Milan, October, 1960

PART I

INTRODUCTION: UNTIL 1919

CHAPTER I

THE PRIMACY OF EUROPE BEFORE THE FIRST WORLD WAR

1. THE NINETEENTH CENTURY BACKGROUND

A distinguished American historian not long ago published a book entitled, *The Political Collapse of Europe* [1]. While such a title, among Europeans in or past middle age, may evoke an instinctive first reaction of emotional negation, to younger Europeans and to nearly all Americans it is but the statement of a condition which is obvious. It is a commonplace and platitude to remark that in varying, but perhaps not too significant, degrees the former so-called Great European Powers have all sharply declined in power to a position incomparably lower than that of the two superpowers of the day; at most, a united Europe, the totality of its former Great Powers outside of Russia, might hope to exercise some balancing or restraining influence upon those same two superpowers. The political structure of Europe, divided into sovereign national entities, appears to many, including Europeans, as so outmoded that it simply cannot continue in existence. It has indeed collapsed.

However that may be, the widespread occurrence of such thinking in itself betokens the occurrence of profound change, or, perhaps better, registers the recognition of a radical alteration in the structure of world power. For it is well to realize how suddenly the new climate has come upon us. Those generations born at the turn of the century or earlier, the representatives of which are still extant in substantial if diminishing numbers, have had their early consciousness conditioned by a quite different sort of world from that which is now familiar. And one should also bear in mind that the normal operation of politics has the effect of leaving in positions of power to the present day a number of these people far out of proportion to their share in the population, a condition which by itself introduces great stresses in the process of adjustment to drastically changed situations.

So radical a change is not absorbed so suddenly. Spectacular events in history, French and Russian Revolutions, unexpected terminations of great wars, for all the accidents of circumstance and personality associated with them, cannot but be the end points and climaxes of

---

[1] Hajo Holborn, *The Political Collapse of Europe* (New York, 1951).

situations long maturing, of deep underlying forces at work, not the less crucial for being often obscure and undetected until their fruit has ripened. It is not the Second World War which catapulted into their present positions of power the United States and the Soviet Union, while correspondingly depressing the former Great Powers of Europe and Japan; that conflict merely served to expose, while doubtless itself contributing to accentuate, the results of a process long under way.

The roots of the change may be sought far into the past. It is not the purpose of the present essay to delve into the record of the prophecies of decline and doom of which pre-1914 literature would furnish many samples. But, confining itself to a nearer interval, that between the two wars, to examine some aspects of what may be called the last phase and stages of the change. After 1919 the prophecies of doom were louder; that of Spengler, [2] and even more than Spengler's book itself the vogue of it for a time, may be cited as illustration of the change in climate. Yet, by and large, the post-1919 world looked to a return to the *status quo ante* and a resumption of the pre-1914 trends interrupted by the accident — stressing accident rather than episode in a continuing process — of an unwanted war.

For some centuries before our own the power curve of Europe as a whole had shown a steadily ascending gradient. From the fifteenth century, when printing and the outside world were discovered by Europe, to cite but two of the more spectacular manifestations of change, a great expansive outburst of energy had gradually made Europe the power house and mistress of the whole planet [3].

Coming nearer to our own day and generation, the immediate historic background of our time may be regarded as the nineteenth century, the period from the French Revolution to the First World War. It is worth pausing briefly to consider the molding trends and forces of that period; they are those out of which the shape of our own time has come. The very shape of our own conflicts and confusions is the result of the intrusion into the mold of older issues of novel conditions, which past struggles themselves helped create.

The French Revolution is a clearly marked episode to which definite dates may be attached. Less definite in time but not less fraught with consequences was that phenomenon, originating in England, to which the label Industrial Revolution has been attached. The appellation is relatively recent, belated recognition of its more diffuse and more gradually revealed impact. Along with it went the rise to overwhelming importance of the "dismal science," economics, better named by its initiators political economy. For all that twenty years ago a book was

---

[2] Oswald Spengler, *The Decline of the West* (New York, 1928-1929). First published in Germany in 1922-1923.

[3] In this context those parts of the non-European world settled by Europeans, more especially, in the light of twentieth-century developments, the United States, must be regarded as extensions of the European complex.

published with the title, *The End of Economic Man*, [4] the present tendency is still, most of all perhaps in America, to take for granted, often unquestioningly if tacitly, the overriding role of economic considerations, indeed to consider man as if he had no other component besides the economic. This last phenomenon is due to the fact that, whatever else man may be, the basic truism must be granted that he cannot live without bread, while the growth and spread of industrial society have created such an intricate and delicate network of world wide interrelations that the task of securing this bread has become increasingly involved and at times seemingly uncertain.

Yet, in the more developed Western countries, the cruder dependence upon the accidents of nature, failures of crops and famines, has been eliminated. The living standard of this West has followed a steadily rising curve, till the point has been reached where the problem is one of management and distribution and the old contest for an adequate share of the goods of the earth could well be rendered meaningless [5]. But the word "adequate" must be stressed, for as soon as we emerge from the stage of satisfaction of the most elementary and basic needs for the sustenance of existence, its content becomes increasingly relative and psychological. The whole story of the modern welfare state is contained in this. Who, but one with a perverse sense of utopian humor, would, a hundred years ago, have thought of suggesting that a set of false teeth was a legitimate claim of the individual upon society and the state?

This may seem a disgression. That it is not will appear when we consider that this modern outlook could not have developed unless two conditions were first satisfied. First, an increase in productivity and wealth such as to bring within prospect of reasonable achievement the conditions that the demand implies; secondly, an awareness on the part of the masses of the existing state of affairs. Industrial development has been the revolutionary agency which has brought the change about [6], not only because of the vast increase of goods which it has produced, but because of the growing consciousness of the masses. This last phenomenon stems in the end from the spread of literacy and

---

[4] Peter Drucker, *The End of Economic Man; a study of the new Totalitarianism* (New York, 1939).

[5] Asia particularly presents a different picture owing to the relation between the rates of increase of population and of production. There are differences in the West as well. The United States and the Soviet Union can easily accommodate far larger numbers than they contain at present. Most of Europe, outside the Soviet Union, is also increasing at a substantial rate without having the nineteenth-century safety valve of emigration and being able to draw to the same degree as earlier on the resources of the extra-European world. A sustained rate of increase may lead to difficulty in Europe as a whole; it has already for some time been a major problem for a country like Italy.

The problem of population has been receiving increasing attention in recent years and the study of it is giving rise to a flourishing literature.

[6] Industry *per se* does not create more food any more than a larger population, but it is industry which has caused the increase to a revolutionary degree of the world wide exchange of goods.

education, developments between which and that of industry the connection has, historically, been close.

Broadly speaking, during the nineteenth century, the word democracy
may be said to have been the carrier of change. The word is older, and
ancient the concept, roots of which may be traced to Locke — and to
the Greek city-states; but this may be regarded as an interesting
illustration of an idea made effective force through the availability of
material means for its realization [7].

Here also, as might be logically expected, in some respects England
led the way. Locke's "people" were assumed to be the well-born and
the competent, and if Voltaire would have put greater stress on
intellectual qualification, the enlightened despotism of his contemporary
Frederick of Prussia was closer to his predilection than the inconceivable
rule of an uneducated rabble. But the concept was elastic in content and
the admirable political evolution of Britain has furnished at least one
instance of its gradual and peaceful extension till virtually no
restrictions may longer be said to hedge it.

When the dust had settled upon the quarter of a century of turmoil
that began with the outbreak of revolution in France in 1789 and
closed at Waterloo and Vienna, it appeared that France had achieved a
result which made her governance not very dissimilar from Britain's.
But the revolution had given rise to an henceforth lasting tradition in
France, and this, combined with the fact that France is of the continent
in a way that Britain is not, made her during the nineteenth century the
European standard bearer of the revolutionary democratic idea or ideal,
of whose struggles she remained the chief battleground. After many
vicissitudes and trials, in 1871 the Third Republic came into existence,
thereafter to become established with increased security. From 1871 to
1914 France was the only Republic among the major states of Europe,
but the Bismarckian and Wilhelmine Reich, for instance, while retaining
the monarchical institution, could not remain immune to the rising tide
of the masses, and even the autocratic empire of the Tsars found itself
allowing the hesitant beginnings of industry and of representative
institutions [8].

France and Britain thus became together the chief carriers and
models in practice of the democratic concept which, viewing the nineteenth century as a whole, came to appear as the inevitable direction in
which the entire world was moving, the "wave of the future" to use

---

[7] Our own time, since the First World War, has witnessed a continuation,
an intensification in fact, of that aspect of democracy which may be described as "material egalitarianism", but at the same time a regression of the
political connotations of the term, witness the totalitarian state. This last
aspect will be considered later in the discussion.

[8] As the case of Britain clearly shows, the monarchical institution is by
no means incompatible with democratic practice. The Low Countries, the
Scandinavian monarchies, and Italy moved along a similar path, but in
Central Europe and Eastern Europe the monarchical institution remained
associated with the existence of strong executive power.

a later day expression. The slogan, "to make the world safe for democracy," of which the United States became the principal exponent during the First World War, was adequate expression of the universally accepted view at the time of the trend of political evolution.

It may therefore seem odd in this context that the chief antagonist of Revolutionary-Napoleonic France, the indefatigable and adamant backbone of anti-French coalitions, should have been this same Britain, apparently nearest France in terms of ideology. Yet the reason is not far to seek, for Revolutionary-Napoleonic France constituted in British eyes a threat to national existence that could not be allowed to endure.

In the context of Anglo-French relations the war waged almost uninterruptedly from 1793 to 1815 is but an episode in the record of century-long conflict. By the beginning of the nineteenth century, Britain and France were, among important European states, those where national consciousness had reached the highest development[9]. But, starting from this basis, the French Revolution, though initially deeply colored by the eighteenth-century cosmopolitan, non-national outlook toward Man and Society, early came to take on a deep nationalistic tinge. It is another commonplace that nationalism as we have come to know it received its main impulse and shape from the French Revolution. This nationalism was destined to be another of the great moving forces of the nineteenth century, and it was fitting that its most outstanding nineteenth-century successes, the achievements of German and Italian unity, should have received their first effective impulse from Napoleon.

Democracy as such need have nothing in common with nationalism, to the more bigoted aspects of which it is even in some respects antagonistic. Yet the connection between the two has been close, chiefly in two respects. The French Revolution had the effect of transferring the basis of sovereignty from the monarch to the nation, with the result that quarrels between states became *national* quarrels, and the polite eighteenth-century conflicts between rulers, who constituted an international of sorts, increasingly degenerated into cruder and fiercer peoples' wars.

In addition, the democratic concept, especially in its egalitarian features, tended to become transferred to the international plane. Not only were all states sovereign, but the fiction of equal rights and voice must be maintained[10]. We shall observe the attempt to codify this tendency in the later institution of the League of Nations.

---

[9] Spain and Holland may be regarded in the same way from the point of view of national consciousness, but the European dimensions of Holland and the decline of Spain excluded either country from the possibility of playing in the nineteenth century a role comparable to those of Britain or France. Likewise, the international significance of the United States did not appear before the First World War.

[10] This raises the fundamental problem of power, central to the whole present discussion, and there will be occasion to observe the operation and consequences of the egalitarian myth in international relations.

Even more, the concepts of the rights of the poor, the dispossessed and the unprivileged, of their legitimate claims upon society, which may properly be regarded as deriving from the democratic idea, also became extended to the comity of nations. Thus came into usage such phrases as "the right to a place in the sun" and "the proletarian nation". This last concept may seem more properly associated with socialist doctrine, which is indeed the case, but for purposes of the present discussion it may not be unfair to link together the democratic and the subsequent socialist ideology, which we shall regard as having been absorbed by the former, especially in the light of developments after the First World War [11].

Along with Democracy and Nationalism, that now much abused term, Liberalism, is often used to describe one of the dominant tendencies of the nineteenth century. The word has been used to cover a wide variety of positions, and the label claimed by antithetic beliefs: the Liberal, or such self-styled, of the mid twentieth century stands on many issues for the very opposite of what his namesake of a hundred years ago accepted. The popularity of the label is itself token of its presumed desirability in the eyes of many. Nineteenth-century Liberalism may be defined in quite specific terms, and associated with concrete doctrines, for instance, *laisser faire,* either economic or political. But, going back to the etymological root of the word, we should regard it here as indicative of an attitude of mind, a general outlook, characteristic of the mind unfettered, hence highly flexible. By the turn of the century, it was the Liberal Party in Britain which had espoused the cause of the welfare state, retaining of its former devotion to unrestricted competition that aspect only which covered the field of foreign trade.

Regarded broadly, the dominant nineteenth-century *Zeitgeist,* or climate of ideas, warrants indeed the use of the term Liberal to describe it. This was one logical, and one might say inevitable, consequence of a development of continuity unbroken going back some centuries. The word science best sums it up. Allowing for continuity and germinal preparation as far as one may wish, it seems fair to say that the period of the sixteenth-seventeenth century saw, if not the birth, at least the real getting under way of the modern scientific development, and, as an accompaniment to it, the scientific spirit [12]. The eighteenth

---

[11] This point may be controversial and there is no intention to minimize or mask the considerable differences in background and derivation between Democracy and Socialism, especially the Marxian version, which are indeed in some respects quite antithetic. Until the Russian Revolution of 1917, Socialism was torn internally between the Reformist and Revolutionary tendencies; but after that event and the birth of the Third (Communist) International it does not seem unfair to say that Socialism has adhered to the democratic concept.

[12] There is no intention to quarrel with the claim that the scientific spirit was in existence among the ancient Greeks. Their Roman successors, however, were not possessed of it, and the tone of the Middle Ages, whatever else it may have been, can hardly be described as scientific. This does

century was much impressed by the achievements of human reason in which it developed what now appears far too naïve a faith. By and large, during the nineteenth century the stream of scientific accomplishment flowed in increasing volume and "faith" in science gained ever more adherents.

Now science cannot claim, nor ever has it claimed, that it can provide answers to the ultimate problems which are the proper domain of philosophy and religion. Such a claim would be senseless because tantamount to the acceptance of an unverifiable assumption. However, Galileo thought that he had good cause to accept the Copernican view of planetary motion, whatever counter evidence the Inquisition might derive from the sanction of Holy Writ. Science could not be prevented from exposing as rank superstition many time- and tradition-hallowed beliefs. With considerable enthusiasm, the Enlightened century attacked superstition and priests, if not the broad concept of religion.

For all that there was a certain religious revival — romantic and sentimental — during the earlier part of the nineteenth century, the former tendency generally prevailed. As science kept accumulating its store of information and enlarging the range of its explanations of phenomena, philosophers simply *had* to take into account its accomplishments, and from the thinkers, through the literate classes, the general belief in the unlimited possibilities of science gradually seeped through the entire society. By the turn from the nineteenth to our own century, homage to the concept of unlimited progress had become a cliché of politicians' speeches and those delivered on commemorative occasions [13].

Science thus operated at two levels. With the growth and accumulation of its contributions it came to secure a place of equal standing in ancient institutions of learning whose tone had been predominantly weighted by the literary disciplines [14]. With the institutionalizing of science, the connection tended to become closer between it and its

---

not preclude the existence of a certain degree of continuity and of certain individuals who were the agents of this continuity. Much work is currently being done on this aspect of the matter by historians of science.

[13] The novelty of the concept of progress is worth stressing. Traditionally, the golden age, or the Garden of Eden, was situated in an unspecified past from which mankind had fallen on less happy days. By contrast, the millennium was now in the future, and accessible through the simple exertion of man's own efforts.

Here also, it would be easy to quote dissenting voices, but the prophets of doom and gloom were not typically representative of the climate of the time; rather, as prophets will be, they were in advance of their day and are only now coming into their own. The normal time lag between the origination of new ideas and views, and their seepage into the common consciousness must be remembered.

[14] It is an important and significant fact that the modern scientific development took place to a very great extent outside the universities whose outlook long remained dominated by the medieval tradition. Individual workers and scientific societies played a very important role in the seventeenth-eighteenth centuries, and the honored standing of science in our modern universities is a relatively very recent development.

derivative applications, applied science and technology. The chemical industry of the late nineteenth century grew directly out of the scientific laboratory. The process which has grown enormously, especially in present day America whose industry will lavishly endow research institutes and foundations, was still young in the nineteenth century, but it had definitely begun. Germany, leader in many fields of science, gave it the first and most marked impulse [15].

But, important as the linkage was, more important still was the already mentioned impact of scientific growth upon the general climate of thought. When Darwin expounded his views [16], they could be drawn upon for support by various political tendencies. The totalitarians of our day have found Darwinism of use to their purpose. But what matters in this context is that if the Darwinian concept jarred many accepted beliefs, this fact was wholly irrelevant to its promulgation.

Somewhat the same effects resulted when certain theologians, predominantly German, began to apply the canons of historical critique to the sacred books of the West. The scientific approach is agnostic and skeptical, hence inevitably opposite to the religious. It need not be inimical in the sense that science will make untenable certain specific tenets of religious belief — this it will do at times and incidentally — but is so in the deeper and more fundamental sense that it tends to undermine the very foundations of acceptance of unverified assumptions.

Marx, who claimed to be scientific, put it as often in the extreme form of an arresting slogan, "religion is the opiate of the people." The new and rapidly multiplying urban masses of workers, increasingly attracted to Socialism, were in large numbers either indifferent or unfriendly to established religion [17]. As to their "betters," the ruling classes, a case might well be made for the argument that ethics and religion have never seriously stood in the way of the operation and exercise of power. The argument that religion is necessary as a *social* binder is old. At best, a polite skepticism came to be the order of the day. In a very real sense Europe was becoming dechristianized. The contest was unequal in view of the concrete and often spectacular achievements that could be credited to the free exercise of the human spirit. Whatever the merits of the new approach, that it was a corrosive and disintegrating force can hardly be denied.

2. THE APOGEE OF EUROPE

But stress was on the growing power of man over nature which he had already gone a goodly distance both toward understanding and

---

[15] The dangers lurking in too close a connection between industry and science, on the score of the fact that he who pays the piper calls the tune, should not be overlooked, but they need not concern us here.

[16] *On the Origin of Species* was published in 1859.

[17] A qualification should be introduced here, especially in the case of Britain, where the Labor movement retained a strong evangelical content, a development to which the non-conformist tradition was favorable.

subjugating to his own purposes and uses. This power of European
man meant power over other men, and the process begun four centuries
ago now reached its apogee and climax. Though the rhythm of its
progress had varied, the movement had never been wholly interrupted.
The first part of the nineteenth century saw it proceed at an attenuated
pace, but the end of the decade whose beginning had seen the united
second Reich make its appearance on the map witnessed a resumption
of the imperial race. The assumption of the imperial title in India by
the British Queen and the French crossing of the Algerian border toward
Tunis five years later may be regarded as initiating the new phase.

As late as 1880, the larger part of the African continent was still
blank *terra incognita* on the map. Five years later, the competition of
the Powers had reached such momentum that it was deemed desirable
to call in Berlin an international conference for the purpose of putting
some order in the anarchic process of scramble for territory. Within
a quarter of a century nearly the whole of the Black Continent was
neatly parcelled out. Asia was the scene of similar pressures from
Europe, and even though partition schemes for China and for the
Ottoman Empire did not bear fruit before 1914, as they did in Africa,
much attention was given to them in European chancelleries. As it
was, China had to give long term leases of small, but importantly
situated, bits of territory; both she and Persia were divided into zones
of foreign influence.

Whatever the reaction to the Powers of the objects of imperial
activity (in the case of China, seat of ancient civilization, it was
definitely one of resentment) the power of Europe must be acknowledged and respected. Moreover, this power was both secure and confident of the validity of its accomplishments. These were the days of
the modern great empire builders, Rhodes, Milners and Lyauteys.

As to the motivation, broadly speaking, the Marxist view that
Imperialism is a stage of capitalist evolution may be regarded as
fundamentally correct [18]. The nineteenth century saw industry spread
beyond the confines of its original British home, though still in
definitely restricted areas, mainly concentrated in Europe [19]. The

---

[18] But in a very broad sense only. The explanation fits well the cases
of Britain, Germany and Japan, less well that of France, where as will be
pointed out, other considerations also entered. Some at least of the Russian
expansion in Asia, to a point comparable to the westward growth of the United
States, is clearly also of a different nature from the ordinary acquisition
of colonies.

[19] By 1914 the United States had become an industrial giant second to
none in Europe, but the relative isolation of the country gave it a role
apart. American imperialism, as manifested in such an episode as the war
of 1898 with Spain, was a pale copy of the European product. Mention
of the Japanese industrial development is also appropriate at this point,
but Japanese interest remained exclusively confined to the Far East.

It should perhaps be pointed out also that when we speak of Europe as
the home of industry, only a part of Europe can properly be taken into
account, what has been aptly called "inner Europe," or "the Europe of

development of German industry after 1870, astonishing in both rate and dimensions, is the most impressive manifestation of the second Industrial Revolution. As industry spread and grew, so with it wealth increased, but also competition sharpened. The play of the traditional incentives, the search for markets, raw materials, and new fields of investment now came into full operation. Other motives existed, the missionary for instance, but they were feeble by comparison with the economic [20].

Most significant was the tone that went with the process, so different from that of present day apology [21]. Kipling expressed it aptly in the phrase "the white man's burden," of which *mission civilisatrice* was the French version. However that may be, we need retain the incontrovertible fact only that Imperialism was one of the ways in which the influence of Europe, economic, political, and ideological, was exported abroad. If we take the word conquest in the broad sense that will include, not only the crude use of force, but also the ultimately more subtly pervasive imposition of ideas and ways of thought and of life, often by willing imitation, Europe indeed had by the end of the nineteenth century [22] conquered the planet.

Much of the conquering was in fact quite peaceful in its operation. The commercial pre-eminence of Britain caused London to become the financial capital of the world. If the City profited handsomely from the services that it rendered, they were valuable services none the less that helped, like the accepted gold standard, the smooth flow of international transactions. For that matter, if Britain held a position of primacy, much European capital other than British found its way to the far corners of the earth [23]. Europe's industrial development, the outward flow of some of her accumulated capital, neatly balancing her unfavorable balance of trade, had served to bring into existence a system that made it possible for her to support a rapidly increasing population [24] on a generally rising standard of living.

---

steam," a region roughly bounded by a line running through Glasgow, Stockholm, Danzig, Trieste, Florence and Barcelona. Europe outside this line, the Balkans and Russia for example, was itself the object of some aspects at least of imperialism.

[20] As to pressure of population, it has been used as a domestically effective political, but not authentic, argument. Germans and Italians, like other Europeans, in so far as they emigrated, went in the main to regions long established in independence, such as the United States and Argentina, not to thickly settled Asia or to tropical Africa.

[21] As Europe finds herself pressed by her formerly conquered colonial subjects, the tendency is reasserting herself to stress the virtues and the positive accomplishments of the conquest. The United States, emotionally anti-imperialist, finds itself going through an awkward stage of readjustment as a consequence of its present world position and responsibilities.

[22] Historically, the nineteenth century clearly ends in 1914.

[23] For an illustration of this, see, for instance, Herbert Feis, *Europe the World's Banker, 1870-1914* (New Haven and London, 1930).

[24] The population of Europe roughly trebled during the course of the century, but the increase was not quite evenly distributed, France being the outstanding exception in the record of growth.

The fluctuations of the economic cycle were regarded as natural part of the normal functioning of an economy successfully operating under the sign of free enterprise, this success being due to the fact that, over the long term, it was an expanding economy. The uninterrupted duration of the process caused it to come to be regarded, in human terms, as permanent.

Europe took pride in her estate of power which, for that matter, went accompanied by intense activity and high accomplishments of her culture. To Europe, especially to Western Europe, came those who would make themselves conversant, through observation and through study in her seats of learning, with the sources of success of the modern world.

Yet we must realize that if it is possible to speak of European ways, and if there was indeed a wide area of common culture deriving from the Graeco-Roman and Judeo-Christian heritage, Europe was sharply divided into discrete units. Of the eight so-called Great Powers [25] of the planet, six were European. As a whole, the European community may be said to have operated in a state of ordered anarchy.

The state was sovereign, meaning by this that no law stood above it. War, consequently, may have been qualified as aggressive or defensive, morally just or the opposite, but in any event not illegal; it was a legitimate tool in the armory of power, sole ultimate judge of the decision to have recourse to it. Between the two great conflicts that enclose the nineteenth century, the Napoleonic wars and the First World war, there were many wars in Europe; but they were all, in comparative terms, of limited range and the damage they caused did relatively little to disturb or delay the general progress of Europe. This is why the period is sometimes described as a century of peace; in relative terms again, it was.

If sovereignty is the denial of law, the result was not nevertheless the chaos that might have been expected. There was an enduring sense, inherited from older days, of the legitimate right to independent existence of all the individual members of the European community [26]. This feeling was not born of any high abstract devotion to justice or

---

[25] Great Britain, France, Germany, Austria-Hungary, Russia and Italy in Europe, the United States and Japan outside. The term Great Power is one which is impossible of objective definition, yet of unmistakable application. Also, it covers a very considerable range of power; the difference was great, for instance, between the power of Britain and that of Italy, usually placed at the bottom of the list and the inclusion of which would even be questioned by some. The test of successful war was the clearest title to admission to the charmed circle. Thus, the Russo-Japanese was earned Japan membership beyond cavil.

[26] The modern state system of Europe, only now in process of marked alteration, is usually traced back to the settlement of Westphalia of 1648. The complete elimination of an important state like Poland in the latter part of the eighteenth century was therefore regarded as a breach of the tacit convention presiding over the relations of European states.

morality, although it may be regarded as having in itself become the basis of an international morality of sorts, but of the recognition that in the preservation of this situation of fact lay the best long term interest of all. It found its best expression in the theory of the balance of power, of which Britain was the staunchest exponent, but really adhered to by all [27].

The preservation of this state of affairs was made possible by the fact that the nineteenth century was innocent of our contemporary ideological struggles, associated with national entities, but the scope of which tends to be world-wide or unlimited. During that century, the Powers pursued what might be described as limited or "reasonable" (in the context of power) interests. The Crimean war was fought for the specific purpose of blocking Russian encroachments at the expense of the Ottoman Empire; Russia's defeat was not exploited to achieve more than that primarily negative aim. In the process of making Germany, Bismarck might gnaw some Danish land and wrest Alsace-Lorraine from France. The Franco-Prussian war was an important enough episode, but France, injured and humiliated though she was, continued mistress of her own affairs and, however diminished, one of the recognized great European Powers. A little earlier, this same Bismarck, having defeated Austria, was anxious to maintain that state's position of power in Europe.

One may speak on the international scene of a state of affairs somewhat reminiscent of that which obtained in the domestic British scene, sometimes labeled the Victorian compromise. The great nineteenth-century political battles of Britain were fought within the bounds of a large area of agreement on the fundamentals of the British system. So likewise, there was a wide area of consent among the Powers in the conduct and aims of their policies. The consequence was that the century, certainly by comparison with other periods, like the sixteenth century or our own, may fairly be described as one of essential stability.

The political counterpart of the economic scene, which last, as pointed out, was rooted in the relatively smooth operation of a free capitalist economy, made it possible in turn for certain ideas, or illusions, to take root about laws governing the operation of power. So long as the state is sovereign, it remains free to denounce any commitments that it has made. Treaties must, in the last analysis, always

---

[27] One of the cardinal principles of British policy may be described as opposition to any union of the continent, hence opposition to any Power, whatever it might be, that seems by way of securing mastery of all, or at least control of too large a part of the continent. Thus, the nineteenth century witnessed the shift of British opposition from France to Germany. The attitude of the continental states has been no different, but there seemed to be greater permanency during the nineteenth century in such conflicts as the Franco-German, for example. There was no dearth, for that matter, of shifting power alignments on the continent. The phrase "Britain has no permanent allies, she has permanent interests only," is hardly characteristic of British policy alone.

depend for their enforcement upon the existence of sufficient force behind them [28], and any state that feels itself able to face the consequences of its action may break or denounce a treaty. To be sure, treaties are subject for their lasting duration to the tacit clause *rebus sic stantibus*; this is but another aspect of the observation that treaties are largely a reflection of the situation, including the relationship of power, existing at the time of their making. That is precisely the point. If conditions are stable, or alter only with gradualness, there is a stronger likelihood that treaties will continue in force for long periods of time; and this condition in turn favors the establishment of the belief in the validity, permanency, even "sanctity" of international obligations [29]. The international character of Belgian neutrality was underwritten in 1839. Maintained for the better part of a century, it had come to take on the utopian aura of "sanctity," and the German violation of it in 1914, on the "realistic" plea that necessity is the higher law, produced in world opinion at the time a reaction of moral indignation which our own age, inured to a climate of instability growing out of a tormented search for a new basis of stability, may find it hard to appreciate to the full.

This last-named episode suggests a reflection which in turn relates to some of the previously discussed aspects of the situation: the existence and weight of public opinion. With the spread of the franchise and of literacy, the feelings and thoughts — especially the former — of the mass must be taken into account. The formation and molding of public opinion therefore had become an important concern of the politician's activity. Clearly, the press, and especially the newspaper press, was bound to play an important role in this development. The place of foreign affairs is a peculiar one in this respect, for public opinion was operating here in a domain relatively more alien to its competence than where the nearer and more readily apprehended stakes of domestic interest were involved.

To be sure, what may be called the popular or mass parties, such as the Socialist, had their organs, presumably devoted to the defense of the interest of the masses. But control of the overwhelming bulk of the press was in few hands, much of it representing specific interests, in addition to which much of it was widely amenable to governmental influence. To a large degree, therefore, the press was an instrument for the molding of opinion into desired shapes rather than a reflection of

---

[28] To be sure, it may be said that no state has yet been found to exist without a domestic police force. But no one, save libertarian anarchists, seriously questions the propriety of applying the law enforcing powers of the state to breakers of the law. In addition, many individual conflicts within the state are settled by the voluntary resort to legal action or by direct compromise on the part of the litigants.

[29] This situation has been discussed ably and at length by Professor E. H. Carr in *The Twenty Years' Crisis* (London, 1948).

its independent reaction [30]. There were appreciable differences to be sure, between say Britain and Russia, but even in a country like France, politically the most democratic of Europe before 1914, the press was very greatly colored by financial and governmental influences. [31]

One thing which it was always possible and easy to do was to appeal to popular prejudice and emotion, particularly to national feeling. Opinion was by no means unanimous in Britain on the score of matters imperial; but the Boer war, especially when it produced local reverses and evoked widespread foreign disapproval, elicited a remarkably unanimous surge of national emotion. Likewise in France, consensus was far greater on the issue of German interference in connection with Moroccan affairs than over the conduct of colonial affairs in themselves, where agreement was in fact non existent.

The consequence of this state of affairs was that foreign policy was conducted in a climate of considerable isolation, not from the realities of power, but from opinion and even from the presumed organs of that opinion, Parliaments [32]. In the democratic countries, Great Britain, France, and Italy, where ultimate decisions lay in the hands of Parliaments, to a lesser extent in Germany where the Reichstag could criticize and debate [33], foreign policy continued in large measure the somewhat esoteric preserve of foreign offices. These closely guarded inner sancta were consequently run along lines of tradition; foreign ministers enjoyed, not indeed complete, but very considerable, freedom of action. Their staffs, among whom competence was generally high, were usually recruited from an extremely thin layer of society, not to say Society. Steeped in tradition and history, pre-1914 diplomats also shared a belief in the reality of the European community. Jealous and punctilious representatives of proud sovereign entities, they had as a group a deep sense of responsibility, not only to the national interests which it was their primary task to defend and foster, but also to the operation of the community as a whole — in the last analysis to the preservation of peace.

---

[30] This should not be misread into a reflection on the qualities of the press, much of which was of a very high order indeed. We are concerned here with that aspect only which has to do with the relation between public opinion and foreign policy.

[31] It should be borne in mind that most European countries before 1914 had few, if any, restrictions on the freedom of the press.

[32] In some respects this made it possible to take greater account of the realities of power and less of the vagaries of a possibly well-intentioned, but probably ill-informed, hence incompetent, opinion. Whether this is the reason for the generally better quality of foreign policy, especially in the democratic countries, before 1914 than after 1919 is a problem worth pondering.

[33] This it did, and although in that country the executive had far greater constitutional powers than in the democracies, the Reichstag might have asserted greater influence had it been capable or willing, following the earlier British model, to make use of the power of the purse that belonged to it.

3. The Hidden Realities

This diplomacy, its ways and its agents, so recent yet so far away, was, like other aspects of the pre-First World War world, manifestation of an order seemingly secure and stable, thought fated to indefinite duration. The view has in fact been expressed that the outbreak of war in 1914 was a calamity unplanned, an accident unwished by any of its major participants. A case can be made for this interpretation. Yet, allowing for might-have-beens, for the role of personalities and circumstances, and without subscribing to any view of inevitability, the fact that Europe erupted into a conflict soon to become world wide and a stable settlement of which has not yet been found, warrants taking a broader historic view of its roots.

There were flaws under the seemingly solid surface of the pre-1914 world. First of all, conflicts among the Powers. Thus, France had not been reconciled to the loss of Alsace-Lorraine; Russia had not abandoned her Levantine ambitions. Yet these conflicts, and others like them, were old and in themselves hardly sufficient cause for open hostilities. The French people, by 1914, less and less thought that the injustice of 1871 should be righted by war. The most consistent opponent of Russia's ambitions at the Straits had been Britain; but Russia and Britain were now, if not formal allies, at least joined in that partnership known as the Triple Entente, the third member of which was France.

This same France traditionally had filled the role of Britain's prime enemy in Europe, and the remarkably successful colonialism of the Third Republic had revived the ancient imperial rivalry. In 1898, the two countries seemed on the verge of conflict [34]; but six years later the two effected what turned out to be an essentially lasting composition of their differences. Even so bitter a quarrel as the Franco-German issue over Morocco had, by 1912, been resolved, although the legacy of it was a renewal of suspicion and resentment between the two countries. A case could be made — and was — for the view that it was a measure of the degree of advanced civilization reached by this Europe that she was able in the last analysis to resolve her differences by means short of the ultimate resort to force [35]. The troublesome Balkans, not quite within the pale of civilization but geographically on the edge of it, might endanger the peace of their neighbors, but as late as 1913 the Powers had successfully managed through their joint action to put off such an extremity.

The differences among European Powers did not, therefore seem, individually, to constitute inescapable threats to the peace. More diffuse

---

[34] Fashoda offers grounds for reflection on the "inevitability" theory of conflict. Had it then come to war, we should doubtless fill our current history books with explanations of the "inevitability" of the clash, "natural" consequence of the preceding background.

[35] Colonial wars were considered in a different category, and, whatever the view of their righteousness and of the rights of non-European peoples, one must grant that, on the whole, they were.

and more dangerous were the mounting pressure and tensions of which the accelerating rhythm of crises was an ostensible manifestation [36]. It has been claimed, for instance, that one of the major, if not *the* major, causes of the war of 1914 was Anglo-German commercial rivalry. Allowing for the fact that there had been a relaxation of the political tensions between the two countries, it is also a fact that the safety valve provided by the colonial expansion had largely ceased to operate for some time before 1914 [37] and that the rapidity and success of the German industrial development created a pressure of explosive quality — explosive because it called for a rate of readjustment faster than the existing mechanism could encompass.

When Britain took the position that she did in the case of the two Moroccan crises, she was moved by the determination not to allow naval bases in German hands on the North Atlantic coast of Africa rather than by considerations of her own commercial stake in Morocco. But why should she have so acted unless from fear of German power, commercial as well as military?

The point has rightly been made that, in 1914, Germany should have been the Power most genuinely devoted to the preservation of peace, for the simple reason that her progress was so rapid and satisfactory that it was folly to risk its continued success on the gamble of war. And much of the story can be written in terms of the clumsy diplomacy of Wilhelmine Germany which managed to bring into existence the very coalition that it professed to fear. Yet, allowing that Bülow was no Bismarck, it was Bismark as much as any one who had helped unleash those forces that his successors could no longer control [38].

Mention must be made here again of that other force, nationalism. The manner in which history was taught to the young in European countries is best described by the French expression *bourrage de crâne*. This was useful when it came to arousing mass opinion. But against this may be cited much interpenetration of culture among the educated, a good deal of cosmopolitanism in the upper layers of society, and in the lower the international and antinational propaganda of Socialism. Most dangerous were those instances of peoples who were increasingly

---

[36] It is the primary task of history to explain how and why that which did happen happened, rather than speculate on might-have-beens. In the light of the sequel to this story the tendency has therefore naturally been to stress this former aspect of the situation; but one should not forget that this inevitable wisdom of retrospect tends to distort, by casting on the present knowledge that the future alone can provide, the reconstructed picture of the present once it has become past.

[37] Which is one of the reasons for the intensity of the struggle over Morocco, it being one of the last non-preempted bits of Africa.

[38] Whether he himself could have, had he been in power, is another of the nice posers of history. It is well to remember that, already during the last years of his Chancellorship, especially after 1887, the too delicately elaborate structure of his diplomacy had begun to show signs of instability, as evidenced for example by the difficulty in managing relations with Russia.

conscious of being under what they considered alien rule which they would shed if possible. Justice, democracy, and freedom could make a heady brew.

Two states were mainly affected by this last mentioned situation, the Ottoman Empire and the Dual Monarchy [39]. Apart from the perennial issue of the Straits, the story of nineteenth-century Turkéy in Europe, the Balkans, could be written as that of the successful struggle for emancipation of the Balkan peoples [40], of which the wars of 1912-1913 may be regarded as the final climax. Their very success, especially the Serbian, had marked repercussions on the condition of the Austro-Hungarian state. That state, from the standpoint of nationalism, of the tendency of the state to become identified with the nation, was an anachronism, and from that standpoint again, it is irrelevant to point out the economic merits of the Danubian creation. Whether reforms, sufficiently extensive in degree and sufficiently early in time, might have saved the Dual Monarchy, is another of history's interesting but futile posers [41].

The fact remained that Austria-Hungary was one of the Great Powers of Europe. Should it come to the worst — as in the end it did — the destruction of the Danubian Monarchy would create such a vacuum and call for such readjustments of power that, by comparison, the transfer of a province could be looked upon as a minor occurrence. Those in Vienna and Budapest who advocated the crushing of Serbia by any means, barring none, had a position that, whatever else may be said of it, was sound in logic; the same is true of those in Serbia who felt that the best, if not the only, hope of achieving their liberating ends was a general European conflagration. Such attitudes fitted ill with the operation of a diplomacy of "reasonable" and limited aims on which they placed unwonted strains. In a sense, the issue was not settled by the radical solutions of 1918, which is why the Danubian problem, albeit in novel shape, was a perennial of the period between the wars.

---

[39] So were the Russian Empire and, to a smaller degree, the German. But there remained the capital difference that the bulks of Russia and of Germany were, in the last analysis, Russian and German respectively.

[40] This introduced complications, for the small Balkan nations were clients of the greater Powers whose rivalries, mainly the Austro-Russian, thus became involved in Balkan politics. In addition, to the extent that they were successful in their primary aim of liberation, the Balkan nations focused on their mutual differences, reproducing on the Balkan stage a smaller edition of the larger European power balance and rivalries.

[41] There were those in the Dual Monarchy who advocated such a solution, both among the ruling (especially German Austrian) group and among the Slavs. But, as often is the case in such situations, the forces of moderation were overborne by the more radical extremes of conversatism on one side, of revolution on the other. What concessions were granted have aptly been characterized as too little and too late, and the assassination of the Arch-duke Franz Ferdinand in June, 1914 was a success for Austrian, and especially for Hungarian, no less than for Serbian, nationalism in their more virulent and intransigeant versions.

These stresses and strains were reflected in the sensitivity of the relations among the Powers. The issues over which diplomacy labored may at times seem trifling, not to say undignified. But if prestige was such a fetish, there was good reason for it; the feeling of insecurity, to use modern psychological parlance, did not allow the diminution of one jot in the recognized standing, lest one setback be prelude to another [42].

The same applies to armaments. The view came to prevail at one time that armaments and munitions makers were largely responsible for war [43]. To be sure, the presence of any weapon is, to a point, a danger; but the deeper reality lies in the fact that there is a demand, because of a felt need, for weapons. Armaments are much less the cause of conflict than the outward symbol of the existence of deep-lying tensions which, in pre-1914 Europe, abounded.

These European tensions, whatever view may have been taken of their true import at the time, were in full evidence to all. But there were other forces of change abroad which, if less clearly perceived, were, for the long term, no less important. In the process of conquering (in the above-mentioned sense) the rest of the planet, European ways and ideas had spread along with European trade and power. The great twin forces that went under the labels of Democracy and Nationalism were beginning to register effects among dependent peoples. China, if not formally dependent, was such in substance, a pawn in the hands of the Powers. Xenophobia ran deep, even though the futile Boxer episode merely served to show how ineffectual she was in terms of power. In 1912, Sun-Yat-Sen showed that she had already travelled far, not in terms of power indeed, but in the direction of acceptance, instead of blind rejection, of the Western outlook as necessary to her own independence and welfare.

Across the opposite end of Asia, the virulent and successful nationalism of the Balkan subjects of the Turks has been mentioned. As they became emancipated from alien rule, Greeks, Serbs, Rumanians and Bulgars hastened to import the trappings, if not the spirit, of Western parliamentary institutions. But even more, among the Arabs, Moslem subjects of the Sultan-Caliph, stirrings of distinct national consciousness were beginning to be noted. The Turks themselves, or at least those among them that appropriated the label "Young," attempted in 1908 a revolution whose ostensible purpose it was to modernize the ancient structure of their tottering state. Constitution and Parliament were their

---

[42] This is why the material content of such a crisis as that produced by the annexation of Bosnia-Herzegovina for instance seems so far out of proportion to the furore that it created.

[43] This view was especially popular, and nowhere more than in the United States, after the First World War. The famous Nye investigation and report of 1935 was at once an expression of it and a source of evidence for its advocates.

first care, Democracy that is, soon to be lost, however, in the greater stress on nationalism, and Turkification [44].

Hardly anyone read serious threats to the position of the European Powers in the performance of Young Turks or of Sun-Yat-Sen. Nor could anyone be charged with lack of perceptiveness for failing to see at the time in those abortive movements the seeds of what have become the great unmanageable problems of our own day, though such seeds they undoubtedly were.

In this story, Japan deserves special mention. Japan, too, had toyed with representative institutions. But more important is the fact that she was the only non Western state successful in appropriating the Western ways of power [45]. For this she was rewarded by the preservation of her independence, a British alliance in 1902, an unexpectedly successful test of power with Russia in 1904-1905, and a general recognition of the fact that she was eligible to Great Power status, hence to Great Power prerogatives. Japan might be a master, or a model, for much of the dependent Asiatic continent.

The Japanese accomplishment, especially in view of the exiguity of Japanese resources, may well command at least respect. But the greatest success story of all during the second half of the nineteenth century is unquestionably that of the United States. Unlike Japan, the United States is vast in both dimensions and resources. From the time the Southern dissent had been suppressed the development and exploitation of these resources had proceeded with equal recklessness and unprecedented effectiveness. There is no cause to rehearse in this essay the economic romance of American growth [46]. We need only retain the consequence that, already by 1914, the United States had become the first economic power on the planet. The statistics of production and commerce were there for all to see, and indeed American wealth and the wealth of individual Americans had already, in the popular imagination, passed into the realm of fable.

Yet in a sense this well known fact had failed to register in Europe. The popular conception of the United States may best be called a parody; in the teaching of history and geography in the schools of

---

[44] Mustapha Kemal finally provided a successful solution of the Turkish problem, but not until the cataclysmic consequences of the First World War had been visited upon the Ottoman Empire. He had belonged to the Young Turk group.

Since such attempts as those of the Young Turks and of Sun-Yat-Sen we have acquired a vast store of knowledge about the effects of the sudden importation of Western democratic procedures among peoples where these processes and ideas have no roots.

[45] The institution of a Parliament did not disrupt the political life of the country, but rather was so contrived as not to break the continuity of ancient institutions and outlook.

[46] It is a significant fact, and one not devoid of consequences and implications, that, allowing for differences of resources and tempo, the great economic developments of the United States, Germany and Japan took place contemporaneously.

Europe little attention was paid to America, and appalling ignorance in its regard prevailed to an astonishing degree even among the educated. That there should have been *any* expectation of Spanish victory in the conflict of 1898 may well seem humorous in retrospect.

But the reasons for a state of affairs that may soon rank among the unbelievable are easy to perceive. It was a simple fact that American contacts with Europe in terms of power had been few and relatively insignificant, certainly by comparison with intra-European relations and differences. The Monroe Doctrine, by none questioned, was expression of a long stabilized relationship, hardly associated in concrete terms with the fact of American power [47]. Before 1914, American isolation was not an object of debate, but a simple condition of fact [48] ; on the American side, the quarrels of Europe, whether national or imperial, were correspondingly the source of little knowledge and less interest. Broadly speaking, and despite relatively (in power terms) feeble essays, the temper of American opinion was anti-imperial; the development of the American subcontinent itself furnished sufficient scope for the expansive energy of the American people, who could in fact use the asset of a large European emigration.

American power was largely potential. There existed a respectable, though by no means unique or overwhelmingly superior, American navy; but the American military establishment was, in European terms, non existent. Why should European Powers have taken notice of such non existent power with which, in addition, their contacts were scant? As to alliances, overwhelmingly important care of the diplomacy of Europe, the word had little meaning, for the need did not exist, where America was concerned [49]. If anything, there was in America the ancient and hallowed caution that foreign entanglements must be eschewed.

The better part of half a century has passed since Europe went to Armageddon, and with the wisdom of hindsight we can easily say that America's growth and the ferment of the dependent world are two of the dominant facts of our day, easily traceable in their roots to pre-1914 conditions, though little appreciated at the time [50].

---

[47] For that matter, the non interference of Europe on the American continent had been as much, and for a long time rather more, a consequence of British rather than of American power.

[48] This is not to say that American foreign relations and foreign policy did not exist and had not even at times, especially in the Far East, been of importance, but merely to stress their proper relative significance in the context of power and imperial relationships.

[49] The nearest thing to it was the tacit, and largely not realized in the United States understanding that led to cooperation with Britain. At the same time, the imporatnce of this situation of fact between America and Britain should not be underestimated, for real community of interest is a stronger binder than formal paper guarantees and signatures.

[50] The other is of course the growth of Russian power. This must be said, however, that while Russian potential, like American, was always vast, the American development has followed a continuous line of growth and was already very considerable before 1914, whereas the Russian has been

4. The Peculiar Position and Role of France

In the sketch that has so far been traced, France has had a place, important but by no means overwhelming. It is generally, and correctly, said that the nineteenth was the British century, meaning by this that if any one Power is to be chosen as outranking all others in terms of world wide influence, that Power certainly was Britain. During the second half of the century, from 1870 to 1914, the central mover — or storm center — of the international affairs of Europe, whether by positive initiative or through outside reaction of contrast, was undoubtedly Germany. But, in view of the general orientation of this essay, in which the role of France will appear central, it is worth pausing a while to consider the France of pre-1914.

We shall not waste time over the hardy perennial of French decadence, moral and other, favorite theme across the Rhine and elsewhere, but the decline of French power, in relative terms at least, does not lie in the domain of the controvertible. One aspect of this decline, perhaps the most outwardly visible, was the demographic.

When one thinks of the centuries-long and overwhelmingly important role of France in Europe, the fact should be borne in mind that, until the turn from the eighteenth to the nineteenth century, France was far the most populous state of Europe [51]. Her population in Napoleon's time stood at some 25,000,000, but from then on the situation rapidly began to alter, most markedly after 1870. At the time of the Franco-Prussian war France numbered 36,000,000, roughly the same as Germany; thereafter, her population remained virtually static, reaching about 40,000,000 in 1914 when Germany had 65,000,000. Her numbers had likewise been passed by Britain's and by Austria-Hungary's, while Italy's were fast catching up. The causes of this phenomenon need not concern us here; the result alone need be registered for population is clearly one important component of power. [52] In addition, with the decline of the rate of growth, the age composition of the population alters, and the French had become much the "oldest" people of Europe.

---

the result of a release which was due to a violent revolution that, by all standards of its own orthodoxy, should have occurred anywhere in Europe but Russia.

[51] It is about the turn of the century that even vast Russia passed France in population. The population of Great Britain was less than half the French at the time.

[52] It has been argued that the biological drain of the Napoleonic wars lay at the root of the French decline. This would seem highly doubtful in the light of the experience of other nations; witness for instance the Russian recovery in that respect after the losses of seven years of war and revolution (1914-1921) and again after the Second World War. Social and economic factors are probably more important.

It is worth noting, in passing, that the French phenomenon of a decline in the rate of population growth is one which has occurred in other Western nations, but that the French came before all others in time.

There has been no dearth of durable Frenchmen, but there was point to the German quip that the reason why France was governed by people in their seventies was that the men of eighty were dead.

Numbers alone, however, are only one component of power, as the powerlesness of China's millions in this period attests. If Europe could easily impose her will on the far greater numbers of Asia, this was in the last analysis because in the use of the *ultima ratio,* the test of force, these were unable (save the Japanese) to offer effective resistance. The bigger guns were the products of the steel mills of Europe; reference has been made to be nineteenth century industrial development of Europe. Here again, as with population, French growth did not keep up with that of the other major industrial states. Next to the British, the earliest and most intense industrial development had been that of Northern France and Belgium. The rate of the French growth held up roughly through the Second Empire, at the end of which France and Germany may be said to have been in comparable positions. But after 1870 the discrepancy rapidly grew wider; by 1914, German industry far overshadowed French [53]. The slower development of industry, therefore, in the case of France compounded instead of compensating the manpower deficiency.

An aging population, a relatively slow rate of industrial growth, go hand in hand — which of the two is cause and which effect, we need not here seek to disentangle — with a conservative society. This may seem surprising when applied to pre-1914 France, generally regarded, and even sometimes looked askance at the time, as the radical state of Europe. In a sense, especially in politics, this view was correct. Radicalism flourished indeed in France; it was partly because of the revolutionary legacy, but even its more extreme forms, for all that France alone in Europe had unrestricted manhood suffrage and that opinion there enjoyed a freedom that some would have called licence, never seriously endangered the state [54]. The Third Republic was *bourgeois,* chiefly of the *petit* variety [55] and many a staunch *dreyfusard,* anticlerical defender of the Republic, was, in matters economic and fiscal, little aware of the new forces abroad in the world. Far less

---

[53] One important reason for the French retardment, but only one, was the deficiency of coal, which both Britain and Germany possessed in ample quantities within their borders. The loss of iron in the annexed territory in 1871 further aggravated the French handicap.

[54] French political nomenclature is misleading. The most typical political mirror of the Third Republic was the Radical Socialist party, a party which did essential work in defending the Republic against its enemies, real or presumed, especially the Army and the Church. But with the secure establishment of the Republic the party became increasingly, and especially in social matters, a middle of the road, not to say conservative, group, apt representative of the dominant petty bourgeois tendencies of French society.

[55] The *grands bourgeois,* the wealthy, existed and wealth wielded not a little influence in France, an influence, as might be expected, of an essentially conservative nature in politics.

liberal politically, backward where political institutions were concerned, Germany was in matters of social legislation a much more advanced and progressive state than France. As has been said, Frenchmen vote left, but carry their pocketbook on the right.

The political history of ninetheenth-century France was, as is well known, troubled. The cleavage going back ot the Great Revolution was not resolved; France had violent political upheavals that Britain and Germany knew not; and even after the Third Republic was securely established, the old division in new forms persisted [56].

But more fundamental than the spectacular raising of barricades in Paris, perennial leader of abrupt changes of régime, was the factor of continuity in basic institutions. Constitutions might come and go and party labels change [57], but the basic framework of administration remained the Napoleonic, which for that matter merely continued and brought up to date in this respect an uninterrupted tradition that can be traced back at least to Richelieu, and even further. France was highly centralized and bureaucratic, more so than any other state in Europe. This bureaucracy, of which much evil has been said, was not in the main either inefficient or incompetent; in many respects it was a source of strength, but certainly in any case of continuity and of stability — too much stability perhaps. Bureaucracies are, by their nature, not agents of revolutionary change, or even of change unqualified. The term "immobilism" has been used ot describe this condition of France; or, less kindly, crystallization, and even ossification.

The wisdom of hindsight is easy and deserves little credit. This relative decline of France, though not totally unperceived, was in large measure hidden — for a variety of reasons. Past history was one: the place of France in Europe had been so large and she had held it for so long. Even after the catastrophe of 1870, grist to the mill of the prophets of decadence, French recovery seemed remarkably effective and rapid. It could be argued cogently that Germany's victory was not so much the consequence of inherently greater strength as of technically superior management: on the basis of existing potential the outcome of the Franco-Prussian war need by no means have been foregone.

There was also much accumulated wealth in France, fed by a lasting tradition of thrift. French banking may not have been as developed as British, or as enterprising as German [58], but the golden content of the

---

[56] The Vichy episode in our time may be regarded as a belated flare up of the *ancien régime,* made possible by the unforeseen circumstances of the moment.

[57] The deep stability of the voting habits of the French electorate has been brought out in various studies among which be cited those of André Siegfried, *France, A study in Nationality* (New Haven and London, 1930) and the excellent recent monograph of François Goguel, *La politique des partis sous la IIIᵉ République* (Paris, 1946).

[58] "Unfortunately, France — although she had been for half a century, next to England, the largest exporter of capital in the world — had never taken care to organize itself as a world financial center. Curiously, on the very eve of the war, the largest Parisian commercial bank effected its ex-

peasant's traditional stocking could finance much Russian railway construction. Paris was able to exert telling financial pressure on the Berlin market at the time of the second Moroccan crisis.

This points to an important fact. German capital found its first and foremost occupation in the domestic field; but in the absence of a corresponding outburst of industrial activity in France, much French capital went abroad [59]. Money is power, to repeat a time worm platitude that expresses a lasting truth, and French money abroad served, to a point, to magnify and distort the true measure of French political power. Though not contesting that the Franco-Russian alliance of 1894 was basically a political agreement growing out of a political situation — German growth and behavior — the role of French loans in forming the connection cannot be gainsaid [60].

This was predicated, of course, on financial stability at home. Napoleon's Franc continued what its creator had made it, and France was ignorant before 1914 of the financial vicissitudes that have been hers since the First World War; the load of her state finance she carried with ease, and even the growing burden of armaments was no source of difficulty. There was no real financial problem before 1914, and the French *rentier*, typical *petit bourgeois* of moderate ambition and limited views, could in all safety entrust his pile to the unquestioned soundness of state funds.

This little man, so representative, is not a heroic figure. Good patriot he may have been, though rather antimilitaristic, but hardly the stuff of which world conquerors are made; the quiet cultivation of his garden was more within the range of his ambition. It was the Third Republic that built an empire second to the British alone. If ever there was truth in the observation that the British Empire was built in a fit of absent mindedness, how much more apt the comment in regard to the French. France did not even have the justification of the commercial urge that applied in the British case. Yet, in the space of thirty years, beginning with the establishment of the Tunisian protectorate in 1881, a huge area in Western and Central Africa was preempted.

British opposition alone, in 1898 at Fashoda, prevented the extension of French influence across the Nile to the Red Sea. The French accomplishment was the work of a handful of men, working with meager means, against indifference and sometimes active opposition at home. As a consequence, France more than ever appeared as a world Power. The real strength derived from imperial expansion, especially in the

change operations in London through the intermediary of the Deutsche Bank". Francis Delaisi, *La bataille de l'or* (Paris, 1933), p. 34.

[59] Interestingly enough, it was not primarily to the development of the vast potential of the French empire that this capital went out, but rather to such places as Russia and the Near East.

[60] Reference may be made on this point to William L. Langer, *The Franco-Russian Alliance, 1890-1894* (Cambridge, Mass. and London, 1929).

failure of more intensive economic development of the colonies, may have been rather less than that derived by Germany from her industrial home growth, but here again the impressive appearance, if only as a patch of color on the map, helped to conceal the true reality[61].

The result of it all was that France pursued, especially after Bismarck's dismissal, a very active and on the whole remarkably successful foreign policy. She was aided in this by the activity of some able diplomats of her own, men like the Cambon brothers in London and Berlin respectively, but most of all by circumstances. After the blood and iron Chancellor had to relinquish office in 1890, the Willhelmine Reich was characterized by a continuation of the outstanding rate of its growth that was accompanied by a clumsy and blundering diplomacy which, more by awkwardness than by design, contrived to convey to others the impression of its aggressiveness and ultimately succeeded in creating the very danger that it professed to fear and was endeavoring to avoid, the much touted *Einkreisung*. When the test came, Germany found ranged against herself all those whom, on the most pessimistic calculations, she might have expected; she was even abandoned by some of her formal allies[62].

France had not set out deliberately to encircle Germany. If her lost provinces were not forgotten, with the passing of time the concrete hope of their recovery had become much attenuated. She wanted mainly to escape from the ring of isolation in which Bismarck had contrived to enclose her. To this end the Russian alliance was welcome. It was soon followed by reconciliation with Italy, whose *tour de valse,* in Bülow's phrase, henceforth put that country in the category of dubious German ally[63], and it was possible for Delcassé to crown his work with the achievement of the Entente Cordiale in 1904. The Entente was no alliance, and it is credit to French skill that British susceptibilities were not pressed too hard. France was naturally pleased to see a similar composition of the Anglo-Russian imperial rivalry in 1907, a consummation beyond her unaided power to contrive, but which quite naturally within her means she assisted.

Mention should be made of the fact, to close this brief survey, that France's prestige and standing were assisted by her position in the broad

---

[61] On important aspect of French colonial policy was the levying of native recruits. This was especially significant in the light of France's demographic problem.

[62] This is not the place to enter a discussion of the war guilt issue. We shall return to it, however, because of its very great political and psychological importance after 1919.

[63] The Franco-Italian agreement of 1900, in regard to Morocco and Tripoli, and especially the exchange of notes of 1902, introduced an element of ambiguity in the position of Italy, amounting to a resumption of freedom of action on her part. Italy, ever devoted to a skilful exploitation of the balance of power, formally continued a member of the Triple Alliance which she did not denounce until 1915.

field of culture. London may have been the financial capital of the world, but Paris was the great cosmopolitan city whither flocked many students, especially from Eastern Europe, who thus became the carriers abroad of French ideas and culture.

It is sometimes observed that Paris is not France, just as New York is not America. In a sense this is true, yet both cities may also be regarded as the quintescence of the respective lands that bear them and both draw to themselves — to an undue extent perhaps — the live cultural forces of these lands. Whatever the relative decline in terms of material power, in terms of culture France fully held her own, a fact to which the standing of the French language bore witness [64].

In the narrower field of science, though by no means supreme or even in some disciplines foremost, France also held her own, but the essential mold of her culture was classical, or mathematical-literary, with outstanding accomplishments in the domain of art: the prestige of the *Ecole des Beaux Arts* and the long supremacy of French painting may serve as illustrations, while long would be the list of names in the purely literary roster. Even in the domain of religion, France, anti-clerical though she may have turned, continued the most lively focus of Catholic thought; she still remained the eldest daughter of the Church.

Characteristic of the tone of this culture was the high standing of and respect for the intellect that prevailed through society, different in this respect from the tone of English speaking countries [65]. The later American phrase "brain trust," with its disparaging overtones, would merely have caused puzzlement in France.

All this betokened a lower standing for the presumably less dignified achievements of commerce and technology and went hand in hand with the lag behind some other countries in the expansion of industry. At the opening of our century France had therefore suffered a very definite, if relative, decline in terms of power. If she was able to maintain an army as large as the German, she could only do this at the price of a longer term of service [66] and of a lower physical standard in the selection of recruits. Clearly this was a makeshift arrangement, no permanent solution.

However, to keep things in their proper perspective, the decline must not be overstressed. Even in terms of mere numbers, France was still a

---

[64] Until the end of the First World War, French was the universally accepted language of diplomacy. English achieved a position of parity in 1919 and the problem of linguistic disaggregation has made much further progress since, until now diplomats can commonly indulge in reciprocal vituperation in their native tongues.

[65] This has nothing to do with the quality of the specific achievements of individuals in one country or another. There was no dearth of outstanding names in science and in literature, though not in art, in England during this period. We are dealing here with the climate of a culture, and in that sense it would be fair to point to the exaltation of the businessman as characteristic of the tone of American culture in this same period.

[66] The three-year term of conscription was introduced in 1913.

large state in Europe. If Germany and Britain outdistanced her in the domain of industry, French industry constituted a very substantial development, while from the point of view of her economy as a whole, France enjoyed the advantages of better equilibrium between agriculture [67] and industry than either of those countries, hence in some ways of lesser vulnerability. The French empire, though underdeveloped, was an appreciable asset. French power was therefore still, by any criterion, substantial.

But what is important from the point of view of the present analysis is the fact that because of circumstances, historic, financial, diplomatic, and cultural, which have been indicated, the degree of the decline of French power was in part concealed. Instead of redressing the balance, the First World War had the effect of exaggerating it in disastrous fashion: real French power was severely injured, apparent power enormously enhanced, by the war. It is this situation, with the ultimate consequence of calamity for France, but not for France alone, that it will be our chief purpose to examine in the following pages.

---

[67] In order to maintain the structure of French agriculture and of the peasant class against the competition of more efficient large scale producers, such as the United States, Canada or Australia, French agriculture has been heavily protected.

CHAPTER II

THE FIRST WORLD WAR AND THE ENSUING SETTLEMENTS

1. THE AMBIGUITY OF THE WAR

On the 28th June 1914 the Archduke Franz Ferdinand, heir to the Austrian throne, was shot in Sarajevo. From the chain of events set in train by that incident the world has not yet been able to recover, for it is not unfair to say that the search is still going on for some sort of new equilibrium to replace that which was broken nearly half a century ago. The collapse of the European order initiated in 1914 and the subsequent failure of attempts to restore that order, or to find solid bases for a new, proceed from the fact that the forces unleashed have so far been unable to come to any stable compromise. And this in turn derives from a duality, born of the war itself, but which, presiding over the peace as well, made it one of unresolved confusion. To a degree, the quarrel is of language for the confronting principles, ideologies as we now like to call them, while using the same words put into them divergent meanings. This is the basis of the most tenacious quarrels. On this duality we must briefly dwell.

The assassination of June, 1914 was the act of individual patriotic terrorists [1], the sort that could with equanimity contemplate a conflict of European dimensions as the best, if not the only, occasion to achieve the liberating ambitions of their thwarted South Slav nationality. If this seems irresponsible behavior in the context of Europe as a whole, it is well to bear in mind that it was also a correct appraisal, correct in the sense at least that the end that was sought was achieved through the means that were used.

Peoples and Power

The Austrian government met the challenge with equal recklessness. Those responsible for the conduct of its affairs belonged to the school that perceived no salvation for the Dual Monarchy save in the ruthless

---

[1] Much has been written on the score of the responsibility of the Serbian government. That individuals in the service of the Serbian state were involved and that the government was less careful than it might have been in supervising their activity, while it may be granted, cannot nevertheless turn the assassination into a state-sponsored undertaking.

suppression of the disintegrating force of nationalism. Whether or not the state might have, by gentler methods, been preserved is by now a wholly hypothetical and purely academic question. We can only record the fact that where Serbians succeeded Austrians failed, and must be content to attribute this outcome to such broad generalizations as that the former were working with, whereas the latter were seeking to oppose and stem, the active forces of their day. But, be that as it may, it must be granted that Count Berchtold's and Conrad von Hoetzendorff's [2] solution of ruthlessness had a case in logic: it was no less than a matter of life and death for the state, for the preservation of which they felt that nothing short of radical surgery was counseled.

From the standpoint of this outlook war had become a necessary means of self-preservation; it was therefore defensive in its essence and the technical act of taking the initiative in its formal declaration became of secondary importance by comparison with the more fundamental fact of the persisting threat constituted by freely agitating, even murdering, Serbian nationalism. For Austria's self-defense Serbia must be destroyed or at least for a long time reduced to acquiescent subservience.

But clearly, on her side, Serbia could hardly be expected to renounce independent existence, however inconvenient this might be to others; if attacked, she could do no other than defend herself, trusting to the good justice of her cause — and to possible assistance from other, more powerful quarters.

Here, in fact, lay the crux of the matter. In isolation, a purely Austro-Serbian conflict, considering the relative strength of the antagonists, would have been a wholly futile performance of foregone outcome. Serbia would likely have yielded as she had done on earlier occasions [3]. But Serbia was not friendless. Russia has shown at times considerable detachment toward the little Slav brothers, the defense of whom could however make a convenient appeal to sentiment at home. The fate of Serbia could hardly be regarded a matter of life and death for Russia; but Russia's interests in the Balkans were of long standing and well nown. In the context of power, moreover, they were legitimate, however much their precise definition might be grounds for debate and compromise. Feeling herself to have sufficiently recovered from the military setbacks of the preceding decade, Russia would not this time accept the implications of such a diplomatic victory as the Bosnian affair of 1908 had represented for her prime Balkan rival, Austria. For the long term, Russia, or at least the then directors of her policy, could easily convince themselves that to prevent another thoroughgoing Serbian humiliation was to defend a vital Russian interest.

---

[2] Respectively the foreign minister of Austria-Hungary and the Chief of Staff of the Austro-Hungarian army.

[3] On two recent occasions, as an aftermath of the Bosnian annexation crisis and after the Balkan wars of 1912-1913, Serbia had yielded to the pressure of an Austrian ultimatum.

At one further remove, the ripples of the Austro-Serbian issue, enlarged to Austro-Russian, reached those two countries' allies. One reason for the Austrian diplomatic success of 1908 had been the unconditional support of Germany on that occasion which had caused Russia to recoil before the prospect of war. In Bismarck's eyes, the initial Austro-German alliance, going back to 1879, was to serve as an instrument of peace. The price that Austria had paid for the promise of German support in the event of Russian aggression had been a partial surrender to German supervision of her policy; Bismarck had conceived the alliance, and in fact used it, as an instrument to restrain Austria as well as Russia.

But the alliance, like any dual partnership, contained the germ of the reverse possibility; to a degree, it was also within Austria's power to influence, even control, German action, and that aspect of the relationship tended to assume increasing proportions as the circle of German friendships became more restricted with the passing of the years.

The conclusion in 1907 of the Anglo-Russian agreement, and with it the formation of the Triple Entente, greatly enhanced in German eyes the value of the Austrian connection. There was talk in Germany of *Einkreisung,* and if the term is more descriptive of German fear than of objective reality, the fear itself had become part of that reality. It had been one reason for German intransigence in 1908 [4]. By 1914, Germany regretted that her support of Austria in 1912 had not been more determined. This must not happen again, and for that matter Berchtold had seen to it that he obtained a blanket German promise of support tantamount to a German surrender of control of her policy into Austrian hands [5].

When it came to the ultimate test, Germany, though with qualms, did not feel that she could afford the loss of standing which pressure on her ally, let alone the threat to abandon the ally, would have entailed for either herself or Austria. Under the overriding pressure of military considerations she took the initiative of an ultimatum followed by a declaration of war against Russia. Yet in her eyes, what with the fear of the *Einkreisung,* this was no aggression, but a purely tactical act of initiative in defense against the aggression of others.

For Russia was not alone. There is much in common between the Franco-Russian and the Austro-German relationships. In 1908 again,

---

[4] That episode is a good illustration of the vicious circle of suspicion into which the relations of the Powers had been drifting. There were divergences enough between British, French and Russian interests; Germany, or better the reading of German intentions, was the strongest cement of the Entente. German suspicions, in turn, and the German attempt to disrupt the Entente, generally served *its* suspicions and thereby strengthened the connection.

[5] This is the famous so-called "blank check" of July 5 whereby Germany assured Austria-Hungary of her support without having taken care to ascertain the precise nature of Austrian intentions.

France had let it be known to her Russian ally that she did not see her way to the ultimate point of military involvement over a relatively minor Balkan issue; the alliance in the event had served as a restraining factor on one if its members, but the test of force between the Central Powers and the Franco-Russian combination had redounded as a consequence to the credit of the former.

Russia's disgruntlement with France as a result, and a possible loosening of their connection, was one aspect of the Austro-German diplomatic success. In France, this did not pass unnoticed and, by 1914, Poincaré [6] represented those forces in the country that, like the Russians, felt that there must be no recurrence of the episode — much for the same reason that Germany felt she must support the Austrian ally even apart from any merits of the latter's case. French feelings were no secret [7], and France, like Russia, was the object of a German ultimatum and declaration of war. France, in her own eyes dragged into hostilities against her will, was to fight in self-defense against a well and long prepared aggression. But here also, from the German point of view, taking the initiative was not so much aggression as merely the result of military necessity and of forestalling the inevitable.

Military necessity went in fact much further where Germany was concerned, one may say to catastrophic lengths. At the beginning of August, 1914, Bismarck's nightmare, the war on two fronts, had finally become reality. The presumed overriding necessities of warfare placed in the hands of the military the power of decision in matters primarily political; no one arose in Germany to contend that war is too serious a matter for it to be left exclusively in the hands of the generals. Hence the putting into application of the Schlieffen Plan, a simple and logical enough conception in its own terms. [8]

The war on two fronts was too risky an enterprise. The way out of the strait was the elimination of one front, and that without delay. Considerations of geography and physical dimensions, plus the likelihood of a quicker mobilization in France than in Russia, all pointed to the desirability of staking on the success of a blow, at once massive and lightning, the destruction of the former country's armed forces.

---

[6] Poincaré had been Prime Minister in 1912-1913 until he was elected President of the Republic.

[7] The second Moroccan crisis in 1911 had confirmed French views on the score of German aggressiveness while the lukewarm support of Russia, repayment of the French attitude toward Russia at the time of the Bosnian crisis, had created concern in France over the solidity of the Russian connection.

[8] The Schlieffen Plan was a purely military scheme of operations and the possibility of a German move through Belgium was no secret to anyone; the French staff, as was its proper function, had formulated its own plans to meet such an eventuality. The decision to put the Schlieffen Plan into effect was, however, a political decision, and it is credit to the greater suppleness of French political direction that it was careful to leave the initiative of technical aggression to Germany.

But the reduction of the French border fortresses might require sufficient time to endanger the whole scheme, dependent as it was on speed. The easier avenue of Belgium and the relatively unfortified northern frontier of France offered an answer. Belgium, to be sure, was neutral, her status under guarantee of, among others, Germany. But, as was frankly avowed at the time, necessity is the higher law the operation of which could not be impeded by such scraps of paper as even a guarantee bearing the German signature.

There was only one flaw in the political implications of the Schlieffen Plan. Moral crimes are not rare in the historic record, and the results of those that have met with success have generally become the new bases of legality and received the sanction of acquiescence registered in treaties. But should the Schlieffen Plan fail to achieve its purpose — the military destruction of France, first, thus opening the way to ultimate German victory — Germany would find herself saddled with the onus of a crime compounded by a blunder; of the two, the latter is apt ot be the less forgivable in politics [9].

Where Belgium was concerned, no one could possibly contend, nor has it been attempted, that her resistance to German demands, then forcible invasion, was any but the clearest case of legitimate self-defense. But matters did not even rest at this point.

As distinct from the major continental Powers, Britain was not involved in the prior formal commitments of alliances, even though her reaction to German deeds and words over the past few years had gradually caused her to drift into joining the circle that Germany so professed to fear. Her imprecise commitments to France were no dependable assurance of her action; none was felt in Paris where instead much anxiety on that score prevailed. A Balkan quarrel, though it had been enlarged to the point where most of the continent was aflame, might not suffice to convince public and parliamentary opinion that national interest was involved to the point where armed intervention was warranted. [10] The Belgian affair changed all this. Even apart from the by no means negligible factor of popular moral indignation at German faithlessness and brutality, clear British interests were now

---

[9] We cannot lay too much stress on the difference between the atmosphere of 1914 and that of our own time in this respect. We have become inured to the fact of shifting alignments in the international domain, nor are we shocked or surprised to find that a non-aggression pact is but a preliminary to the aggression of one of the participants against the other. But the world of 1914 had known a long period of stability (the guarantee of Belgian neutrality, for instance, remained good for three quarters of a century) during which it had become possible for the concept of the validity, even "sanctity", of treaties to strike root.

[10] While Britain had become increasingly involved through military conversations and naval arrangments with France, the nature and extent of her commitments remained imprecise. Even such commitments, moral rather than legal, as existed were not known to all the members of the government, let alone to Parliament or the public.

at stake: defense of the Low Countries neatly combined with defense of the respect for international obligations. For these defensive purposes, the peace-minded British peoples engaged in war.

Thus, with one interesting exception, the Italian [11], all the major European Powers found themselves engaged in war at the beginning of August 1914. More by accident than by design, the catastrophe toward which Europe had been drifting and for which she had been making mounting preparations, yet which neither her peoples nor their leaders in general can be said to have contemplated with equanimity, let alone actively desired, had, as a consequence of a breakdown in the operation of power relationships, finally come to pass.

The moral of the tale which has been summarized is simply this: all the initial participants in the war could genuinely feel that they had been driven to wage, not a war of conquest but one for the defense of their lands and their homes, however loud might be the cries of *Nach Paris!* and *à Berlin!* that accompanied the troops entraining for the frontiers. This indeed was essential, all the more so as it soon began to appear that all the technological and economic arguments used to prove that war of such dimensions must of necessity be brief were obviously fallacious. To keep in operation the monstrous machine that made unprecedented, undreamed of, and ever growing demands on all the resources of the nations, morale must be maintained. No better sustainer of it could exist than the persisting conviction of all that their plight was none of their making but the result of the inescapable necessity of defending themselves. The early publication of documentary evidence, the so-called Rainbow Series, in which all belligerents shared, was designed precisely to that end [12].

Yet, however much all the belligerents agreed that they were fighting a defensive war, along with this negative purpose went a desire to secure themselves against the dangers, real or imagined, that their opponents represented. The war was a test of power between the two

---

[11] Italy was a member of the Triple Alliance. In 1914 she alleged the defensive character of the alliance to justify her neutrality. The case was sound in law, granted the aggressive nature of Austria's action toward Serbia, but of at least equal importance was the fact that, ever since the turn of the century, Italy's loyalty to the partnership had become doubtful. Adjusting itself to the changing nature of power relationships, Italian policy reflected the fact that Italy considered her interests better served by a freer position "on the fence" between the crystallizing rival groupings. There will be further occasion to dwell on the Italian position and activity.

[12] These various official publications, blue, white, yellow, etc., books, consisted of highly selected and sometimes high-handedly edited documents. They were but the beginning of a long drawn out controversy, the magnitude and consequence of which were destined to overflow beyond historical dispute into the realm of active politics.

great rival combinations into which Europe had for some years been split [13].

The Central Power grouping would break the ring that had contained its growth. The precise fate of Serbia, in the event of Austro-German victory, would, whatever the details of the settlement, in any event sanction her destruction as a focus of South Slav agitation and thereby consolidate the creviced structure of Austria-Hungary. Whether Serbia was annexed or merely humbled into abject acquiescence, her defeat would open the road to the East. Austria's interests in the Balkans and Germany's in the Ottoman Empire could then join hands to build a mighty structure: *Mitteleuropa* would be reality and its imperial tentacles would reach out to Baghdad.

We need not at this point consider what additional concessions would have been extracted from France, Belgium, Russia and Britain; whether or not Germany should annex the mining resources of the Briey Basin and control Liége, for instance, in any event the result of the successful — and defensive, one should remember — breaking of the *Einkreisung* would be a colossal enhancement of German power that would place Germany in a position of unquestionable mastery over Europe, even though Britain, France and Russia could in diminished form continue their separate and independent existences.

Should things go otherwise, results of a comparable nature but favorable to the Entente, would come about. The initial thinking of the Entente was not in terms of the destruction of either Germany or Austria-Hungary. But there was much, short of this, that could be accomplished. Perhaps the clearest and most simply defined result would be the recovery by France of the lands lost in 1871; such was the battle cry of France. But of no less importance would be the breaking of the long hovering German threat; what precise measures would have to be taken to implement this consequence, there was time to consider.

The breaking of the German threat would be the great achievement of the Entente of which it was in fact the cement. Britain did not covet German land in Europe, but if past experience were any guide, imperial matters would command more of her attention. For one, the threat of Berlin-Baghdad, pointing toward the head of the Persian Gulf, could be expected to be definitely removed. What else and how much more might be done throughout the Near and Middle East would depend upon clarification of the Ottoman role in the conflict. Meanwhile, the British position in Egypt could be made more precise through the formal establishment of a protectorate over that land [14]. As to German naval power and the commercial rivalry that German economic growth had

---

[13] Italy having excluded herself from belligerency at the start, the fact of war clearly called for a further reappraisal of her position among the Powers. How she went about doing this will appear below.

[14] The establishment of a British protectorate over Egypt was proclaimed when Turkey entered the war on the side of the Central Powers.

been to Britain, it could be expected that both would sustain appreciable setbacks. Britain's by now traditional position of power primacy would be confirmed, although the precise manner of registering this fact was not clearly defined.

The prime focus of Russian interest was not German, save in so far as German power has been at the center of this entire tale. The Balkans and the Ottoman Empire offered more concrete fields of endeavor; one clear, if negative, gain would redound to Russia from the breaking of the Austrian or Austro-German position in those regions. Beyond this, it might be reasonably expected that some concrete, though yet unspecified, advantage would be sought.

The details of adjustment in the event of victory by either side would provide ample scope for the exercise of diplomatic ingenuity. There was ample room for manoeuvre, but the general aims of the belligerents may be considered to have been those just indicated [15]. The war could thus be looked upon in the light of either of two wholly distinct aspects: as a primarily defensive enterprise entered upon through no choice of its participants, what might be called the peoples' view, or as a contest of power that fitted into time worn patterns, what might be called the power, or foreign offices, view. But the two views need not a first be necessarily antithetic, as the foregoing discussion of initial war aims shows.

There was another possibility which stems from the consideration of the past record of many wars fought to an inconclusive compromise of stalemate. But this possibility was not to be entertained on any side until a long time had elapsed and the weariness induced by the frightful price that the war exacted, material as well as human, led to prosaic second thoughts of possible accommodation in some quarters at least [16]. The initial reaction to the outbreak of war on all sides was a curious combinations of unbelieving dismay that the incredible had happened and of enthusiasm in confident expectation of soon-to-be-achieved victory.

Power and Principles

Success generally attended at first the arms of the better prepared Central Powers, but it was limited success tantamount to failure of the initial German plan. After the Marne and the stabilization of the fronts during the latter part of 1914 the war became a test of endurance.

---

[15] There were naturally a number of smaller issues, the fate of Serbia, for example, which would have to be taken into consideration when it came to making specific plans for the future.

[16] The very fact that the defensive character of the war was stressed by all belligerent governments, if for no other reason in order to bolster the morale of their respective peoples, made it all the more difficult to effect a compromise which might be tantamount to an admission of the futility of the whole undertaking.

Would the Entente, of necessity on the defensive, succeed in mobilizing its own greater potential and other to which it had access and as a consequence seize the initiative? The fact that it eventually did, albeit through unexpected vicissitudes, is in brief the story of the war and of the ultimate allied victory. It does not fall within the compass of this essay to tell once more a well known tale, some aspects of which alone are relevant to its purpose.

Many wars have been fought to a stalemate, but peoples' wars, stressing simple emotion and high moral purpose, promote the desire for clear success. Nevertheless — and here we can see in operation the fact that though peoples might elect Parliaments their control of foreign policy was remote and indirect — as has just been indicated, the First World War did not find the participating governments thinking in terms of unlimited aims, or the total destruction of adversaries. The war falls within the category, for the first three years at any rate, of what might be called classical conflicts with specific and limited, though possibly extensive, results. There was in addition the fact that a consequence of the initial stalemate was on both sides an effort to break it by introducing novel forces, sucking an increasing number of neutrals into the maelstrom of war.

The Diplomacy of the War

Until 1917 the task of diplomacy may well be regarded as a continuation and an extension of its peacetime effort to organize alliances. The Central Powers achieved the notable success of Turkish, then Bulgarian, intervention on their side. The collapse of Serbia, following this last in 1915, gave them uninterrupted control of territory reaching from the North Sea to the Persian Gulf: Berlin-Baghdad was made reality.

The Allies on their side secured the addition of Italy, Rumania and Greece to their ranks [17]. None of these interventions accomplished the purpose of breaking the original stalemate, but naturally gave much scope to diplomacy. The diplomacy of the Allies tended to be more active and intricate, owing to the fact that it had to reconcile powerful divergent interests, whereas in the opposite camp matters were relatively simplified by the fact that the direction of the war, in all its aspects, remained to an unusual degree in German hands.

It should also be pointed out that these interventions, in so far as they could be justified by the new participants, must be so rather in terms of national interest and advantage than of inescapable defense as was the case with the original participants of August, 1914; they therefore tended to emphasize the factor of specific and limited aims in

---

[17] Japan entered the war in August 1914 on the strength of her British alliance but her role remained strictly confined to Far Eastern operations

the struggle. The Italian is a good case in point. Having declared her neutrality at the outset, the issue from that point became for Italy how best to profit from the conflict, whether by continued neutrality or by active participation on the side of the Allies. She conducted negotiations with both sides, mainly in Vienna and in London, the outcome of which was that she went to war in May, 1915 as the result of a carefully drawn up contract, the Treaty of London of the preceding month.

That arrangement promised Italy certain definite gains in the event of allied victory: the acquisition of the *Irredenta* still under Austrian rule, the Trentino and Trieste, somewhat extended for good measure beyond lines of nationality so as to procure a further advantage in the form of virtual control of the Adriatic, and some undefined colonial compensation. It could be argued — and was — in Italy whether participation in the war was the best way to further the national interest, but nobody could claim that the country was defending herself from attack [18]. As a result of these concrete, but limited, gains Italy's position would be enhanced and she might proceed to the purusit of a more active policy in the Balkans. But it was implicitly assumed that the Dual Monarchy, if correspondingly diminished, would survive as an entity and as one of the major Powers of Europe.

The consequences of German victory doubtless would have been far reaching. They certainly would have established German primacy in Europe and quite possibly have laid the bases for the ultimate control and organization of the whole continent in accordance with German interests and wishes. The prospect was not one to be lightly dismissed; it was in fact largely responsible for the world wide coalition that resulted in Germany's ultimate defeat. Since Germany was beaten in the end, what she might have done with victory may be left out of our considerations.

The Allies on the other hand did win the war and what they planned to do with victory is worth dwelling upon. Fear of German designs and power was the cement of the grand coalition whose members otherwise nurtured widely divergent aims, not to say inconsistent desires. The reconciliation of these often contradictory and rival aims was the task of allied diplomacy, the results of which alone need be retained here. While peoples were urged on to fight for the narrow and immediate, though vital, end of self-preservation and the broader and more remote achievement of general right and justice, the compromise between their purposes was essentially an exercise in the relationships of power.

---

[18] It could indeed be argued that a victory of the Central Powers would have constituted an eventual threat to Italy. There was force in this argument but such preventive action as Italy was taking in that interpretation was very different from the defensive position of the initial belligerents. It is of interest that even after her intervention the division of opinion continued, with the consequence that the war never commanded in Italy the enthusiasm of unanimity that it did elsewhere. This, needless to say, weakened Italian purpose and is one of the explanations of the country's behavior both during and after the war.

The fact should not be minimized or ignored that the Allies enjoyed some authentic moral advantages over the Central Powers. The chief of these, inherent in the map of Europe, lay in the fact that "oppressed" nationalities were to be found in far greater numbers under the rule of the Central Powers than among the Allies. [19] Nationalism was no allied invention, but the espousal of self-determination could be a useful asset to the allied cause. Crude power and pure principle do not mix well; Pascal's ideal, where force and justice are harmoniously united, often yields place to a condition where the latter is but a conveniently used adjunct of the former.

At any rate, by 1917, a whole network of agreements had come into existence among the Allies, charter of the future or, perhaps better, mortages on its shape. Britain had no claims on the continent. That France should recover Alsace-Lorraine might be regarded as foregone, the simple redressing of a wrong, but further acquisitions along the Rhine would be another matter. In 1917, France exchanged acquiescence to a Russian free hand in the East (meaning Poland) for the *quid pro quo* of her own free hand where the Western frontier of Germany was concerned.

Perennial doubts among the Western allies on the score of Russian loyalty to the alliance, combined with Russian suspicion of these Powers' designs in the Near East, resulted in their granting Russia her long cherished wish of outright control of the Straits. This happened in 1915 [20]. Prospective Italian gains have been listed; the Allies looked upon them as a high price which the enhanced position of Italy, engendered by the war stalemate, induced them to grant in their hour of need [21]. Likewise, Rumania secured the promise of Transylvanian gains [22].

In the imperial field the operation of the power factor was less impeded by extraneous considerations. Britain and France agreed between themselves on a division of German colonies in Africa, Italy

---

[19] There were no alien minorities in either France or Italy; there were substantial minorities in Russia and one might also include the Irish in the same category where the United Kingdom was concerned. As against this, there were French, Polish and Danish minorities in Germany; but, most of all, the various minorities of Austria-Hungary constituted together a majority of the total population of the state. As to the Ottoman Empire, the dominant Turks were a minority in it if one allow Arab in the same category as other nationalisms.

[20] This is one of the best instances of the effect of the war upon the relationships of power, which the details of the negotiations between Russia and her Western allies illustrate even better.

[21] The initial Italian demand for the bulk of the Eastern Adriatic shore was cut in half mainly as a result of Russian opposition.

[22] The Polish question was a universal poser. Both sides in the conflict favored the reconstitution of the country provided it could be done under their own, either Central Powers or Russian, control. The Franco-Russian agreement of 1917 was related to this issue.

to receive some minor balancing advantage [23]. When it came to the Ottoman Empire, the final solution of the problem of the Straits just indicated was natural prelude to the demise of the Sick Man of Europe, still possessed of substantial Asiatic holdings. Arab dislike of Turk was exploited, mainly by the British who enjoyed the advantage of physical proximity and whose imperial contingents constituted the bulk of the forces that fought the Turks in Asia. The result was tantamount to British control of the bulk of the Arab world. But, despite the advantage of physical presence, Britain could not ignore other interests at the Eastern end of the Mediterranean: a sphere was carved out for France in Syria and, subsequently, Italian interests were adjudged priority in Southern Anatolia [24].

Such were the arrangements made among the Allies during the first three years of the war. They provide in their totality a good illustration of the adjustment of contending forces effecetd through the function of diplomacy; they may be viewed as an exercise in the pure operation of power. Their eventual failure was not the result of faulty diplomacy in their original contrivance, but of the intrusion of circumstances and events, some of which might have been foreseen while others were largely unpredictable.

The Ideology of the War

These various arrangements, for Europe and outside of Europe, were not revealed in public at the time, adhering in this respect to the accepted prewar diplomatic practice to which the fact of war gave added justification. But we meet at this point the same duality or conflict that might be labeled peoples versus power. Not that peoples are invariably good and power an unmitigated evil, or that one need accept the naïve view, so popular after 1918, that the removal of secrecy would by itself suffice to cure all ills. Peoples — their component individuals, that is — indeed will vote in favor of "good" in the abstract, but when their interests are touched will fight for them no less than states. The point is rather that power operates according to its own laws. Where friction would be likely to arise would be over the incomprehension by peoples of the operation of power representing their collectivity.

The simple peasant or worker of France could with ease grasp the necessity of preventing the German seizure of his home; he could even

---

[23] Japan having entered the war, her position, also enhanced by the diversion of British and other power, secured for her the heirship to Germany's place in the Far East, a result that was of much concern to the United States.

[24] As this last item indicates, the partition of the Ottoman Empire was not confined to its non-Turkish parts. France also was to have a zone (Cilicia) in Turkey proper, which would abut on a Russian sphere south of the Caucasus. This series of arrangements was concluded with the allotting of the Italian sphere in April, 1917 and the statement of the Balfour Declaration in November of the same year.

evince enthusiasm for the recovery of the French soil of Alsace, though in pursuit of this last aim he would already wish to qualify the extent of his sacrifice. To ask him to die for Russian Poland or for Syria would be an altogether different story, though at this point the qualification is relevant that he could easily be roused to at least deep resentment if convinced that his reluctance to die for a French Syria might merely result in the latter becoming a British prize.

This French example could be multiplied and extended to universal application. How were governments, foreign offices, and diplomats to operate in these conditions? The millions in the various armies locked in conflict were in their overwhelming numbers simple peasants and workers — especially the former; they were the bulk of cannon fodder on which, as year passed into year, ever growing demands were made; whose loyalty therefore it was essential to maintain through simply stated slogans rather than subtle and involved considerations of power balance now or in the future. It cannot be gainsaid that much that has just been described of the work of diplomacy, if publicly revealed, would have furnished telling ammunition to those who saw the war as a clash of rival wicked forces unconcerned with the peoples whom they were exploiting. Such views could have found ears all the readier that the prolongation of war and its insatiable demands inevitably and by themselves tended to induce doubts and weariness of purpose [25].

Into all this the year 1917 introduced novel forces in the shape of events centering on what were destined to become the two Great Powers of mid century. In March, 1917 the Tsar abdicated in Russia; in April the United States entered the war on the side of the Allies; in November a second revolution in Russia was prelude to the withdrawal of that country from the war. From the standpoint of allied military fortunes what may be regarded as the exchange of the broken-down and exhausted organism that was 1917 Russia for the unlimited resources, the skills, and the organizing ability of the United States was to prove eminently worthwhile; it insured total victory. We are not here concerned with that aspect of things but with others for the long term not less pregnant with consequences and likewise intimately related to the element of power.

The Russian Bolsheviks who seized power in late 1917 were dedicated to a clear and simple view of history in general and of the current conflict in particular. Their actions were logical consequences of their

---

[25] The international position of Socialism had been virtually destroyed in 1914 when all the Socialist parties among the belligerent countries gave priority to their respective national allegiances. But, as early as 1915, Socialists had begun to recover from this setback and a series of meetings was initiated in Switzerland. Such activity was naturally not calculated to bolster the warlike determination of the belligerent peoples and was as a consequence looked upon with disfavor by the governments who feared that it might strengthen whatever defeatist tendencies existed in their respective countries.

beliefs. The war to them was but an episode in the murky record of capitalist exploitation and rivalry; conflict along national lines was senseless, made possible alone by the lack of understanding of the masses who should instead join hands accross the borders and unite against the class of their masters, be they German, French, British or Russian. To a degree, these views gained some ground among troops of the Central Powers, of whom their own command became distrustful, but not sufficiently to disintegrate their armies and to cause revolution in Vienna or Berlin. Indiscriminately, and with consistency, the same appeal went out to all from Russia, ex friend or foe, but failed to turn world war into world revolution. Pending the day when light would come, the first task was to save revolution in Russia — at any price: harsh terms of peace, indemnities, lost land were but details in the balance which, for that matter, was soon to be redressed [26].

If the appeal from Russia to all the belligerents failed, the impact of the revolution abroad was none the less considerable. What with war weariness and the fact that Marxist views had for a long time commanded widespread adherence in Europe, the various governments were naturally and properly concerned with the danger of defection at home. One way to meet this threat was to stress the defensive character of the war, the designs of the enemy [27], and above all clearly to proclaim to the world the aims for which the war was being waged. All this had much to do with British Prime Minister Lloyd George's speech, designed to precisely that end, of January 5, 1918 [28].

History has taken comparatively little notice of Lloyd George's declaration. This is because within three days of it another statement of a very similar nature was presented to the American Congress. President Wilson's Fourteen Points have been famous ever since he broadcast them to the world.

It has been pointed out before that German victory would have been the likely prelude to German control of at least the continent of Europe. In view of the constitutional structure of the German state, of its deeply embedded military tradition, which the success of German arms could but have reinforced, there was good enough reason to fear such an outcome. Britain's motivation is obvious which caused her to fight Wilhelmine Germany for the same reason that she had fought Napoleon's France; her own past historic experience, codified in foreign office

---

[26] The early Bolsheviks, idealistic though they may have been, were also very realistically aware of the factor of power. This is the explanation of their various tactical moves and dealings, with the Allies and with the enemy, all designed to serve the larger end of preserving their own control, hence the revolution in Russia.

[27] This was at once simple and awkward. The Bolsheviks, in order to establish their contention about the nature of the war, set about publishing the various secret partition agreements, the content of which has been indicated above.

[28] Appropriately, this program was announced in an address to the Trades Unions Congress.

tradition, made clear and strong her purpose in the struggle. Once more, as on other occasions, Britain found herself in the enviable — if understandably, to others, irritating — position where the narrow defense of self interest merged in the broader and higher value of the defense of justice.

Taking into account the technological advance of the century, the threat contained in the possibility of German dominance of Europe had implications that reached beyond Britain to the whole wide world [29]. This would constitute adequate justification for American concern with the European conflict and, in a way at once fundamental and simple, it may be said that America's interest was basically the same as Britain's. Very likely this will be history's long term verdict on the score of the causes of the intervention of the United States in 1917.

Yet this verdict, if true in a deeper sense, also contains a misrepresentation. For two things must be borne in mind about the United States of 1917. Great as its power was, that power had for the most part remained in military terms potential, and, by comparison at least with the activity of European foreign offices, the quip made in description of popular feeling in Britain that foreign affairs are something, usually not pleasant, that happens to other peoples, had even greater applicability in the American milieu. By comparison again, one may be allowed the slight exaggeration that America had had little foreign policy for the simple reason that there had been little need of one. Isolation was not a hard-fought-for moral virtue, but a condition as pleasant to contemplate and enjoy as the innocent charm of adolescence — whatever may be said of the persistence of innocence in grownup manhood.

America, moreover, in a sense more than any other land, had long been dedicated to the democratic practice. The fact is of capital importance, for the consequences of it, in some respects later disastrous, are writ large in the record of our time. In the eyes of the American people, whose European nationalities had on the whole with surprising thoroughness and ease dissolved into their newly acquired allegiance, "the quarrels of Europe are not our quarrels". With little cause to be acquainted with the intricate details and history of what often seemed from a distance petty feuds, let alone be involved in them, the first emotional reaction to 1914 had quickly yielded to the more normal wish for neutrality, and this popular attitude was strongly reflected in the representative governmental bodies. Constitutionally, the American Senate has a powerful voice in the conduct of foreign affairs, with the consequence that an unusually unenlightened electorate was a rather

---

[29] The world-wide repercussions of European conflicts are no novelty, as the record of four centuries attests. What was new at the time of the First World War was the degree of technological development just mentioned on the one hand, and the existence of Great Powers outside of Europe on the other.

more powerful force in this field than was the case even in the democracies of Europe.

The view that the outcome of war in Europe might affect America's future was conspicuous by its absence, and the Presidential election of 1916 which retained Wilson in the White House was fought under the slogan, among others, "he kept us out of war". Some diplomatic contact with the warring nations was unavoidable, but it was of a limited nature, largely concerned with specific matters that touched on concrete American interests, mainly the rights of neutrals in wartime. On that score, there was controversy with both sides. But Germany suffered a disadvantage inherent in the fact that the effectiveness of her action at sea depended on the use of the relatively novel weapon, the submarine. That some aspects of submarine warfare ran counter to accepted rules was for Germany awkward, just as Belgian neutrality had been awkward in 1914. The German solution was again the same: necessity is the higher law. Over the specific issue of unrestricted submarine warfare the United States declared war on Germany in April, 1917 [30].

The purely military contribution of America to the First World War was destined to be relatively small; there was no time for it to be other. But the total influence of America's intervention was enormous; it was in fact decisive. On this we shall not dwell, but we must stress other aspects of its significance. This foremost, the unique position of the United States among the belligerents. The fact that it refused to style itself ally but insisted instead on the phrase "allied and associated powers," bespeaks awareness of this unique position. If some could see in the insistence on distinction a reminder of the phrase, "I thank thee Lord that I am not like unto other men," it was nevertheless expression of the simple fact of authentic difference.

For whatever may be said of American motives in intervention, this is incontrovertible: even if one allow the judgment that ultimate security was at stake, the fact remains that America did not seek for herself any such concrete advantages as her associates did, and as have been outlined in the above mentioned network of agreements [31].

---

[30] This is no place to enter the vast controversy in which America allowed herself to become involved after the war, or to assess the unrealistic search for scapegoats that was it manifestation. If the Morgan loans and the profits of industry are invoked, it may be rejoined that the good wages of industry and the high price of wheat seemed no less attractive to the beneficiaries of those bounties. We shall therefore rest content with the view that America went to war in defense of what seemed her interest, be this taken to mean the long term consequences of German victory that must be avoided, the defense of her rights as a neutral, or the more narrow and immediate commercial and financial stake developed in the conflict.

[31] A French case might be made with conviction for the line of the Rhine, and an Italian one for the Brenner frontier, to mention but two illustrations. Even if one allow these, which is stretching considerably any concept of justice, the imperial agreements must depend for their justification on the concept of power. To say that such is the consequence of the inherently different situations of Europe and America, true as it is, amounts to a mere tautological emphasis on these differences.

The circumstances of the time of American entry into the war, where Europe was concerned, the stress on moral values, freedom, democracy and justice, were thus calculated to a nicety to give America a role of leadership among the belligerents. Such a place, through her leaders, she evinced no reluctance in assuming. In this respect it may be seen that the two great events of the year 1917, revolution in Russia and intervention by America, tended to have a similar effect on one aspect at least of the course of events [32].

Thus it came to pass that one important consequence of the American intervention was greatly to emphasize the ideological character of the war, and America became the natural spokesman for all the Allies, placed by the circumstances and the desires of their own peoples in the necessity of accepting American leadership. Ideological, like other, struggles are fought with the weapons of power, but the stress on principle has the effect of making them less amenable to compromise [33]. This we now realize and it is quite the fashion in our day to extol the greater merits of the more limited designs of power alone, more easily content with balance.

Lest we lose our sense of perspective, it is well to recall that the outlook of forty years ago was born of a revulsion at what seemed the sordid operation of power, unable in the resort to forestall disaster. That outlook had the great asset of drawing for its sustenance on a deep desire of man. Naïve it may have been, *noble candeur* as Clemenceau aptly described it, yet for a brief day at least a potent force in the magnitude of the tide of response that it evoked regardless of nation, of color, and of creed. Nor will it do, in denigrating fashion, to argue that all the while America was merely following the line of her best interest. If it be the best interest of America that the world be at peace and open to her trade, this may be called America's good fortune; surely no cause for complacency in Americans, but none the less a fact from which others may derive benefit as well [34].

America disclaimed any quarrel with the German people, as with any other people for that matter. Still rooted in the eighteenth-century view of man, of universal type and perfectible, the American view held

---

[32] It must not be forgotten that the Russian Revolution was at first viewed with sympathy by the Western democracies for it tended to bolster their own moral position in so far as they presented themselves as opponents of undemocratic German militarism. Equally naturally, the fact of defection under Bolshevik leadership was viewed mainly, in the light of its military consequences, as betrayal.

[33] This phenomenon is well illustrated by the conflict that grew out of the French Revolution and by the long drawn out religious wars of the sixteenth century.

[34] A good deal of this may be said to hold after the Second World War with the important qualification that, owing to her deep involvement in the present harsh contest for power, much in the same way that European Powers used to be involved, the strength of America's moral appeal has been greatly weakened.

that all the German people needed was to destroy, or have destroyed for them, the superstructure of their military state and their undemocratic constitution. Let them but once embrace the blessings of the democratic way and they, like all who did likewise, would be devoted to the arts of peace. Democracy meant peace, the great aim of the war therefore was "to make the world safe for democracy," and since this was the avowed purpose of the current struggle, it was also "a war to end all wars".

The battered wisdom of retrospect and failure may make it clear to us that such views were not so much ideas or ideals born in cloistered seclusion from reality; they were the expression of historic tendency combined with a failure to appreciate the novel realities to which the nineteenth century had yielded, a misunderstanding of the true nature of power, and an inadequate appreciation of the unique and exceptional nature of the political evolution of the English-speaking peoples. But all this does not alter the reality of the vision of 1918.

Be that as it may, and however lofty the motivation, a war was on which must be fought and won. The heights must then be descended and the realities, however mean, of frontiers, trade, finance, even for a while and in places bare existence, must be attended to. Mention was made before of Lloyd George's now largely forgotten speech of the 5th January, 1918, largely forgotten on account of President Wilson's resounding manifesto of three days later.

2. The Ambiguity of the Peace

Background of the Peace

The fact that it was Wilson's rather than Lloyd George's statement that caught the world's imagination was the result of two conditions, one moral and one physical. The first, just indicated, derived from the position of disinterest of the United States where material advantage was concerned; the second from the power of America, for the first time fully translated from potential into actual.

No clearer illustration than this situation could be cited of the duality which, accentuated by the circumstances of the war itself, was about to color the peace as well. Had a state of affairs in the world's troubled record of strife been reached where force and justice were at last united, and was as a result the promise of the future, the bright new day of universal peace, about to come to life? Many thought so, and the phrase "New Order," freely bandied about and in earnestness coined, is characteristic of the temper of the moment. Or was this a case of one more Utopia which, like earlier ones, would soon dissolve in face of the hard facts of power?

It was to take less than two decades to furnish a definitive answer to these questions. But if the debate has long been stilled, the reality of the duality, especially in late 1918 and early in the following year, must be stressed for it was precisely because of it that there prevailed over the peace a confusion that may in the end be said to have resulted in making the worst of both worlds: defeat and discredit of the ideal, unable in the last resort to control power; but also power operating in confusion, in machiavellian guise appropriating to its own purposes the attraction of spurious and debased ideal [35].

The high point of illusion, naturally enough, occurred during the brief interval between the termination of physical hostilities in November, 1918, and the peace congress that opened two months later. One fact stands out which adequately bears witness to the quality of the prevailing atmosphere. In December, President Wilson, having decided to participate in person in the peacemaking process, arrived in France [36]. He used the time before the formal opening of discussions to visit Britain as well as Italy. His tour of the Western capitals was a triumphal progress that revealed the degree to which the promise that he had come to personify had captured the imagination and support of the masses. There was danger in this and governments were anxious over what seemed to them a potential challenge to their control of their own peoples [37].

Some aspects of the conditions that constituted the immediate background of the peace warrant consideration. They may conveniently be put under three heads: the Fourteen Points themselves and their significance; that of the subsequent armisitce contract; finally, the true state of power relationships at the end of the war.

What has been said thus far sufficiently explains why Wilson's Fourteen Points are a historic document of prime importance. There is no cause to analyze their genesis [38] or the detail of their content; it

---

[35] The best illustration of this last result, with which there will be cause to deal later at length, is furnished by the case of Italian Fascism and of German Nazism which drew much of their strength from their appeal to perverted ideal.

[36] This decision of President Wilson, and the wisdom or lack of wisdom of it, have been the subject of much debate, especially in the United States. The decision was primarily due to the fact that, in the last analysis, Wilson trusted none but himself to fight for the things he believed in. It raised certain awkward issues which stemmed in the main from the American constitutional structure: the relatively minor one of Wilson's own position vis-à-vis the chief allied delegates (Chief Executive or Prime Minister), and the more troublesome one of his position at home, as Chief Executive and party head. The election of November 1918 had rebuffed Wilson's appeal to the American electorate to return a Democratic Congress as the surest way to strengthen his position of American representative abroad. This last incident may be regarded as an illustration of the intrusion of politics and power (domestic in this instance) into the operation of higher purpose.

[37] In Rome, for instance, pretexts were found to frustrate Wilson of the promised opportunity to address the populace.

[38] The Fourteen Points have been denigrated as an instrument of propaganda. This, of course, they were, but that does not invalidate their significance o rinterest, for, as pointed out before, it was a simple fact that

will suffice to say that they may be regarded as the culmination or climax of the nineteenth-century trends of Democracy and of Nationalism. Their essence may accordingly be summed up under two heads. The greater part of them amount to sanction of the right of peoples to independence, self-determination, in enumerated specific instances. This is important, for it has been pointed out before that the allied war aims until 1917 had contained no such far reaching intention as the complete destruction of Austria-Hungary, for example. Clearly, however, American advocacy of the independence of Czechs, of Poles, or of any other authentic ethnic group for that matter, had an authority unchallenged by any possible suspicion of ulterior motives of selfish gain [39]. It was principle that Wilson was advocating, and simple principle at that, reducible to elementary justice. There was such a thing as a Polish people; why then should Poles be ruled by Russians, Germans or Austrians if they would rather rule themselves? Why, indeed?

There is to this a simple answer, namely that Poles (or whatever group one may wish to insert in their place) are not fit to govern themselves and if allowed to do so would merely become a focus of instability and a likely cause of conflict around them. This view, in many cases, is not to be lightly dismissed; but who in 1918, or for that matter now, that holds public office, would dare openly so to declare? [40] This fact itself is measure of the degree of strength achieved by the democratic myth or, if one prefer, the rising of the masses [41].

---

the majority of subject peoples were under the rule of the Central Powers. The principle of nationality was indeed useful to the Allies but hardly a synthetic invention of theirs.

It is to the point to recall that most of the Fourteen Points were not primarily creations of Wilson's brain, but were abstracted by him from the report drafted by a group of American technicians, the Inquiry, under the sponsorship of Colonel House. In this connection, the explanatory gloss elaborated by Irving Cobb and Walter Lippmann for use at the time of the armistice negotiations must also be borne in mind.

[39] It is worth pointing out that, in their espousal of the principle of self-determination, the Fourteen Points retained a considerable element of flexibility. In the case of the subject nationalities of Austria-Hungary, for example, they could have been reconciled with arrangements short of full independence. The full support of this independence, with its consequence of the total destruction of the Austro-Hungarian state, was only slowly and gradually accepted by the Allies including the United States. It received a decided impetus from the meeting of a Congress of Oppressed Nationalities that took place in Rome in April, 1918.

[40] The idea that some peoples or races are superior to others is no novelty. The easily derived corollary that it entitles such superior peoples to rule inferior ones had tended to fall into disrepute, but we have witnessed the crudest revival and application of it in our own time at the hands of Nazi Germany.

[41] It has become the fashion, in America for one, to berate the limitations of nationalism. This, however, should be seen in the context of certain rather vigorous manifestations of America's own nationalism and of the

America's espousal of self-determination was in addition further strengthened by the impartiality of the American outlook. Thus, to cite one example, the Fourteen Points acknowledged the justice of Italy's acquiring Italian lands under Austrian rule, but those alone and no more, thereby implying American rejection of the inter-allied arrangements entered into before America's participation in the war [42].

In addition to the underwriting of self-determination in a number of specific cases, there were other provisions in the Fourteen Points. They may be regarded as further expressions of the same general principles of justice, democracy, right of peoples to control their own affairs, all rooted in the last analysis in the optimistic view of the nature of man. Thus, the old secret diplomacy was to be forever banished [43]; it was undemocratic, hence dangerous. To cap it all, an association of nations was to insure the future reign of peace among men, introducing at the international level the clear benefits that the rule of law provided within states. No one at first seemed to be much concerned with the inner inconsistency that the concept of a sovereign subject to the rule of law contained, a dilemma to this day unresolved [44].

This then, the Fourteen Points, was to be the charter of the New Order which the Allies, granted victory, professedly desired to make of universal application. To repeat, the attraction of the prospect was great. Of the genuineness of Wilson's intentions there is no cause to doubt, and this may be extended to the general American desire for a peace that would be lasting because of its justice. It was appropriate that America, Wilson, should be the bearer of the world's great hope. Wilson was sensitive to this; with typical American suspicion of outsiders he even felt that he was better representative of the hopes of the

---

continued espousal in America of nationalism where it can present itself as anti-imperial.

It is also worth noting that the Soviet state has managed to combine lip service to the principle of self-determination with the most effective control of non-Russian nationalities. This may be regarded as adaptation to novel circumstances and is part of a later story.

[42] Here was clearly a potential hornets' nest and it was over the issue of Italian claims that there occurred the sharpest clash during the peace negotiations in 1919, Wilson resting his case on an appeal to the Italians to accept the New Order. It is of interest that Wilson, testifying before the Senate Foreign Relations Committee in 1919, denied prior knowledge of the Treaty of London, a fact which, save in the narrowest technical sense, could not have been possible. For the details of this story we may refer to the author's *Italy at the Paris Peace Conference* (New York, 1938).

[43] It is significant that the first of the Fourteen Points advocated "open covenants, openly arrived at". The naïve interpretation of this statement by the popular mind and by the press in 1919 has given rise to much disillusion and many second thoughts. That all negotiations cannot be conducted *coram populo* would seem obvious and is generally granted, and as to the continued role of secret diplomacy it is perhaps unnecessary to comment.

[44] There were some other provisions among the Fourteen Points, such as for instance the rather loose advocacy of Freedom of the Seas (Point II). They may be regarded in the broad sense as derivatives of the principle of freedom.

world's peoples than their own governments. And for a moment this may even be said to have been sound appraisal. But only for a passing moment.

Before proceeding to observe the mutual impact of this outlook and of the realities of the peacemaking process, mention must be made of the contract that the armistice involved, for that too was significant as a source of later confusion. Little notice was taken at first by those in charge of German destinies of the Wilsonian proclamation — so long at least as hope of victory was still entertained by them. This they gave up after the failure of their last offensive in July, 1918, soon followed by a clear turning of the tide of war. To make the story brief [45], the German government approached the American with a view to arranging a termination of hostilities preliminary to the making of peace on the basis of the American program. At this point several things happened.

An armistice being a military matter, after a while the Germans were properly referred to the Allied Supreme Command which proceeded to draw up its terms. These were tantamount to total surrender in that Germany was required to yield the means — her arms — of resuming the struggle. The outcome of the war could no longer be in doubt, and since the German rulers of the day, saner than those of 1945, were not wedded to the vision of a grandiose *Götterdämmerung* if victory was not vouchsafed their arms, they opted for surrender.

But, alongside this clearly defined military situation, there were political implications. The German request to Wilson produced from him the inevitable query to his associates: did they accept the Fourteen Points as the bases for the cessation of hostilities preliminary to peace? [46] Some brief, though at times heated, sessions in which participated Colonel House and the governmental allied leaders yielded formal agreement to the Wilsonian charter [47].

---

[45] For a detailed analysis we may refer to Frederick Maurice, *The Armistices of 1918* (London and New York, 1943) and particularly to Harry R. Rudin, *Armistice 1918* (New Haven, 1944).

[46] While it is correct to say that the Fourteen Points had become the charter of allied war aims, there is none the less an important distinction between that broad acceptance and the narrower, specific, one may say legal, commitment that was involved in the exchange of formal notes between governments.

[47] For all that the intent of the Fourteen Points was clear there was room for interpretation. The British, the French and the Italians all had reservations to make. It is in connection with this that the Cobb-Lippmann explanatory comment was elaborated.

Colonel House resorted on this occasion to the threat of separate American action in the event of failure of agreement on the basis of the Wilsonian program. The result was that he won the day and the Fourteen Points were formally accepted by the Allies with only two minor reservations, one British to Point II and one French in regard to the meaning of "restoration" in Point VIII . On the failure to register the Italian reservation to Point IX, on House's plea that it was not relevant to the German armistice, there will be occasion to touch again.

Thus the situation stood when the guns were silenced on the Western front on the 11th November of the year 1918, four years and three months after they had been first unleashed [48]. Meanwhile, the last days of the war had also witnessed startling changes within the German Reich. Kaiser Wilhelm had abdicated, fled for shelter to Holland, and a Republic was installed in place of the Empire. Whether or not this was properly to be called a revolution, considering the relative orderliness with which so radical a change was effected, one might debate. But this change in Germany raised some interesting issues.

For one, the final act of surrender was almost simultaneous with that of the Republic's birth. The effects of this contemporaneity were to be considerable in the future, for the twin myths were already beginning to be nurtured that the old army had never been defeated in the field (it was still on enemy soil when hostilities ceased) and must therefore have been betrayed, stabbed in the back, preferably by Socialists, initial bulwarks of the newborn Republic [49]. But, more immediately, the German people who, in their own eyes, had never been guilty of aggression in the first place, had now gone the length of ridding themselves of the very things that the Allies professed to be fighting against, militarism and arbitrary government. A peace of justice could therefore not entail for Germany — or so it was soon to be argued — retribution for non existent guilt. Such at least were implications that could be read into the Allies' profession of their faith.

At any rate, once the armistice had been signed, the clearly indicated next step was the calling of a peace congress. This was done, and the Peace Conference of Paris formally opened just two months after the coming of the German armistice into force. With the perspective and experience of our own day we may smile in wonder at the contemporary complaints at the duration of the delay — two months.

The unique position of America and the prestige of American views have been indicated, as well as the strength they derived from the universality of the appeal which they contained. When it came to the task of writing some at least of these views into the formal instruments that are treaties it would be futile to pretend that had such views been mainly sponsored by the Rumanian delegation, for example, they would have carried the same weight. But, like them or no, whatever predilections the American representatives might have, these must be at

---

[48] Separate armistices had meantime been concluded with Bulgaria (September 30), Turkey (October 30) and Austria-Hungary (November 3). These raised the question of the validity of the Fourteen Points in relation to these countries. However, the fact that Germany was the main enemy and that the commitment to the Wilsonian program was made in connection with the negotiation of the German armistice, clearly implied a moral, if not a strictly legal, commitment to this program as the basis for the general, rather than the purely German, settlement.

[49] The significance of this cannot be overstressed and the disastrous consequences of these myths of which Nazism made the most, for Germany and for others, will be considered later.

least examined with deference. In simple form, the American influence in the shaping of the terms of peace would certainly be of the greatest consequence owing to the fact of American power. If force was to be used in furtherance of justice so much the better for the future of mankind, but force it was again that was decisive.

The relationships of power at the time of the termination of hostilities are therefore of overriding consequence. This, to be sure, is but a truism; one, however, worth stressing because of much that was illusion in the atmosphere of the day. What precisely then were these relationships of power? One fact stands out at once that in itself was consequence of the complexities of this relationship.

For all that Wilson had expressed the view that interest divides, rather than unites, men and nations, the diversity of interests within the victorious coalition was too considerable for it not to be obvious that the reconciliation of these interallied divergences would constitute a major and complicated task. It would clearly be the best card of the enemy, sanctioned by traditional precedent, to make the most of allied differences and to inject new ones where possible. The lesson, or presumed lesson, of Talleyrand's success at Vienna a century before had been well learned — perhaps too well.

The decision was therefore made to exclude the enemy from the peace table around which would sit the victors alone. But the victors alone represented a world-wide coalition. Reasons of practicability of operation sufficed to demonstrate the impossibility of arriving at decisions within a parliament of some thirty sovereign nations which could only have reproduced the disabilities of an eighteenth-century Polish Diet. Power and responsibility are inseparable, and so it happened that the process of peacemaking was essentially in the hands of the five Great Powers associated in victory, the United States, Great Britain, France, Italy and Japan [50].

But even more: of the five two played but minor roles of self-effacement. The war had indeed been world wide, but the central arena of disturbance as well as of active hostilities had been European. Japan had little concern with European matters, chief objects of the peace; if she could have her way near home, others might decide as they wished elsewhere [51]. In Europe proper, the formal disintegration of the Austro-Hungarian Empire emphasized the fact, erroneously to a degree, that *the* great problem of the peace was Germany. But Germany

---

[50] The Peace Conference, to be sure, met a times in Plenary session. But these occasions were few, essentially formal and perfunctory, and played no part whatever in the making of decisions.

[51] Essentially, in 1919, the Japanese had their way. Since their allies were committed, it was left to Wilson, who was not, to do battle against the Japanese attempt to encroach upon China. It suffices here to mention that, as a result of their skilful management of the situation, Wilson lost the battle. One consequence of this was the Chinese refusal to sign the Treaty of Versailles.

was no overwhelming concern of Italy which, in addition (again measure of power), elected to play an even less important part than she need have. Focusing her attention on relatively small Adriatic matters, she took the general position of acquiescing in and underwriting the decisions of others where most things were concerned [52].

The result was this: the power of the great areopage of nations devolved into the hands of five, in reality three. Three men in fact, for with the elimination of the foreign ministers early in the proceedings, discussion and ultimate decisions were largely left to the heads of the three delegations of America, Britain and France. Wilson, Lloyd George and Clemenceau, the Supreme Council, peacemaking adaptation of the directing body of the war, the Supreme War Council, in the spring of 1919 held in their hands the shape and future of the peoples of Europe, if not of most of the earth [53].

Before this body, supreme tribunal and highest court beyond appeal, there came the multitude of issues that war and victory had raised [54]. The responsibility was commensurate with the power. This in itself was neutral fact, the consequences of which need by no means be necessarily **nefarious.**

---

[52] It is a fact, as interesting as it is curious, that Italy, or at least the directors of Italian policy at the time, chose to concentrate in narrow and legalistic manner on the Adriatic problem, and even on some limited aspects only of that problem. They lacked the breadth of outlook that might have caused them at least to make a bid for a position of leadership in the large region open to outside influences as a result of the demise of Austria-Hungary.

[53] Once we come to so small a group as the Big Three the role of personality becomes important. In fact it was, and much has been written about the Three. Keynes' famous sketches in *The Economic Consequences of the Peace,* brilliant distortions, especially where Wilson is concerned, are perhaps the single best known account. Allowing for the role of personality, however, we shall confine ourselves to the interplay of the larger forces in operation.

[54] Clearly, the Supreme Council could not have the technical competence to pass on the issues involved in most problems, territorial or other; its ultimate powers of decision were political in their essence. The Supreme Council took, therefore, the only possible course, that of appointing a number of *ad hoc* commissions, mainly staffed by technicians or "experts", to draft recommendations.

These commissions did in effect the bulk of the work that was finally embodied into the text of the treaties of peace, work which incidentally was in general of a high order of quality. The Supreme Council accepted for the most part the work done by the technical committees, reserving to itself the ultimate power of decision and also the handling of certain highly controversial matters where the Great Powers were primarily concerned.

This mode of operation, inevitable consequence of the complexity of circumstances, in itself raised the interesting and highly important issue of the increasing role of technical competence in the operation of modern government and of international relations. A whole body of practice has thus come into existence which is by way of affecting the very fundamentals, not only of operation, but even by indirection of principles involved.

The Peace That Was the Outcome

The settlements contrived in Paris have almost receded into the relatively safe domain of history, whither the accumulation and rush of subsequent events have relegated them. Yet this stands out that neither they nor later efforts in the same direction have so far furnished the world with the bases of a new stability. This failure then remains imporatnt, and for a time it was the fashion to heap abuse and scorn upon the work of Paris, convenient whipping boy of later discontent.

The failure to restore durable peace is an obvious fact that cannot be gainsaid. Perhaps the simple truth might have received greater attention that no treaty, charter, constitution or scheme, be it devised in heaven, can by itself, as if endowed with magic, establish suddenly the reign of Utopia on earth. What is done with the instrument, how, when, by whom, can from the same tool draw wholly diverse effects. The operation of this process will be later examined as in fact one of the purposes of this essay.

Nevertheless the shape and nature of the tool are not without importance; used well or poorly, constitutions can in themselves be potent factors. For that reason, those settlements arranged in Paris, which after all did constitute the formal charter of the future, deserve being considered in some detail, a task made possibly more fruitful by the passage of time.

Our age is both articulate and vocal, and out of the large gathering that was called to draft the terms of peace a flood of literature has issued in the form of recollections and memoirs, to say nothing of the duller stream of more official publications. Yet, for all this plethora of information, it is an interesting fact that no adequate and comprehensive history of the peacemaking has to this day been written [55]; the raw materials of the tale are there, however, for anyone to use.

---

[55] The basic material for the history of the peacemaking lies in the official record of the proceedings which have been published by the participating governments. The American publication is *Foreign Relations of the United States, The Paris Peace Conference, 1919* (Washington, 1942-1947, 13 vols.); this supersedes the earlier valuable collection of David Hunter Miller, *My Diary at the Conference of Paris* (Privately printed, 1928, 20 vols.).

The work edited by H.W.V. Temperley, *A History of the Peace Conference of Paris* (London, 1921-1924, 6 vols.) remains fundamental, and Paul Birdsall, *Versailles Twenty Years After* (New York, 1941) is a convenient, documented, one-volume account that draws upon subsequently available material; it may be cited alongside F.S. Marston, *The Peace Conference of 1919, Organization and Procedure* (London, 1944).

The literature is vast that has grown out of the Paris congress, but the following more limited works may be cited among the more basic ones: R.S Baker, *Woodrow Wilson and the World Settlement* (New York, 1923, 3 vols.); Thomas A. Bailey, *Woodrow Wilson and the Lost Peace* (New York, 1945); Mermeix, *Le Combat des Trois* (Paris, 1922); Harold Nicolson, *Peacemaking, 1919* (London, 1933 and 1943); David Lloyd George, *The*

If, as pointed out earlier, there was hope and elation abroad toward the beginning of 1919 there was also bitterness and resentment. What more natural than that such feelings should thrive best in Paris? The accidents of the course of the war had made France the chief and ultimate battleground whereon victory was at last secured. For this distinction France had paid a high price; a section of her land, materially the richest since industry was largely concentrated there, had been thoroughly ravaged. It was perhaps convenient for others, friend and foe, that France should have been the chief battleground; in French eyes, this constituted a valid claim on others, at the very least priority of claim against the vanquished enemy.

Not only wealth, but men, had France lavishly furnished to the common cause. Not French alone indeed were casualties, but among the Allies the French proportion was markedly the highest. 1,360,000 killed out of a population of 40,000,000, a static and aging population at that, constituted a drain the magnitude of which may be difficult to encompass, to say nothing of further millions in varying degrees crippled or disabled [56]. The phrase "bled white" was in this case no metaphor.

France's claim to recognition of her contribution to the joint enterprise of war and victory was acknowledged by her associates. It was one reason for making Paris the seat of the peace congress, suitable symbolic recognition of the French role [57]. There was criticism, then and especially later, of the choice of Paris, whose atmosphere overcharged with emotion, "poisoned" said some, was inimical to the coolness and calm that the making of a sound peace demanded. The point should not be overstressed [58], but whatever influence the

---

Truth about the Peace Treaty (London, 1938, 2 vols.); Charles Seymour, ed., *The Intimate Papers of Colonel House,* vol. IV (New York, 1928); André Tardieu, *La Paix* (Paris, 1920), translated as *The Truth about the Treaty* (Indianopolis, 1921).

[56] It is impossible to place too much stress on the consequences of this fact. The American reader may stop to consider what the impact would have been on the American mood and feeling had some 4,000,000 young Americans been killed in the war; whatever the precise effect, that it would have been profound can hardly be doubted.

In addition to the large absolute loss, the aggravating factor must be taken into account that France was the one country whose reproductive rate had long been so low as barely to maintain the level of the existing population. A comparable loss in a country with a high reproductive rate, like Russia for example, would have had an entirely different impact.

[57] The other reason, more prosaic though equally important, was the physical convenience of its location, established center of numerous agencies connected with the direction of the war.

[58] It may be pointed out that the "khaki" election of December, 1918 in Britain constituted a marked display of emotionalism; in America there was at first not a little criticism of the too soft treatment of Germany. To be sure, a sharp change of feeling was soon apparent both in Britain and in America, and this in turn might be cause for some interesting reflections on the score of such commonplaces as French fickleness versus Anglo-Saxon stability.

atmosphere of Paris and of France may have had on the proceedings, the role of France was bound to be of prime importance in both their evolution and their outcome. Therein lay a distortion. To put it simply, the place and role of France were in large measure due to recognition of past services. Natural as this may have been in the circumstances, the future would also naturally tend to organize itself on the basis of what relationships of power would in that same future prevail. In the Europe of 1919 French power was relatively considerable, not to say overwhelming. Had this been a true expression of a long term condition, peace organized around French power would have been a reasonable enough conception.

As it was, the supreme irony lay in the fact that victory itself had served to place French power into this "false" position, for victory had been purchased at such a cost as to do that power the most serious injury, a greater and more lasting injury in fact than defeat had caused some at least of the vanquished. Cruel as it may be at times — this is a case in point — the future cannot organize itself mainly on the basis of rewards for the past. This state of affairs was sensed, and in some cases clearly realized, in France. The consequence was an effort to capitalize on the present, an attempt to crystallize the advantageous moment into a lasting future.

Clemenceau, leader of France, was a disillusioned old man who clearly understood these things. The rhetoric of victory did not for him conceal the more basic reality that underlay the future. To him, France shared in victory, to which indeed her contribution had been both great and honorable, but which this contribution alone would have been wholly inadequate to procure. It was the lucky accident of circumstances, membership in a world wide coalition, that had put France in a momentarily and unexpectedly fortunate situation. Clemenceau understood and respected power: Germany could not forever be held down, but the advantage of the fleeting moment must be made to yield the most that could be extracted from it. The advantage after all was real; with good luck, French power might remain in control and for perhaps a generation secure the peace. If that could be achieved, Clemenceau felt that he would have deserved well of his country; thereafter, the future would have to look after itself, as best it could meet its own problems [59].

Such aims were clearly conceived and limited in purpose. How implement them then? In the atmosphere of 1919 and for some time thereafter they commanded sufficient support among French opinion to permit the conduct of a consistent foreign policy based on them [60]. But

---

[59] Clemenceau's own reflections on the peace may be found in his *Grandeurs et misères d'une victoire* (Paris, 1930).

[60] It was the Chamber elected in 1913 that discussed and ratified the treaty of peace. The French election of November, 1919, comparable in some respects to the British election of December, 1918, produced the *Chambre bleu horizon*, dominated by the National Bloc. Reflecting the impact of wartime emotion, the election resulted in a marked shift to the

even in the matter of making the peace France had to take into account the other current realities of power, American and British.

The American and the British approaches to the peace were not identical, but there was between them sufficient common ground to make it possible for them to join with relative ease. Lloyd George was mercurial and nimble, little hampered by the deficiencies of his own knowledge of the world outside the British sphere; he had besides able advisers and the tradition of the foreign office was strong. For electoral purposes in 1918 he might be willing to allow the impression both that he would "hang the Kaiser" and "squeeze Germany until the pips squeaked"; by May, 1919 he was fully alive to the dangers (from the British point of view) of too much squeezing.

Broadly speaking, it may be said that the British approach to the problem of the postwar period fitted into the traditional pattern of Britain's European policy: no one must dominate the continent; for that purpose, fighting the Kaiser had been the same necessity as defeating Napoleon. The negative purpose once accomplished with the achievement of military victory, the enemy must not be destroyed — though a modicum of precautions against the possibility of his renewed aggression might be taken — for that would be tantamount to robbing victory of its (British) purpose: Britain does not fight so much *against* any one as *for* the preservation of the balance of power. Call it *divide et impera* or defense of the equal right of all to existence, the specific manifestations of Britain's policy will be the same. The fundamental fallacy, in 1919, of the traditional approach will be examined later together with the disastrous consequences, not least for Britain, of stubborn adherence to it.

This British approach — perniciously in one type of view, quite genuinely in another — easily lends itself to excursions into the realm of ethics, at which point contact was also easy with much of the American outlook and many of its representatives. It has been pointed out that when the statement is made that Britain is the staunch defender of small nations the statement, in considerable measure true, is largely so because it gives expression to a long standing British interest. It is also expression of the greater measure of nineteenth-century British power. A similar position now befitted the United States, and largely for similar reasons, if anything reinforced by the fact that America even less than Britain had any interest in or knowledge of the details of the local quarrels of Europe.

By its very nature the Anglo-American approach is conducive to stressing the element of trust, all the more because of underlying confidence that, should the trust turn out mistaken, there is sufficient power in reserve to redress the error. To Britain, the recovery of Germany, up to a point at least, was desirable from the standpoint of British interest,

---

Right, with a strong stress on nationalism, whereas in the 1913 legislature the anti-nationalistic and anti-militaristic tendency had been strong.

whether commercial or political. To Wilson, now that the Kaiser and his generals were gone, the German people were largely purged, soon to be welcome in the comity of nations. This may be added: if ever there is to be a fundamental change in the military tradition of the German people, the Anglo-American approach of confidence will make this easier than that approach that first insists on retribution, compensation and atonement. Wherein lies the proper balance between justice and mercy? Wherein, for that matter, lies precisely justice, and how far is the victim to bear his damage for the sake of the rehabilitation of the aggressor? The relevancy of such considerations may be argued; that they received varying weight in different quarters must be obvious.

At all events, the foregoing makes it clear that sharp divergence between France on one side and Britain and America on the other was a most natural phenomenon in 1919. If we confine ourselves to the large view of fundamentals rather than to awkward and irksome detail, it must be granted that the divergence is honest difference of opinion, expression of diverse historic experience, diverse geography, and estimate largely correct of diverse magnitude of power. [61]

In concrete terms what happened then was this: France, conscious of her weakness in the future, wanted insurance against recurrence of aggression, as much insurance as might be obtained, barring no limit. It must be remembered that, in 1919, the view of initial German aggression in 1914 went generally unquestioned in America and in Britain, whatever optimistic views may have been taken in those countries of the future of German democracy. The French desire for security seemed therefore legitimate. The question was how give it satisfaction in a form that would at once be adequate and reasonable?

In narrow military terms, control of the line of the Rhine was a clear and concretely realizable objective; in those days of comparative sanity and moderation, no one seriously spoke of the physical destruction of Bismarck's achievement of German unity. But even so restricted an aim as the Rhine boundary raised what seemed at the time insuperable obstacles. The triangle of territory enclosed by the frontiers of France, Luxembourg, Belgium, Holland and the purely German segment of the Rhine River was German land; the Allies had made themselves the champions of nationality [62]. Even any device

---

[61] Britain's estimate of her own relative power seems to have been in great measure incorrect, a fact that the Second World War may be said to have definitely established. The 1919 British estimate was colored by historic precedent; in addition, if one assume a *de facto* combination of British and American power — an assumption which, over the long term and when it comes to really fundamental matters, does not seem unwarranted — the British estimate might still be regarded as valid.

[62] What there was of desire for separation in the Rhineland was of negligible consequence, though not altogether synthetic. The French attempt to magnify and exploit the tendency redounded in the main to French discredit.

A measure of the disintegration of international morality during a quarter of a century may be obtained from a comparison of the arrangements of

whereby military control alone of the Rhine would have remained in French hands would not be entertained by Wilson; tension ran high in March when Clemenceau dubbed him pro-German [63].

But on the one hand Clemenceau was realist enough to bow to the reality of American power, while on the other America and Britain had the means to satisfy the desire of France which, for that matter, could not be coerced beyond a certain point. Out of this situation a compromise was born. The German Rhineland would be demilitarized as well as a fifty-kilometer zone on the right bank of the river; the left bank would be occupied for a term of years by allied forces but would otherwise remain integral part of Germany; but most important, against the possibility of renewed German aggression France would have the assurance of American and British support.

Per se the compromise was excellent: German nationality was respected; if Germany should really become converted to the ways of peace, as some would fondly hope, then the guarantee need never come into effect; in the opposite case, clearly the joint power of America and Britain was ultimately worth far more than the more immediate but also much more limited asset that the Rhine barrier in French hands constituted. The prospect might in fact be adequate deterrent to aggression even if the thought of it was entertained by Germany [64].

That American signature to a treaty is not valid until Senate ratification; that the American electorate had given Wilson a rebuff in the election of 1918; those were issues of domestic American concern with which it would have been hardly proper to confront the American

---

the Treaty of Versailles with those effected since 1945 where Germany is concerned. The present practice of the wholesale removal of populations for the purpose of altering the ethnic composition of territory was not entertained in 1919 when this contribution of Nazi Germany, since emulated by others, would have been regarded as a mere return to barbarism. The approach of 1919 was still in the main to fit frontiers to peoples rather than peoples to frontiers.

[63] Wilson had gone back to the United States in mid-February to attend to domestic matters; when he returned to Paris a month later the work of the various commissions was well advanced and the Supreme Council proceeded to the business of final decisions on this work and on the issues which it had reserved to itself. Among these the French problem was the first and most important.

[64] While it may be granted that the combination of British and American assistance meant far more power available than the useful, but limited, asset of the Rhine line in French hands, the arrangement raised an important issue that later developments have brought out in sharper relief.

British and American power, save at sea, is normally potential rather than actual; also, especially in the case of America, it is remote from the scene and raises the problems of availability and of transportation. Granted that it may be sufficient to redress even an initial defeat — as was the case in the Second World War — there remains the crucial consideration that the prospect of ultimate liberation has doubtful attraction by comparison with the possibility of successful initial resistance. In some ways, therefore, the greatest value of an Anglo-American guarantee lies in its deterrent effect upon aggression.

President in the spring of 1919. We must not here anticipate that story, but shall content ourselves with the reflection that compromise does not necessarily solve a problem. It puts it off, as this one did, and for the time made possible continuation of the peacemaking process. What it is significant to retain of the episode is the illustration that it provides of an adjustment in the relationships of power, an adjustment limited however to the relations among three participants only.

The same issue was basically at the root of the discussions that surrounded the drafting of the Covenant of the League of Nations. This above all was America's contribution, Wilson's more narrowly and personally, to the future. The details of frontier disputes and kindred matters, about which he himself was generally uninformed, were for the most part boring, dull necessity that had to be accepted, better dealt with if possible through technical advice, disinterested and competent. But the League was something in a wholly different category; if the concept of the desirability of the institution of some rule of law among nations was not new, the attempt to write in into formal treaties was [65].

To Clemenceau especially, hard bitten veteran of French and international politics, the League concept had more in it of *noble candeur* than of practical usefulness. It was one more case of deferring to American wishes because of American power that the drafting of the Covenant was not only taken seriously, but received priority among the various problems of the peacemaking.

The prospect of instituting the reign of lasting universal peace had understandable attraction in 1919, especially at the popular level. Not that leaders and rulers had a condemnable predilection for war, but that greater experience and knowledge induced greater reserve among them. However, since the American President would have it so, there was nothing for it but to take up the matter in earnest. The more flexible British approach deriving from more favorable circumstances made it relatively easy to produce Anglo-American agreement on the League whose Covenant emerged as an essentially Anglo-American document. But not until considerable battle had been done. And in this instance also the battle was largely one between the Anglo-American view on one side and the French on the other [66].

---

[65] Without going into the history of proposals and schemes aiming at the establishment of universal peace, it is worth recalling that, during the earlier part of the war, prior to the American intervention, the concept had found its strongest advocates among Republican ranks. The course of events makes it proper, however, to associate the active sponsorship of the League with Wilson and to give him credit for the effort to translate the idea into reality.

[66] In addition to the general references given in note 55, mention should be made here of David Hunter Miller, *The Drafting of the Covenant* (New York, 1928, 2 vols.) and of A. Geouffre de La Pradelle, *La Paix moderne, 1899-1945* (Paris, 1947).

This was a wholly natural outcome of circumstances, for the French view in brief was this: the League, if the new institution was to have meaning, could only derive such from the creation of real law-enforcing power at its command. This view had the asset of irrefutable logic combined with the drawback that really to create such an instrument as the French proposed presented well-nigh insuperable difficulties. To repeat again, the difference was simply this: France did not feel that she could entrust her security to anything but the protection of adequate and well-defined force, be that her own or that of whatever organization might come into existence; but in any case the stress was on the *prior* organization of both the force and the mechanism that would set the force into operation in the event of need. America and Britain shared a greater willingness to place their trust in moral force in lieu of ironclad prior material guarantees; should moral force prove inadequate, they could still retrieve their position behind the joint protection of geography and of time. It has been indicated that the Anglo-American view generally prevailed in the matter in 1919 [67].

In passing, it might be pointed out that the simultaneous creation of a League charged with the maintenance of universal peace and of an Anglo-Franco-American alliance was perhaps not devoid of a certain inconsistency. It was only reasonable perhaps to allow that the League was an untried instrument; that, in itself, was also simultaneous confession of doubts of its effectiveness [68].

And finally, again in passing, it is impossible to refrain from pointing out the change produced in the American position by change in circumstances and technical conditions after a second world war. No longer feeling so secure, America, still favoring the League now dubbed United Nations, has essentially espoused the French position of 1919 which might be summed up in the slogan, security comes first. What else would anyone, other than an unconditional pacifist do, in similar circumstances?

It is quite true, of course, that perfect logical consistency is no inevitable requirement of politics, the very lack of it being sometimes an asset. The failure of the League will be a later story. At any rate the League was born and launched on its career. Novel instrument that all recognized it to be, embodiment of many hopes, its future would inevitably depend upon the manner in which its directors would operate the tool.

---

[67] The fact is not devoid of irony that while Wilson was far more sanguine about the possibilities of the League than were the French, he it was who opposed French efforts to give the League real power. This situation becomes easily understandable, however, in the context of American historical tradition and of immediate American political necessities, matters which Wilson had to take into account and which, to a degree, he himself reflected.

[68] It might also be pointed out that there could be no possible defense in logic of the inclusion of the Monroe Doctrine in the League Covenant. Here again, the necessities of American domestic politics received recognition, but again only because others felt that American wishes must be deferred to.

It is not the purpose of this treatment to rehearse the history of the peacemaking in all its details and aspects; rather to draw upon that story, as upon earlier and subsequent records, for purposes of illustrative interpretation. But a little more must be said before we turn from the peacemaking to a discussion of the operation and use that was made of the peace instruments.

The subject of Reparation was destined to a troubled history and, for a time, to play a large role in the politics of postwar Europe. No one doubted in 1919, even on the German side, that Germany and her allies were liable for the war damage. Point VIII of the Fourteen Points explicitly mentioned "restoration" in connection with the restitution of Alsace-Lorraine to France and, to make assurance doubly sure, the French had obtained the addition of a covering explanatory clause with a view to avoiding any limitation of the German liability.

When it came to drafting the concrete terms of the peace, two questions confronted the congress on the score of Reparation: what should Germany pay? What could Germany pay? There was much discussion of these and no final agreement on either "should" or "could", save that they would not in any event coincide. The outcome was Part VIII, the Reparation section of the Treaty of Versailles, the principal effect of which was the establishment of a commission charged with the task of furnishing answers to the should and the could, mainly to the latter which was in addition to be clarified by answering the further questions, how and when? [69]

Mention must be made at this juncture of the fact that this entire section of the German treaty was introduced by the since famous article 231 which specified:

> The Allied and Associated Governments affirm and Germany accepts the responsibility of Germany and her allies for causing all the loss and damage to which the Allied and Associated Governments and their nationals have been subjected as a consequence of the war imposed upon them by the aggression of Germany and her allies.

This is known as the war guilt clause; it became the source of extended controversy, a boon to the historic craft, and a millstone to the operation of practical politics [70]. The reason for the innovation that the introduction of such a statement in a peace treaty constituted is revealing. Here was no traditional war indemnity, simple penalty con-

---

[69] The Reparation section of the Treaty of Versailles specified certain payments and deliveries in kind that had to be made immediately. These, however, were but a token and a relatively minor matter by comparison with the immeasurably larger amounts that would be involved in the final total of Reparation.

[70] The distinction between the assertion of responsibility by one side and the acceptance of the consequences of this assertion by the other, while valid, is essentially irrelevant in view of the widespread popular acceptance of the statement as establishing a connection between the moral judgment and a liability deriving therefrom.

sequent upon defeat, but again the mere implementation of justice. We shall have occasion to dwell upon some of the consequences of the innovation; the whole debate on responsibility for the war in large measure grew out of it. At the very least, it was an invitation to the German people to seek to rid themselves of the judgment visited upon them, with the added incentive that the destruction of the moral basis for Reparation would have the logical consequence of exonerating them from the material obligation of payment.

Yet the war guilt clause was in legitimate line of derivation of the New Order that was being established and of which the League was another manifestation. Not revenge and the crude operation of power were to set the tone of the future, but justice and high minded morality. The point is not so much that here was a mistake, though it is easy to perceive that in the final reckoning the precise opposite effect to that intended was achieved, since the arrangement helped shift the argument to a plane far more suitable to protracted recrimination; it is rather that here was a manifestation of the heed paid to popular emotion, to the democratic factor of the mass coming into its own. America was the best qualified and clearest spokesman of the new condition of which the war guilt clause is one expression. Here was clearly as good an illustration as can be produced of the duality that prevailed in the peace.

But perhaps the sharpest instance of the interrelation of power, or better of the awkward mixture that power and principle can achieve was that provided by the Italian case, which for that reason will be briefly mentioned.

Italy, it will be recalled, had joined the Allies in 1915 as the result of a definite contract, the Treaty of London of that year. She had fulfilled her side of the bargain by going through the war to its victorious end. She was now entitled to the fulfilment of the promise that her allies had made. Nothing could be much clearer or much simpler, nor did Britain or France ever seek to question the validity of this argument, which that of the sanctity of treaties could only serve to bolster. Was it not Germany's dishonoring of her signature in the Belgian case which had largely contributed to Britain's intervention in order to uphold the sanctity of international obligations?

But in 1915 America was neutral; her intervention two years later did not make her a party to interallied obligations then existing. On the contrary, we have seen the United States taking the leadership in the attempt to organize the New Order and the manner in which this affected the process of peacemaking. The Fourteen Points in fact made special provision for the Italian case by stating that "the frontiers of Italy should be drawn according to clearly recognizable lines of nationality" (Point IX). In concrete form, such lines of nationality could not possibly coincide with the line of the Treaty of London. What then to do? The matter was in the hands of the Supreme Council in April, just after the "French problem" had finally been resolved through the compromise previously indicated.

There is no room to go into the intricate details of a controversy the essence of which, however, is simple [71]. To Wilson — he was dealing with the situation himself though relying on his "experts" for advice — the issue was a simple one of right versus wrong: why should the South Slavs, a small nation besides, hence especially liable to sympathy from him, be made the victims of Italian greed? The Treaty of London did not stand for justice, being another instance of old time wicked power politics; simply brushing aside awkward considerations of detail, he would have the Italians themselves abandon it [72]. Here were the makings of a beautiful debate on the high plane of principle: the sanctity of treaties versus the right of self-determination. Yet, in more prosaic reality, a test of force between America and Italy [73].

The possibility that Italy could bend America to her will need not be considered. But was the reverse achievable? Having declined to use the instrument of economic and financial pressure [74], Wilson's direct public appeal to the Italian people brought to him nothing but bitterest disillusion [75]. Thus the outcome was stalemate: America preventing Italy from obtaining the frontier that she wanted, the issue of that frontier remained an open question [76]. The course of this dispute was

---

[71] As indicated earlier, this episode has been treated at length in the author's *Italy at the Paris Peace Conference.*

[72] The debate was fed by such complications as the fact that the issue had not been settled whether, strictly speaking, the Italians had or had not legally bound themselves to the Fourteen Points. Also, the fact that Wilson himself had agreed to the Brenner frontier for Italy in the north, might strengthen the case for compromise but certainly weakened his moral position.

[73] The Italians were aware of all this; not overimpressed by the New Order, they recognized American power and were prepared to compromise. The basis of the compromise in Orlando's view would have been his yielding of the section of Dalmatia allotted to Italy by the Treaty of London in exchange for Fiume, specifically excluded by that same treaty. The fact that Fiume was partly Italian in population made it possible to invoke the principle of self-determination at this point. But Orlando's tactics which consisted in opening his case with a demand for all the Treaty of London benefits, on the plea of treaty obligations, *plus* Fiume, on the plea of nationality, merely served to arouse violent indignation in Wilson who saw in them nothing but unprincipled disingenuousness.

[74] The possibility was in fact considered, but although this was 1919 and not the nineteen fifties, the argument was already used of the danger of Bolshevism in Italy if the country was too hard pressed, an argument of which the then leaders of Italy were not loath to make the most.

[75] His Manifesto of April 23, 1919 resulted in an explosion of over-heated nationalism in Italy. This appeal constitutes a pathetic document, being at once so right (in the context of Wilson's own assumptions) and yet so beside the point. It brought home to Wilson the degree to which his feeling that he was a better representative of the wishes of the well-intentioned masses than their own governments was already by this time erroneous. This is only one, but one of the clearest, aspects of the tragedy of Wilson.

[76] And this continued so long as the American position remained the same. It was shortly after the American election of November, 1920, which brought a repudiation of the administration in office, that direct negotiations between Italy and Yugoslavia settled the issue, again on the basis of a

an important object lesson on the score of the complications that the
psychological factor of an aroused public opinion could introduce in
the relations among peoples; here certainly was one of those imponderables that the simpler, more purely rational, considerations of the
material components of power would have to take increasingly into
account in future. To cite but one example in anticipation, we shall
observe the repetition of the same phenomenon in the case of Italy again
in connection with the Ethiopian affair of the nineteen thirties.

That the task of making the peace was vast was fully realized even
before it started; so much so that there was thought of drafting a preliminary treaty that would with expedition make possible the formal
termination of the state of war. Precise detailed arrangements could
then at leisure and with calm be attended to. But more by accident
than plan it was found that during the spring of 1919 most matters
had become so far advanced that gathering together the work of the
various commissions, plus the decisions of the Supreme Council, the
material for a German treaty was available. The result was presented
to a German delegation in May; some brief, but essentially unimportant,
exchanges occurred, and on 28 June, 1919 the Treaty of Versailles was
signed. The fact that this was the anniversary of the Sarajevo assassination, specific occasion that had opened the conflict; the fact that
the locale of the ceremony of signature was that same Hall of Mirrors
in which the birth of Bismarck's Reich had been proclaimed; all this
was adequate expression of historic continuity. The valued richness
of tradition seen through a different lens might also be described as
the dead hand of the past [77].

The German treaty, of necessity, attended to matters purely German
only. There was much else to do, which may be put under two heads.
The same gathering that had produced the Treaty of Versailles went on
to draft similar instruments for the remaining enemies, Austria, Bulgaria,
Hungary and Turkey in the order mentioned [78]. But there was, in
addition, the problem of the new Russia. The idea of having Bolshevik
Russia represented at Paris was only briefly entertained and what
happened finally was this: along the northwestern borders of Russia
the emergence of various non-Russian national entities had been made
possible by the combination of Russian chaos and of Russian defeat at

compromise that may be regarded as an expression of the existing balance
of forces at the time.

[77] The continuity was carefully preserved in 1940 when the ceremony
of the signature of the Franco-German armistice was a careful reproduction
of that of the signature of the German armistice of 1918.

[78] The treaties with Austria and Bulgaria were signed in 1919, but the
signature of the Treaty of Trianon with Hungary was delayed until June,
1920 as a consequence of the temporary establishment of a Bolshevik government in Hungary in 1919.

As to Turkey, the Treaty of Sèvres, signed by the Sultan in August,
1920, was a dead letter from the beginning and peace with Turkey was
not really established until 1923 when the revolution led by Kemal succeeded
in procuring the complete independence of Turkey proper. The Ottoman
Empire, like the Austro-Hungarian, did not survive the war; to that extent
the settlement of 1920, where the former was concerned, held good.

German hands. The Baltic states were in German control until Germany's own final defeat. Quite naturally, the Allies annulled the treaties that the fortunes of war had made it possible for the enemy to impose in Eastern Europe; however, they recognized the newborn states and, though not without some difficulty, secured the withdrawal of German forces from them. Bolshevik Russia they did not recognize at first, but lent instead assistance to various "white" groups and armies that were fighting the revolution. This left it to the newly emerged Baltic states, plus Poland and Rumania, to come to terms directly with Russia, which they all did, except Rumania [79].

Appraisal of the Settlements

In the popular imagination the idea gained wide currency that the Paris congress, even more narrowly the Treaty of Versailles, was responsible for the total settlement of the First World War. This view is obviously erroneous, since there were a number of other instruments besides the German treaty, as the preceding pages have shown. Nevertheless, there was a certain degree of validity in the popular misconception, owing to the fact that Russia, absent from Paris, was largely at the time a vacuum of power to which scant attention was paid, which in fact it would have been difficult to bring into the total picture precisely because of the uncertainty that her inner chaos presented. At the same time Germany loomed far the largest entity, whether in terms of wartime performance or because of the fact of her continuing existence contrasted with the fate of the Austrian and Ottoman Empires. Thus, the German treaty loomed correspondingly more important and it was in addition the model for the other settlements elaborated in Paris. Versailles is therefore not unreasonably used as a label to describe a whole system, the whole new organization of Europe.

In view of the importance of that settlement, comparable in its dimensions and purpose to those of Vienna and Westphalia, some appraisal of it is warranted. This we can do, moreover, with the advantage of perspective and of whatever wisdom the passage of time may have granted.

It was for a long time the fashion, especially between the two world wars, to lay all the ills of the world at the door of Versailles. Renewed warfare has served to focus attention on matters of more immediately pressing significance. The problems of our day, since the termination of the main hostilities in 1945, have in large measure relegated to the realm of academic discussion the value of Versailles, although the contemplation of many occurrences in the last two decades has caused

---

[79] Taking advantage of the Russian chaos Rumania seized Bessarabia. Soviet Russia refused in this case to give *de jure* recognition to the Rumanian acquisition which thus remained *de facto* in Rumanian hands until the Second World War.

an occasional glance of wistfulness to be cast back at what can but appear as the relative sanity and moderation of 1919.

If we take the larger view, rather than concentrate on the details of Fiume, Teschen, or Danzig, this will appear at once. The map of Europe as it was redrawn in 1919 constituted the nearest approximation ever attained to the identification of political with ethnic boundaries. No one denied the Germanness of Germans and from this followed the respect of German territorial integrity. Germany, to be sure, lost some lands, but the loss was generally warranted. Even the most controversial of these, the "bleeding frontiers" of the East, of which so much was heard during the twenties, was, on the basis of German census statistics, predominantly inhabited by Poles.

Or take the case of Danzig, initial starting point of the Second World War. The original decision in Paris was to make Danzig Polish; this did not seem unreasonable in view of the recognized necessity that Poland have secure access to the sea, a need which the Fourteen Points themselves had acknowledged (Point XIII); against the admitted awkwardness of a territorial splitting of Germany, there was the greater awkwardness that would have been a Poland blocked from the sea by a thin strip of German land [80]. Yet even this wholly defensible solution was not adopted, for in deference to the Germanness of Danzig a compromise was effected whereby Danzig was set up as a free city, neither German nor Polish, but under League control.

A more reasonable compromise than this could hardly be conceived. It is, to be sure, but one illustration, but it has been chosen on purpose because more has been heard about it than about many others and because of the fame associated with Danzig. This is not to say that *all* territorial arrangements were invariably manifestations of the highest fairness and wisdom [81]. Hungarian grievances on this score, though in Hungary overstated, were on more solid ground than German. On more solid ground, that is, if one accept the criterium of nationality as the proper test of justice in the matter of drawing frontiers [82].

---

[80] To make matters even worse, such an arrangement would have necessitated the inclusion in Germany of territory not predominantly inhabited by Germans; according to the German census statistics of 1910 the since famous Polish Corridor had a majority of Polish population.

[81] The large triangle of territory bounded by lines running from Danzig to Trieste in the west, from Riga to Odessa in the east, and the Balkans proper in the south constitutes an almost hopeless problem when it comes to the drawing of frontiers.

[82] It is perhaps unnecessary to point out that an absolute application of the principle of self-determination in the matter of frontier drawing would in many cases merely result in absurdities. Economic, historic and strategic considerations cannot be totally ignored; in the end there is no other criterion but that of reasonableness in effecting some compromise between various valid arguments. The same applies to the case of areas of mixed population, such as the Banat of Temesvar, for example. As stated in another connection, the suggestion that populations be moved in order that frontiers might be neater was wholly alien to the thinking of 1919, still generally colored by the humane and civilized outlook of the nineteenth century.

And this points to a fundamental consideration. If German grievances received more attention than others, and if Danzig was the occasion for a renewed outbreak of war, the reason lies therefore not in the abstract validity of the grievance but rather in the fact of power. One might indeed take the position that while it may not too much matter that Hungary was discontented, to irritate Germany was unwise because Germany was more likely to be in a position to back her wishes with substantial power at some future time. Such an approach should not be dismissed, though few would care openly to espouse it, for it is tantamount to acceptance of the primacy of the rights of power.

Not the map of 1919, then, but the principle of self-determination that lay behind the drawing of that map is what ought to be challenged if the frontiers of the postwar are to be criticized [83]. This indeed may be done; there is nothing sacrosanct about the principle the discovery of which is relatively recent. Not so recent, however, but that it embodies much of the historic trend since at least the French Revolution. The settlements of 1919 in this respect were a culmination, conceivably a high point, after which other forces may appear to have become more powerful determinants of change [84].

Many would think so now who, whether they be Marxists or not, put the greater stress on economic factors. Such stress, now often greater in the so-called free West than in lands formally dedicated to the Marxian gospel, justified as it may be, is after all but recognition of the complexity of the relationships that have come to prevail in the operation of the material life of nations and of men. This is not new, though the complexity has been fast increasing, and this also can now be understood: the world of 1919 thought to a large extent of merely returning to the stable relationships of pre-1914 when the gold standard everywhere prevailed as the fit symbol of the existing stability.

That the seemingly static equilibrium was a false image; that the marvelous nineteenth century growth of population, industry, and trade was perhaps passing accident, made possible by the special simultaneous existence of a set of favorable circumstances that served to conceal the fragility of what had come to look like settled permanence; all this was far better understood after another breakdown and as the result of analyzing the reasons for the failure to return to those conditions of pre-1914.

---

[83] The contrast between the preservation of the essential bloc of Germany and the total disintegration of Austria-Hungary is enlightening at this point. It is sounder to say that the war itself grew out of the tensions of nationalism in the Dual Monarchy than to say that that state was destroyed by the war and the subsequent peace.

[84] The answer to this must clearly be left to the future, especially when one contemplates the revival of national tensions in Europe with the recovery after the Second World War and the strong nationalistic component in the movements for emancipation among peoples. What the relations of India and Pakistan, for example, will turn out to be over the years makes for interesting speculation. The Israeli case is perhaps too obvious to need comment.

It still happens today that economists make fallible predictions, but undeniably we have learned a great deal since 1919. The economic thinking of the time was, with few exceptions [85], relatively primitive and naïve. This is at most explanation, if not justification, of what would be universally regarded as some of the economic absurdities of the peace of 1919. Upon them we shall touch again, but this may now be added: economic provisions of treaties are changed with relative facility; after 1919 the process began almost before the ink was dry on the signatures of the treaties. It is otherwise with territory which has seldom changed hands save as the aftermath of armed conflict.

That the peace settlements of the First World War were susceptible of improvement few would care to deny. But this is not to say that they were the instruments of wickedness that legend was to make of them [86]. It is perhaps not amiss to recall that the Covenant of the League was part of the treaties of peace. Much as this arrangement has been criticized, the fact remains that here was a contribution, a novel experiment, which the characterization of noble in purpose became rather better than that other experiment which a later American President so described.

The League has failed, we know, and we can analyze its short-comings and discourse on the causes and manner of its passing. Some of those very things will have to be considered later in this essay. But none of it was in 1919 irrevocably preordained. Germany to be sure was disarmed and placed on probation. Why should she not? She had after all violated Belgium, dictated Brest-Litovsk, and unquestionably threatened to establish a military dominance over Europe. At the very least, a large contribution could in all fairness be demanded of the German people, moral to the restoration of confidence, and physical to the reconstruction of Europe. If it were to be true that they had genuinely espoused the ways of democracy and of peace, then, after

---

[85] Keynes is the most famous among the critics of the economic aspects of the peace and his *The Economic Consequences of the Peace,* which appeared as early as 1920, achieved immediate notoriety. Broadly speaking, it may be said that the best economic thinking of the immediate post-war was British. This is only natural, for Britain's position of dependence upon the conditions of international exchanges made her aware earlier and more keenly than others of the consequences of such attempts as that to collect enormous cash reparations from Germany, for instance. Even Britain, however, had still much to learn about international financial relationships as is shown by what is now generally considered her mistaken return in 1925 to the pre-1914 gold parity of the pound.

[86] The persistence of the legend is of interest as evidence of the inability to revise once-established categories of thought. One might quote Secretary Dulles' words at the quadripartite Berlin Conference on January 26, 1954: "We then [in 1919] believed that the way to exorcise the evil from the German spirit was to occupy Germany, demilitarize German, impose upon Germany humiliating discriminations so she would always be a nation apart, branded openly with the stigma of Cain". (*New York Times,* January 27, 1954). Allowing for flights of rhetoric and for the changing necessities of the day-to-day conduct of American foreign policy, Mr. Dulles' is a curiously colored description.

a term of years, their victors also could be expected to disarm and Germany would return as an equal to the community of nations.

This to be sure could be debated, as it was indeed. The reality could not be ignored of the strong feelings that the fact of war itself had aroused. Imponderables perhaps, but not for that less effective elements of the practical politics of nations after 1919. Or perhaps some would say that such considerations are irrelevant in the face of the more concrete realities of power. This is precisely what we wish to consider and we shall have occasion ot examine how large the psychological element looms in the politics of modern nations.

But, above all and to repeat once more, this must be borne in mind. Good or bad in themselves as they may have been, the settlements that closed the First World War were in large measure instruments that could be used in a variety of ways. This fact is more important than their specific shape. No more than any other treaties, past or future, could they forever freeze the *status quo*. This, then, is what we shall now do: trace through the coming years the manner in which the use of the instruments that were forged resulted in the failure of which the recurrence of war was evidence, with in passing an eye also to the question, why would fate have it so? [87]

---

[87] Perhaps it should be pointed out again that the discussion contained in this chapter does not purport to be a complete history either of the war or of the peace settlements. The omissions are numerous and they are deliberate, the purpose of the present essay being to analyze certain aspects of historic development by drawing upon the total content of the story for purposes of illustration.

PART II

———

THE FALLACIES CONCEALED

CHAPTER III

THE FALSE PEACE: VERSAILLES TO LOCARNO

1. EUROPE AFTER THE WAR

The Revolt of the Masses

It is at present, and for some time, especially since the First World War, has been, a well-nigh universally accepted view, in the United States and in many other countries as well, that peace is a desirable condition; correspondingly, war is a state to be avoided save in the most stringent necessity of self-defense. [1] But whatever added validity the modern tools of war may have given to this desire for peace, it is worth reminding oneself that such a view has by no means commanded universality of acceptance either in time or place. Even leaving aside the fatalistic belief that war is an inevitable evil, the more positive assertion that it has been at least an instrument of progress has had over the centuries many supporters.

Quite apart from the traditional importance of the military class and the time-honored stress on the military virtues, [2] this interpretation is not to be lightly dismissed. If, on the moral level, war serves to bring out the worst as well as the best in man, likewise on the material level its consequences are mixed. The view that there are no victors in modern war, already voiced before 1914, [3] may prove to be correct

---

[1] The sources of such a view of war are complex. The impact of war itself and the havoc caused by it is one, but only one. Such an explanation would have validity in Europe, but hardly in the United States where the anti-war feeling was no less strong. The feeling is perhaps to be associated with a particular stage in the evolution of society.

Another aspect of the matter which the experience of the last thirty years has emphasized and clarified is the difficulty of defining aggression, and correspondingly self-defense. This fact, combined with technical developments, speed, range and effectiveness of weapons, has produced a situation where, even in the United States, the thought of preventive war can be considered without producing the automatic reaction of rejection that it did, not many years ago.

[2] Taking the history of Europe as a whole since the days of Rome, it may be said that it is only quite recently that the military and the stress on military virtues have lost their place of eminence in the structure and outlook of society.

[3] The classical illustration is the famous book of Norman Angell, *The Great Illusion,* first published in 1910.

in future; it cannot be said to have so far been conclusively and un-qualifiedly established.

To take the clearest case of all, there is little question for instance that the United States benefited materially from both World Wars, in the clear and simple sense at least that the productive capacity of the country, most basic source of wealth, was vastly augmented under the impact of the demands of war; there can be little argument that the fact of war gave an added impulse to what might be regarded as the normal rate of growth of the country. Taking the purely economic, or statistical, view of the matter, the cost of this gain, even allowing for human loss, has been small. The consequences are writ large in the present position of world power of the United States. [4]

The case of Europe may seem different. Indeed it is, as there will be occasion to examine, but in Europe also the war was a great promoter of change. Moreover, despite the loss, this change was not mere retrogression, but rather acceleration of trends that may be called basic in the evolution of the Western, in fact the whole, world. [5] Granting that the war grew out of the clash of national, imperial, and economic rivalries, its effects were considerable on that most important nineteenth century phenomenon best put under the general label of "rising of the masses" or "emergence of the mass man," phenomenon to which those other labels, democracy, socialism, technology and science, popular press and popular opinion, should also be attached.

Of necessity, the war had been fought by these masses. Strong as were among them the influence of the national idea and the nationalistic virus, other influences had been at work as well, among which the Marxist was one of the most important. [6] July 1914 had dealt a heavy blow to international socialism, but it has been pointed out that with the prolongation of hostilities the movement made some recovery and attempted to resume its former role across and above frontiers. [7] The events that took place in Russia during 1917 gave it a renewed impulse as well as a novel direction. What had been the Revolutionary wing of the movement was now in actual control of a particular government

---

[4] The uniqueness of the position of power of the United States was more clearly marked after the First than after the Second World War when Russian power presents a serious challenge.

[5] This may be described as progress if the word be taken in its etymological sense, neutral from the standpoint of moral values. Whether this "progress" be improvement or the reverse is an issue that need not be considered at this point, though the reminder may be relevant that the contention that the world is drifting toward perdition is an old and hardy perennial.

[6] It may be pointed out that the Churches, especially the Roman Catholic, for all their loss of influence with large sections of the population, and for all their antagonism to the Marxist view, have nevertheless an element of the inter- or supra-national in their essence. Thus the Vatican took what might be described as a detached view of the conflict and had been generally favorable to a peace of compromise.

[7] See above, pp. 54-5.

from which began to issue indiscriminate appeals to ex friend and foe to emulate the Russian example.

If these events inevitably put new stresses on the Socialist parties among the belligerents, they also served to give sharper focus to the discontent of the masses, discontent that was fed by the dreary prospect of endlessly renewed demands for further sacrifice. These effects were deeply felt on the continent of Europe, [8] but it was in Britain that Lloyd George envisioned the future as "a world fit for heroes to live in." What could this mean save the holding out of hope as reward for the sacrifices demanded of the people, albeit in the form of pie-in-the-sky glibness? A world safe for democracy, the war to end wars, all these were part of the same effort to maintain the allegiance of the masses to the war effort by raising correspondingly high their hopes.

The propaganda was highly successful in raising these hopes, oblivious of the fact that, in belligerent Europe at least, the first and most immediate effect of the war was destruction and waste plus an accumulation of debt rather than expansion of productive capacity. Demobilized soldiers upon returning home were apt to find less of pie-in-the-sky than of the more prosaic search for a job. [9] The widespread disillusion seemed fertile ground in which to sow the seeds of Bolshevik propaganda, and concern was great among governments lest the seeds take root and bear fruit.

Mention has also been made before of the immense, if evanescent, popularity of President Wilson among the European masses. To a degree — anticipation of the roles of Russia and America after another Armageddon — Wilson and Lenin emerged as two pole stars for peoples at once confused, wearied, and hopeful. [10] With the unexpected turn of American events, the repudiation by the American people of the short-lived excursion into world leadership, the Russian star assumed greater proportions in the international firmament as its establishment at home was made secure.

Much that we hear at present about the danger of Communism in Europe had its counterpart immediately after the First World War. The Russians entertained high hopes of the possibility of revolution in Germany and for a time devoted considerable effort to the furtherance

---

[8] The growing consciousness of weakness in Austria-Hungary, the Reichstag Peace Resolution of 1917, the situation in France and in Italy in 1917, may be cited as illustrations.

[9] The shortage of civilian consumption goods caused by the war had created an accumulated demand which gave a boost to industry immediately upon the termination of hostilities. But this artificially pent up demand once satisfied, by about 1921, the more serious problem of long term adjustment had to be faced and a depression ensued. though of minor dimensions by comparison with the great depression of the thirties. Also. the nature and intensity of the stresses of readjustment varied considerably from country to country.

[10] A good description of this atmosphere may be found in Quincy Howe, *The World Between the Wars* (New York, 1953).

of that end. [11] The Italian Socialists trebled their parliamentary representation in the first potswar election in 1919. But in Hungary alone was a Bolshevik regime under Bela Kun successful in establishing itself. Under allied pressure, even this episode turned out to be but a passing incident. In the end, revolution, if it could not be defeated in Russia proper, was not on its side capable of achieving success beyond the dimished borders of this Russia wherein the *cordon sanitaire* successfully contained it.

It will be noted — which should not be surprising — that there was a marked correlation between the degree of the revolutionary danger and the intensity of the disturbance resulting from the war. It was in defeated Germany that revolution was essayed and in defeated Hungary that it was temporarily successful; among the victors, Italy, the weakest, was the most shaken and the first to yield her existing institutions to a novel experiment. [12] The older-established, deeper-rooted and wealthier, democratic systems of Britain and France continued essentially unaffected in their fundamentals by the impact of war; but even in these countres the effects were deep though not violently revolutionary in their manifestations. The decade of the twenties was to witness in Britain the true emergence of the Labour Party [13] and the displacement by it of the Liberals, destined henceforth to virtual extinction. As early as 1923 Britain had her first Labour Prime Minister in the person of Ramsay MacDonald, and the more flexible operation of British politics was to prove capable of absorbing the necessary far reaching changes the impact of which was to lead the more rigid French structure to the stalemate of impotence that characterized it even more after the Second World War.

But this is anticipating our story. The stresses to which the French system was subject will appear as a factor of great consequence for Europe as a whole during the decade of the thirties. The preceding decade saw the French system operating in traditional fashion and with seeming success. There were strikes and labor unrest in France after the war, but no serious threat to the regime as such. But be it in Britain

---

[11] Germany was and is the king pin in the Communist scheme of world revolution, a logical enough view in the light of the degree of industrial development of that country and of its crucial and central position in Europe. In the period immediately following the war there were actual attempts at violent seizure of power in Berlin as well as in Munich, but these were suppressed with relative facility.

[12] The danger of Bolshevism in Italy in 1919 and after was much exaggerated, particularly by Fascism which had a vested interest in exploiting the myth that it had saved the country from Communism. The fact remains, however, that the existing democratic system of Italy was incapable of maintaining itself.

[13] The Labour Party existed before the war but its strength in Parliament was so small as to have little effect on the operation of the normal two-party (Conservative and Liberal) system. It is one of the interesting aspects of the operation of British politics that the emergence of Labour did not lead to the establishment of a three-party system, save for the relatively brief period during which the Liberal Party was dwindling into insignificance.

or in France, outwardly least disturbed, in Germany or Italy, where revolution threatened or was thought to threaten, or in Russia where revolution took control, the power of the rising mass was everywhere a force that must increasingly be reckoned with.

This raised a problem, the full import of which was not adequately perceived at first, the problem of how to deal with, or control, the mass and mass opinion. In the immediate aftermath of war it seemed as if the slogan "to make the world safe for democracy" were in a fair way to being made reality. The Russian Revolution, the precise course of which was for that matter still uncertain, and the dictatorial nature of the newly installed Soviet regime, could be explained, or excused, on the basis of the peculiar conditions, mainly the backwardness, of the Russian milieu. [14] But in mid Europe, in Germany and in the new states arisen out of the disintegration of Austria-Hungary and the territorial losses of Russia, the story was everywhere the same of constitutions patterned on the classical model of the West.

After the lapse of forty years we are more ready to accept the fact that democracy may not be equally suited to all times, circumstances, and peoples; and that even if democracy is assumed *in abstracto* to be the "best" political system, its successful functioning cannot be divorced from certain preconditions — political maturity, a sense of responsibility are among these — which a slow evolutionary process can alone produce. There was in 1918 some of the same aura about "democracy" that used to be attached to the word "constitution" a hundred years earlier. Similar disillusions were destined to ensue.

The Italian case is an enlightening illustration. After four years of what might be described as groping confusion the country surrendered itself to Fascism. Mussolini did not so much save the country from Bolshevism, though he exploited the Red bogey to the full in obtaining conservative support and financial assistance, as he promised a way out of an impasse. [15] The stress should be put on "promised", for the Fascist program — if such a name can be used to dignify a jumble of

---

14 The new Soviet regime put at first considerable stress on world revolution which it did its best to foster. But the chief immediate effect of Moscow's activity was to create an open split among the various Socialist parties of Europe. As a consequence, those elements in Socialism which had sufficient sympathy for the Russian Revolution became Communist parties, henceforth servilely subservient to Moscow, while the more conservative, or evolutionary, wing of Socialism constituted the Socialist parties. These latter may be regarded from this time as definitely integrated into the Western tradition of democratic parliamentarianism of which they became some of the staunchest supporters.

15 It must be remembered that Mussolini became Prime Minister in accordance with the proper functioning of the existing Italian constitution. Entrusted by the King with the task of forming a government, his ministry was endorsed by Parliament. But it is also well to recall that the Chamber had only thirty-five Fascist deputies in it. No clearer illustration could be given of the voluntary abdication of a democracy, acknowledging its own incapacity to function.

incoherence — could mean all things to all men. Yet the incoherence was in itself significant. Fascism was an opportunistic adaptation to circumstances which gradually shaped it into a system. If the national idea was exalted there was not a little socialist content in Fascism, of which the name of the German version, National Socialism, is a far apter characterization.

Nationalism and Socialism had been traditional opponents, standing at opposite poles of the political spectrum. To join them may have shown confusion, but it may also be regarded as a stroke of genius. To point to the class struggle as futile waste while diverting the conflict into new channels by stressing the discrepancy between haves and have-nots at the national, instead of the social, level was evidence at least of a shrewd understanding of popular psychology. Doctrinaire Marxists might refuse to be taken in, but many among the little-thinking mass would respond. If Fascism did not command very high enthusiasm in Italy, neither was the opposition to it impressive. [16] And one would hesitate to say that Nazism did not command the allegiance of a willing majority of the German nation. The effort to persuade through education and propaganda could be bolstered by an elaborate apparatus to suppress opposition and coerce dissension. All in all here was a new response to novel circumstances. The mass had risen; it would not be denied its rights, but instead outwardly exalted; it would not be denied the suffrage or kept illiterate as in days of yore, but on the contrary encouraged — even dragooned — to share the benefits of press, radio and cinema, all carefully controlled and edited by the state. These are no doubt bitter and unsuspected fruit to the naïve believers in the mere spread of literacy, education and the suffrage as the simple and easy panaceas that would bring the millennium on earth; our time has clearly shown the resourcefulness of unforeseen adaptability to the problem of the rising of the masses. [17] Passing transitional aberration, one may hope and wish, but undeniably a great reality and force risen out of the ashes of the world of 1914.

The use of wilfully and deliberately distorting propaganda in lieu of education combined with ruthless suppression of dissent are most undemocratic methods. But between them and the free play of beliefs

---

[16] And the high point of popularity of the regime was reached during the Abyssinian episode when sanctions were decreed by the League of Nations against Italy.

[17] The Soviet system has shown, if anything, even greater refinement and thoroughness in the combination of persuasion and coercion than either Fascism or Nazism. The common element is strong between the three systems, that the word totalitarian best describes. There remains, however, the important difference that Communism established itself through violent revolution and had behind it a long established philosophy, whereas the Italian and the German systems came to power through the smooth operation of the existing constitutions in their respective countries and can hardly be said to have had behind them a *prior* system of thought comparable to the Marxist.

and ideas, [18] characteristic of democracy, there is this much in common that in both systems the role of the mass and its opinions, however the latter engendered, is receiving overwhelming attention. Even Britain, oldest and most stable of democracies, indulged in the khaki election of December 1918, though the consequences of this emotional manifestation were neither drastic nor lasting. Likewise, France in 1919 elected a Parliament that reflected the emotions of war. The *bleu horizon* Chamber gave way in 1924 to a more normal representation of the French nation, but we shall see the later disastrous effects of the expression of popular opinion in France, opinion that was free, but also confused, bewildered, and as a consequence divided into a fatal stalemate of resulting inaction.

Considering the long-term trend which has been put under the label of "rising of the masses," a trend to which the war had given added momentum, the chief concern of these masses can be said to have had two dominant aspects; these may be described as the economic and the national. The first expressed itself as a demand for jobs and for improved conditions of work in general, the claim now given virtually universal recognition which has led or is leading under all flags and all systems to the welfare state.

The economic effects of the war were many, but what best describes their totality is the word dislocation. The purely negative aspect of war, waste and destruction, had been impressive; yet it is also clear that the recuperative capacity of modern industry had been underestimated. To take but an example, among the Western states France had suffered far the greatest physical damage. For that reason, France was entitled to receive the largest share — 52 percent — of German Reparation. But in actual fact the physical reconstruction of France was effected with both success and speed and largely independently of the German contribution. Regarded purely as an economic matter, and all considerations of justice and morality left aside, it may be said that France was fully capable of absorbing the damage of war. The financing of this same reconstruction was another matter, however; it led in the end to the devaluation of the franc to the extent of 80 percent of its prewar value. Such inflation and the repudiation of debt that it represented did not go without causing profound social stresses and readjustments. [19] In varying degrees, the French experience was typical

---

[18] The fact should be neither concealed nor underestimated that much that is broadcast through the mass communication media, press, radio, television, etc. in the democratic countries can only be described as propaganda in the pejorative sense of the word. The theory that all opinions should have their day in court and that, as a consequence, truth will out and triumph is an assumption that some would say requires a strong dose of optimism to stomach. The assumption works well enough in times of relative quiet; in periods of stress it is apt to suffer.

[19] Germany underwent the complete destruction of her currency before a new stability was reached. British finances were handled better than either

of that of most belligerent countries. Both within and among countries, the old relationships of trade and finance were disrupted, some of them permanently. [20]

If the war had given rise to high expectations among the masses where their economic affairs were concerned it had also aroused national feeling at the popular level. The desire for peace, given expression in the slogan "the war to end war," may have been shared by friend and foe alike, but the very desire received irreconcilable expressions when it came to the terms of this peace. The same thing which to an overwhelming section of French opinion meant mere security and simple justice, appeared in German eyes as revenge and unwarranted punishment. Opinion once aroused — and the necessities of war itself caused governments to seek to arouse it — it was no easy matter to backtrack. Many were, and are, the occasions when statesmen had to plead, sometimes genuinely and other times not, the necessities of domestic opinions and parliaments as obstacles to their acceptance of arrangements the desirability of which was, and is, by them recognized. [21]

Enough has been said perhaps to give some indication of the difficulties that faced postwar Europe as a consequence of a century of progress in the form of giving growing recognition to the rights of the common man. The world of 1815 presented by comparison an infinitely simpler and more manageable picture. [22]

If Lenin would be the Messiah that would lead the world to salvation as a consequence of the proper understanding of the operation and effects of economic factors, it may be said that for a time at least his chief rival was Wilson. He, too, could save mankind, but the stress in

---

French or German, but in some respects Britain, dependent as she is on foreign trade, was saddled with a more difficult and lasting problem than either of those countries.

[20] The changed international position of the United States from that of debtor to that of *the* world's creditor, direct consequence of the war, is one which to this day remains an unresolved problem.

[21] The illustrations that could be given of this are legion. The American return to isolation after the First World War and the disastrous demobilization after the Second World War are good examples of the influence of opinion. Much of French action, or inaction, after the Second World War can be explained on the same score. Conversely, a regime like the Nazi, where opinion is controlled and manufactured instead of freely expressed, found it possible to make a pact with Poland in 1934, an arrangement that German opinion would hardly have countenanced under the Weimar regime.

[22] Which is one reason at least why the settlements of 1815 proved more lasting than those of 1919-1920. This is not be misunderstood as an argument in favor of the *ancien régime*, but the fact has to be faced of the difficulties, complexities, and shortcomings that attend the operation of a democratic system; simple and naïve optimism of the eighteenth-century variety clearly will not suffice, and the refusal to acknowledge this is one of the best ways to invite the dangerous shortcut of totalitarianism. Mention is apt at this point of the recently republished reflections of Wilfred Trotter, *Instincts of the Herd in Peace and War, 1916-1919* (London, 1953).

his case was on universal and lasting peace. The strength of this appeal will not be stressed again; it found concrete expression in the League of Nations. The very imperfections of the peace were to be mitigated and might be redressed by this agency. The Saar and Danzig were not annexed by France and Poland respectively: the League would supervise their future ; though far reduced in numbers, minorities still existed in Europe, but the new states had been forced to accept the novel curb of minorities treaties, over the execution of which the League again would stand watch. Ex-German overseas possessions and much of the Arab world were turned mainly to the control of Britain and of France: but they were dubbed mandates and ultimate title to them rested in the League, to whose Mandates Commission the mandatories were accountable for their stewardship.

Bearing the record of the past in mind, these were truly revolutionary innovations, provided, however, that they would become living realities. The qualification is important and it impinged, as pointed out before, on the unanswered question: how would the power of the League be made effective and wherein did that power lie? The League had no distinct and separate existence beyond the collectivity of its members. Real power lay in these members' hands and the control of it was not surrendered; the question therefore might be phrased: would these rise to a higher view than narrow and immediate interest for the sake of the common, in the long term their own individual, good? A vicious circle appears at this point which no way has so far been found of breaking. The League, however sanguine one might be about its prospects, was obviously an untried instrument; could those possessed of power, the Great Powers, be expected to exchange the safety that their own means provided for the guarantee of the problematic decisions of a parliament of nations? [23]

Whatever the future might hold in store, one thing was clear: the world of 1919 was still a world of nations and the relationship of power among these nations, pending the day when power might be brought effectively under the rule of law, remained of paramount importance. It is therefore necessary to have a clear picture of the extent of existing power and of the precise nature of its distribution; this is especially the case after 1919, for the state of affairs that emerged from the First World War was in some respects unique and unprecedented.

---

[23] The result, not surprisingly, has been a compromise — unanimity rule in the League, veto in the United Nations — that provides an escape for the Great Powers. It is another consequence of the same situation that the most genuine supporters of world organization, whether League or United Nations, have been and are the smaller Powers. This is, in the last analysis, but a recognition on their part that their security cannot be entrusted to their own power. What the effects may be of a condition where all, great or small, come to feel that their own means are incapable of ensuring their safety, a condition that may have in effect already been reached, makes for interesting speculation.

The Relationship of Power

When peace was finally restored after the Napoleonic episode the professed purpose of its provisions had been a return to the *status quo ante* the French Revolution. If many of the effects of that disturbance could not be undone, in terms of the power distribution and organization of Europe the Congress of Vienna may be said to have been largely successful in the achievement of its aim: the picture of 1815 did not radically differ from that of 1789. Many of the effects of war could no more be undone in 1919 than those of the French Revolution could a hundred years earlier; in that sense the war had been a powerful and lasting promoter of change. But in terms of power distribution based on a return to the *status quo ante,* 1919 was radically different from 1815. An important distinction must be made at once between immediate circumstances and long term reality.

For the European members of the victorious coalition victory had served an essentially negative purpose. They had prevented Germany from ousting them from their former positions but this had only been achieved at a high, not to say disastrous, cost to themselves. Britain had no illusions about the fact that her former position of primacy of power had passed to the United States. [24] But, even more important, because it touched upon the issue of the sheer necessities of existence, was the fact that the delicate and successfully operating balance under which Britain had grown and prospered had been destroyed. The multiple relationships of trade were altered, irretrievably in some cases; markets lost to Japan or the United States for instance were not to be recovered, while much of the foreign investment had been consumed. These losses were less dramatically obvious than the ravaged cities of France; their effect was no less and even in some ways more lasting: cities could be rebuilt, trade might not be regained. After the war Britain was permanently saddled with sick industries, depressed areas, and an irreducible minimum of unemployment. [25] Little wonder that the great interest of British policy was not security or Reparation, but general economic restoration, not least of Germany with whom her trade relations used to be so important. Beyond a question Britain issued from the war substantially diminished.

The appearance of victory was even more misleading where France was concerned. The point has been made earlier [26] that, prior to 1914,

---

[24] Her acceptance of naval parity with the United States, in lieu of her former insistence on the two-power standard, was clear evidence of this recognition. The fact that this was done with good grace is credit to British political realism.

[25] The sound — by orthodox standards — management of British finance and the return of the pound to the 1914 gold parity in 1925 tended to give a misleading picture of the British position. The costly effort entailed in the reestablishment of the pound had but short-lived results; gold payments were again suspended in 1931.

[26] See above, p. 37.

a combination of circumstances served to mitigate and conceal the relative decline of France's power among European states. Quite correctly, France had felt that in the event of conflict she must not face German power alone; the war had found her joined by more allies than her fondest dreams could have envisioned. Her contribution to the common victory had been lavish in blood, in treasure, and in the form of providing the chief and final battleground; but the very fact that it had taken the joint efforts of such an immense coalition went to show that the discrepancy between her own power unassisted and the German was even greater than it had been thought to be. The elation of victory, such as it was, went accompanied by an acute consciousness of weakness, hence fear and an unsatiable craving for guarantees of security.

Not only this, but the war itself had caused, through the losses sustained, a further diminution of French power. The economic damage, if repairable, had been immense, and the significance of the manpower loss was particularly serious because of the unique demographic condition of France. This, too, has already been mentioned. In brief, it is not unfair to say that the cost of victory had caused France, for the long term, a graver injury than that of defeat had caused Germany.

By contrast, Germany was indeed defeated, but the record of her military performance was such that all would grant its high order and that it could, for Germany, be source of future confidence in her own strength. Just as French victory had been procured through the assistance of a world-wide coalition, so likewise Germany had only succumbed under the weight or overwhelmingly superior numbers and resources. When she signed the armistice, warrant of her defeat, Germany was still in occupation of large sections of the victors' territory; her own sacred soil knew not invasion and as a consequence she had suffered none of the destruction at home that had been the lot of some victors, France most of all. [27] If her manpower loss was large, proportionately comparable to the French, this must be set against a totally different demographic picture. Again for the long term, the record of the war was calculated to instill confidence rather than fear in Germany. [28]

Quite other was the picture of Germany's chief ally. Austria-Hungary had simply ceased to exist. Her power was truly destroyed, presumably in lasting fashion. The states that emerged from her demise all fitted into the category of small European Powers. From the standpoint of the power structure of Europe, the outcome is best summarized by saying that Balkan conditions had extended into the very heart of Europe. But the consequences of Balkanization were great, for they

---

[27] It is little wonder in the circumstances that the legend soon prospered in Germany that her defeat was not a genuine one but the result of unfortunate accidents, such as betrayal at home (the stab-in-the-back myth) and broken allied promises (the not-lived-up-to armistice contract based on the Fourteen Points).

[28] Another war has shown how correct these estimates of power were.

meant that a huge vacuum of power had been created where one Great Power had formerly held sway. Power, like nature, may be said to abhor a vacuum. Traditionally, the Balkan states had been pawns in the game of greater Powers' politics, pawns which in turn could use, or at least sway, the actions of these greater Powers to their own purposes, as the circumstances of the outbreak of the great war themselves had shown.

Traditionally also, or at least for some considerable time before the war, *Mitteleuropa* had been a German or German-Austrian dream. Now that the Dual Monarchy was gone would not Germany, especially a Germany set back in her essays at *Weltpolitik,* more than ever tend to regard this area of fragmented power as the natural sphere of her activity, all the more so that from the point of view of rational economic relations, the area may in a sense be said to have been the logical complement of the German economy? If Danubia, because of the existing state of power there, was in 1919 cause of less attention and concern than Germany (because of the latter's potential), for the long term again the future of that region constituted a problem no less serious than the German.

If Balkan quarrels had had such widespread repercussions, that was because Great Powers's rivalries, mainly the Austro-Russian, were in them involved. Austria was now gone, but what of Russia? When the dust of conflict had settled over the chaos of war and revolution [29] it appeared that the frontiers of Russia had been considerably pushed back to the East. Much of the work, some of it going back to Peter the Great, of her penetration into Europe had been undone with the loss of the Baltic provinces and Bessarabia and the reconstitution of an independent Poland. But large and important as these losses were, the greater core of Russia, unlike Austria-Hungary, still remained intact. [30] What its future would be, constitutionally or otherwise, was uncertain; but whether Lenin stayed, or even should a Tsar return, it seemed only reasonable to expect that some sort of order would eventually return to this vast land; so great are its dimensions and resources and such the numbers of its people that one could count on Russia becoming at least an important factor in world affairs no less than she had been before the war. But, in view of the existing chaos, huge losses and far

---

[29] This may be said to have taken place with the conclusion of peace between Russia and Poland by the Treaty of Riga in March, 1921. Although there was still much seething unrest and some changes took place in Eastern Europe after the Russo-Polish peace, these changes were relatively minor and the larger international issue of Russia's place and her frontiers may be regarded as having become stabilized.

[30] Strictly speaking, one should henceforth speak of the Union of Socialist Soviet Republics (U.S.S.R.) of which Russia proper, the Russian Federated Socialist Soviet Republic (R.F.S.S.R.), is merely one of the members. We need not be concerned here with the genuineness, or lack thereof, of the constitutional changes that took place in the former empire of the Tsars, and just as Austria is often used when strict accuracy would demand Austria-Hungary, so likewise Russia will often be used here in lieu of the U.S.S.R.

reaching disintegration of all aspects of life and government, this certainly would take some time to happen. [31]

Meanwhile, the more immediate picture of the power reality was vastly different from what it might be expected to be after some years of recovery. In 1920 or 1921, when the various settlements had restored at least formal peace, the simple fact is that there was no power where three of the six Great Powers of Europe had been. The Danubian Monarchy was gone for good. Russia, as indicated, presumably would recover, but only in some possibly remote future. If the potential of Germany remained considerable, in 1919 Germany was defeated, disarmed and quite powerless; moreover, unlike Russia, she was subject to legal disabilities and supervision by her victors, the effects of which might, if these wished, be of considerable duration.

Britain knew her loss and her diminution, but she could also contemplate the reality of very solid gains. If her trade had lost some overseas markets, more radical by far had been the severance of Germany from her own overseas connections where she had been a feared competitor. The German naval threat found its way for the most part in British custody; pending its final disposition, the scuttling by its crews that sent it to the bottom of Scapa Flow Bay constituted in some respects the simplest and most convenient solution of the problem of its fate. The long tradition of imperial growth was crowned by the establishment of paramount British control or influence throughout the major part of the Arab section of the former Ottoman Empire, [32] while Russia had conveniently eliminated herself from the Straits by denouncing and renouncing the 1915 agreement with her allies which had granted her their possession. [33] Germany's total eviction from Africa,

---

[31] Mention should be made of two more states in order to complete the picture of the relationships and distribution of power in Europe. Italy was rated formally a Great Power, and while this position might be questioned, she retained considerable importance. Although the war put a great strain on her meager resources, with consequences that have already been mentioned, her basic position of power may be said to have been essentially unchanged, save in one important respect. Now that the European balance of power had been destroyed, with it had gone the chief asset of Italian foreign policy. She might therefore, for the long term and irrespective of regime, be expected to favor a restoration in some form of the earlier condition.

New Poland, with a substantial territory and a population of some 35,000,000, was clearly in a different category from the minor European states. If the visions of Great Power role, entertained by an overheated nationalism, may be looked upon as delusions of grandeur, her potential and her location between Russia and Germany gave her very considerable importance. However, her long subjection to three different Powers presented her at first with the great problem of internal integration and organization.

[32] The French had received the Syrian mandate, but even there they had been induced to accept a revision of boundaries that placed Mosul in British-mandated Iraq. Even in Syria, the Arabs, if they could not have their first choice of independence, would have opted for British, rather than French, control as their second.

[33] The Russian zone south of the Caucasus, recognized in the Sykes-Picot agreement of 1916, naturally had the same fate.

of relatively minor importance in economic terms, seemed, immediately after the war, in terms of strategy, not a negligible gain. Taken in their totality, these advantages, around 1920, appeared to contain considerable substance.

France may have mourned her dead and with sound instinct feared the future, but she too had substantial gains to contemplate. Above all the fact that the defeat of Germany was of a nature that surpassed the wildest expectations that could have been entertained in 1914. Her insatiable thirst for reinsurance had led to the Anglo-American guarantee in lieu of her control of the Rhine. When this failed, there still was left the Treaty of Versailles which gave legal sanction to serious guarantees. As was stressed by Clemenceau and Tardieu during the debate on ratification in the French Parliament, for fifteen years French troops were entitled to occupy German soil. This temporary occupation was to insure the execution of the terms of the treaty; only upon faithful German fulfilment would it terminate. In the opposite event, constituting a breach of the treaty, France would be entitled to prolongation of the guarantee. And even if there were no more than doubts about German intentions, French legal and diplomatic ingenuity still might, when the time came, find ways of maintaining the guarantee. [34] There was even the League, and although, in this case as well, France had yielded to Anglo-American preference and tended to regard the novel instrument with a considerable measure of skepticism, the League was after all a guarantor of the *status quo,* or at least that aspect of it could be stressed. [35]

If we allow for the case of Italian power, seemingly little minded to assert itself far beyond the immediate confines of the country, of real and effective power in Europe immediately after the war, Britain and France between them shared close to the totality. It was no accident that these two countries, so long at odds over the centuries, had been allies during the war just ended. Basically, even before 1914, they had become powers of conservation, essentially on the defensive against the encroachments of new rising entities, among which the German was the sharpest challenger. Joint victors and beneficiaries of the fruits of victory, clearly both had the same basic interest in trying to enjoy their possessions in a climate of continuing peace. Injured and relatively diminished in a fundamental sense as they both were, their power was still considerable. Had they acted in unison, which they did not, they might conceivably have succeeded either in enforcing the peace that had been made or in leading Europe through a peaceful transition of change.

---

[34] This, to be sure, would be a matter of will, as much and rather more than of legality, but that is a later part of our story.

[35] The American abstention, leaving Britain alone to defend the Anglo-American point of view, had the effect of correspondingly strengthening the French position in League councils.

But in any event the power picture of Europe was an anomaly as a consequence of the virtual destruction of the power of three of its former major units. That two of these while momentarily powerless were not destroyed, hence would some day return to claim their rightful place of influence, made for an awkward state of things; Europe could after all not wait in a suspended state for the day when Russia would recover and Danubia had found some new stability. [36]

For the long term therefore it may be said that there were three major problems for Europe, which may be labeled the Russian, the German, and the Danubian or Central European, or that of the legacy of the demise of Austria-Hungary; this meant that no lasting stability could exist until these three regions had found their proper place within the whole. These large problems found expression in the concrete form of a myriad more localized and immediate issues. Whether or not Germany would accept the return of Alsace-Lorraine to France, she certainly was not reconciled to her Polish border, whether in the Corridor, in Danzig, or in Silesia. [37] Not to frontiers alone did Germany object; the whole treaty of peace was viewed by her, with virtual unanimity, as an unfair *diktat,* on the score of disarmament, of Reparation, of lost colonies, no less than on that of her frontiers in Europe.

The frontiers of Poland might be characterized as a collection of problems. That Poland should be at odds with Germany and Russia was no more than might in any event be expected, but she was not on good terms with either Lithuania or Czechoslovakia, new states issued like her from the war. [38] This last named country was the object of claims from Hungary, growing out of the presence of some 1,000,000 Hungarians in Slovakia, while similar grievances were for like reasons entertained by Hungary against both Yugoslavia and Rumania as well.

Out of the necessity deriving from her weakness Russia had come to terms with her new neighbors, save Rumania, from the Arctic to the Black Sea. That did not mean that she, any more than Germany, was truly reconciled to her new boundaries. It has been pointed out that Italy felt disgruntled and cheated of the fruits of victory. She had only absorbed a quarter of a million Austrians and three times that number of Slavs. That Italy should feel aggrieved was little consolation to Yugoslavs and to Austrians, who felt in turn that they had only yielded

---

[36] It was within the power of the Allies not to destroy German power, but the Russian and Danubian problems were largely beyond their control.

[37] The Silesian frontier was only settled after a plebiscite held in Upper Silesian in 1921. The division of the territory that ensued was not accepted as just in Germany, owing to the fact that the area as a whole had produced a German majority.

[38] The successful repelling of the Russians had made it possible for Poland to extend her eastern frontier so as to include large numbers of non-Polish population. From Lithuania Poland seized the capital city of Vilna and she entertained a grievance against Czechoslovakia over the division of Teschen.

to superior force and circumstances. The list of outstanding issues could be long extended.

That war should leave behind itself a train of bitterness is no less than can be expected; but, to return once more to the comparison with 1815, the state of things in Europe after the First World War differed from the post-Napoleonic mainly in two respects: in the abnormal power situation, and in the fact that all European states had now to take into their calculations and the formulation of their policies the fact that the masses had risen. How then did Europe proceed to organize herself?

2. BACKGROUND AND EMERGENCE OF THE FRENCH SYSTEM

The fact has been mentioned that the bulk of effective power in Europe at the end of the war lay in British and French hands, and that, even in unison, such power would have been taxed by the task of maintaining the organization of Europe. In actual fact, odd and strained as such a situation would have been, something far stranger came into existence which may best be described by the label "French system."

The End of the Wartime Alliance

It is appropriate at this point to cast again a glance at the United States. The importance of the role of America in procuring victory, then in shaping the peace, has been sufficiently stressed before, but one particular item must be mentioned again, the compromise whereby the French desire for security had received satisfaction through the tripartite arrangement whereby America and Britain jointly promised France their assistance in the event of renewed German aggression. This was the price for which France had yielded in the matter of the Rhine guarantee.

The abstract excellence of this solution was marred by the condition of domestic American politics which it had failed to take into consideration. When, in the summer of 1919, the treaty of peace with Germany came up for consideration in Washington, a great debate arose in the American Senate. It does not fall within the compass of this story to rehearse the dramatic course of this great debate, the result of which alone is of relevance to our purpose. [39] The debate, as

---

[39] There is not a little irony in the fact that the clash of personalities between President Wilson and Senator Lodge had much to do with the failure of ratification. Lodge was skilful enough not to offer frontal opposition, but to propose instead amendments to the Covenant of the League. Wilson may be said to have fallen into Lodge's trap, for it was in the end his stubborn adherence to an all-or-nothing attitude that prevented ratification of the treaty as a whole. On this point we may refer to D.F. Fleming, *The United States and the League of Nations* (New York, 1932) and to K. Schriftgiesser, *The Gentleman from Massachussetts: Henry Cabot Lodge* (Boston, 1944).

is known, did not hinge on the quality of the terms of peace imposed on Germany — that was an afterthought — but turned entirely on the issue of the safeguarding of American sovereignty which underwriting of the Covenant of the League some feared it might curtail. The net result was that America refused to ratify the Treaty of Versailles.

This result was at once unexpected and awkward. It may be idle to speculate on what the effect would have been of America's participation in the novel experiment that the League represented, but some consequences of the American abstention were immediately obvious: the League, for one, received a body blow almost from its inception. [40] But more important still, League or no League, was the significance of the rejection on the score of what it meant as to America's intentions vis-à-vis the rest of the world. In 1919, America was beyond question *the* greatest Power in the world. America might, formally and in theory, try to renounce contact with the rest of this world; in practice the attempt was meaningless, for the effects of abstention, though different, were bound to be quite as considerable as those of the most active and deliberate participation. From the time of the First World War, when America tipped the scales of the conflict in Europe, no history of the subsequent European record can have meaning that would ignore the role and influence of the United States. [41]

Not only did America decline to ratify the treaty of peace with Germany, but the treaty of guarantee with France never even emerged from the committee stage for debate on the floor of the Senate. This is a measure of the little interest that the arrangement commanded in American eyes at the time, but the consequences of American indifference were a serious matter. A treaty after all involves more than one partner; the reinsurance treaty was one part of a bargain between America and France, and the French part of it had been delivered in the form of provisions written into the Treaty of Versailles. Little consolation could France derive from the study of American constitutional processes and the contemplation of their operation in this instance. Nor would it serve to indulge in recrimination or to point out that Wilson had been less than wise in making the commitment that he had made. The simple fact, from the French point of view, was that France had been deprived without compensation of an important guarantee. [42] However consti-

---

[40] The absence of Germany and Russia was serious enough in an organization that professed universality; but to have it disowned by its very creator raised the question of its validity.

[41] The American return to isolationism is easy enough to understand in the context of past American history and experience. The futility of the effort has been realized and the consequences of this realization accepted, but not until the experience of another world war, a war to the precipitation of which the very effort at withdrawal was not without making some contribution.

[42] The point might be made that, independently of any American guarantee, it would not have been a wise thing for France to try to maintain permanent control of the Rhine. This may well be argued, but clearly was irrelevant at this stage.

It may be worth pointing out that, as with the matter of the desirability —

tutionally (in American terms) this had been done, France had been defrauded, and her reaction could hardly be other than one of resentment and frustration.

Beyond this what could France do? Coercing America or denouncing the Treaty of Versailles that she herself had signed was hardly within the domain of the feasible or the practicable. Her only alternative was to insist on strict enforcement of the German treaty which, if applied to the letter, provided by itself quite serious guarantees. Thus, by indirection, the American action, or rather inaction, was calculated to foster in France an attitude of intransigeance toward Germany. In addition, France could see to the maintenance of her military establishment; she could also look for any available substitutes for American help in the event of need. And these, as we shall see presently, were forthcoming.

But the consequences of the position taken by America went even beyond these results. The nature of the tripartite arrangement was such that, in the event of American refusal to implement it, an escape clause would also exonerate Britain. Britain elected to avail herself of this provision. No better evidence could be cited of the fact that Britain failed to recognize the broad and fundamental similarity of her position and basic interests with the French. [43] This, too, was in a way quite understandable; it was one more example of the not unusual fate of coalitions: held together by a common danger, the removal of that danger robs the association of its chief purpose and leaves its members free to focus on their other divergent interests. The German danger had, for the moment at least, unquestionably been eliminated. By comparison with the record of Anglo-French wartime coöperation, that of difference was of much longer duration; it was a bare twenty years before 1918 that open conflict had seemed a possibility. Twenty years — or even less if we take the date of the formation of the Entente in 1904 — is a very short time in the life of nations and it is no cause for surprise that Britain in so short a period should fail to grasp the true extent of the change that had taken place in her position — just as America could not realize at first that isolation was irrevocably ended.

The German danger had not in British eyes the same obsessive quality that it had for the French. Fitting into the context of the past record, it seemed more in the nature of repetition of earlier and by now familiar experience; Britain had survived the Armada and the

---

or inevitability — of involvement abroad, in the specific case of France, America has returned to the Wilsonian arrangement of 1919. France, now as then, is anxious to have the American guarantee, but to a degree the tables have been turned as a result of changed circumstances. If anything, it is America who is now pressing for the Atlantic Aliance, of some aspects of which it is France (with others) who is critical.

[43] The Anglo-French alliance, into which the Entente had been transformed during the war, remained in vigor, but the British decision could not but put a strain on it, being clear indication of British qualifications and reservations.

Napoleonic peril, rising thereafter in each case to greater heights of power. Germany had risen and fallen like her predecessors (in the British view and aspect of the story). Should new dangers arise from new quarters, and should even the German danger recur, they could and would be dealt with in their time. The imperial British approach did not envisage with cordiality, but rather with suspicion of their impracticality, schemes of indefinite duration, hard bound commitments, a heaping up of guarantees seeking to freeze the present into the future. [44]

Moreover, as pointed out before, if the threat to Britain, be it from Spain or France or Germany, must be removed when it became too great, the source of the threat itself must not be destroyed, but merely put back in its adequate place. Else the result would be mere substitution of one danger by another, hence frustration of the true British purpose. [45] Not obsessed, like France, by a clear picture of superior German power, Britain, once the emotionalism of war had very quickly subsided, could contemplate with equanimity, even desire, a restoration of Germany to a position of equality among the Powers, an outcome which could in addition be presented as a manifestation of the British devotion to fair play as much as credit to realistic British empiricism. To this may be added the fact, of no little importance, that German trade, hence German economic recovery, seemed a clear and important British interest.

In comparative terms, trade meant little to France. Commercial interests there were in France and they had definite views and influence when it came to such matters as German Reparation, but taking the broad view it may be said that the political approach had definite primacy in French eyes. German power was the obsession; anything that would curb, diminish, and control that power had attached to it the criterion of "good"; correspondingly, anything that would restore, enhance, or liberate that power was to be opposed. If the economic

---

[44] Excursions into the field of national psychology are strewn with pitfalls, but an important, if elusive, reality exists in these "national" characteristics. It is worth pointing out that if the British respect for, and obedience to existing law is rather greater than the French, the French attachment to the forms of legality tends to be stronger and more rigid than the British.

[45] Here again, this was tantamount to a misreading of the changed position of her own as well as of France's power. The fundamental difference between the post First Word War situation and earlier ones was that neither British nor French power was any longer rising — in relative terms at least — but precisely the opposite. This points to the basic tragedy of the British position in both world wars, which makes so apt the Churchillian title, *Triumph and Tragedy*, the fact that the consequence of the very victory achieved is to raise for Britain a problem no less difficult than that of which victory has disposed. On this score, reference may be made to the penetrating review of *Triumph and Tragedy* which appeared in *The New Yorker* magazine of December 12, 1953.

recovery of Germany would tend to increase German power — and what else could it do? — so much the worse for economic recovery. [46]

More sensitive to the significance of economic factors, the British also feared that poor economic conditions in Germany might open there the door to that other danger, of which we hear so much more in our day, Bolshevik revolution. France was not too impressed by this argument. For the moment at least Germany could be controlled to the extent of blocking revolution. [47] The Communist danger, however, did exist; to deal with it meant a further extension of the commitments of French power, beyond Germany, into Eastern Europe. [48] It was France that inaugurated the policy of the *cordon sanitaire* vis-à-vis Soviet Russia.

For all the divergence of their outlooks Britain and France had an important element in common, a profound revulsion toward the fact of war and a correspondingly deep and sincere desire for lasting peace. [49] But even this common desire found divergent expressions: in France it meant an intensified wish for security, hence greater suspicion of and effort to control Germany; in Britain it found expression in a tendency to relax and trust, to forgive and forget both the unpleasant memory of war and the circumstances that had brought it about. [50]

The result of this state of affairs one might be tempted to describe as a comedy of errors had not the final outcome been renewed tragedy. In the early stages of the postwar, British policy contrived to achieve the results opposite to those intended. For the stress on German recovery, the insistence on what was regarded across the Channel as unwarranted softness, had the effect of making France feel less secure and correspondingly to make her all the more rigid and intransigeant.

---

[46] This may seem like blind stubbornness and in a way it was. Two things may be said on this score: first, the reality of economic necessities is more pressing and easily perceptible than long term and somewhat problematic considerations of power; second, the passage of time and subsequent events have shown French fears to have been justified.

[47] Revolutionary attempts of the Left had been successfully checked in Berlin in March, 1919 as well as in Bavaria in April without even the intervention of outside forces.

[48] France had assisted Poland in repelling the Russian invasion in the Russo-Polish war of 1920-1921. The broader significance of the Franco-Polish alliance will be considered later.

[49] The attraction of peace was great to all peoples at the end of the war, but the desire for "peace at any price" if anything increased in Britain and in France with the passing of the years, whereas a different climate developed elsewhere. This common feeling may be taken as evidence of the common defensive position of the two countries vis-à-vis the rest of the world, but the underlying reality of the similarity of position was not consciously apprehended until very late — too late — on the British side.

[50] This may be related to the curious phenomenon that appeared early in Britain and that is best described as a feeling of guilty conscience where Germany was concerned. The debate on war guilt, fed by the work of the revisionist school of historians, so prosperous in both Britain and America, and the widespread acceptance of the view that Germany had been unjustly treated, are part of the same story.

The effects of this intransigeance were to retard German recovery even in the purely economic domain. France wanted the British alliance, but not at any price; for the moment at least she had superior power, she was in fact almost the only effective power on the whole continent of Europe.

If British action may appear absurd — since it was from Britain's own point of view self-defeating — there is this to be said for the British case: must one unquestioningly accept the French view of an unreconstructed Germany, of the necessity of everlasting suspicion and control of her? Was not the true solution of, among others, the problem of French security to be found in a changed Germany, in final liquidation of the Franco-German quarrel, in true reconciliation of the age-old foes? This may be viewed as a generous, as much as a rational, hope. Unfortunately, in this case as in others, the weight of past history could not so easily or quickly be lifted. On both sides of the Rhine feeling ran strong and deep. What else could it have been? If the hope is to be realized, time alone, a long time, can bring such a result about. Meanwhile, even a reformed and peacefully minded Germany could have no other foreign policy than one aimed at restoring her position among the states of Europe; even a trusting and generously minded France could do no other than insist on adequate precautions. [51]

The question may be raised, why did not France pursue a policy of reconciliation toward Germany? Whatever the longer future might hold, for the nearer present it was undeniable that Germany was impotent. Was it not more unrealistic to think that Germany could forever be controlled than to gamble on the possibility that generosity would be reciprocated? Might not this be the very thing that would serve to establish in secure control in Germany those elements which on their part favored peace and reconciliation? Such forces after all existed, whatever their uncertain strength, difficult in any event of accurate assessment, might be. [52]

---

[51] One need not take a hopelessly fatalistic view of the problem of Franco-German relations — any more than of other international problems. The world does move and the nature of its problems changes. No better illustration can be given of this than the record of Anglo-French relations during the past half century. What must be realized, however, is the importance of the time element, and the limitations of a purely rational approach, especially when dealing with masses and their feelings. To point out that peoples "ought" to feel otherwise than they do may be as sound as it is irrelevant.

[52] The establishment of the Republic and the constitution of Weimar Germany were predominantly the work of the Left, supported by the Center. Depending upon the course of events, these forces might be strengthened or weakened with the passage of time. Undoubtedly, a policy of distrust would make their task more difficult vis-à-vis German opinion, although one should guard against assuming the validity of the converse proposition: there could be no assurance that a policy of leniency toward Germany might not merely be taken advantage of.

Part of the answer to this question has been given by pointing to the aroused state of feeling which the necessities of domestic politics made it impossible to flout, beyond a certain point at least. But there was more to it, which is perhaps made clearest by a comparison with the state of affairs after the Franco-Prussian war of 1870-1871. Having defeated France singlehanded, Bismarck took enough guarantees and precautions against her possible revenge; his ungenerous policy has indeed been much criticized as unwise. However, France was not disarmed and Bismarck would after a time gladly have resumed normal, or even amicable, relations with her, provided only that she renounced the thought of undoing the results of defeat.

But if Bismarck considered such a policy — and he might well have been far more generous than he was — it must be borne in mind that post-1871 Germany felt no fear of French power, of French power alone at least with which she quite rightly considered that she was capable of dealing. By contrast, the post-1919 situation presented a paradox: France was the victor — one of the victors at least — but the victor now feared the vanquished, correctly estimating the long term deficiencies of its own power. It is up to the stronger to allay the legitimate fears of the weaker; but how could that be done when, for the moment, the (ultimately) stronger was shorn of power which lay all in the hands of the (ustimately) weaker? This comes back to the fact, earlier mentioned, that the war itself had, despite victory, rather increased than reduced the discrepancy between the basic and lasting sources of French and German power. To this extent the victory was a false picture of reality. [53]

The war it will be said, quite truly, was more than a Franco-German contest, that particular aspect of it being but one component of a much larger conflict. But the American withdrawal and the relative one of Britain left France alone to a degree all the more contrasting with the record of the wartime alliance. What more natural in the event than that alternative solutions should be looked for by France?

Clearly, these alternatives, if they existed, were to be found on the continent of Europe. Something must be said at this point of Italy, already touched upon. Though basically weaker, and for that reason more strained by the war, Italy after all was also among the victors, and, next to France, constituted the one organized force in Europe. In a sense, Italy's victory was far greater than France's; if her prime enemy is considered to have been Austria-Hungary, the irrevocable demise of that Power was something of an altogether different character from the shackles, however stringent, to which German power was subject. Attractive vistas of expanding influence were opened up in Central Europe and the Balkans. Since, in addition, it might be expected that Germany would try to secure some at least of the inheritance of the

---

[53] The overall comparison between the Franco-Prussian war and the First World War would stress contrast rather than similarity, but on the limited score of the Franco-German relationship the point here made is valid.

Austro-Hungarian influence in those quarters, the future possibility of German danger might seem a common point of interest between France and Italy. [54]

But it must also be remembered that Italian policy had been founded on two cardinal principles: the maintenance and exploitation of the balance of power was one; never to be on the side opposite Britain was the other. This made for natural affinity between the policies of Britain and of Italy, an affinity that the pre-1914 record bears out. Like Britain, Italy was impressed after the war by the momentary distribution of force; no question for the moment that the equilibrium of power was destroyed. Italy therefore tended to share in large measure the British view that it was desirable to restore the balance of power through opposition to or curbing of the French. In concrete terms, this meant a limited support at least of German rehabilitation. It was not long before Italian complaints and disgruntlement over the "mutilated" victory began to be vented against France. [55]

The French System

America, Britain and Italy exhausted the list of available Great Powers when France came to envisage the possibility of alliances; but there were other possibilities. As early as September, 1920 a military agreement was concluded between France and Belgium. This may be regarded as both logical and natural in the circumstances. The pre-1914 guarantee of Belgian neutrality had been destroyed by Germany; in Belgian eyes the protection of French power was an obvious alternative. [56] Belgium is a very small Power, but whether from the point of view of strategy or from that of her resources, considerable relative to

---

[54] To a point this was so, but to a very limited degree only. Like France, Italy remained opposed to the *Anschluss* through nearly the entire interwar period.

[55] Being Italian, this resentment led to louder vocal expression and to local incidents and manifestations which had no counterpart in the more dignified and reserved British milieu. These were small matters, although the operation of the press tended to exacerbate popular feeling on both sides of the Alps.

On the score of the French policy and position toward Italy two things must be said. One, the French attitude of condescension toward Italian power, however justified it may have been, led to a policy that was somewhat cavalier and ungenerous — in the matter of colonial compensations, for example — and proved a sharp irritant to Italian opinion and feeling. To that extent the French behavior may be called unwise. But, on the other hand, and second, the French view that concessions to Italy, rather than purchase her gratefulness and loyalty, would be likely to create a demand for more, was basically sound.

[56] Belgium would have liked a tripartite arrangement involving Britain as well as France, but in the face of a British refusal fell back on the French connection alone. This British refusal is another aspect of the British withdrawal from commitments, of which the refusal to implement the French guarantee, after the American default, was a similar expression.

her size, her integration into the French defensive system was clearly valuable to France.

In older days, mainly in the seventeenth and eighteenth centuries, France had cultivated connections with three Powers which played a large part in the affairs of Eastern Europe, Sweden, Poland, and the Ottoman Empire, as a counterweight to Central European, mainly Habsburg, power. [57] Sweden was gone, a small Power quite content with the neutrality to which it was dedicated; the Ottoman Empire had finally collapsed and dissolved, the issue at the moment being whether even a small part of it, the purely Turkish, would succeed in freeing itself from subjection to the European victors. But Poland was again on the map. The difficulties of definition of the frontiers of the new Poland are known; they were greatest where Russia was concerned, but after the defeat of the Red armies in August, 1920, direct agreement established the Russo-Polish frontier as well where it was to remain until 1939. [58]

Poland, for obvious reasons of geography and history combined, was faced with two dangers, the German and the Russian. Considerable as her dimensions were, and whatever her exaggerated claims to Great Power status, clearly her potential power, under any conditions that could be described as normal, was not in the same category as either the German or the Russian, let alone the two in combination. Vis-à-vis Germany, and in view of the intensity of German feeling where the Polish frontier was concerned, Poland had precisely the same interest as France in keeping Germany under control.

But Poland, for the long term, feared Russia quite as much as, and rather more than, Germany. France, around 1920, was the chief exponent of the policy that in our day America has called containment. [59] By her position and dimensions Poland was the natural master piece in such a policy, and France had assisted Poland in repelling the Russian invasion in 1920. [60] Here then were two cardinal issues on which Polish

---

[57] Francis I was the first to establish the connection with the Turks as early as 1535. When Hohenzollern had definitely displaced Habsburg power in the nineteenth century, the Russian alliance was for France the pre-1914 version of the same traditional policy of promoting a counterweight in the East for Central European power.

[58] The formal peace of the Treaty of Riga was not signed until March 12, 1921, but the war had come to an end with the signing of the preliminaries in the preceding October.

[59] France had given support and assistance to the counter-revolutionary forces in Russia; after the failure of the White armies, she went over to the policy of containment, then dubbed *cordon sanitaire*.

[60] It is of interest that the Allies had urged on Poland a policy of moderation where Russia was concerned. The famous Curzon Line was the concrete expression of this advice. When Poland, sorely pressed, appealed for help, Germany refused to allow the passage of allied troops to go to her assistance. An allied mission was sent to Warsaw, where General Weygand did an effective job of advising the Polish armies.

and French policy saw eye to eye. What more natural than that a Franco-Polish agreement should be signed in 1921? [61]

In this agreement the two governments declared themselves "both desirous of safeguarding, by the maintenance of the treaties which both have signed or which may in future be recognized by both parties, the peace of Europe, the security of their territories and their common political and economic interests." Having paid due respect, as came to be the fashion in the international instruments of the period, to the League of Nations, [62] the heart of the agreement lay in this provision:

> If, notwithstanding the sincerely peaceful aims and intentions of the two contracting states either or both of them should be attacked without giving provocation, the two governments shall take concerted measures for the defense of their territory and the protection of their legitimate interests, within the limits specified in the preamble.

Some phrases are worth underscoring. *Maintenance of the treaties* as the best way *to safeguard their security and their interests* is one. The word "both" in the central article could only apply to a German attack; "either" took care of a possible Russo-Polish conflict as well as of German action against one or other ally. The treaty of alliance was in ostensible intent defensive — certainly so on the French side — and if the stress may have differed, greater on Germany for France, greater for Poland on Russia, that aspect of the matter was not apparent for some years.

From Russia, Rumania had taken possession of Bessarabia; [63] this gave her an interest similar to the Polish. A defensive alliance between

---

[61] The agreement was dated 19 February 1921. The text of it may be found in a variety of places. One convenient source is the *Survey of International Affairs, 1920-1923* (Oxford University Press, 1927), pp. 503-4.

This publication, covering yearly periods thereafter, and edited originally by Professor Toynbee and accompanied by the parallel *Documents on International Affairs,* may be cited as the best and most convenient single source of information for developments in the international field. Publications in that field are legion, but one other extremely valuable source that deserves mention is the weekly, *L'Europe nouvelle,* published in Paris.

[62] The treaty was duly registered with the League. Such an agreement as the Franco-Polish, like all regional agreements, raises an important issue on which there were and are two schools of thought. It can be viewed as bolstering the general purpose of the League (or the United Nations), incapable of dealing effectively with all issues at all times and places; or it can be regarded as weakening the general purpose of the larger organization through the implied distrust of its ability to fulfill its purpose of the general preservation of peace.

[63] In the case of Rumania, by contrast with Poland, Russia declined to recognize the new frontiers, but the Rumanian acquisition of Bessarabia was recognized by the Supreme Council of the Allies in a statement of 3 March, 1920.

the two countries, that specified a military convention as well, was signed in Bucharest on March 3, 1921. [64]

Czechoslovakia, another Polish neighbor, might be thought to have had a similar interest to the Polish where Germany was concerned. [65] But, around 1920, the issue seemed less pressing, and for that matter no German territory had been lost to Czechoslovakia. Carved out entirely from the body of the defunct Dual Monarchy, Czechoslovakia tended at first to show more concern with other lands that had been part of the Empire. Fear of a Habsburg restoration, combined with opposition to the claims of Hungarian revisionism, she shared in common with both Rumania and Yugoslavia. From this situation was born the Little Entente, so-called because it could be regarded as a smaller edition of the larger pre-1914 combination. The Little Entente was based on three similarly-worded bilateral treaties among the three countries, which specified their purpose of preventing changes in the terms of the Treaty of Trianon with Hungary. [66]

France had no particular quarrel with Hungary and there had even been indications of a lenient inclination on her part at the time of the peace making. [67] But now that the fate of Hungary had been settled the chief French interest in the form of maintaining the peace through preservation of the *status quo* applied to Hungary as well and would operate in support of the similar interest of the Little Entente countries. Some at least of the aims of Hungarian revisionism were perhaps not unreasonable, but any satisfaction of it would have had the value of dangerous precedent that could be used by the German desire to modify the terms of peace. Versailles must remain an intangible charter, and, for consistency's sake, along with Versailles all the other instruments of peace as well.

Here lay one source of strength, the greatest single one in fact, of the French system. [68] Out of the war there had emerged a group of

---

[64] Rumania fitted well enough into the policy of the *cordon sanitaire*, but she had no direct contact with Germany. French interest in her was correspondingly weaker, and a formal connection between the two countries was not established until 1926.

[65] Polish-Czech relations were not good, disturbed mainly by their differences over Teschen, which obscured their fundamental common interests vis-à-vis Germany. In addition, Polish-Hungarian relations tended to be friendly, while the opposite was the case between Czechoslovakia and Hungary. A Czech-Polish agreement of February, 1921 was never ratified.

[66] The Czech-Yugoslav treaty was signed on 14 August 1920, the Czech-Rumanian treaty on 23 April 1921, and that between Rumania and Yugoslavia on 7 June 1921. This last treaty, in addition, made reference to the Treaty of Neuilly with Bulgaria as well as to the Treaty of Trianon. Threatened action by the Little Entente was instrumental in the failure of Archduke Charles' attempt to return to the throne of Hungary.

[67] Cf. Francis Deák, *Hungary at the Paris Peace Conference: The Diplomatic History of the Treaty of Trianon* (New York, 1942).

[68] The French system of alliances was only perfected after some time with the conclusion of Franco-Czech (January 1924), Franco-Rumanian (January

states in Europe which had in common the desire to preserve for themselves the benefits that had been reaped from victory. What more
natural than that this strong and fundamental interest should bring
these states together? The reality of this common interest might in fact
be thought a stronger bond than formal treaties of alliance; there was
nothing artificial, synthetic, or transitory in the bond, expression as
it was of a simple condition of fact. For the rest, the totality of power
residing in the combination of France plus her allies was considerable,
whether in terms of numbers or resources, and might be thought
adequate to the prevention of change. Many thought so indeed who
felt that too much power lay in one place; the phrase "French hegemony"
was expression of this view.

The False Bases of the French System

In the end, as we know, this system proved incapable of performing
the task that was its prime purpose: preservation of peace through
preservation of the *status quo*. But it is not mere wisdom after the event
that could perceive some fundamental flaws and vices in the system
from its very inception.

With the definite exception of Belgium in the West and to a considerable degree of Czechoslovakia, the Eastern members of the French
system had in common the fact of their economic backwardness, or
underdevelopment as the more urbane current expression goes; [69] they
were all primarily agricultural countries. French capital had played
an important role before 1914 in the development of such a country as
Russia and had been at the same time one factor in maintaining the
French influence in that country. That capital and that influence were
now lost, but France, though impoverished, still had considerable
resources; she could therefore resume her role of lender to the East.
This in fact she did though hampered by her recurring financial difficulties. French lending served in part to finance the armament of
France's allies; to that extent it was militarily useful, but economically
unproductive where the recipients were concerned. [70]

The economic life of these countries was based on the exchange of
their agricultural products for manufactures from abroad. The French
economy was ill-designed for the establishment of a strong current of

---

1926) and Franco-Yugoslav (November 1927) agreements, but, as indicated,
the more important consideration was that of a common outlook which
existed from the beginning in the form of devotion to the preservation of
the *status quo*.

[69] Like France herself, Czechoslovakia enjoyed the advantage of an unusually well-balanced internal economy, all the more striking in view
of the dimensions of the country.

[70] Here also Czechoslovakia was in a different category. Possessed of
the important Skoda armament works, in which French capital had an
interest, she could not only attend to her own needs but supply others as
well.

trade with the new French dependents whose economies fitted more naturally into the German. In the existing state of things, Central and Eastern Europe constituted a logical sphere of German economic penetration. This might be looked upon as in the category of a fact of life. Should it come to the test of force, France could see to the prior military equipment and organization of her Eastern allies, [71] but in the organization of their economic life she was ill-fitted to play a major role.

Perhaps more serious than economic deficiencies were those that might be called political and psychological. France herself was an established democracy and the impact of war had apparently not placed undue strains of her system of government which continued unchanged after the war's conclusion. In the flush of the democratic wave that accompanied allied victory, the new states gave themselves constitutions largely resembling the French model. It was not long before it became clear that a democratic constitution was not *per se* the magic nostrum it had been thought to be. Again with the exception of Czechoslovakia, more evolved politically as well as economically, dictatorship in more or less overt form made its appearance in Poland, Rumania and Yugoslavia. [72] Clearly, such domestic instability raised a question about the effectiveness of these countries as allies.

But most important of all was the French position itself. First of all French resources and power. These had been injured by the war, but they remained considerable. The France of 1919 was no longer the France of Napoleon; there could be no question of herself controlling for long the whole European continent, and it was precisely the awareness of the deficiency of power that led France to embark upon the organization of the system that has just been described. If America and Britain chose to return to a policy of total or relative isolation where the European continent was concerned, France could not for a moment consider the obvious absurdity of withdrawing from Europe. France therefore *had* to have some positive policy with regard to the rest of the continent; this meant not Germany alone, but everything else in Europe as well. Moreover, the existing state of power being what it was — its peculiar condition has been noted — France being *the* effective power, there was relatively little choice in the outcome: in one form or another it was only natural that the organization of Europe should have French power as its center. The network of alliances was the outward expression of an existing state of fact; it was expression of the common interest of its participants and fitted in addition into the traditional pattern of France's policy in Europe.

---

[71] Quite naturally, French military prestige stood high after the First World War and there was a correspondingly high demand, even apart from alliances, for French military guidance and advice.

[72] This may be regarded as, in varying degrees, the combined result of political inexperience and internal nationality problems.

But the alliances were not associations of equals. To a dangerous degree — the future would show this — the whole system depended on the strength and soundness of the one member that was the keystone of the structure: remove France from it, the structure lost its meaning. Under the best of circumstances and with the staunchest and most sustained determination, one may doubt whether in the end French power would have been equal to the task of "controlling" Europe. Certainly the solution of the three great problems of Germany, Russia, and Danubia could not be considered final. But even to sustain the system as it was France must show determination and willingness to act. Should Poland, for example, be threatened France must give her effective assistance, even if that should mean taking the initiative of action against Germany.

At this point we run into an initial and constitutional vice of the French system. The outward appearance of French policy may have recalled Louis XIV or Napoleon, but at bottom France — the French people — were in a chastened and defensive mood; they truly wanted peace, as much as possible they wanted to be left alone. This could not be. For power does not consist of divisions and arms factories alone; without the wilingness to use them, all these necessary trappings become futility. To be sure, France was eager to have the Polish alliance; but she tended to think too exclusively in terms of the additional assistance that Polish arms would furnish to her own. Poland quite naturally thought first and foremost in terms of her own defense and security. The fact is that French power was in potential a considerably greater asset to Poland than the reverse.

Enough has been said in other connections of the delicate relationship of alliances, of the possibility that they contain for either member of controlling the policy of the other. The Polish case in this respect is enlightening. When a plebiscite was held in Upper Silesia in 1921 it was largely French influence that was instrumental in procuring a decision advantageous to Poland. [73] This may have been due, as was claimed, as much, if not more, to the French desire to weaken Germany as to the wish to strengthen and please Poland, though undoubtedly it had those effects. But the case of Vilna is clearer. France had no special interest in Vilna being Polish rather than Lithuanian; she would prefer reasonableness in the matter, but she would not antagonize her

---

[73] With a certain amount of justice, Lloyd George complained of the pro-Polish attitude of the occupying French forces, but there was point to the French rejoinder that Britain would render a more useful service by herself having a larger force in Silesia. This is an interesting illustration of Britain's effort to extricate herself from, or reducing as much as possible, her commitments on the continent, leaving French power in a position of effective influence, and at the same time objecting to the use of that power. Responsibility and power cannot be divorced so easily.

ally in the face of Poland's marked determination, let alone use force ot coerce that ally. [74] Examples could be multiplied.

Such things served to conceal the true reality which lay behind the false bases of the French system, false in that the system rested on insufficiency of power and, even more, on insufficiency of aggressive will. France was conservative and backward looking; looking to the past for a model, she would freeze the present if possible. Yet for the moment she did have power, more than any one else in Europe. As much from the operation of circumstances as from deliberate and calculating plan France was thus placed in this false position.

This must be added. If there were those in France who with complacency recalled visions of Napoleonic glory, they were not typically representative of the French temper of the day. That the French atmosphere should have been one of fear rather than of confidence and elation might be taken as unconscious apprehension of the true state of things. But abroad there was little understanding of these French fears, the accepted picture being rather that of hegemony, that like all such was to be feared, combatted, and when possible checked.

3. THE FRENCH SYSTEM IN OPERATION

The picture of hegemony was certainly the one that was prevalent among the English-speaking peoples, and this was all the more resented by them that they were conscious of having made a large contribution to the common victory, of which France was now thought to be taking more than fair advantage. In British eyes, this victory was being robbed of its purpose since the effect of it had been to establish another effective dominance of the continent of Europe. Seen from America, France was in effect denying the common proclaimed purpose; her stress on military power, now that German militarism had been destroyed, made her appear as the embodiment of the very evil that had just been destroyed. Alliances such as the Polish could not be seen as motivated by genuine defensive wish, but rather as devices for meddling where none was needed with a view to enhancing the reach of French control.

By contrast with the instability and fickleness often associated with France among the English-speaking peoples, the change in their own temper can only be regarded as bewildering. In a surprisingly short time, in both America and Britain, the feeling became widespread that France was the chief trouble maker and obstacle to the restoration of peace; her everlastingly reiterated fear of Germany and her insatiable

---

[74] The issue of Vilna came up before the League and in the end Polish intransigeance had its way. Such an outcome inevitably cast doubts on the League and gave point to the charge that it was in disguise an instrument that served the interests of the Great Powers who had been victorious in the war and who would use it either to maintain the *status quo* or to alter it to their advantage only.

desire for guarantees and reinsurance could not be understood; these were instead suspected, and, correspondingly, not a little sympathy began to redound to the benefit of defenseless, downtrodden, and abused Germany.

The degree of mutual misunderstanding is difficult to exaggerate. The rapidity and extent of the change in the American and British attitude was, from the French point of view, no less difficult of acceptance. The feeling was strong in France that the country had born the heaviest burden of the war and that her allies or ex-allies were reaping the benefits of victory while refusing to share the costs of the continuing preservation of peace. This may be granted: whatever might be said of the validity of the prevalent French view of the German danger and of the quality of specific French policies and actions, the French view that some clear scheme was needed for the general organization of Europe, specifically the French interest in Eastern Europe, stemmed from sounder instinct than the seemingly easier, but ultimately more dangerous, approach that sought to ignore the existence of a multiplicity of admittedly awkward issues. The solution of difficult problems is rarely enhanced by the mere denial of their presence.

Where Germany in particular was concerned, for Britain and America to expect France merely to shed distrust and fear, to shift instead to hopeful trust, was neither realistic nor even wholly fair. If it was true that Germany had been a real and a common danger — and how deny this after their own participation in the war? — then France remained the first line of defense and the most exposed position. If the defeat of Germany had been a necessary accomplishment, then all the victors shared in the benefits of the outcome; America and Britain in particular were beneficiaries of a system that after all did preserve international peace and order.

But Britain and America in their hearts knew not fear. Yet, possessed of power as they were, if they found fault with the French system, their power they might use to institute another. Good or bad as French policy may have been, it was *one* logically consistent whole. Merely to undermine and oppose the French system, without having a workable substitute to offer in its place was tantamount to irresponsible levity that past history might help understand, but future history could only judge with severity.

In the abstract at least there is much to be said for forgiveness and reconciliation. If, in fairness, France could not be expected to bear the cost and run the risks of such a policy, might not American and British power have made a contribution toward its implementation? Here we come back once more to the 1919 proposal of an Anglo-American guarantee. Whether in that or in another form, why not give France the most far reaching insurance imaginable — the more extensive the less likely would it be to have to be implemented — then use the guarantee to exercise control over those manifestations of French policy that seemed objectionable? [75] The corollary of course would have to be accepted that the Banat, Danzig, or Teschen were not faraway places about which one need have no concern. Had Britain had in Silesia a force comparable to the French, British views in regard to the solution of that problem could also have carried weight comparable to the French.

An interesting illustration of the quality of the existing relationship was provided by the Conference held in Washington at the turn of the year 1921 to 1922. The initiative of this meeting was American and its main purpose was somewhat remote from the acute concerns of Europe at this time: the meeting had to do with naval matters. The war had caused America to create a vast military establishment, and if the end of hostilities had seen the virtual disbandment of her land forces, the naval part of it was more lasting. But the temper of post-First World War America was not at all belligerent; rather she would eschew responsibilities of power and the view gained wide popularity of the danger that arms in themselves constituted: the road to peace, one major road at least, was through disarmament. Where Europe was concerned, historic tradition made disentanglement psychologically easy, [76] but there was also a tradition of active interest in the Far East, of which the Open Door policy was the clearest expression. In that quarter, Japan had used with skill the circumstances of the war; the imperial and imperialistic manifestations of Japan's expanding economy and power were natural matters of American concern. [77] How deal with them? Could some agreement be contrived that would protect the American position while avoiding the cost of naval competition?

The Washington Naval Conference dealt with the related matters of Far Eastern affairs and naval disarmament, or more accurately the

---

[65] This may seem an oversimplification and in a sense it is. Such a policy would have required both skill and tact to operate it and we can see at present how awkward it is to deal with even negative aspects of French power. We shall have occasion to see the hesitant British efforts to operate such a policy of mediation, but the central point is valid that British policy, especially at first, and American policy throughout, remained policies of negation.

[76] The view in fact achieved popularity that intervention had been a mistake which America had been "bamboozled" into making. This, combined with the naïve assumption that if one action is wrong the opposite must be right, led to the policy of isolation. Responsible statesmen might have been expected to know better and one may well speak of a failure of leadership in America after 1920. At the same time, the outcome may also be regarded as an enlightening, if not encouraging, manifestation of the operation of the democratic process. The leaders may have failed to lead, but they and their policies accurately reflected the predominant wishes of the electorate.

[77] As indicated earlier (p. 65, n. 51) Japan had had her way in China and the better of the United States at the peacemaking.

limitation of naval armaments. [78] Five Powers were involved in this, the United States, Great Britain, Japan, France and Italy, the only naval Powers of importance, and the chief result on the second score was the agreement on certain ratios of capital ship tonnage among them. These were 5.25:5.25:3.15:1.75:1.75, corresponding to the order in which the Powers have been named. America and Britain were to have parity with each other [79] and so were France and Italy.

Two of the five Powers were dissatisfied with the outcome, Japan and France. With Japan we need not be concerned, but the French case has relevance to our story. France did not regard as fair permanent ratios based on the existing state of the fleets, for the reason that the inevitable wartime concentration on her part on the land war had caused her relatively to neglect her maritime establishment, which had as a result fallen to a comparatively lower estate than before 1914. [80] The French view received scant attention in Washington, though a degree of compromise was effected on "existing strength," and France (though not alone) was instrumental in preventing the agreement on naval ratios from being extended to smaller surface ships and to submarines, the poor man's weapon. [81]

There was another source of French disgruntlement in Washington, the parity with Italy. The American argument vis-à-vis Japan, that parity would have meant Japanese superiority in the Pacific owing to America's commitments in two oceans, seemed applicable on the smaller Atlantic-Mediterranean scale between France and Italy: overall parity would result in Italian superiority in the latter sea. Like Britain, though again on a smaller scale, France had imperial obligations such as Italy

---

[78] Far Eastern affairs fall outside the range of this essay. Certainly where France was concerned they were of secondary interest by comparison with European. Their chief interest in the present discussion, and the reason they are introduced at this point, is the illustration that they provide of the French position and of France's relations with others, this last especially important in view of the central position of France in European affairs.

[79] Britain's policy toward America has, over a long period, been the intelligent one of accepting with good grace the American rise to power, a policy which may be said to have paid good dividends. It was partly in deference to American predilection that Britain abandoned the Japanese alliance after the First World War.

[80] This touches also upon a very long term factor in French policy. Time and again, especially in her century-long conflict with Britain, France had to give inevitable priority to land warfare at the expense of naval development, which ever remained the prime concern of Britain. It may have been a logical division of labor during the war for France to concentrate on land while Britain looked after the sea, but the consequences of this as they appeared in Washington were all the less palatable to France. The British effort on land had for that matter been very substantial and, together with the extent of Britain's naval establishment, was to a point a measure of Britain's greater resources, a fact even truer where America was concerned.

[81] Although the franc had recovered to some extent during 1921 (from about 17 to about 12 to the dollar), French finances were beginning to show the strain of the postwar burden.

did not have. Skilfully from her point of view, Italy took the (apparently) simple and (to America and Britain) attractive position that she would readily agree to any degree of reduction provided only that she have parity with France. The effect of all this was to place France in isolation as the one possible stumbling block on the path to agreement to so desirable and virtuous an end as armament reduction. In the event France yielded, but the yielding under pressure rankled. The value of agreements obtained in such conditions may well be questioned. [82] The significant things to retain of this episode — one to which too much importance should not be attached for that matter — are two : the position in which France found herself on this occasion; the fact that, in her own judgment, France did not feel she could afford to stand in isolation. This last was clearly related to the French estimate of French power.

Britain, France and the German Problem

Briand returned to France before the Washington proceedings were ended. Apart from his lack of success in an uncongenial and not-too-friendly atmosphere, he had to meet Lloyd George in Cannes in January to take up matters of greater immediate interest to France. That meeting and its outcome are of considerable significance in the present tale, but before dealing with it it is necessary to go back a little.

Once America had made clear her determination to withdraw as an active participant in the affairs of Europe, the effective power residing in that continent, as pointed out before, was largely concentrated in French and British hands. The great immediate problem was viewed

---

[82] France's isolation at Washington came to her as something of a surprise and was all the more resented for that reason. It should be pointed out that the French case seems to have been poorly prepared and based on certain misconceptions. Briand, the chief French delegate, occupying the posts of Prime and Foreign Minister, was quickly disillusioned in his expectation of Anglo-American differences in which France could have played a role of mediation.

The primary source of information for the French side of the Washington Conference is *Documents diplomatiques: Conférence de Washington, juillet 1921 - février 1922* (Paris, 1923). The fullest, though to be used with critical care, account of Briand's career is the six-volume work of Georges Suarez, *Briand, sa vie, son œuvre* (Paris, 1938-1952).

It may be pointed out that, if matters naval had second priority to land armaments in French eyes and, partly for that reason, made at least limited agreement possible, the French position was both more assertive and stronger when it came to the discussion of disarmament on land, a subject not even approached at this time. Also, which is at once natural and humorous, that the primarily naval Powers found it easier to perceive the virtues of disarmament on land than on the sea. America and Britain were willing to enter agreements for the limitation of naval armaments, but only if these agreements sanctioned the margin of their own superiority. The absolute is after all less important than the relative degree of armed power.

as that of Germany — Russia and Danubia, important as they were, or would be, were less pressing.

The story of European affairs may therefore be said to have been dominated at first by that of the relations between Great Britain, France and Germany, or, in different form, by the contrasting British and French views of how to deal with the German problem. The world duel has been aptly used to describe the nature of the Anglo-French relationship.

Sufficient has been said before to explain the fundamental differences between the two approaches and the reasons, stemming from past history and current economic need, that induced Britain to take a view far more lenient than France's of the proper way to deal with Germany. The specific points of difference and debate may be put under the heads of the two great issues of the time, Security and Reparation. [83] Britain did not deny that the Treaty of Versailles remained the formal charter that determined the status and the obligations of Germany. But a treaty, like any other legal instrument, is subject to interpretation, which may be legalistic and narrow, as was the French, or lenient and broad; in addition to which justice may be tempered by mercy.

Security at first was the simpler matter. The disarmament of Germany was proceeding apace, [84] but Reparation was more troublesome. The treaty of peace itself had not settled the matter, and the Reparation Commission created by the treaty was at work on its appointed task of coming to concrete decisions. There is here no cause to retell a long, intricate, and on the whole dreary, tale which has been rehearsed many times; [85] it will suffice to recall its highlights, bearing in mind the general orientation of this discussion.

By January 1921 the Reparation Commission had completed the first part of its task: definite figures had been reached which formed

---

[83] The divergence between British and French policies after the First World War has, as much as any one single factor, been the cause of the subsequent breakdown; the importance of this divergence cannot be over-emphasized. It has been the subject of important studies among which two are outstanding: Arnold Wolfers, *Britain and France Between Two Wars: Conflicting Strategies of Peace Since Versailles* (New York, 1940) and W.M. Jordan, *Great Britain, France and the German Problem, A Study of Anglo-French Relations in the Making and Maintenance of the Versailles Settlement* (London, 1944). As a general analysis the work of Bertrand de Jouvenel, *D'Une guerre à l'autre*, 2 vols. (Paris, 1940-1941), covering the period to 1931, is highly stimulating.

[84] There was indeed a certain amount of controversy on that score also, due in the main to French suspicion. There were some breaches and delays in German execution, but they were of minor consequence and one may say that Germany was quite soon effectively disarmed.

[85] The literature on Reparation is extensive. It may suffice to refer here to such adequate summaries of the whole tale as Karl Bergmann, *The History of Reparations* (London, 1927), translated from the German, *Der Weg der Reparation* (Frankfurt-am-Main, 1926); John W. Wheeler-Bennett, *The Wreck of Reparations* (London, 1933); and the extensive French work of Etienne Weill-Raynal, *Les Réparations allemandes et la France,* 3 vols. (Paris, 1948).

the bases of negotiation between the Allies and the Germans. These were protracted and laborious and were not brought to a conclusion until Germany was confronted with an allied ultimatum on May 5, 1921, which threatened Germany with the enforcement of sanctions in the form of the occupation of the Ruhr district. Germany was powerless and when confronted with allied unity she could hardly do otherwise than she had done at Versailles, that is accept. One day before the expiration of the allied ultimatum, on May 11, Chancellor Wirth, having obtained the consent of the Reichstag, notified the Allies of the German acceptance. [86]

During this period, and also throughout 1920, there had been numerous exchanges between the Allies and the Germans as well as among the Allies themselves in the course of a long series of conferences. [87] Whatever differences these had brought out among the Allies [88] — and such there were — they were not such that allied unity could not be preserved. The outcome was the agreement finally embodied in the so-called London schedule, which set the total of German Reparation at 132,000,000,000 gold marks. [89] The belief, or the hope, that the matter of Reparation was at last settled since all now knew where they stood and that the problem was henceforth reduced to the mechanics of collection and payment was soon to be dispelled; as much as closing a chapter, the London agreement was the opening of a period of confusion and recrimination destined to end in a sharp break.

After Germany had promptly discharged the initial payment of 1,000,000,000 marks, trouble was not long in appearing. There was on the one hand difficulty among the recipients: France was dissatisfied with the allotment of this initial payment of which she was to have no

---

[86] There had been negotiations throughout this period between the Allies and the Germans and a substantial abatement of the initial claim presented in January, but the two sides were unable to come to agreement, hence the ultimatum.

[87] This was the beginning of the innovation described as diplomacy by conference. Prime and foreign ministers, and often financial ministers as well, frequently met in person, thus reducing the scope of the operation of the traditional channels of diplomacy. Much hope was entertained for a time from these direct contacts, clearly resulting from increased facility of transportation. Enough time has elapsed to show — what might have been expected — that personal contacts, while they may speed up and facilitate negotiation, can also have the opposite effect. In addition, the peripatetic nature of ministerial office has drawbacks of its own.

[88] As on other occasions, the Germans proved on this one to be their worst enemies. The foolishly arrogant behavior of Stinnes at the Spa Conference in July, 1920 served to bolster the French contention that Germans were intractable and incorrigible, amenable to the argument of superior force alone.

[89] It is not necessary to go into the details of the London arrangement, but there is relevance to the observation that the present value was given to be no more than 50,000,000,000 marks (*Survey of International Affairs, 1920-1923*, p. 147). There is also significance in the provision that required the German government to reimburse the duty levied on German exports by the British customs.

part; on her side she proceeded to make a direct agreement providing for the partial discharge of the German obligation in the form of direct reconstruction by Germany of the destruction in her northern provinces. [90] But inter-allied bickering would have little point unless German contributions continued to be forthcoming. One harbinger of financial strain in Germany was the behavior of the mark on the currency market. Fairly stable during the first half of the year at about one-tenth of its prewar value, the second half of the year saw the beginning of the process of its final disintegration: from July to October the value of the mark was halved, and that halved again in November. The reason for the fall was partly psychological but there were none the less solid grounds for concern over the future of the German currency. [91]

These circumstances led to a meeting in December in London between the British and the French Prime Ministers, Lloyd George and Briand, a moratorium on German payments, and a further meeting between the same two men that took place in Cannes in January, 1922.

The Cannes Conference, that met from January 6 to 13, marks an important turning point in the story of Anglo-French relations. Formally, it was a meeting of the Supreme Council; it was to deal with Reparation, but its objective, in British eyes especially, was much broader, no less than laying the bases for the economic reconstruction of Europe. The focus of the British interest was economic, and from Lloyd George's point of view the problem was how to secure French assent to his plan. What Britain wanted above all was trade; this meant in turn economic health and stability in Germany; also the reestablishing of some contact with Russia.

---

[90] This agreement, known as the Wiesbaden agreement, was signed by Loucheur, French minister of liberated regions, and German Foreign Minister Rathenau on August 27, 1921. The provisions in it which made it possible to defer crediting Germany with the value of reconstruction seemed detrimental to the interest of other recipients and there was opposition to it, particularly in British quarters. There was opposition also from French industrial interests desirous of retaining the French market for themselves.

[91] There was some recovery in December, half way between the October and the November marks, as it appeared that Germany would have some temporary relief from her Reparation obligations.

The story of the German currency, and the causes of its collapse, is a complex one where it is hard to disentangle and allot the share of the various contributing factors. Domestic German financial management certainly was one, and so likewise was the Reparation burden (the two are by no means unrelated). From this it was easy to argue that the collapse was a device deliberately used to escape obligations (the popular French view) or that it was entirely the result of unreasonable pressure with a view to wrecking the German economy (a popular German view of French motivation and policy).

In addition to the previously cited references on the subject of Reparation, mention is appropriate at this point of the famous book of John Maynard Keynes, *The Economic Consequences of the Peace* (London, 1920), to which may be added the companion critique by Etienne Mantoux, *The Carthaginian Peace, or the Economic Consequences of Mr. Keynes* (New York, 1952)

France at this time may be said not to have yet clearly perceived the relation between the two aspects of her German policy: France wanted both Security *and* Reparation. On the score of the last, the prevailing French view was still that Germany must, can, and shall pay; there were rumblings of discontent in Parliament, which hampered the freedom of manoeuvre of the government in making new arrangements and concessions, however necessary they might be, and even had it wanted to make them. In the French interpretation, German difficulties were but expressions of German bad faith and ill will, hence proof that Germany had not mended her ways and therefore remained a danger: to this extent did Reparation overflow into Security. There was also some suspicion that Britain feared the possibility of too close a Franco-German economic integration such as the Wiesbaden agreement might presage. [92]

Lloyd George, shrewd and hardened veteran of politics, was the last to fail to appreciate the necessities of domestic politics, in France or elsewhere. France, from his point of view, may have been a nuisance, but since she could not be coerced she must be appeased. Britain had it within her power to make a valuable contribution in the form of returning to the 1919 guarantee that, behind the shield of American default, she had declined to ratify.

While pushing his scheme for general economic reconstruction in the form of laying the groundwork for a more inclusive meeting than was taking place at Cannes, Lloyd George submitted to Briand the proposal of a British promise of full assistance in the event of German attack, though, adhering to British tradition, Lloyd George's memorandum made clear British reluctance to assume commitments elsewhere in Europe. [93]

Perhaps a certain inner inconsistency may be detected in the British offer which stemmed in part from the "fear" of too much French power

---

[92] "It was felt in London that France had sufficient power to exert an attraction on German weakness. To weaken France became an imperative of British policy. How to go about it? By playing on France's weak point, her obsession with security," Bertrand de Jouvenel, *D'Une guerre à l'autre,* vol. I, De *Versailles à Locarno,* pp. 244-45. This is an important point, but the answer to the question it raises is not forthcoming, and may never be. The British documentary collection covering the period since 1919, undertaken after the Second World War under the editorship of of E.L. Woodward and Rohan Butler, *Documents on British Policy, 1919-1939,* of which the first series (1919-1929) will cover this episode, has not yet reached this point. For that matter this publication includes certain categories of documents only. Without in any event attributing to British policy the consistency of a clearly thought out machiavellianism, it is enlightening to consider in this connection the instinctive reaction of suspicion toward the European Coal and Steel Community and the consequent British refusal of participation.

[93] The British memorandum also pointed to the desirability of settling *all* outstanding issues between the two countries. In concrete terms this meant the Near East, about which more will be said presently.

yet at the same time offered France the "protection" of British power; connotations of aloofness or superiority might be detected or suspected in this. The logic of the refusal to see the implications and the necessities of Central European commitments would, in French eyes, be conspicious by its weakness. Briand's reaction, expression of the continuity of French policy and harking back to pre-1914, was to suggest a "reciprocal" Anglo-French guarantee to be accompanied by a military convention. The French position had logic on its side; it was in addition conditioned by the necessities of French domestic politics.

For Briand was aware that the very fact of his negotiation was a source of suspicion in Paris. The second half of 1921 had brought France disillusion on the score of German Reparation, a suspicion, however unwarranted, of having been taken advantage of and tricked through the device of technicalities, and the feeling of isolation at the Washington meeting rankled. Briand did not have a chance to pursue his discussion very far. From Paris he received the news of two parliamentary motions. The finance commission of the Chamber "reminded the government of its undertaking not to agree to any future sacrifices" in the matter of Reparation; the *Gauche Républicaine* group of the Senate wanted to be sure (shades of 1954!) that any Anglo-French alliance would not impair the existence of "a strong national army." [94] Worse still, Briand received a summons from the French President, Millerand, to come to Paris in order to furnish explanations. He went, and having attended on the 12th a session of the Cabinet followed by one in the Chamber, without even waiting for a vote in Parliament, he resigned.

Briand's succession as Prime Minister and at the Quai d'Orsay went to Poincaré. The same Parliament remained, but the change meant somewhat more than the customary French ministerial reshuffles; the contrast between the two men was significant as well as symbolic. Briand's success in politics had been the result of intelligent suppleness; quicker and more versatile than thorough, he excelled in the politician's art of compromise. Like many French politicians, his evolution had been from the Left toward a more central position. During the war, his natural bent for accommodation had led him to entertain the possibility of negotiations. Though not disloyal — precisely wherein lies the difference between disloyalty and honest dissent? — this tendency to compromise made him suspect in the eyes of some. The spectacle of war had aroused in him a mood of revulsion rather than of heroic exaltation; already at this time it might be said that if there was any possibility of conciliation or softness where Germany was concerned, Briand would be the man to pursue such a course. Little wonder that the mere fact

---

[94] The incident of Briand's appearance in the company of Lloyd George on the golf links at Cannes is an amusing one, but revealing. Admittedly, Briand wielding a golf club was a fit object for humorous treatment; the picture was played up as symbolic of a French policy of subservience, and the French phrase may be recalled, *le ridicule tue*.

of his negotiating with Lloyd George did not appeal to the *bleu horizon* Chamber. Briand, not a fighter by temperament, understood and withdrew.

Poincaré had had a brilliant career in French public life, in spite of the rigidity of his personality. Little loved, he was by all respected; he was the embodiment of many virtues, not all attractive, characteristic of that bourgeoisie that was the traditional backbone of the nation. Precise and meticulous, honest and conscientious, intelligent and legalistic (the law was his profession), staunch anti-clerical republican, on the score of Germany his views were definite and clear and not subject to modification. France had a treaty — this charter could be used in court; France had power — this power should be used to enforce the letter of the law; justice and her good right were synonymous. [95]

Such a man was apt choice as representative of the prevailling temper of the country and even more of the dominant tendencies in Parliament. Finance he understood, but economics less, in this respect also typical of the French milieu. Lloyd George would not "bamboozle" him, and the wiles of the fickle little Welshman would be vasted on the humorless stolidity of the dour Lorrainer. Poincaré's tenure of office — in French terms it was long, lasting from January 1922 to May 1924 — was to witness the most thoroughgoing experiment in the use of French power and the climax of the Anglo-French duel. That episode must now be related.

The Anglo-French Duel

When Poincaré assumed the reins of power, France, under British prodding stood committed to a meeting of European states [96] — Germany and Russia were to participate — whose basic purpose it would be to examine the problem, primarily in its economic aspects, of European reconstruction as a whole. Poincaré did not go back on the commitment, but set to work instead circumscribing and limiting the scope of the conference to be held in Genoa. At a preliminary meeting with Lloyd George in Boulogne he obtained agreement on safeguarding "the rights of the League of Nations, of the treaties signed in France after the

---

[95] There were severe critics in France of Poincaré's prewar policy, to the point that in some quarters the label *Poincaré-la-guerre* became popular. The implications of this were unfair, but there was a deeper element of truth in the charge. Only in the sense, however, that, having accepted the premise of German aggressive intent, Poincaré likewise accepted the logical consequence that force must be met by force. This was an issue of what we have come to call appeasement. It is often not realized that to argue about appeasement *per se* is essentially meaningless; what matters is the validity of the premises on which appeasement or the opposite policy is based.

[96] Turkey was refused admission, being considered an Asiatic Power, but the British Dominions were to participate. The United States was also invited but, in keeping with the current policy of isolation, declined the invitation.

peace and of the rights of the Allies to Reparation"; in brief, the *status quo* must not be tampered with. [97]   Lloyd George might not be loath to let France place herself at Genoa in the position of being *the* obstacle to European reconstruction; Poincaré was aware of this and Barthou was directed to use his influence with other delegations to prevent such isolation; the Little Entente states, Poland, and the Baltic states had expressed their attachment to the sanctity of existing treaties.

The story of the Genoa meeting, full of interest and intricacy as it is, may be summed up in the one word, fiasco.   In so far as Lloyd George was genuinely desirous of furthering economic recovery and alongside it of promoting a softening of the war-generated passions — and that such was his hope is not open to question — his purpose was undoubtedly frustrated; this same result was a corresponding success for Poincaré and his policy. [98]   Lloyd George, followed in this by a considerable section of British opinion, was incensed and resentful [99] and made no secret of his feelings.   Precisely what passed on May 6 between himself and Barthou, upon the latter's return from Paris, became the subject of debate and recrimination, but the statement that "Mr. Lloyd George replied severely, saying in substance that the Entente between Great Britain and France was at an end," sent to the [London] *Times* by Wickham Steed on May 7, and which appeared under the headline "Wrecking the Entente — Premier's Threat to France," is hardly an exaggerated description of the state of Anglo-French relations at this point. [100]

As it turned out, the most startling episode of the Conference was not provided by the Anglo-French divergence.   The announcement that a Russo-German agreement had been signed at Rapallo on April 16 created the stir that might be expected of it.   This agreement may be said to have been the response in both the German and the Russian cases to the feeling that neither country would succeed in obtaining concessions from the other Powers.   The denial of the existence of secret or

---

[97] The general lines of Poincaré's policy were clearly defined in his reply of February 1 to the Italian invitation to the Conference, his memorandum to the British government of the preceding day, and the instructions to Barthou, the chief French delegate at Genoa.

[98] To a degree, France was isolated and even embarrassed when she chose to force a showdown on a Belgian resolution insisting on total restoration by Russia of foreign-owned private property, and even before this it was Barthou who had had a sharp exchange with Chicherin, the Russian Foreign Minister.   The fact remains that France was both able and willing to prevent agreement.

[99] Garvin in the *Observer* (April 30) used the phrase "Kaiser of the Peace" in referring to Poincaré in an article entitled "Reconstruction for Ruin."

[100] Wickham Steed, Editor of the [London] *Times* at the time, was pro-French in the sense that he believed in the necessity of preserving the Anglo-French alliance.   For a full account of this episode which incidentally throws not a little light on Lloyd George's character and methods, see *The History of the Times*, vol. IV, *The 150th Anniversary and Beyond*, Part II, 1921-1928, pp. 664 ff.

military provisions in addition to those of the published terms of the agreement did little to mollify the irritation generally produced by this unexpected development. [101] Both Germany and Russia were still under a cloud; for the two great outcasts of Europe to join their impotence could have little immediate effect; yet there was no need of the knowledge that the passing of twenty years would provide to give point to the long term French fears that the prospect of a Russo-German combination aroused. [102]

The French victory at Genoa, if such it was, was a negative one. Merely to foil schemes for the reconstruction of Europe could in itself be neither an end nor a policy. Even apart from the Russo-German warning, there were indications that others might tire of pure negation and veer to the British view. Britain herself might go further and implement the threat contained in Lloyd George's hint of direct and independent dealings with Germany. To be of value and make sense French policy must carry its implications farther. France's, or Poincaré's, contention was that the real difficulty arose from Germany's unwillingness to recognize her defeat and to accept its consequences in the form of faithful execution of the terms of peace. [103] German resistance should therefore be broken through the device of convincing Germany of its futility. Franco-British coöperation could continue, was indeed desired, provided only that Britain would cease fostering German hopes of evasion; failing this, France could and would do without Britain. This may be called a large and bold view, based as the event would prove on a false estimate of French power, especially of that component of power, will, but a consistent view none the less. If anyone in France was to essay such a policy, Poincaré was the man for the task. Where Germany was concerned, before and after Genoa, he himself had

---

[101] The German explanation that this was one specific contribution to the professed general purpose of the conference, whether given seriously or with tongue in cheek, can only be described as humorous. The agreement was at the same time a clumsy piece of diplomacy and a gesture of desperation, especially in the case of Germany more immediately hard pressed than Russia at the time.

[102] Even in 1921, there was more point to these fears than was admitted for a long time. Quite apart from the advent of Nazism and its doings, the position and views of conservative groups in Germany, and especially of military circles, is relevant in this connection. On this score, two valuable studies may be cited: John W. Wheeler-Bennett, *The Nemesis of Power: The German Army in Politics, 1918-1945* (New York, 1953), and Benoist-Méchin, *Histoire de l'armée allemande*, vol. II, *De la Reichswehr à l'armée nationale, 1919-1936* (Paris, 1938).

[103] There were also French complaints on the score of the German failure to disarm. Strictly speaking, these complaints were justified, but in effect Germany was thoroughly disarmed at this time. As Lord d'Abernon, the British Ambassador in Berlin remarked, if there was little point to the French complaints, there was also no sense in Germany not fulfilling the letter of her obligations, since that merely served to give the French case validity without procuring her any compensating benefit.

the determination that the effort demanded. Before tracing the course of the attempt and its fate a brief digression must be introduced, for differences over Germany were but one aspect of the Franco-British duel which was simultaneously being fought in a wholly independent quarter, the Near East.

The background of this issue lay in the wartime agreements and in the peace settlements dealing with that part of the world. [104] The war had destroyed the old Ottoman Empire and its Arab part had been removed from the control of Constantinople, finally to emerge either in formal independence or under mandates. Anglo-French rivalry in the Near East is an old and long story; it fills the nineteenth century during which it may be summed up as a tale of gradual French retreat and British progress. The wartime record of British diplomacy in the Arab world was somewhat less than straightforward, however much, as Balfour apologized, wartime necessities might account for it. In Syria and in Palestine, French and Jews respectively could easily suspect — divide et impera is an ancient device of empire — far darker machinations than were ever even contemplated. At all events there was disgruntlement on the French side, mainly directed toward Britain, over the Near Eastern settlement, disgruntlement that genuine Arab opposition did little to allay. [105]

The rest of the Ottoman Empire, Turkey proper, or Anatolia, had been largely carved into spheres of influence, French and Italian, while the Greeks were in Smyrna and an independent Armenia as well as an autonomous Kurdistan were to arise; the Straits were to be internationalized although the Sultan remained in Constantinople. Helpless and personally weak, Mehmed VI signed the Treaty of Sèvres in 1920. But already a year before this happened, in 1919, Mustapha Kemal had begun to organize in the interior of Anatolia the Turkish Nationalist Movement and forces of resistance.

The details of the romantic tale of Kemal's success story do not belong in this treatment, the Anglo-French aspect of which is alone relevant here. The focus of Kemal's opposition was the Greeks, and behind the Greeks the British who supported them as well as the Sultan by whom Kemal had been outlawed. It came to open war between his forces and the Greek; the latter's initial successes in 1920 turned to defeat in 1921 and culminated in their complete rout and literal ejection from the mainland of Asia Minor in August, 1922.

Interestingly, the British and French attitudes toward Germany were in a sense reversed in Turkey. Here it was France that took the realistic position of recognizing the rise of new forces and sensibly coming to terms with them, while Britain obstinately remained attached to the

---

[104] See above, pp. 53, 99.

[105] A very good account of the postwar situation in the Near East may be found in the volume *The Moslem World*, being volume I of the *Survey of International Affairs* for 1925. See also, H.N. Howard, *The Partition of Turkey, 1913-1923* (University of Oklahoma, 1931).

pursuit of impossible and unrealistic ends. [106]   After some military encounters in the French zone of Cilicia in the spring of 1921, France opted for coming to terms with Kemal; in October, 1921 Franklin-Bouillon signed in Ankara the agreement that bears his name and as a result of which France relinquished her Cilician sphere of influence. [107] The British view of these French dealings is best described in the British phrase "not cricket" and Near Eastern affairs had contributed not a little to Lloyd George's irritation with France.

Worse was in store, however. Having ousted the Greeks from Asia Minor, the Turkish Nationalists, understandably elated, turned toward the Straits where they faced the allied occupying force. Lloyd George could find no support in any quarter for his policy of making a stand. The French forces, physically present alongside the British, were ordered withdrawn by Poincaré, and the Italians having done likewise, the British were left alone. [108]   French behavior at this juncture seemed to the British little short of treacherous, but Poincaré was not impressed by the remonstrances of the British Foreign Secretary, Lord Curzon. What sort of policy had Britain been following in the (to France) far more important case of Germany? Curzon, in his own person, was an apt representative of the dignity and pomp of a proud empire; too much so perhaps. His personal encounter with Poincaré was attended by an outspokenness unusual in the dealings between statesmen of the old school; but he had found his match, if not more than his match, and emerged from the meeting thoroughly deflated. [109]   These personal encounters between British and French statesmen, Lloyd George and Barthou, Curzon and Poincaré, were both indication and measure of the degree to which the Entente had disintegrated. But they made one thing clear: British recriminations and lecturing had, if anything, the opposite effect to that intended.

In the dealings of nations with each other, recriminations may succeed in poisoning the atmosphere and making more complex and difficult the task of diplomats; the latter find it best to retain a more dispassionate estimate of the true facts of power. In British eyes, France may have been a nuisance, her fears and policies unreasonable; she may have had exaggerated views of what she could accomplish. But it was also clear that Lloyd George's policy, be it in Germany or

---

[106] French action was also motivated by concentration on the German problem, hence the desire to curtail commitments; it had the additional advantage of checking Britain at the same time.

[107] Meanwhile, in March, Kemal had made an advantageous agreement with Russia from whom he obtained the contested districts of Kars and Ardahan and assistance for the war. In June, Italy, taking a position similar to the French, evacuated the zone of Adalia which had been allotted to her.

[108] The British stood their ground, and the Turks, wisely deciding not to force the issue, concluded the armistice of Mudania (October 11) with them and with the Greeks.

[109] An interesting account of some of these exchanges may be found in Carlo Sforza, *Makers of Modern Europe* (Indianapolis, 1930).

Turkey, was attended by something less than success. Just as France might try to carry to its logical conclusion the policy of asserting the full weight of her power, so likewise Britain, who after all also had power, might also use it to the full. Failing to do this, the greater French determination of the moment resulted in British setbacks. Discontent had been mounting in Britain and the Conservative component of the wartime coalition, continued after the election of 1918, had been growing increasingly restless. Events in the Near East helped crystallize this discontent; the Conservative decision to withdraw from the coalition brought down Lloyd George, who was succeeded by Bonar Law and a purely Conservative administration, Curzon remaining at the Foreign Office. [110]

The change of government in Britain had no effect on France's policy under Poincaré's firm guidance. The French view of the virtues of a firm policy of intransigeance toward Germany was not accepted in Britain, but neither was opposition to it increased: France would have to become convinced of the error of her ways through witnessing their consequences, be these a complete breakdown. For the immediate future, this made it easier for Poincaré to adhere to his course.

The Ruhr Episode

Such a breakdown was nearing. The story of Reparation need not be followed in its wearying details during 1922; it will suffice to say that Poincaré found ample occupation for the exercice of his legal talent in the numerous, lengthy, and ably drawn up papers that he penned on the subject: they added up to a closely reasoned indictment of German remissness. The effects of this policy were soon apparent; they may be observed most simply and clearly on the course of the German currency during that year. By the middle of it the mark had lost half of its value at the beginning; the summer saw that cut by three quarters, after which the final débâcle may be said to have got under way. Between September and December the value of the German currency was cut more than 80 percent; it stood at some 34,000 to the pound and 7,000 to the dollar.

These clear signs of financial disintegration were, to Poincaré, mere added evidence of German ingenuity attempting to evade its obligations. [111] If Germany was undergoing hardship that was no cause for

---

[110] Curzon was bitterly disappointed at his failure to be offered the Prime Ministership to which he considered himself entitled. The disruption of the coalition was followed by general elections in November which endorsed the Conservatives.

[111] A great deal which is now commonplace in economics and finance has become so as the result of an analysis and understanding of the experiment of Reparation and the aftermath of war in other instances as well. It was relatively little understood at the time, even by such people as Poin-

sentimental pity, being no more than just retribution: France, too, had suffered, and that, be it never forgotten, at German hands. Through the length and breadth of the country, indefatigably went Poincaré making Sunday orations reminding his countrymen of the essential justice of their cause that he was so staunchly defending. There was nothing for it but to show determination and strength, enforce France's good case with the weapon of strict adherence to legality until Germany's will to resist and evade had been broken by a stronger French will.

As the year 1922 was drawing to a close Poincaré was prepared for the supreme test of his policy. A substantial part of German Reparation was at his time in the form of deliveries in kind. For a variety of reasons certain deliveries of timber had fallen behind schedule. Cutting across the tangled discussion of further moratoria and of the reorganization of German finances, this concrete fact was now seized upon by France. The meeting of the Reparation Commission of December 26, 1922 was the occasion of one more Anglo-French passage at arms, the issue being whether Germany was in default, thereby opening the way to the application of sanctions under the provisions of the Treaty of Versailles (Part VIII, Annex II, art. 17). Sir John Bradbury, the British representative on the commission, characterized the situation with both accuracy and wit when he pointed out that

> The fact was that this trumpery accusation was only before the Commission at the moment as a preparation for an offensive in other fields. Since, in the tenth year of the war, Troy fell to the stratagem of the wooden horse, history recorded no similar use of timber. The situation was at present somewhat different; it was the fifth year of the peace and the city under attack was not Troy, but Essen. [112]

But to charge Poincaré with pettiness alone would be to miss the real point. To be sure, the specific issue was Reparation, and within Reparation the relatively insignificant matter of timber and telegraph poles, but behind the trifle lay the overwhelmingly important matter of a test of strength between France and Germany.

The French delegate and Chairman of the Commission, Barthou, faithful spokesman of Poincaré with whose views he was himself in close agreement, was unmowed. He put two motions to a vote. The first, registering the fact that Germany had not executed in their entirety the deliveries of timber to France during 1922, was approved unanimously. But the second, to the effect that this non-execution constituted

---

caré. It is true, nevertheless, that there was a definite element of irresponsibility in the management of German finances. As Poincaré put it, Germany's capacity to pay was determined by "her policy and her good will."

[112] Cited in *Survey of International Affairs, 1920-1923*, pp. 191-92. The belief was widespread that France was bent on seizing the Ruhr, but Poincaré was perhaps credited with more far reaching ends than really were his. In his typical narrow and legalistic manner, he was assiduously pursuing the limited purpose of forcing Germany to pay Reparation.

a German default — and all agreed "default" meant "voluntary default" — received the assent of the Italian and Belgian representatives while Sir John Bradbury opposed a decided "no." The consequences of this were not long forthcoming; on the 11th of January, 1923 the French occupation of the Ruhr began.

In the English-speaking world feeling ran high. The French action seemed to many at once brutal, heartless, and petty, unqualified abuse of power, and not a little sympathy redounded to impotent, defenseless Germany. [113] It was on the very date (January 10) when the French government notified the German of the forthcoming occupation [114] that the American Army of occupation of the Rhineland was recalled. But the British reaction, at the official level at least, was different. During the exchanges between Poincaré and Bonar Law, the latter made it clear that he took a dim view of the consequences of the French attempt and the prospects of its success, but that the alliance remained in existence. Did Britain have the power and the will of bending a determined France to the acceptance of her own wishes?

France, after all, was not alone in the Ruhr. At this time Belgian policy was working in close coöperation with French (vide the Genoa meeting), although somewhat less rigid, and Belgian forces went alongside the French. The Italian case is more interesting. The advent of Mussolini to power two months before these events had brought no alteration in the course and aims of Italy's diplomacy. At heart, Italy preferred the British to the French position, in addition to which Italy was thinking of the day when German power would be restored to balance French; she would rather let France bear alone the weight of German resentment. But Italy recognized power: France had power and the will to use it; Germany was impotent; Britain would object and moralize but not act. What if France should succeed? Italy therefore felt that her interest would be best served by aligning herself with France on this occasion. [115]

---

[113] French opinion was not unanimous in supporting the policy of Poincaré, but the popular reaction in Britain and America rankled. Whatever might be thought of specific policies, the conviction that she had been originally the victim of German aggression was held with near unanimity in France. It may be pointed out that instances are not few of an inverted sympathy, vide the frequent attitude toward criminals, which causes concern to focus on the shortcomings and difficulties, preferably psychological, that "explain" crime or aggression, forgetting in the process the rights of the victim. "Justice" takes on a peculiarly distorted meaning in this context.

[114] France had insisted on "productive guarantees." Strictly speaking, what was done was to send a "mission of control" and to establish a customs barrier between the Ruhr territory and the rest of unoccupied Germany. The mission was accompanied by military forces that would insure its safety and freedom of operation. Ostensibly, therefore, the "occupation" was not a punitive military measure, but merely one intended to assure the direct collection of Reparation.

[115] Hedging to the last, Italy did not send troops into the Ruhr, but insured her presence through the sending of some technicians.

It is of interest to quote from a lengthy analysis sent to Mussolini by the Italian Ambassador to Berlin. This document reveals in addition the relatively objective and dispassionate Italian view, which was also that of many other dispassionate observers. Wrote Frassati,

The freedom, and therefore the possibilities of our foreign policy, derived before the war from the interplay of the balance of opposing European forces.... The world conflict has destroyed the European equilibrium and erected on its ruins a formidable hegemony. With the collapse of the three greatest powers, Germany, Austria and Russia, two of these without armies of any significance, all three finally destroyed, from their ruins and their partial dismemberment there having emerged a group of powers that surround and oppose them— as they are opponents, or at least lukewarm friends, of Italy — France with a war-tempered army ever ready to march, with a decisive political and military preponderance over that group of powers by her brought into existence for the furtherance of her imperialistic ends, exercises today such a hegemony as modern history has not known....

. . . .

The only substantial obstacle to the establishment of the French continental empire would be a well-organized and therefore politically powerful Germany. But the views and the aims of France with regard to the possibility of such an obstacle are clearly perceptible. Either, by taking advantage of the financial disintegration of Germany, she will succeed in taking possession of German industry, or, forcing the latter into the orbit of her own interests, she will enforce her will on the entire country; or else, pursuing her policy, she will push disintegration to its extreme consequences [subsequently explained to mean the disintegration of German territorial unity]. [116]

It is all here, the exaggerated view of French power, and even more of the intentions of that power; the charge so often heard in those days of French militarism and imperialism, of French hegemony on the continent of Europe. If Poincaré had a point when he objected to the view that France was "suffering from the two diseases which other nations sometimes attributed to her, and which alienists considered complementary, namely megalomania and persecution mania," [117] the outward manifestations of French policy could justify the picture of hegemonic intent. Yet it remains true that controlling, or perhaps better, organizing, Europe was in French eyes the inevitable corollary of that supreme, but negative, desideratum, preventing German aggression, rather than the manifestation of a positive plan of expanding power such as might be credited to Louis XIV or Napoleon.

For the moment, at the beginning of 1923, the great test of the French policy of intransigeance was under way. Britain, like France

[116] Frassati to Mussolini, 11 November 1922. I Documenti Diplomatici italiani. Seventh Series, 1922-1935. Vol. I (31 October 1922 - 26 April 1923), Doc. 103.
[117] Quoted in Survey of International Affairs, 1920-1923, p. 199.

possessed of effective power, was the one state capable of leading an effective opposition. The great Anglo-French contest, and the chief pre-occupations of European diplomacy at this moment, had two foci, Germany and Turkey.

This last may be disposed of briefly, being more eccentric and relatively secondary. After the Greek disaster, the armistice of Mudania, and the change of government in Britain, that country may be said to have accepted the inevitable and decided to cut its losses. On its side, the new Turkey of Kemal, if it was highly nationalistic, strictly adhered to the distinction between nationalism and imperialism. The destruction of the Ottoman Empire it accepted as irrevocable: the Arabs would have to work their own salvation and deal as best they could with the mandatory Powers. [118] On that basis agreement was not difficult to reach. Briefly, in Turkey proper, Kemal had his way, and the Treaty of Lausanne in July, 1923 was the international birth certificate of the new state, destined to be a rare and on the whole unusually successful example of a nationalism at once intransigeant, enlightened, and reasonable. [119] In the course of the negotiations leading to the Lausanne agreement, the Turks proved themselves shrewd and hard bargainers, but Curzon and the British representatives contrived to retrieve some of the British position.

The British may have fought the Turks while the French came to terms with them and even gave them assistance, but the Turkish outlook was cool and realistic rather than sentimental; correctly, the Turks judged that in the foreseeable future Britain would be a more significant factor than France in the Near and Middle East. [120] France on her side, especially at this moment, was naturally more concerned with matters nearer home, specifically Germany and the Ruhr affair.

Germany was a far more bitter source of contest than Turkey and the German problem proved much more recalcitrant to solution. The occupation of Essen [121] by the Franco-Belgians on January 11 was the opening of a new chapter in the story. The area under occupation,

---

[118] The story of the French mandate in Syria and of the difficulties that France encountered in that quarter does not belong in this discussion, but the fact should be mentioned that French suspicion of British opposition and intrigues died hard.

[119] Which is the reason why Turkey, in contrast with the Arab states for example, has achieved the position and status of respected Power that she currently enjoys.

[120] The Italian reaction, for one, to the Near Eastern situation, as it appears in the above-cited volume of the *Documenti diplomatici,* is interesting. Here also Italy aligned herself on the whole with France, whose suspicion of British machinations she shared in part. But she also suspected the possibility of an Anglo-French understanding as the result of which France had been recognized by Britain a free hand vis-à-vis Germany in exchange for giving Britain a free hand in the Eastern Mediterranean.

[121] Shortly extended to include the entire Ruhr region as well as some other points on the right bank of the Rhine.

physically small enough (some 60 by 30 miles), was the heart of hearts of German industrial power, concentrated in it to a degree without parallel. [122] The allied control commission, the M.I.C.U.M. (*Mission interalliée de Contrôle des Usines et des Mines*), was the agency through which Poincaré's "productive guarantees" were to be collected; it expected the coöperation of the existing German administration, threatened with severe penalties in the event of failure to obey its orders. The purpose of the undertaking was clearly to break Germany's resistance, that was claimed to be wilfull, to the discharge of her obligations.

This was in effect a renewal of war, with the important difference that, save for Belgian assistance, France faced Germany single-handed. But in the absence of German armed forces the test could not be military. The first German reaction was, at all levels, one of indignation and non-compliance. In addition to protesting against the occupation that it claimed was illegal [123] and suspending all further deliveries on account of Reparation, the German government resorted to the only weapon at its disposal, passive resistance: not only would it subsidize its own officials, as well as strikers in the mines and factories, but legislation was enacted imposing penalties for coöperation with the occupying Powers. These, however, were not deterred by the wholesale adherence of the local population to the policy of non-coöperation: trials, imprisonments, fines and expulsions (these reached 150,000) were their reply; it was war indeed.

The observation gained currency in many quarters that coal cannot be dug with bayonets, implying that in the lack of local German coöperation the French attempt would result in failure by the standards of its professed aims; this was to take too limited a view. The MICUM took over the direct operation of mines and railways, importing its own technicians for the purpose: considering the difficulties of the undertaking, the results, though far short of full operation, were remarkable and a source of surprise. But, to repeat, what mattered was the test of wills. [124]

---

[122] It produced some 80 percent of Germany's coal and the same proportion of steel and pig iron, as well as containing 10 percent of the country's population.

[123] The issue of legality, though it remained abstract and academic, was widely debated. Interestingly enough, it was not brought up officially by Britain until six months had passed in a note of Lord Curzon in August, 1923.

[124] The episode of the Ruhr has caused much ink to be spilled. In addition to the previously cited references on the general subject of Reparation, the following may be mentioned as especially relevant: *Un an d'occupation: L'œuvre Franco-Belge dans la Ruhr en 1923* (Düsseldorf, 1924); Paul Tirard, *La France sur le Rhin. Douze années d'occupation rhénane* (Paris, 1930); Jacques Chastenet, *Raymond Poincaré* (Paris, 1948); *Gustav Stresemann: his diaries, letters and papers.* Vol. I: *The Battle of the Ruhr* (London, 1935); Paul Wentzcke, *Ruhrkampf, Einbruch und Abwehr im rheinisch-westfälischen Industriegebiet* (2 vols., Berlin, 1930); Hans Ronde, *Von Ver-*

For a variety of reasons, Germany was less able to withstand the strain of the occupation than France the loss of Reparation payments and deliveries. The most immediately obvious effect was financial. The policy of passive resistance was costly; in the circumstances, and with not a little levity, the German government let loose the printing presses. The result is easiest perceived in the precipitously declining curve of the value of the mark; [125] especially from July to November the decline was fantastic in both its rapidity and dimensions. The consequences of this were in turn numerous and equally fantastic, not least in their social manifestations; the word chaos best sums them up. One could hardly any longer speak of state finances under such conditions; taxation covered but a fraction of the budget. Inflation of this kind does not particularly affect the real wealth of the nation, within the confines of which it produces, however, the most arbitrary readjustments. If the middle class was severely injured, many a wealthy industrialist could contemplate with equanimity a state of affairs from which he could draw benefit, while his mobile wealth found the protection of escape abroad; this was the heyday of Stinnes' economic empire. Chaos it was nevertheless that could not be of long duration.

There were besides other sources of concern to the German government. This initial solidarity of passive resistance which had united all segments of the people, labor as well as industry, after a time showed disquieting signs of disintegration. Might not the great industrialists of the Ruhr come to (to them) satisfactory terms with the occupying Powers, and through such arrangements might not French capital obtain a foothold in German industry? [126] Was this perhaps the real, if concealed, aim of French policy?

At an entirely different level, more purely political, the very fabric of the unity of the nation was strained. In the Rhineland, separatism

---

sailles bis Lausanne (Stuttgart, 1950). The works of Jordan and Wolfers, cited above, are also relevant, and the diary of Viscount d'Abernon, the British Ambassador in Berlin, *An Ambassador of Peace* (3 vols., London, 1929-1930), is full of valuable and interesting information.

[125] It is best illustrated in the following table of monthly average value of the dollar during 1923

January	13,700	July	294,000
February	26,300	August	2.950,000
March	21,275	September	53,000,000
April	24,400	October	1,481,000,000
May	45,500	November	2,320,000,000
June	100,000	December	4,405,000,000

These figures are based on those given in the Federal Reserve Bank publication, *Banking and Monetary Statistics* (Washington, 1943), p. 671.

[126] Without pushing the parallel too far, it is interesting to note that the present European Coal and Steel Community, a French initiative, has been accepted by Germany at a time of political weakness. Independently of the professed purpose of this experiment, the question remains open of the ultimate location of the controls in the organization.

reappeared. If it was disavowed by the Belgians in Aachen, it seemed a sturdier growth in the Bavarian Palatinate, while Bavaria proper was the scene of confusion reminding one of the cry *los von Berlin!* [127]

The retort attributed to Poincaré when confronted with the picture of disintegrating Germany, "let there be chaos!", whether or not authentic, is not unfair description of his reaction. He was unmoved. Let Germany discover the consequences of her deeds, her arrogance, her trickery and her ill will; her financial collapse was contrived, a deliberate device of feigned bankruptcy; all she need do was to give evidence of her willingness to meet her obligations: the issue was psychological and moral rather than economic and financial. What early German approaches were made with a view to negotiating a way out of the impasse he flatly rejected: there was nothing to negotiate about; let Germany begin by complying with the directives of MICUM instead of supporting opposition to them. The issue of passive resistance became the touchstone of success between the two contestants.

Such ruthless determination brought results. German national feeling may have been seething with the indignation of impotent rage; necessity, as had been said in Germany on other occasions, remains the higher law. Stresemann replaced Cuno as Chancellor and his first speech before the Reichstag, on August 14, gave indication that the policy of passive resistance, for which his predecessor had stood, might have to be altered. At the end of the following month the legislation relative to this resistance was suspended and the suspension of deliveries for Reparation was withdrawn. In October and November the MICUM was able to enter into specific local arrangements.

The author, or the instrument, of this new German policy was no treasonable separatist. Stresemann was one of the leaders of the small but influential *Deutsche Volkspartei,* a party of the moderate Right associated with large industrial interests such as Stinnes'. Neither Stinnes nor Stresemann were suspect on the score of the authenticity of their German patriotism, or nationalism. But they were also realists, as big business is apt to be, and Stresemann clearly perceived that the approach to the solution of Germany's economic difficulties must be political. His policy, which nowadays would be dubbed appeasement — and such it was — in brief was this: France had shown that she had the power and the will to bring chaos to Germany; Germany did not have the power to prevent this outcome; French pressure would only be lifted if France became convinced of German willingness to fulfill German obligations. The first step on that path must be outward surrender. To this extent, therefore, it may be said that by the end of 1923 Poincaré's policy had been crowned with success.

---

[127] It is perfectly correct to say that Rhenish separatism was an essentially artificial growth, largely dependent upon French support, to whose discredit it ultimately redounded. The fact remains nevertheless that there were certain native elements willing to avail themselves of this support and that Berlin did not know to what lengths the support of France would go.

The success was at once less and more than intended. Breaking Germany's will to resist was for Poincaré a means to an end, the end being ostensibly to collect Reparation. Whether the end would be achieved time alone could answer; that would depend both upon the nature of the new economic and financial arrangements that would have to be made regarding Reparation and upon the fulfilment of these new arrangements. [128] The limitations introduced into this aspect of the French success through the initiation of the Dawes Plan will be indicated presently. But the political and moral aspect of the matter, the means, was of great moment, and there was point to the French observation that

> Incontestably we have gained a material victory, but we have also gained a moral victory of perhaps even greater importance. The truth is that the occupation of the Ruhr has profoundly modified the mentality of the Germans. From now onwards, they see the French and the Belgians with other eyes. [129]

How far and how permanently German mentality had changed, this also time alone could tell. The French success, whatever one might think of the manner of its achievement, was impressive, all the more so for having been contrived virtually single-handed. [130] Poincaré has been charged in some French quarters [131] with giving up the fruits of victory when they were well within his grasp. The accusation does not seem well founded. The attempt to pursue the advantage to the point of the physical disintegration of Germany by using further force does not seem realistic: the fact of German unity can in our day no longer be denied. If some French penetration of German industry might have been accomplished, more important for the long term were two things: had German mentality really been altered? Would the determination of French will persist and, if future occasion demanded, would it again, as in 1923, assert itself?

---

[128] With the complete collapse of the German currency there was nothing for it but to wipe the slate clean and make a fresh start. The famous and notorious Dr. Schacht, able if nothing else, successfully managed this operation. A new currency, the Rentenmark, was introduced (the old mark was officially stabilized at the rate of 1,000,000,000,000 to 1) which was immediately accepted and achieved stability.

[129] Cited in *Survey of International Affairs, 1924,* p. 292. The point should be made that the mentality of the Germans and their view of the French and the Belgians may indeed have been affected by the Ruhr episode, but perhaps not entirely in the direction and in the manner meant in the above quotation.

[130] Belgium alone had closely adhered to France, and even Belgium had had reservations and always kept an eye on Britain between whom and France she sought to find some meeting ground. Italy agreed with Britain at heart but deferred to French power. Among ex-neutrals and the English-speaking peoples the Ruhr episode marked the height of French unpopularity, which was considerable.

[131] On this point may be noted the discussion of the Ruhr episode in J.-B. Duroselle, *Histoire diplomatique de 1919 à nos jours* (Paris, 1953) and in the previously cited works of Jouvenel and Chastenet.

Outside of France the Ruhr episode has often been regarded as a failure. This view is largely incorrect, based on the limited aspect of failure to collect Reparation directly and immediately out of the Ruhr itself. [132] If one can speak nevertheless of failure, or of France being robbed of her victory, this only holds for the long term prospect. The reasons for failure, if failure it was, were of two kinds, foreign as well as domestic. Briefly, they must both be considered.

The Limitations of French Power

If France had power — power of which an exaggerated view was held in many quarters — she also suffered from certain disabilities. The task of healing the wounds of the war to the land, physical reconstruction, was undertaken promptly and carried out on the whole with both effectiveness and success. But the quality of the management of the operation was in other respects deficient. The point is perhaps best expressed by the contrast between the pictures of French and of British finance, in turn reflection of different qualities of both economic management and thinking. The return of the pound to its gold parity in 1925 is commonly regarded as having been economically unsound; the fact that this was possible, however, was the result, apart from the extent of British resources, of sound and careful husbanding of these resources. One aspect of it was the British willingness to resort to direct taxation which was increased in sensational fashion. The commonly held view that the French do not pay taxes is incorrect; what was — and is — true is the considerable unwillingness to reform the basis of taxation, which may have served in the days of pre-1914 but no longer after the impact of world war.

When, in March 1919, the wartime exchange control arrangements had been abandoned by America and Britain — the fact and the timing were both resented in France — the franc quickly declined in value; at the end of 1920 it stood against the dollar at roughly one-third of its prewar rate, while French internal prices had somewhat more than quadrupled. A number of illusions colored French financial thinking, not only at the popular level, but even in quarters where a better and quicker apprehension of what had happened and was happening might have been expected. With the end of the war, the tendency to resume the "normal" game of politics had effects on finance: the claims on the exchequer arising from this same war, be they for reconstruction or war pensions, were of an altogether different order of magnitude from pre-1914 demands on state finance. But this caused little concern, for the popular slogan was "Germany will pay." Pending the day when Reparation would be collected, a special and separate "budget of

---

[132] There were certain French illusions, especially at the popular level, that resulted in disappointment on that score; clearly, what mattered was the long term settlement and German payments over the years.

recoverable expenditures" would conceal the disequilibrium of national finances. The expectation was also widespread that the loss of value of the franc was a passing matter and that it would return to the full gold value that it had had since its creation by the first Napoleon; had not this happened both after 1848 and after 1870? The franc of *Germinal* was a popular myth. The national debt and the wartime deficits continued to accumulate, but for a time confidence persisted and the state had little difficulty in borrowing the necessary funds.

During and immediately after the war some of the borrowing had been foreign, American primarily and also British. The matter of inter-allied debts was to prove a troublesome issue, no less than Reparation, and some of the same misconceptions prevailed in both cases. If it ever was true that sentiment and finance make a poor mixture, no better illustration of this can be found than in the story of Reparation and war debts. The former issue was bedeviled by the moral approach: in French eyes, the German financial obligation was moral in its origin. War debts involved allies instead of enemies and a less rigid outlook might have been expected from the creditors. Nevertheless, in the long term, America, the universal creditor, expected to recover the loans that she had made to her allies. [133]

At this point complications entered which could only serve to embitter relations without contributing to financial settlement and recovery. If one takes the view, then prevalent in America, that she had entered a war wherein she had neither obligation nor interest, with the result however of procuring allied victory, then clearly these allies ought to be grateful and only too anxious to honor their obligation. But if one takes the view, common to these allies and particularly French, that the war had been a joint enterprise wherein America too had a stake, then, in view of her late entry and small military contribution, a financial contribution was the least that could be expected from America. Debate between these points of view is wholly futile since they derive from fundamentally antithetic premises. Depending upon the glass through which he was being viewed, the same character could appear as generous Uncle Sam or hard hearted Uncle Shylock.

The United States had not pressed its allies for immediate repayment, and the debts remained as contracted pending arrangements that

---

[133] Not surprisingly perhaps, in view of the greater understanding of international finance in that country, the soundest economic thinking on the score of Reparation and war debts came from Britain. In August, 1922 Balfour declared Britain's willingness to forego the wartime debts owing her as well as her share of German Reparation if the United States would in turn forego the British debt to it. In view of the American refusal, Britain would only collect an amount sufficient for the discharge of her own obligation even though on balance she was a creditor.

It may be noted that, while the matter of the First World War debts has never been formally disposed of, the institution of Lend Lease during the Second World War was based on American acceptance of the allied view of the First World War as a joint enterprise.

might even involve some recognition of the debtors' difficulties though no remission of principal amounts. In 1922 the American Senate constituted the World War Debts Funding Commission while France was preparing for the showdown that was to take place in the Ruhr in 1923. In French eyes, there was far more "justice" in the collection of German Reparation than in the payment by her of the American debt; but to have to pay the latter while not collecting the former seemed in the nature of insult added to injury. However, not only was America adamant in refusing to acknowledge any connection between the two sets of obligations, [134] but America, like Britain, felt at this time that France was the chief obstacle to the general economic recovery of Europe. The widespread opprobrium of which France was the object in 1923 was to a point disturbing; financial pressure could be more concrete.

It is at the very time when German resistance was breaking that Poincaré accepted, on November 30, 1923, the proposal of the American President to submit the whole question of Reparation to a committee of experts. It is significant that, during 1923, the franc had fallen from 13.70 to nearly 20 to the dollar, half of this fall having taken place in the last two months of the year. [135] Moreover, by this time, doubts had begun to appear in France about the financial effectiveness of the policy of German coercion. The confident assumption in the solidity of the franc was shaken and, as usual in such circumstances, the psychological factor entered to aggravate the very condition that it feared. During the first ten weeks of 1924 the franc fell from 19.92 (January 2) to 27.20 (March 12) to the dollar and from 85.64 to 116 to the pound. With the German example of runaway inflation so close, immediate measures seemed imperative. As it happened, the situation was retrieved with ease on this occasion; [136] by early May the franc had nearly doubled its value (15.23 to the dollar).

Meanwhile, the committee of experts, sitting in Paris from January to April, under the chairmanship of the American, General Dawes, had brought in its report, soon to be accepted. Its specific features need not be considered here. What was significant was that it implied considerable yielding by France. Not so much in purely financial terms, for the

---

[134] Relatively little was heard at this time of the transfer problem which, justice and sentiment aside, applied to all international financial obligations. The American action in raising the tariff is a measure of the quality of American economic thinking at the time.

[135] This is not to be construed as an organized American drive against the franc, but merely a result of accumulating French financial difficulties, which however neither America nor Britain were minded at this time to alleviate.

[136] A $100,000,000 loan had been secured which was used to combat speculation. Poincaré's sound advocacy of doing away with the distinction between the ordinary budget and the "budget of recoverable expenses" and the work of the Dawes Committee, completed in April, had created a favorable atmosphere in financial circles both in France and abroad.

prospect of definite payments had attraction by comparison with the uncertain outcome of continued single-handed coercion, but just because, in view of this single-handed attempt, France now was to renounce the possibility of resorting to similar action in future. This may properly be called a setback for Poincaré.

The story would not be complete without a glance at the domestic French scene. The limited aspect of financial danger has just been mentioned; we shall soon meet it again. But there were broader considerations. When the French had initiated the occupation of the Ruhr, on January 11, Poincaré had been endorsed in the Chamber by a vote of 452 to 72, Communists and Socialists alone being in opposition. [137] A vote of such proportions is as impressive as it is rare; it could be read as near unanimity in the Chamber, though not necessarily in the country. The 1919 house was now nearing the end of its term; general elections were to take place on May 11 in which the dominant issue was not so much the Ruhr affair as Poincaré's policy in the broader sense. For a distinction must be made at this point. The desirability of collecting German Reparation was no issue where the French electorate was concerned, but the manner of doing this and the immediate consequences of the attempt were something else again.

Poincaré might claim success for his policy of coercion which had brought about a German surrender; but the concrete results of this surrender, forthcoming payments under the Dawes scheme, lay in the future. What was immediately perceptible to the average French elector was that no Reparation was being collected at the moment, that the franc had been threatened, and that there had been a flat increase in taxation. In addition to which France was to a degree isolated and highly unpopular in many quarters, most importantly in the English-speaking countries. America and Britain may have been unwarrantedly soft in their approach to Germany; the fact remained that the influence of America, even if unofficial, and that of Britain, had been large, not to say dominant, in the making of the new arrangements — jugglery and tricks of international finance thought some in France — over which the name of Dawes presided.

Disgruntlement born of failure, or even seeming failure, turned against Poincaré and his policy. Napoleon or Richelieu with ruthlessness used power; they had at their command greater relative power than Poincaré did have, nor were they hampered by the fetters of an opinion that no twentieth-century government of France could ignore. Moreover, the Richelieu-Napoleon tradition, if it was rightly associated with France, was but one aspect of modern France; the Great Revolution may have turned patriotic and even nationalistic, but its legacy remained strong of eighteenth-century optimistic humanitarianism. The Wilsonian outlook and appeal had evoked a very large and genuine response in France as elsewhere, and when France was now being

---

[137] There were also some 30 abstentions, among them that of Herriot.

accused of abusing her power, when she was widely charged with being militaristic and imperialistic, the charge at most applied (so far as it applied) not to France as a whole, but to one half, or part, of her. The other part, or half, democratic, libertarian France, had strong attachments to the English democratic development which had been for it both inspiration and model. [138] In the contest between the outside, especially the English-speaking, world and Poincaré's France, half of France was prepared to lend a ready ear to the outside. [139]

The outcome of this combination of circumstances was a victory for the *Cartel des Gauches,* or perhaps better a defeat for Poincaré, his policies, and, broadly speaking, the Right. This did not mean an overwhelming repudiation by the electorate, [140] but in terms of the distribution of parliamentary seats the change was impressive. The *Cartel* was represented by some 100 Socialists, 40 Socialist Republicans, and more than 130 Radical Socialists, next to whom sat some 50 Independent Radicals. [141] In opposition were somewhat over 200 deputies of the moderate Center and Right facing 30 odd Communists at the opposite extreme of the House.

From the beginning of the century the standard bearer of lay liberal republicanism had been the Radical Socialist party. It was now again the largest single group in the Chamber and it was natural that the Prime Ministership should devolve to its leader, Edouard Herriot. This is in fact what happened when Herriot, on June 14, took over from Poincaré the two offices of Prime and Foreign Minister. It did not happen, however, until a relatively small, but significant, event had occurred. The triumphant *Cartel,* defender of popular rights against would-be dictators, was determined to force the resignation of President Millerand, suspect of being desirous to assert greater powers for the

---

[138] We are dealing here with imponderables, difficult of precise measurement but no less important for that reason. To a degree, also, the above is an oversimplification; the French situation being complicated by a strong injection of nationalism into the revolutionary, humanitarian strand. In the cases of both Poincaré and Clemenceau the national component was dominant, yet they were both staunchest republicans. Another connection, even more complex and elusive, between English and French developments, is that between protestantism and the anti-clericalism of the Enlightenment variety which have a point of contact in their attitude toward the Catholic Church organization.

[139] There will be occasion, somewhat later, to observe a wholly different manifestation of this same phenomenon of the response of a section of French opinion to outside influences and ideologies.

[140] Much could be accomplished as a result of electoral deals and combinations with a relatively small shift in votes. The mechanism of French electoral laws is for that reason a perennial object of debate and manipulation. In this instance, the Left showed greater cohesion than the National Bloc of 1919.

[141] This group, resuming the appellation of "Radical Left," was of somewhat doubtful allegiance. It could fairly easily align itself with those to the Right or the Left of itself and for that reason commanded a critical position.

executive. The result was accomplished through the simple device of what might be described as a parliamentary strike. No one commanding a majority would accept the Prime Ministership; conversely, the parliamentary majority would have no dealings with anyone else designated by the President. Helpless President Millerand resigned. [142] If this was an assertion of the popular will, the observation has point that dictatorship can have various forms; that exercised by a parliament has dangers of its own.

Thus we see here at work the influence in the conduct of foreign policy of forces operating mainly on the more limited domestic scene, deep-rooted and fundamental aspects of the French milieu as a whole. But France as a state among states was a whole and a single unit. If it is one of the more attractive aspects of freedom that men may be allowed to differ, if it may be regarded as a good that there were men in France who could disagree with the outlook of Poincaré — enough of them in fact to oust him — those who welcomed his defeat, in the country as well as outside, failed on the whole to take the proper measure of two facts: one, the degree to which the entire edifice of Europe rested upon French power; the other, the fact that divergence and hesitancy on the use to be made of French power at its very source, France herself, could have no other effect than to lessen its effectiveness.

In any case, the French election of 1924 marks the closing of a chapter in the history of the postwar that bears the sign of Poincaré and his policy. A new approach must now prevail.

---

[142] This was not quite the end of the story, for when it came to the election of a new president to replace Millerand the Senate, though it too had a majority of Radicals, would not accept Painlevé, the choice of the *Cartel* majority in the Chamber. The result was the election of the President of the Senate, Gaston Doumergue, a dependable but more colorless and less-committed-to-the-Left Radical. This incident is a good illustration of the nice complexities and adjustments of French politics.

CHAPTER IV

THE ERA OF ILLUSIONS

1. POSSIBLE ALTERNATIVES

France and Germany

The international picture of Europe as a whole during the year 1923 had unquestionably been dominated by the course of the Ruhr episode, more broadly by the issue of Franco-German relations. These continued to be of paramount importance. The broad aims of the foreign policies of the two countries were unaltered: France still wanted both Reparation and security; Germany could not but want the lifting of the disabilities that were still her lot. But the events or 1923 had placed these Franco-German relations in a somewhat novel context.

Poincaré's France had, well-nigh single-handed, broken the German will to resist. Yet Poincaré himself had seemingly judged it necessary to allow British and American [1] intervention in the effort to find a way out of the impasse into which the problem of Reparation had run. This was widely interpreted as acknowledgment of defeat of the French policy of coercion, a view only in part correct. For a different interpretation could be given of the course of the episode. If France had to acknowledge that one cannot indeed dig coal with bayonets, meaning that the "productive guarantees" had not immediately produced either much coal or ready cash, Germany on her side had to admit that she was both alone and impotent. French policy may have aroused resentment, even at times indignation, in Britain; these feelings were not translated into anything stronger and more useful to Germany than verbal and moral support. They did little to stop French bayonets.

Might not the Ruhr affair, for all the intense feeling aroused in Germany, yet serve a useful purpose? This, in a sense, was the moderate

---

[1] During this period Aemerica continued to adhere to the isolationist policy inaugurated in 1920. She took nevertheless an interest in the affairs of Europe, even though she would not actively participate in them. General Dawes was a Chicago banker, and it is precisely the fact that he was American that was supposed to guarantee an impartial, purely "business," approach to the problem of Reparation, instead of the charged political and emotional approach of those most immediately involved. Moreover, whatever the official position in regard to matters political, there remained the question of the debts owed America and the American commercial interest in Europe.

British view to which the government may be said, broadly speaking, to have adhered [2]: on both sides of the Rhine there had been much unrealistic thinking; Germany would have to acknowledge the fact of French power, France would have to accept the realities of the German and of her own economies. Unpleasant as the operation was, the Ruhr and its consequences might yet serve to burst the abscessed bubble of unreality and clear the path to a saner outlook .

On the German side Stresemann gave every indication that such a realistic approach was his. Whatever his long-term wishes or his ultimate hopes, he understood that politics is the art of the possible and must deal with the present. His coming to the Chancellorship [3] had marked a change in policy that was radical and that it was courageous to advocate in the German atmosphere of the day: passive resistance was abandoned. The next step consisted in endeavoring to convince France of Germany's honest intent; beyond that Stresemann had no control over French policy and reactions.

On the French side Poincaré's preconceptions were not subject to easy alteration. Yet he, too, had to a point yielded when he accepted the proposal of an independent committee of experts to examine the whole issue of Reparation. Since France had the effective power, she was the more immediately important factor if any change were to be effected in the tone of the Franco-German relationship. But change in France there seemed to be as well.

The victory of the *Cartel des Gauches* in May 1924 could fairly be taken as French repudiation of Poincaré. Herriot was now leader of France, adequate symbol of a different orientation as well as of the degree of change that might be expected: he had been one of a handful of abstainers — not an open opponent be it noted — when the Chamber had overwhelmingly endorsed Poincaré about to embark on the experiment of the Ruhr. In more senses than one the figure of Herriot looms large on the French scene during the entire period of the interval between the two world wars. A man of broad culture, in the best tradition of his country, he could with both authority and grace speak and write about French literature or Beethoven; where Poincaré had meant austere adherence to principle in all aspects of life, Herriot

---

[2] After the breakup of the coalition government at the end of 1922 and the general election in December, a straight Conservative government was in office, first under Bonar Law, then under Baldwin. The hope was ever reviving in Germany that Britain would give her concrete support; this hope was periodically fed by British words and similarly deceived by British deeds, or their absence; thereby, the perennial of British duplicity was also perpetuated. Actually, we have a continued manifestation of the traditional and pragmatic approach, more intuitive than carefully planned, of the British policy that had prevailed before 1914.

[3] This office he only retained for a few months, but once he had vacated it in November, 1923, he remained at the foreign office, in a Cabinet headed by Chancellor Marx, and continued to direct German foreign policy until his death in 1929.

evinced a greater liking for its amenities and comforts. Principles Herriot did have though the conviviality of his nature made for a softer approach to problems and to peoples, perhaps even at times for weakness. [4] The eighteenth-century benevolent outlook toward Man was his. He was appropriately the leader of the party in French politics that regarded itself as the prime guardian and defender of the Republic and the keeper of the sacred tradition of the Great Revolution; quite correctly so in a sense, for the Radical Socialists were the representatives *par excellence* of the small bourgeoisie of France; not of wealth, large industry or the workers. Rather conservative therefore in matters of social policy, they cherished the revolutionary slogans about "the people"; to these they paid lip service and they had made one of their mottoes, *pas d'ennemis à gauche*. Compromise and accommodation, beginning at the grass roots, a dose of what may be described as the Tammany type of politics, not overrigid a concern about matters financial, the domestic field rather than the foreign was the familiar habitat of the Radical Socialists. The weaknesses contained in all this will appear both presently and later.

Herriot, long mayor of Lyon, was no small town politician; he kept the foreign ministry to himself as well as the Prime Ministership. His accession to power was welcomed across the Rhine and elsewhere where Poincaré had become the symbol of the accumulated unpopularity of French policy. The foreign interpretation was correct though its expectations were too sanguine. Herriot and his Radicals [5] after all were French; whatever eighteenth-century-derived optimistic view of human nature may have been theirs, they certainly had reservations on the score of conservative Frenchman and of German man in general. Poincaré's methods were wrong, his ultimate aims were not: the French claim to Reparation had not become less sacred after the 11th of May.

The great question therefore and for the longer term remained across the Rhine. Had Germany really changed? Had she given up her conquering and domineering ambitions? How judge such an imponderable? Profound constitutional change in Germany beyond a question there had been; in form at least the Weimar Republic was as democratic as any state that called itself such. If the constitution was secure — but was it? — it did not seem unreasonable to expect that the German people in their mass would henceforth prefer to devote themselves to the tasks of peace. If their own country had not been invaded, their casualties in war had been proportionately of the same order as the French; that might well be a sobering experience. Tradition may run deep, but national

---

[4] It may be worth noting that it has been one of the accomplishments of Nazi Germany to convert Herriot to the intransigeant view of Germany as shown by his record after the second World War.

[5] The Socialists had joined the *Cartel* for electoral purposes, but, adhering to their traditional policy, refused to participate in the government, with the result that its composition was overwhelmingly drawn from Radical Socialist ranks.

characteristics, so-called, are cultural phenomena rather than immutable facts of creation.

Comfort and hope might in fact be derived at this point from the French example itself. France, too, had had until quite recently a not unimpressive military and militaristic record. But, even before 1870, critics of this tradition had become increasingly vocal, and, after the defeat, once the French people had come (politically at least) into their own, their pacific intent had become ever more assertive; the Republic had broken the power of the army in the state. The Republic, before 1914, was predominantly anti-militaristic as it was anti-clerical, and the dominant tone of much of the French milieu was one of scant regard for the military and of dislike for military service. Another war, far more disastrous though victorious, had greatly magnified the revulsion toward the fact of war. Nothing was wider of the mark than the widespread picture of a militaristic and imperialistic France often harbored abroad during the twenties.

To be sure, it might be remembered that the infant steps of the Third Republic had long been faltering. Twenty years after Sedan it had semed for a moment possible that the handsome general on horseback might sweep the country with the cry of *revanche*. The penalties imposed upon Germany after the First World War were immeasurably more severe than those visited upon France by the Peace of Frankfort; France's international isolation had been the work of Bismarckian diplomacy, but otherwise France remained mistress in her own house; she could rebuild her army and her recovery was swift. In that relatively relaxed climate the Republic had taken root and prospered. But if a like development was to be wished in Germany there was point to the contention that the best way to foster it from the outside was to encourage the forces of change, the liberals, the democrats, the Left in general, who had started the Weimar experiment on its course, by not saddling the country with impossible economic demands and the perpetual reminder of moral condemnation. Liberal and pacific forces did exist in Germany; their strength might be uncertain and difficult of accurate assessment, but they might grow and prosper as they had done elsewhere. The temper of a people cannot be expected to change overnight; a generation is but a brief span in the life of a nation. [6]

---

[6] In addition to which it must always be remembered that any people, in ordinary times, always contains a large section largely a-political, the weight of which only asserts itself in time of stress, but which in normal times will let well enough alone and accept passively the established form of the state.

A quotation of Viscount d'Abernon's diary, under date of 13 March, 1922, seems apropriate here: "No one that I have met here would think a successful war morally reprehensible; nor would any one advocate a war likely to prove unsuccessful, on the ground that it was morally defensible." D'Abernon, *op. cit.*, p. 291. This judgment carries all the more weight that Lord d'Abernon, if not the biased pro-German that he was pictured in France, certainly did not lack sympathy for Germany.

Such considerations would commend themselves to Herriot and to the majority of the *Cartel,* far more at least than to the tendency that they had just displaced. But this only brings us back to the central factor of power. Had France felt more secure in her own strength, had the relationship between herself and Germany truly been reversed — not at the moment only, but for the longer future — then she might have felt more inclined to run the risks inherent in a generous policy of trust and a broadminded relaxation of the controls that fettered Germany.

To quote from Lord d'Abernon again, as early as 1922:

> One of two views must be adopted: either Germany must be regarded as a danger and be held in check by military conventions and by overpowering force, or Germany must be regarded as an ex-enemy whom it is desirable to treat with fairness and generosity in order to strengthen the elements of peace and reconciliation within her borders. It appears difficult, if not impossible, to frame a policy reconciling these conflicting conceptions. [7]

That is precisely the point. Under Poincaré's leadership France had tried the first policy; under the combined pressures of outside opposition and of her own divergences she had renounced that policy. But she was not prepared for an abrupt reversal to the opposite extreme. It is in any case the primary and most elementary task of any government to insure order within the country and adequate defense toward the outside. However much the France of Herriot and the *Cartel* might agree that in the end there must be reconciliation based on mutual trust, for the immediate present existing rights and guarantees might be enforced with greater reasonableness and laxity, [8] but by no means abandoned. Perhaps it might be put this way: it was too much to ask of either France or Germany alone to make the whole contribution to the reestablishment of normality; the purely negative reaction of outsiders of mere criticism, mainly of France in those days, was of less than no value.

The League of Nations

It is with this background and in a general atmosphere of qualified hopefulness that the new government was inaugurated in France. In concrete terms, there were two, related but distinct, specific matters that must be dealt with: the Dawes Plan and the evacuation of the Ruhr.

From January to April the committee of experts [9] had been at work

---

[7] D'Abernon, *op. cit.,* p. 271.

[8] The coercive measures accompanying the occupation were relaxed by such actions as amnesties and the return of expelled individuals.

[9] Actually, there were two committees, presided over by General Dawes and by Mr. Reginald McKenna, respectively. The second committee was relatively unimportant and it is the report of the first committee, the Dawes Plan, around which discussion centered. Even in this first committee much of the work was directed by Sir Josiah Stamp. Owing to the Belgian and Italian tendency to support the British view, the Dawes report may be regarded as largely British, or Anglo-American, in inspiration, and its adoption a definite success for the Anglo-American view of Reparation.

in Paris, after which it had presented its proposals. Pending the forth-coming French election, the first reaction came from Germany: Strese-mann considered the Dawes proposals an adequate basis of discussion; speaking in Hanover, on April 29, he made it clear that political questions had priority in his eyes over economic: Germany must at all costs first rid herself of the stranglehold of the occupation.

On the French side, even before the election, there had been a notice-able improvement in the atmosphere of Anglo-French relations. [10] The advent of Herriot could only strengthen this tendency; he and Mac-Donald had much in common in their outlooks and philosophies. There was little difficulty in accepting the Dawes scheme itself, but Herriot, with the home situation in mind, felt that he could not consent to evacuation except in exchange for some other compensating guarantee. [11] The two issues were inextricably linked and agreement on evacuation proved somewhat difficult to reach. But reached it was finally, with the help of MacDonald's mediation, on the basis of a compromise that put off the evacuation of the Ruhr for a year.

From this point, despite some secondary additional complications, [12] the question of Reparation and the particular phase of it that the Ruhr episode constituted may be considered essentially liquidated. [13] As the event was to prove, the Dawes scheme was successful, in the sense at least that from the time of its coming into force German Reparation payments were regularly forthcoming, with the result that the trouble-some issue was removed from the realm of politics and emotion; the "business" aproach to an essentially economic question seemed war-ranted. This was a marked success and a justification of the Anglo-

---

[10] It is worth noting the changed tone of Poincaré's communications in the Anglo-French exchanges that took place in 1924 before he relinquished office. In Britain, Ramsay MacDonald had become Prime Minister in January, following the Conservative setback at the election of December, 1923. It is an interesting fact that Anglo-French relations became easier after this, despite the greater sympathy for French policy in Conservative than in Liberal or Labour ranks. To be sure, in view of the past relation-ship between Curzon and Poincaré, the removal of the former could only make matters easier.

[11] The matter of evacuation was complicated by the fact that, in addition to the Ruhr itself, there was the question of the evacuation of the towns of Duisburg, Düsseldorf and Ruhrort, occupied by way of earlier sanctions in March, 1921, as well as by the fact that the Cologne zone, under British occupation, was due for evacuation five years after the coming into force of the Treaty of Versailles, that is in January, 1925. This zone was situated between the Ruhr and the rest of the occupied Rhineland.

[12] These grew out of the issue of the control of German disarmament which was reported to be unsatisfactory. On this score France was supported by the Conservative British government that succeeded MacDonald in November, 1924. However, the regions occupied as sanctions were evacuat-ed in July-August, 1925, but the matter of the Cologne zone was disposed of only in connection with the Locarno agreement.

[13] The final chapter in the story of Reparation, from 1929 to 1932, of relatively secondary importance in the context of the present discussion, will be mentioned later.

American point of view which on the whole had won the day. In any case it may be said that, after 1925, the economic aftermath of the war seemed to have been successfully absorbed; Europe, the whole world for that matter, could for a spell entertain the illusion that the course of its interrupted progress had been resumed. The fallacies that underlay the artificial prosperity of the second half of the twenties, in particular the peculiar and unsound relation of the American to the world's economy, were not to be revealed for some years. [14]

In view of the conditions that confronted him, Stresemann was quite right, from his own and the German points of view, when he gave priority to political over economic problems. To regain her freedom of action, Germany had first of all to liberate the Ruhr: securing this result was worth a high price and many concessions. [15] But it is also true that satisfactory economic conditions and a prosperous state of international trade are powerful solvents of political divergence. To the extent that it had helped the general economic health of Europe, the solution of the Reparation issue helped to create a climate more favorable to the relaxation of political tensions, especially where the three most important members of the European community at this time, Great Britain, France, and Germany were concerned.

That did not mean, however, that the perennial of French security had been removed from the category of unresolved issues. The cautious behavior of Herriot in dealing with the evacuation of the Ruhr has been mentioned; he knew that within his own party he would not find support for too far reaching concessions, and, farther to the right of the Radical Socialists, the *Gauche Républicaine* had been rather ambiguous with respect to Poincaré during the election. Nevertheless, it remains true that the general orientation of French policy after the 11th of May was more favorable to the internationalistic approach of general pacification. In a different quarter, France at one time had been the chief advocate of the *cordon sanitaire* policy toward the Soviet Union. Herriot, who had personally visited Russia, was not unfavorably impressed and proceeded to implement the Radical policy of *pas d'ennemis à gauche,* in

---

[14] Despite the official isolationist position of the United States, the state of the European economy continued to be of considerable interest to America. At the level of governmental relations there was the issue of the wartime debts; these were funded during the years 1923-1926. But American capital was highly interested in the possibilities of foreign investment. The seeds of the Dawes scheme may be found, as early as December, 1922, in an address delivered by Secretary of State Hughes to the American Historical Association in New Haven in a fruitless effort to forestall the impending French occupation of the Ruhr. America persisted, however, in her official refusal to acknowledge any connection between the problem of German Reparation and that of interallied debts.

[15] It must be emphasized that there was genuine concern in Germany over the precise nature of French intentions, a concern given real point by the French support of Rhenish separatism.

the foreign domain as well by recognizing the Soviet Union in October, 1924. [16]

The great hope that President Wilson had brought with him across the ocean and that had been given concrete form in the League of Nations could not but be dimmed by the events of 1923. Nevertheless its possibilities, if dormant, were not dead. The League existed and had established its home in Geneva. As pointed out before, in the absence of America, Russia, and Germany from its membership, the fate of it was largely in the hands of Great Britain and France. The central point of the 1919 debate between the Anglo-American and the French views has been indicated. [17] The question raised by France — in simplest form: what power did the League have and how could such power be effective? — if difficult of answer could not be evaded. There was behind the question the strength of obvious logic; pending a satisfactory answer to it, there was also for the moment the reality of French power which one could hardly expect merely to surrender and yield to general trust and gentle hope in the goodness of man.

Nevertheless, in this instance also, the French camp was to a point divided, a part of it at least not unresponsive to the British outlook. Simplifying somewhat, it may be said that this tendency had prevailed, or at least had been enhanced in 1924. In Britain, too, though the matter was simpler because security was not felt as an issue as it was in France, the year 1924 had brought a change that would enhance the prospects of the broad internationalist and pacific, not to say pacifist, outlook. Ramsay MacDonald, leader of the Labour Party, was now Prime Minister. [18] Labour and its Liberal allies were on the whole rather less sympathetic to France in general, and to Poincaré's France in particular, than were the Conservatives, [19] but Poincaré had used much

---

[16] The international revolutionary ardor of the Soviets had considerably cooled by this time. Lenin himself had inaugurated the New Economic Policy and the country's energies were absorbed in the task of domestic reconstruction and, at the higher political level, by the struggle over the succession of Lenin. The ultimate victory of Stalin over Trotsky in that contest put the stress on "socialism in one country". Concurrently, toward the outside world Soviet policy became one of live and let live. Trade with other countries and formal recognition by them were both welcome. For the rest, the chief concern of the Soviet Union remained the possibility of a capitalist coalition and in that context Franco-German differences were also welcome.

[17] See above, pp. 73-4.

[18] The Conservatives still constituted the largest single group at Westminster but the circumstances of the election of December, 1923 had been taken as a repudiation of the Conservative administration. The result was a coalition Labour-Liberal government.

[19] We are touching here again on elusive, though important, imponderables. At the cultural level, France and things French were more alien to the rank and file of Labour, which combined an internationalist outlook in abstracto with a greater insularity of individual experience. The best example of uncongeniality, to put it mildly, in higher Labor ranks, is perhaps that of Philip Snowden. By contrast with the dourness of Snowden, MacDonald, as time was to show, displayed not a little response to the softer aspects of existence.

softer language in his exchanges with MacDonald than with Curzon. With the advent of Herriot in June there was established a broad area of congeniality, at the intellectual and ethical level at least. The visit of Herriot to Checquers, one of the first acts of his Prime Ministership, was a highly successful as well as a pleasant occasion. A greater contrast could hardly be imagined than that between the couples Curzon-Poincaré and Herriot-MacDonald. Would these two men, both adept in the use of fine, if perhaps somewhat vague, phrases, abandoning the harsh "realistic" approach of power, succeed in dragging Europe out of the bog into which *Realpolitik* had mired her, through a fresh approach make a reality of peace and of Geneva? There were high hopes in many quarters.

Before recounting the sequel, it is necessary to go back a little in time. One understandable result of the war, as mentioned, had been the widespread popular dislike and suspicion of arms. The Covenant itself pointed to the hope of disarmament, and from its very beginning the League Assembly had instituted a Permanent Consultative Commission to look into the armament question. The first result of this activity was a clearer realization of the difficulties of the problem, which a Temporary Mixed Commission, appointed by the Council in 1921, went on to deal with in its political, as well as more limited military, aspects. By September, the third Assembly of the League adopted the famous Resolution XIV which is a very good expression of the progress of the discussion and of the prevalent thought of the time on the subject. This Resolution made the chief following points:

1. Reduction of armaments could only be successful if general;

2. In view of the special position and problems of many states, reduction of their armaments would be a function of any corresponding increase that could be given their security;

3. This guarantee of security could be provided by a general defensive agreement, of universal scope, "provided that the obligation to render assistance to a country attacked shall be limited in principle to those countries situated in the same part of the globe." In cases of special danger detailed arrangements could be made on that basis.

To a considerable extent this was endorsement of the French view, the view of most continental states for that matter, that disarmament depended on security, therefore could only follow the achievement of the latter or be a function of its extent. Such a position may be called inevitable; but how does one arrive at an arithmetical coefficient of security?

The Resolution ended by indicating a preference for a general treaty, allowing that limited (i.e. regional) arrangements were permissible. In other words, the French system of alliances, still in process of formation, or the Little Entente, could be regarded as contributions to security, hence facilitate the reduction of armaments.

The drafting of a Treaty of Mutual Assistance was the next step. [20] The draft was before the League in 1923 and the Council resolved to have it submitted to members (in September) as well as to non members (in December). The replies, forthcoming in the next few months, were, not surprisingly, expressions by the various states of their respective positions in the matter of security: briefly, it may be said that their support of the Treaty was in direct proportion to the degree of insecurity that they felt to be theirs. [21]

It is worth noting as significant that the French acceptance bore the signature of Herriot rather than that of Poincaré. If both men, and the tendencies that they represented, were equally desirous of insuring their country's security, it took the former to respond to the appeal — and the risks — of a novel experiment that would make this security and its basis collective. The risks were not perhaps too great since the French system of alliances was not to be abandoned, but was instead endorsed as a concrete contribution to the broader general purpose; but undeniably there was a shift of emphasis at least. How would Poland for instance, number one member in the system, respond? And if Poland did not, what then of the French system?

In the event, the British position was crucial. Britain herself, or the United Kingdom, is but a part, although the heart, of that vast and unique combination, the Commonwealth, whose extent at the time embraced one quarter of the planet. The political evolution of the system was following the course on which it had for a long time been set of increasingly asserted independence on the part of its outlying members: the voice of the Dominions must be heard before London could answer. It takes little effort of the imagination to appreciate the fact that the Rhine, not to mention the Vistula, seemed rather far removed in Ottawa, Melbourne, or the Cape. To the Dominions, the new proposal looked like the prior, and unnecessary, assumption of burdens and commitments without perceptible compensating advantage.[22]

---

[20] The text of this treaty was the outcome of much debate and discussion in which Lord Robert Cecil of Britain and Colonel Requin of France were the chief contributors.

[21] France, Belgium and Czechoslovakia were favorable; a number of East European states felt that the increase of their security was not sufficient to warrant further reduction of their existing armaments; ex-neutrals and the members of the British Commonwealth objected that too great an extension of their obligations was involved; Italy and Japan had reservations on regional agreements and on the definition of aggression; Germany could assume no commitments since she was disarmed; the Soviet Union adhered to its "negative" attitude toward the League as it was constructed; the United States gave a categorical refusal.

[22] This condition persists in our own day, and the British reluctance to participate in continental arrangements, be they the Coal and Steel Community or the Common Market, uses as an argument — or pretext — the British connection with the Dominions whose interests are diverse and divergent.

But it was not the Dominions alone. British opinion at home had failed to register the altered facts of power as well as the more concrete developments of the military art. The British people felt secure behind the Channel moat; if they might choose to help others, the idea that they in turn might need assistance was largely alien to them. The phrase, "our frontier is on the Rhine," was not to be used until more than a decade had passed, and the French view of the unity of Europe in the sense of the inextricable interdependence of the relations of its members seemed rather like a French pretext for interference where none was necessary, a polite shield for French hegemony. With France and Belgium some limited commitment might be made; even that would appear in the guise of a generous contribution for which no counterpart was to be either asked or received. [23] In Britain therefore also the concept of collective security embodied in the Treaty of Mutual Assistance seemed to imply enlarged responsibilities for which no compensating gain was visible. [24] Whether or not the British government had to reflect this widespread sentiment and yield to it, the fact is that it did — Britain, like France, is a democracy — and there is irony in the fact that it fell to the internationalist MacDonald to reject the Treaty in July, 1924. [25] It is hardly an exaggeration to say that the British action was tantamount to the death warrant of the attempt.

Despite this setback, the atmosphere was now different; the team MacDonald-Herriot, in Geneva and to the world at large, stood as a symbol of the altered mood to which they in turn felt an obligation. The two Prime Ministers explained their views at the League Assembly in September; these were still far apart, but it proved not beyond the skill of others to find between them common ground. [26] The result, to make a long story short, was the Protocol for the Pacific Settlement of International Disputes, commonly known as the Geneva Protocol. This was submitted on October 1 to the Assembly which, after debating it for two days, unanimously recommended its adoption.

The essence of the new device was the attempted solution of the dilemma between security and disarmament; this was done by intro-

---

[23] French thinking in that respect was more realistic and advanced. It is revealing that in the Anglo-French exchanges after the war, the French approach of mutual assistance and protection appears to have generally been regarded as a fiction that must be entertained to humor French pride rather than as corresponding to an existing reality.

[24] It was quite true that, in view of the extent of the Commonwealth and the primarily naval basis of her power, Britain was likely to find herself called upon to intervene in no matter what quarter of the globe trouble might arise; and, finally, the non-membership of the United States in the League raised at least the possibility of an issue with that Power in the event of the use of British naval power for blockade purposes, for instance.

[25] The publication of the British note was followed by a very interesting debate in the House of Lords on July 24 in the course of which the issues and the currents of opinion were neatly brought out.

[26] The credit for this goes primarily to the representatives of two small Powers, Beneš of Czechoslovakia and Politis of Greece.

ducing the concept of arbitration: the trilogy "arbitration, security, disarmament" became the simple and attractive slogan to which all were asked to rally for the final exorcising of war. Any dispute between states would henceforth be arbitrated unless it fell under the jurisdiction of the Permanent Court of International Justice. [27] Refusal to accept arbitration, or the verdict of arbitration, would be considered tantamount to an act of aggression. In the event of such, the Council, by a majority of two-thirds of its members, would decide upon the sanctions to be applied to the aggressor and the Council's decision would be binding upon all members.

This last provision was important for it represented a substantial strengthening of the powers of the League; the unanimity rule was done away with in the Council whose decision was in addition binding, whereas before it could only "recommend". The everlasting French desire for guarantees could focus on this last aspect of things; the British reluctance to face unpleasing possibilities could console itself with the thought that so many hurdles had been created on the path to open conflict that it was unlikely to occur. Although this was 1924 rather than 1960, [28] it may be said on balance that the greater concession was the French, for there always remained the possibility that delay might insure the success of aggression, and the old platitude has lost none of its validity that possession is nine points of the law. Time would tell whether France was making a valuable contribution to world peace or had allowed herself to be lulled and "bamboozled" into surrendering the best guarantee of peace — her own as well as that of others — the effective force that she could control and draw upon in case of need.

No piece of legislation can by itself insure the reign of order, whether inside or among nations, but in the general consensus of opinion the Geneva Protocol was a valuable and promising contribution. Small states, quite naturally, will prefer a general guarantee of their safety, *provided they can count on it,* to that of any one Power or group of Powers with the dependence that it entails for them. The unanimous

---

[27] The essence of the compromise between the British and the French views lay in this: stress was put on the one hand on all the means that would prevent a dispute from reaching the stage of open conflict (this appealed to the British reluctance to undertake prior commitments that would involve the use of force); if, however, all these safeguards proved insufficient, then regional arrangements (the French alliances) could come into play; but then again the functioning of this ultimate resort would not be automatic, but only operate after the signatories of the Protocol had been called upon to apply sanctions by the Council.

[28] "Indirect" and "internal" aggression are later contributions to international relations that did not loom large in the thinking of 1924. Also, the passage of thirty years, with the technological developments that have taken place during the interval, has clearly made obsolete much of the emphasis on procrastination and delay. Consequently, we hear much more of the *déclenchement automatique* (automatic coming into operation) of defensive means that was a French favorite thirty years ago.

endorsement of the Protocol by the Assembly was followed by a number of prompt ratifications, the French among them. Once more, the British position was crucial. As fate would have it, the weight of tradition was to win the day in Britain against the risks and the attraction of novelty that broader vision and imagination might have entertained.

The reticence of the British reaction to Geneva has been explained in connection with the discussion of the Draft Treaty of Mutual Assistance. The advent of a Labour-Liberal coalition to power had not altered in Britain the general state of feeling where foreign, especially European, affairs were concerned. [29] It was MacDonald himself who asked postponement of the discussion in Geneva until the session of March, 1925. [30] The coalition that ruled Britain, a makeshift and rather uncongenial device, met defeat almost immediately after the endorsement of the Geneva Protocol by the Assembly. The ensuing election in November produced a clear Conservative majority that was to remain in office for the remainder of the decade. Stanley Baldwin was Prime Minister while Austen Chamberlain held the Foreign Office.

If the general temper of the British electorate in matters of foreign policy was unchanged, Conservatives and Labour represented none the less somewhat different tendencies. Paradoxically it may seem, Labour was at once more insular (or provincial) and more internationalist than the Conservatives. The broad and more utopian approach of Geneva appealed to it more than it did to the Conservatives; to the extent that you could work for universal peace and for the good of Mankind, you need know less about the specific problems of remote Polish Man or share and understand the concerns of none-too-congenial French Man; with equal impartiality all would be equally provided for. This nebulous, to a degree Messianic, outlook did not commend itself to the more realistic Conservative approach that preferred to deal with more limited segments of reality: the whole world, universal peace, these lacked concreteness; France, the Rhine, the Empire, these were precise and apprehensible objects with which policy could deal with meaning. This last approach had, in addition, the advantage of the pragmatic way commonly associated with the British mind.

The combination of the general British outlook, Conservative predilection, and the preferences of the outlying Commonwealth, had the effect of causing the new government of Britain to reject the Geneva Protocol: this was the sense of Austen Chamberlain's speech which he

---

[29] Especially since the critical issue of the election of 1923 had been that of protection.

[30] Pressure of unfavorable Dominion reaction, of which Canada was the foremost exponent at this time, was a factor again. One issue raised by the Dominions was that of possible League interference with their immigration policies. More fundamental, however, was the fact that the Dominions did not feel the urgency of security in the same way that the continental states of Europe did. Senator Dandurand, the Canadian delegate, gave clear expression to this feeling in Geneva when he said: "our house is fireproof, far from inflammable materials."

delivered before the Council of the League on March 12, 1925. [81] The British decision had been known for some time; its formal announcement, nevertheless, caused widespread and genuine consternation, for hopes had been raised high that were now being dashed. What the course of events would have been had Britain chosen to throw the weight of her power and influence in favor of strengthening, instead of quenching, the wave of enthusiasm and hope that had begun to rise, can only be idle and fruitless speculation. But there is point ot the charge that if the existing state of affairs, more specifically the French system, was irksome and objectionable, here was an opportunity to embark on a path that would alter it; France seemed willing to run certain risks. Here was a case indeed where Britain had it in her power to make a positive conrtibution, but in the test declined to make it. Could France, in fairness, be asked to bear, apart from British participation, the main burden and risks of possible reconciliation?

Of the validity of this charge the British government was not unconscious. All the more reason for seeking some constructive alternative that could be a concrete contribution to the cause of peace. The results of this effort will appear presently; they are writ large under the banner of Locarno.

2. LOCARNO AND ITS SIGNIFICANCE

The Locarno Treaties

At the time of their visit to the United States at the end of June, 1954 Prime Minister Churchill and Foreign Secretary Eden were both startled at the violence of the American reaction to Sir Winston's earlier suggestion of a Far Eastern Locarno. It was reported that in the course of a White House function, Sir Anthony was prompted to observe to an American table neighbor that "we did not realize that Locarno was a dirty word in America." It seems to have been widely forgotten in America that Locarno, and the so-called spirit of Locarno, have stood in many eyes for all that was best and most hopeful on the international

---

[81] The British position took some time to assume formal shape owing to more immediately pressing preoccupations of the Foreign Office at the time the Conservatives assumed power; these had to do mainly with relations with Russia (the famous Zinoviev letter had played an important role in the election) and with Egypt (the Sirdar, Sir Lee Stack, had been murdered in November).

It is of interest that Chamberlain received strong support at Geneva from the Italian delegate. Fascism, though peaceful at this time, being fully occupied with the task of domestic consolidation, was generally and on principle inimical to any attempt that could be interpreted as tending to freeze the *status quo*.

scene of Europe between the two world wars. [32] Locarno, its origin, and most of all its true implications and significance, in retrospect clearly perceptible, must be looked at with care as one of the grand climaxes and turning points of the whole course of Europe between the two world wars.

There has been considerable discussion of the genesis of the Locarno agreements, centering on the question whether the initiative that led to their conclusion was German or British. It can be safely asserted that the origin of them lies in Germany and that various circumstances led Britain to accept and even actively support the proposal, [33] to which circumstances again caused France to be converted. Basically ,the scheme grew out of the German effort to mitigate the effects of the unequal contest between French intransigeance supported by French power on one side and German powerlessness on the other. Hence the persistent effort to introduce third parties into the situation.

As early as December, 1922 the German Ambassador in Washington approached Secretary of State Hughes with the suggestion that Germany and France should pledge themselves toward the United States not to resort to war for a generation. Even apart from the awkwardness of German diplomacy, which gave Poincaré occasion to describe the attempt as a "clumsy manoeuvre" when the suggestion was passed on to him, [34] the fact that it took place at the very moment when France was determined to essay the policy of coercion made it in any case **untimely.**

---

[32] The source of the American confusion probably lay in the fact that Locarno was followed by the admission of Germany to the League. From this the parallel is drawn that a Far Eastern Locarno would be preliminary to the admission of Red China to the United Nations. American feeling being what it is on that score, it is easy to equate Locarno with appeasement; and since, moreover, the Far Eastern Locarno suggestion was attractive to the British and the French who were the great appeasers of Germany at Munich, this last name, and all that it symbolizes, becomes linked with Locarno. That is, of course, one way of reconstructing history. It would be difficult to find two more divergent spirits than those that presided over Locarno and Munich, and it would be interesting to recall the very diverse American reactions to events of 1925 and of 1938.

[33] It has been said that Britain, more specifically Lord d'Abernon, the British Ambassador in Berlin, was responsible for Germany having made the initial proposal. This view had currency especially in France where Lord d'Abernon was regarded as highly pro-German. Of Lord d'Abernon's sympathy for and understanding of Germany there can be no question, nor of the fact that he was strongly in favor of the scheme. His close acquaintance with the German leaders, whose confidence he enjoyed, put him in a position to give advice and guidance to them. His memoirs, previously referred to, are full of valuable and interesting information on this particular subject.

[34] Even d'Abernon agreed that the qualifications to refrain from war "for a generation" and "without plebiscite," well enough meant as they may have been, were indeed clumsy and calculated to arouse suspicion. Chancellor Cuno gave public notice of the attempt and of its failure in a speech in Hamburg on December 31, 1922.

Yet the seed was planted. Despite, or perhaps just because of, the state of Franco-German relations during 1923, the suggestion was reverted to on two occasions during that year. A variant in May, when Britain, Japan and Italy were brought into the picture in addition to the United States, and again in September, when Stresemann was Chancellor, met the same fate. From his own point of view, Poincaré was altogether consistent: the intrusion of third parties could only complicate and weaken the pursuit of his policy, which was precisely the German aim.

Stresemann understood and bowed to the inevitable. The year 1924 brought about a considerable change, the manifestations of which have been recounted. With Reparation removed from the domain of active controversy, Stresemann was bent, as he openly avowed, on restoring Germany's full freedom of action: immediately, this meant evacuation of the Ruhr. The changed climate of 1924 had led to the discussion, which has just been related, of schemes for the general preservation of peace linked with the reduction of armaments, schemes which were all centered around the League. [35] The Geneva Protocol, specific form of the Genevan discussions, was meant to be of universal application; but German disarmament was the object of definite provisions that were written into the treaty of peace. The particular issue of the evacuation of the Ruhr had become linked with that of Germany's fulfilment, or lack thereof, of the disarmament clauses of the peace; the report on which the allies were basing a note to Germany [36] on that score was known to indicate German default on a number of points.

German disarmament and the dimming prospects of the Geneva Protocol were the immediate background of the negotiations about to be resumed and the final outcome of which was to be the Locarno Pact. The new spirit in France, of which Herriot was the symbol, was after all a fragile growth. The words that he used at the end of January, though lacking the harshness that would have been Poincaré's, were all the more significant coming as they did from him: Germany had not lived up to her disarmament obligations, "our establishment on the Rhine is the essential and, also, the last condition of our security"; "remember the dramatic circumstances that have faced us since the settlement of the war. Remember that France has constantly had to discuss peace with a dagger an inch off her heart"; "as first conditions of this [world]...

---

[35] Another German line of approach was to seek admission to the League. A German note of September 29, 1924 was sent to the states members of the Council. It is of interest that in this note Germany stated her wish to discuss some preliminary questions, all of which added up to her restoration to full equality with other members through the lifting of whatever disabilities she was subject to. Nothing came of the attempt at this time. The Council's reply to Germany came in March.

[36] The note was dated January 5, 1925 and denied the German contention of her note of September.

peace, I want the security of my own country." [37] Was there not danger that the nascent plant of improving relations might be killed before it had a chance to strike solid root? Worse still, might not a renewed Anglo-Franco-Belgian agreement be in the offing?

There were German approaches to Britain where greater understanding and sympathy might be expected, but Chamberlain would not assume the risks of secret negotiations that might give ground to French suspicion. [38] France should be approached directly. Consequently, on the 9th of February, 1925 the German Ambassador in Paris submitted his country's proposal to Herriot. The German scheme was purposely loose and flexible; the gist of it was an undertaking by the Powers more directly concerned to guarantee the inviolability of the Franco-German frontier. [39] This may be taken as the effective opening of the negotiation that was to be concluded nine months later.

There was no immediate or direct French response, but one inevitable question immediately arose: what was the significance of Germany's offer to accept her Western frontier without making a similar commitment in the East? On March 6, Count Skrzynki, the Polish Foreign Minister, was in Paris to consult the French government.

It is at this point that we rejoin the earlier story. Chamberlain's speech on the 12th at Geneva, which finally buried the Geneva Protocol, had also the effect of making clear that whatever might be accomplished in the direction of enhancing security must be more modest in scope than schemes of universal application: diplomacy could concentrate all its efforts and attention on the German problem. [40] Just because it was she that had been primarily responsible for the failure of the promising effort that the Protocol seemed to be at one point, Britain was the more anxious to make some substitute contribution; she would thereby decrease the onus that attached to her action. During the course of a

---

[37] Speech of January 28, 1925. It may appear odd to have France speak of "a dagger an inch off her heart" at the time when French troops were deep in Germany. Coming from Herriot, this is all the more convincing expression of the reality of the long term French fear. The fact is worth mentioning that Chancellor Marx had had not a little difficulty in securing acceptance of the Dawes scheme in the German Reichstag. He had finally obtained it with the support of the Nationalists, but their price was an official statement to the effect that no reconciliation was possible so long as Germany had not been exonerated of the false accusation of war guilt. This somewhat strange procedure may be understandable in the context of the necessities of German domestic politics; but it naturally aroused suspicion in France, as did the fact that the German press on the whole revealed a remarkable dearth of any effort to understand, let alone agree with, the legitimate bases of French fears.

[38] The British government at this time stood solidly with France on the score of the German default in the matter of disarmament.

[39] The original proposal made no mention of Belgium.

[40] France had been the first to ratify the Geneva Protocol, but she was not irrevocably wedded to that scheme. To her, universal security was of value only in so far as it would take care of the German problem. To return to that problem alone was therefore no very difficult readjustment.

debate in Commons, on March 24, Foreign Secretary Chamberlain proceeded to reply to criticism and to expound his government's foreign policy. He took a very kindly view of the German proposal on which he put the best construction; stressing good faith and good will, he pointed out that Germany, of her free will, now offered to accept the *status quo* for her Western frontier, and that if she did not feel that she could undertake a like commitment in the East, in that quarter also she was willing to renounce the resort to force in favor of peaceful methods of change. [41] In any case, Anglo-French negotiations got under way in regard to the German proposal.

These negotiations were shortly interrupted by a change in the French Cabinet, which brought Painlevé to the Prime Ministership with Briand at the Quai d'Orsay, [42] the same Briand who three years earlier had been evicted for his supposedly too great subservience to Britain. But times, and to some extent French feeling, had changed. The direction of French foreign policy was to remain in Briand's hands without interruption almost until his death six years later.

Briand's personality is therefore quite important; it has been touched upon before. If Briand lacked the broad and deep culture of his immediate predecessor, of the art of politics and of the use of words, which the quality of his voice enhanced, he was master — to an unusual degree even for France. Briand was a man of the Left; compromise and accommodation were highly congenial to his nature. There was therefore no cause to fear that under his guidance the novel direction of French policy would be altered. However, Briand too was French and the exchanges that ensued between Paris and London are reminiscent of those that had taken place during the prewar years. Without going into their wearisome, though not uninteresting, detail, the gist of them may be summed up in this: Briand persistently endeavored, at times almost high-handedly, to involve Britain into larger commitments of guarantees in Eastern Europe, which Chamberlain with equal persistence endeavored to avoid. On the basis of France's retaining the liberty to assist her Eastern allies and of Britain's retaining the liberty of implementing her guarantee to France in that event, agreement was reached on the French note that went to Germany on June 16.

---

[41] This was largely echoing the German line of reasoning which, for that matter, was not uninfluenced by British advice. Much indeed depended on good faith. The French reaction tended to be rather that the German proposal was tantamount to notice that Germany *would* seek modifications of her Eastern frontier, a view that the German press did little to weaken.

This is also the time when the death of President Ebert caused a presidential election to take place in Germany in March, with a second balloting in April. The election of von Hindenburg to the Presidency had the effect that might well be expected in France, no less than in Poland and in Czechoslovakia.

[42] For the sake of continuity of exposition, French domestic developments during this period, in so far as they have a bearing on the discussion, will be considered later.

The German reply was a whole month in returning (July 20) and when it did was generally considered a poor exercise in diplomacy. [43] The Anglo-French discussion thereupon resumed, the specific center of it being the definition of aggression, behind which lay the usual question of the circumstances in which the British guarantee would come into operation. The solution, a distinction between "flagrant" and "doubtful" aggression, made it possible to send a French answer, British endorsed, to Germany on August 24. Agreement was sufficient by this time to procure immediate German acquiescence to the meeting in London of a committee of jurists on September 1 for the purpose of drafting definite texts. This task proved easy and was promptly done and invitations were sent to the allied powers to a meeting that took place in Locarno from October 9 to 16. [44]

The successful outcome of the Locarno meeting was due to the adequate work of the prior diplomatic preparation and to the prevailing "spirit of Locarno," which meant the readiness of the participants to deal with each other in a mood of accommodation and compromise. This manifested itself in the easy direct contacts among individuals, preferably in pleasing circumstances and surroundings — whether the Briand-Luther conversation in a country inn at Ascona, or the lake excursion on wich British, French and Germans went together — a condition which enhanced the belief in the virtues of personal diplomacy and diplomacy by conference at the higher levels. Some issues were still outstanding when the statesmen gathered at Locarno; they reduced themselves to two: the conditions surrounding Germany's admission to the League, and the precise nature of France's relation to her Eastern allies. The first proved the more troublesome, but was resolved by falling back on the provision of the now defunct Geneva Protocol that a member's obligation would be a function of "the degree which its geographical position and its particular situation as regard armaments allows" (art. 11, par. 2 of the Protocol). Thereafter, Germany proceeded to negotiate directly with the Czechs and the Poles, and the series of instruments that together constituted the Locarno Pact was signed in the evening of October 16, 1925. [45]

---

[43] Even Lord d'Abernon found this an occasion to bemoan the limitations of the German mind. The delay and the tenor of the German note are again traceable, in part at least, to the domestic German situation. The government was a precariously balanced coalition whose task was made more difficult by the fact that it was trying to follow a foreign policy of conciliation, hence more congenial to the Left, with the support of the Nationalists. The statement of policy issued by Stresemann's own *Deutsche Volkspartei* on July 2 was an expression of the compromise that he had had to make.

[44] The list of invitations included Czechoslovakia and Poland, a fact which took Germany by surprise, but Stresemann decided to bow to the *fait accompli* with good grace.

[45] After the initialing at Locarno the ceremony of signature took place in London on December 1 and ratifications were subsequently forthcoming.

In addition to the final protocol signed by all, that is by Britain, France, Germany, Italy, Belgium, Czechoslovakia and Poland, there were three categories of instruments:

1. Five annexes consisting of

The main Rhineland Pact or Treaty of Mutual Guarantee between Germany, Belgium, France, Britain and Italy;

Two identical Arbitration Conventions between Germany and France and between Germany and Belgium, respectively;

Two identical Arbitration Conventions between Germany and Poland and between Germany and Czechoslovakia, respectively.

2. A draft collective note to Germany from the other participating Powers regarding the interpretation of article 16 of the Covenant of the League.

3. Two identical Treaties between France and Poland and between France and Czechoslovakia, respectively.

The first annex, or Rhineland Pact, was the most important of the various agreements and is often, mistakenly, thought of as the whole of the Locarno arrangement. It provided for a guarantee by all the signatories of the frontiers established between Germany on one side, Belgium and France on the other, by the Treaty of Versailles, *including the provisions of that treaty that established the demilitarized zone of Germany* (art. 1). [46] The three countries renounced the resort to war save in the case of self-defense or in discharge of League obligations; self-defense was specified to include a flagrant violation of articles 42 and 43 of the Treaty of Versailles that established the demilitarized zone of Germany (art. 2). Any differences between Germany on the one hand and France or Belgium on the other were to be settled by peaceful means (art. 3), and the arbitration conventions specified in detail the procedures to be used. The undertaking was placed under the guarantee of the contracting parties (art. 5).

In article 4 lay the heart of the treaty. It provided that

a. an alleged breach of article 2 of the treaty or of articles 42 or 43 of the Treaty of Versailles was to be brought before the Council of the League by the aggrieved party;

b. the Council, upon finding the complaint justified, would notify the signatories who would come immediately to the assistance of the aggrieved party;

c. in the event of a flagrant violation of article 2 of the treaty or of articles 42 or 43 of the Treaty of Versailles by one of the contracting parties, "each of the other contracting parties hereby undertakes im-

---

[46] Italics throughout this discussion are, needless to say, the author's.

mediately to come to the help of the party against whom such a violation or breach has been directed *as soon as the said Power has been able to satisfy itself that this violation constitutes an unprovoked act of aggression* and that by reason either of the crossing of the frontier or of the outbreak of hostilities or of *the assembly of armed forces in the demilitarized zone* immediate action is necessary." The Council in any event would be seized of the question, report its findings, and all would abide by its recommendations *"provided that they are concurred in by all the members other than the representatives of the parties which have engaged in hostilities."* [47]

The Franco-German and Belgo-German Arbitration Conventions implemented in elaborate detail article 3 of the treaty and the German-Polish and German-Czech Arbitration Treaties were identical with them. [48]

The Collective Note, in reply to Germany's request for clarification of her position under article 16 of the Covenant, stated that the signatories interpreted that article to mean that "the obligations resulting from the said article on the members of the League must be understood to mean that each state member of the League is bound to co-operate loyally and effectively in support of the Covenant and in resistance to any act of aggression to an extent which is compatible with its military situation and takes its geographical position into account."

Finally, the identical treaties between France and Poland and between France and Czechoslovakia had for their main provision (art. 1) that in the event of either participant "suffering from a failure to observe the undertakings arrived at this day between them and Germany, France and reciprocally Poland [Czechoslovakia], acting in application of article 16 of the Covenant of the League of Nations, undertake to lend each other *immediate aid and assistance, if such a failure is accompanied by an unprovoked recourse to arms."* Furthermore, should the Council fail to reach a unanimous decision, "and in the event of Poland [Czechoslovakia] or France being attacked without provocation, France, or reciprocally Poland [Czechoslovakia], acting in application of article

---

[47] The remaining articles specified that the treaty did not affect the rights and obligations of the signatories under the Treaty of Versailles, the London agreement of August 30, 1924 (Dawes Plan), or the Covenant of the League whose function remained unimpaired. The treaty was to remain in force until the Council, upon the request of one of the signatories, found, by a two-thirds majority, that the effectiveness of the League's protection made it superfluous. The British Dominions and India were not bound by the treaty unless they chose to signify their acceptance. Finally, the treaty was to come into force upon deposit of all ratifications at Geneva and after Germany's entry into the League.

[48] Save for an additional article (art. 21) reiterating the position of the signatories vis-à-vis the League, a similar provision being part of the main treaty of which Poland and Czechoslovakia were not signatories.

15, paragraph 7, of the Covenant of the League of Nations, will immediately lend aid and assistance." [49]

L'Equivoque de Locarno

What precisely was the meaning of all this?

In the perspective of thirty years it is clear that Locarno was a failure, and it is also possible to trace the reasons for this failure. But it is also well to reconstruct the atmosphere of 1925, to recall that "the spirit of Locarno" was once concrete reality. Perhaps the greatest immediate significance of Locarno lay in the contrast between the mood that made it possible and that which had prevailed until shortly before its conclusion. The latter had laid stress on freezing the *status quo* and securing the fruits of victory. Locarno, to be sure, did not free Germany from the consequences of her defeat, but clearly it contained the hope of rehabilitation, where the stress of Versailles had been on retribution. Therein lay a danger; in the words of an acute contemporary French observer: "It is a dynamic agreement. Hence the risk of a double misunderstanding. On the French side reluctance to develop its consequences; on the German side exaggerated hopes." [50] How far and at what rate would France proceed on the road of further concessions? How much would Germany expect in the way of further concessions and how soon would she expect them?

For Germany had paid a price, in her own eyes quite high, for the sake of Locarno. From any objective standpoint, it might be said that there was little merit in Germany's renouncing of Alsace to which she had no rightful claim; [51] the fact remained that those were numerous in Germany who did not accept this view, to say nothing of that other long ago voiced by Treitschke that the people of Alsace *were* German and that if they were not aware of the fact they should be made to realize it, by coercion if necessary. The nature of a belief is not altered by a

---

[49] It was also specified that these treaties in no way impaired the rights and obligations of the contracting parties as members of the League, and that they were concurrent with the main treaty of mutual guarantee of the Western frontier of Germany.

[50] Alfred Fabre-Luce, *Locarno sans rêves* (Paris, 1927), p. 94.

[51] Despite controversy, the facts about Alsace are fairly clear. The native speech of Alsace is Germanic and Alsace did not become French territory until the seventeenth century. By 1871, however, the annexation to Germany was unanimously protested by the Alsatian deputies in the French Assembly; the protest was continued by the Alsatian representatives in the German Reichstag. Needless to say, a half century of German rule had left its mark and there had been a certain amount of German immigration into Alsace. After Alsace returned to France a certain amount of friction grew out of the French tendency to high centralization and uniformity, applied at times with more rigidity than tact, in religious matters for instance. All factors considered, it may be said that the statement in the Fourteen Points that the wrong inflicted by Germany in 1871 should be righted (Point VIII) was a fair one.

signature on a piece of paper. The fact remained also, however, that Stresemann was willing to sign the statement and was capable of finding a majority to support him, though this in turn might be qualified by considerations of passing expediency.

The German willingness to abide voluntarily by articles 42 and 43 of the Treaty of Versailles may be seen as a more authentic sacrifice, a genuine contribution to the allaying of French fears. It must be remembered that there had also been genuine fear in Germany that Poincaré might seek to use the combination of superior military power with economic pressure to bring about the physical disintegration of the Reich.

German concessions were French gains. [52]   French skepticism in regard to the long term dependability of German declarations was the counterpart of German reticence in their making; yet in France, too, Briand was willing to put his name to Locarno, and he, too, could find a majority in the French Parliament for its ratification. France retained the security granted by military advantage; [53] if, as she professed and basically was true, no aggressive intent was to be feared from her, then the Anglo-Italian guarantee could only operate in her favor.

Germany, to be sure, had declined to underwrite the acceptance of her frontiers with Czechoslovakia and Poland as she had those with France and Belgium. That was more than she would or could undertake at this time. This in itself could be regarded as notification that she did not accept the permanence of those frontiers. She made no secret of the fact that it was her hope to alter them some day; but this result she would endeavor to procure by peaceful means alone — how often have frontiers thus been changed? — and in the meantime she signed the two arbitration treaties with those countries, whose alliances with France were so to speak formalized as part of the Locarno network of agreements.

Here in fact lay the crux of the matter: Locarno constituted a definite modification and weakening of the system under which Europe had been functioning, the French system so-called. Even forgetting for the moment the subsequent phenomenon of Nazi Germany and its curious contributions to the practice of diplomacy, suppose that, as a result of German demands and pressure, trouble should occur on her Eastern frontier. Poland was fortified by her French alliance, duly registered with the League. But French support of Poland could be effective only in the form of French military action in Germany. At that point, what

---

[52] Acceptance of the Belgo-German frontier as permanent meant likewise abandoning the claim to Eupen and Malmédy, but the dimensions of this claim made it a minor issue in any event.

[53] German disarmament was not affected by Locarno, not directly at least, but this first step toward the rehabilitation of Germany was inevitably a precedent and a preliminary for a demand on her part of the lifting of remaining disabilities.

would happen in Britain and in Italy? [54] The latter country in all likelihood would pattern her behavior on that of the former, which made Britain the crux of the matter once more. Would Britain then decide the case was one of flagrant aggression that warranted her immediate intervention, or would she call the matter doubtful and let it go to the Council with all the possibilities of procrastination, tergiversation, and delay, during which a *fait accompli* might change the whole situation? There were in Britain those who, even at this time, thought German grievances in the East well founded.

Clearly, the result of Locarno was to alter the balance between Britain and France; the relationship between them was no alliance with reciprocal commitments but a one-sided guarantee given by Britain. To be sure, France could proceed alone and get involved, on the calculation that Britain could not afford a French defeat. But this might be rash speculation; what if Britain should feel that it was best that Poland yield, and through her reticence succeed in holding France back? [55] What then of the whole French system? At the very least, Britain had achieved a possibly important voice in the operation of that system; to that extent she had modified and weakened it. [56]

Poland was well aware of these possibilities as shown by her immediate reaction to the initial German approach to France. Even apart from the possibility of armed conflict, to the extent that Franco-German differences were composed while Polish-German still remained, a wedge had obviously been driven by Germany into the Franco-Polish connection. The same considerations applied to all of France's Eastern connections. If France should really come to feel secure, why should she be concerned about the fate of distant countries? It was all very well to present Locarno as a contribution to general security and peace, to hope and argue that if *the* great sore point of Europe, that of Franco-German relations, could be healed then other tensions would in turn be easier of alleviation. They might indeed — on German terms.

The stress at the time was not so much, as it was to be later, on collective security and the indivisibility of peace. But could peace really be established on the Rhine without regard to the Danube or the Vistula? To the extent that Germany was encircled by the network of connections

[54] There was relatively little response to and interest in Locarno on the part of the Fascist government which participated in the arrangement rather for the negative reason that it would have injured Italy's prestige not to do so.

[55] This is not a forecast of what happened ten years later, based on the easy advantage of knowledge of what, in 1925, was the future. These considerations were very real at the time, particularly in France and among her allies.

[56] It could of course be argued that this was precisely what was needed since there could be no stable and lasting European settlement based on the French system. The soundness of this argument would in turn depend on the validity of the assumption about the future course of Germany on which it was based.

the heart of which was in Paris, Locarno was a German victory in that the tightness of the net had been loosened, though it had not been broken. Stresemann regarded Locarno as but a step, the first of many that must follow, on the path of his country's full restoration to complete freedom and equality.

But need it be a French defeat? That would depend on many factors. One of these remained in France, where it consisted not so much or only in the preservation of militarily superior power, as in the will, should need arise, to use that power. There were voices in France critical of Locarno, who felt that the country was trading substance for shadow, but, even apart from utopian enthusiasts for peace and for Geneva and its works, there was a body of feeling, timid and weary, which would have liked to persuade itself that vigilance could be relaxed, that the burdens and costs of a security that meant arms, alliances, perpetual distrust of Germany and the ill-will of much of the outside world, need not forever be carried. These people, though without sanguine glee, accepted Locarno, at least with some relief. To repeat, as seen at the time, Locarno is best described, not as a French defeat, but as a modification of the French system. In the French assent to this change lay the French concession. It was very considerable [57] and, to a point, it may be said to have represented a yielding on the part of French power, unwilling or unable to carry on the burden, both physical and moral, that for a time it had assumed.

The other factors lay outside of France, primarily in Britain and in Germany. They, too, as much as physical, were moral factors. Britain, as pointed out before, knew not herself the French feeling of insecurity; from her own point of view, she had achieved a very satisfactory arrangement: her new commitments had little added substance since, in any event, a genuine recrudescence of German aggression, *limited to the West,* she was bound to oppose; [58] under the sign of Geneva she had in large measure regained the place of arbitrator or mediator between France and Germany, a place that fitted into her traditional policy of fostering a continental equilibrium. In Britain, Germany could hope for a considerable degree of sympathy and understanding for many of her remaining grievances, whether imagined or real.

This is not to imply sordid calculation on Britain's part; at worst miscalculation and unawareness of existing reality. Nor is it necessary

---

[57] The factor of the weight of world, especially English-speaking, opinion which had been highly and vocally critical of Frency policy must not be underrated. Herriot, Briand, the Left generally, were highly sensitive to this, and to the extent that they succeeded in recapturing foreign good will for France their policy had positive value. Whether good will would, in the hour of need, translate itself into mere ineffective sympathy or something more concrete, time alone could tell.

[58] Austen Chamberlain, who did much to make Locarno possible, may be described as pro-French in his orientation, and in British eyes Locarno appeared as a substantial contribution to French security.

to read base motivation in Germany, where the crux of the matter lay. That Germany would strive for full emancipation and complete restoration of her place could be a surprise to no one, French or other. The question was: how would Germany interpret her "rightful" place in Europe? Would the securing of untrammelled equality be an end point or a mere stepping stone in the process of expansion that had been interrupted by the war? Would a "reasonable" revision of the Polish frontier remove her grievance in that quarter, or did she look upon all Central Europe as her rightful preserve? Germany, like any other large nation, contained all sorts of views and many possibilities deriving from a large mass whose uncertain allegiance circumstances would ultimately determine. [59]

The answer to these questions we now know, but in 1925 the future was as always wrapped in speculation and mystery. The reception of Locarno in the world at large was highly favorable. [60] The spirit of Locarno about which much was written in glowing and romantic terms *was* a reality. Locarno was not an end point, the closing of a chapter, but rather the beginning of a new, truly a dynamic agreement, which, if it was to have any meaning, must initiate the era of real liquidation of the war. Therein lay its *équivoque* for it gave rise to expectations of developments of contradictory directions that men and circumstances could in the end not reconcile.

---

[59] The question of Stresemann's real motivation and intent has been the subject of considerable controversy. It is an interesting question, but of little importance in the context of the present discussion for the reason that, given the fact of German inferiority, German foreign policy at this time could hardly be other than one aimed at the restoration of Germany's position through the elimination of the disabilities that were hers as a consequence of defeat. Methods might differ, and so might eventual hopes and intentions, but the preliminary task of rehabilitation was in any case the inevitable first aim that was bound to be pursued by *any* German foreign minister. The latest contribution to the Stresemann controversy is Hans W. Gatzke, *Stresemann and the Rearmament of Germany* (Baltimore, 1954).

[60] It was welcomed in the United States, officially and otherwise. The reaction of the Soviet Union was the most discordant note, and this was the logical consequence of the everlasting Russian fear of a coalition of capitalist states. Russia at this time took a contemptuous view of the League, which it regarded as a pious fraud devised by the victors of the war. Russia had generally espoused the German opposition to the existing system, and the possibility that Germany was liquidating her Western quarrels correspondingly increased in Russian eyes the fear that Germany might turn her ambitions to the East, possibly as the spearhead of the dreaded capitalist coalition.

Despite Locarno, Germany was still impotent at this time, and she was careful not to sever her connection with Russia, but rather to reaffirm it; this allayed only in part Russian dislike and suspicion of Locarno.

3. THE FORKING OF THE ROAD

German Hopes and French Hesitations

The hopes raised at Locarno were high. The story of the next few years can be written from two wholly antithetic standpoints: the elements of ultimate failure can easily be traced in the contemporary record; but the prevailing contemporary view was on the whole rather one of success. In 1925, the possibilities were open. In any event, however, the second half of the decade marks a pause in the longer tale of continued drift toward disaster. For that reason, the story of the years immediately following Locarno will only be touched upon sketchily. Some high points in it and some of its tendencies must nevertheless be recorded.

The Locarno agreements were to come into force upon Germany's admission to the League, a logical consequence and a symbol of her acceptance by others on a position of equality. Though this might appear a gain for her, she tried to extract from it further advantage. Not until the evacuation of the Cologne zone had been agreed upon were the Locarno agreements and the proposal to apply for admission to the League submitted to the Reichstag. [61] Her application for admission, submitted in February, could not be acted upon at the March session as intended, [62] but in September she was duly received amid general rejoicings. Throughout the proceedings Briand had loyally supported Germany's candidacy; her final admission to Geneva was occasion for one of his more famous flights of oratory. Having extolled the spectacle of collaboration in a common will to peace on the part of peoples so shortly locked in deadly struggle, he concluded: "Away with rifles, machine guns and cannons. Make way for conciliation, arbitration and peace!" The thunderous applause that greeted these words, like the whole Genevan atmosphere of high hope and elation, is difficult to reconstruct and realize after the lapse of thirty years. This was the heyday of Utopia, but not starry-eyed utopians alone, many

---

[61] This was the price for Nationalist support in that body. Germany failed, however, to obtain repudiation of the war guilt clause and assertion of her competence to have colonies.

[62] The difficulty arose out of the question of giving Germany a permanent seat on the Council. This issue furnished an opportunity to some of the smaller Powers to jockey for position. The difficulty was not resolved until the composition of the Council had been altered by enlarging its membership, thus making room for three semi-permanent members. Even so the episode led to Brazil's departure from the League.

It is significant that Poland was one of the candidates to the Council whose claim it was thus possible to satisfy. The Polish claim was not wholly a matter of prestige and of an exaggerated Polish view of Polish importance, but a reflection of Poland's dislike of Locarno and its consequences. It was in May, 1926 that Pilsudski effected the coup d'état which, after some fighting in Warsaw, placed him in effective, though not ostensible, control of the country.

sober men as well, allowed themselves to believe that it might after all be true that the world was entering upon a new era of which the Wilsonian idea was the living expression and symbol.

Of the genuineness of Briand's peaceful intent, of his desire for reconciliation, there is no cause to doubt. If, for the longer term, what mattered was the true nature of the German complex, at the moment it was still France that held the upper hand through her superior force in being, while Germany had a long way to go before her remaining disabilities were lifted. She was therefore bound to be for some time in the position of demandant of concessions that it was largely within France's power to grant or to withhold. The French saying, *la façon de donner vaut mieux que ce qu'on donne* (the manner of the gift is worth more than the gift itself), is relevant at this point. On the score of the Versailles *diktat* German opinion remained well-nigh unanimous. Clearly, there was danger in letting the impression take root in Germany that whatever gains were achieved were victories extracted from French weakness, concessions made by France with reluctant ill-will and undiminished suspicion. Correspondingly, there was, or at least might be, rich reward in strengthening the forces of peace and reasonableness in Germany — such existed, though their strength was uncertain, variable, and difficult of assessment — by showing to the German people that France was willing to trust and accept. To that end, a *grand geste,* one that would shut its eyes to minor breaches of the letter of the law rather than focus on the failure to deliver some telegraph poles, or even on the German fondness for goose-stepping, that would not haggle pettily for compensating guarantees in exchange for every little concession, might be appropriate.

This Briand understood; a policy of the *grand geste* had for him an undoubted appeal. [63] What beautiful speeches could be made at Geneva, with the world for an audience, on the subject of peace! Such speeches Briand did make, and the combination of the choice of his language with the manner of his delivery endowed the atmosphere with a seeming reality that the retrospect of cold print and subsequent events make appear wholly evanescent. In politics Briand was an artist; witty and quick, he enjoyed playing on his listeners as a conductor with an

---

[63] It has been claimed that Briand's inclination was skilfully exploited by Stresemann by whom he was merely duped. The point is one that can be debated and is beyond possibility of definitive settlement. Even if one allow that Stresemann exploited Briand's soft disposition for all that it was worth, the fact remains that the *grand geste* was never made by France and that other developments, largely beyond the range of either French or German control, intervened to prevent such hesitant reconciliation as there was from bearing fruit. On Stresemann and Briand the appraisal of Austen Chamberlain, crediting them both with honest intentions, is of interest. Cf. Austen Chamberlain, *Down the Years* (London, 1935). Professor Renouvin's judgment in *Les relations internationales 1914-1945,* vol. II (Paris, 1949) that from 1924 to 1930 "it was Germany that led the game" need not be taken as more than an expression of the fact that it was indeed Germany that took the initiative in pressing for concessions and change.

orchestra. Not for him dry facts and statistics, or the dull mysteries of finance of which he was largely innocent — for this he could depend on his trusted assistant Philippe Berthelot whom he brought to the Foreign Office. [64] His method and approach is well illustrated by his reported comment to Stresemann at Thoiry that the bulky file of information cataloguing Germany's breaches of the disarmament provisions he had put in a corner of his office without ever looking at it.

Throughout the customary changes of Cabinets in France, Briand uninterruptedly continued at the Quai d'Orsay for almost seven whole years, from April 1925 to January 1932. The continuity of policy that this long tenure indicates and the tone of this policy partly depended on an ambiguity that Briand's skill at compromise served to conceal and to prolong. He had secured in France a broad support for Locarno, but, while defending it, had taken care to mollify the doubts of those who saw no virtue in trusting Germany by pointing to the effective guarantees that remained in French hands. In any case, Briand was circumscribed and fettered by the circumstances of the Parliament and opinion with which he had to operate. When the *Cartel* won the election of 1924 it was not so much the ultimate aims, as the methods, of Poincaré that the electorate had repudiated, and by no means by an overwhelming majority.

The Left was now in control, but it too had its limitations which were not long in making their appearance. An element of doctrinaire intransigeance existed in it that caused it to revive what should have been outworn issues at the expense in part of the more pressing and novel problems of the day. One may respect and understand the good democrat's fear of a strong executive, though doubting that Millerand would have been the instrument of dictatorship in France. Forcing him out of office may have been defending the Republic; more prosaically, it had the earmarks of petty partisanship and of parliamentary tyranny. The episode was of minor importance save as an indication of the sort of issues that commanded attention in French politics. How dangerous was the return of some of the religious expelled twenty years earlier? [65] How dangerous, likewise, would it be to have representation at the Vatican, or how necessary was it to enforce strict adherence to the religious laws of the Republic? The Left had done good service in behalf of the Republic, but the Republic could not be regarded as being under serious threat from the loud enough noises that issued from the *Action Française* and Daudet's *Camelots*.

The Republic had bigger fish to fry. In matters of social legislation, for instance, there was room for considerable improvement; here the

---

[64] On Berthelot, see Auguste Bréal, *Philippe Berthelot* (Paris, 1937).

[65] These men, as French citizens, had answered the call to the colors and served loyally during the war. For this they earned respect, and it was felt by many, not only devout or conservative Catholics, that a strict application of the law in their case had more in it of petty partisanship than of fairness.

Socialists might have been expected to play a large role, but while there was much in their programme that was sensible, they too were not devoid of the doctrinaire tendency that would indulge in easy but sterile and largely negative attacks on the money powers — *le mur d'argent* (the wall of silver) was the phrase of the day, forerunner of the Popular Front's *deux cents familles*. [66]

Financial matters were in fact a danger point; the near panic of March, 1924 has been mentioned, and if Poincaré had managed to retrieve the situation, this in itself had influenced the results of the election and did not augur well for the future: it is one of the sacred laws of democratic politics, French no less than American, that to increase taxation on the eve of an election does not help the party in office. The advent of the Left, with its likely greater stress on social problems, and the expenditures that these entail, was naturally not welcome by the generally conservative money powers. The franc which had stood at 15 to the dollar just before the election dropped to 19 by the end of May. The causes of this fall were largely psychological.

For two years after this the picture was one of growing financial disorder which served to bring out the inner divisions of the Left and its final downfall. The rhythm of the crisis may be followed most simply through the decreasing value of the currency. During the course of 1925 the franc lost one-third of its value — from about 18.50 to 27 to the dollar; it was essentially financial pressure that brought down Herriot in April, 1925. The Left remained in power with Painlevé, then Briand, in the Prime Ministership. The rapid succession of Finance Ministers makes an interesting contrast with the stability of the Foreign Office. [67] The real difficulty arose from the divergence between Socialists and Radical Socialists who could not agree on a fiscal program, a situation that reflected one of the most deep-rooted and troublesome cleavages of the French body politic.

The *mur d'argent* was indeed a reality, but not the simple one that was often depicted. It consisted not only of banking and big business interests, but included as well much of the Radical Socialist party, those of whom it has been said that they vote Left but carry their pocketbooks on the Right, devoted equally to the soundness of the currency and to the shirking of taxation. Not surprinsingly, this was reflected in Parliament in the form of Radical ministers of Finance refusing to adopt the Socialist program for the taxation and control

---

[66] It would be grossly unfair to lay the blame for France's economic and financial troubles, then or later, wholly or primarily at the door of the Left. If it is true that there is greater respect for financial soundness, in the orthodox sense of balanced budgets at least, in administrations of the Right, it is also true that French business interests, large and small, have been generally retrograde in their thinking.

[67] From April, 1925 to July, 1926 the finance portfolio was held in succession by Joseph Caillaux, Louis Loucheur, Paul Doumer, Raoul Péret, and again Caillaux.

of wealth. The rapid turnover of the finance ministry was merely outward symbol of a stubborn refusal to face the real facts. But these
facts, too, were stubborn; French finances and the franc ultimately
could not escape them.

The crisis came in 1926. All of Briand's powers of compromise and
persuasion were wasted in this field largely alien to his competence.
From 27 to the dollar at the beginning of the year the franc fell to
almost 36 at the end of June, a 50 percent depreciation since the advent
of the *Cartel*. Then came panic; attempts to repeat the 1924 operation
merely ended in the waste of foreign funds (another Morgan loan);
French capital was increasingly fleeing to the shelter of safer foreign
havens, thereby making worse the condition that was the initial cause
of its flight. When Briand asked for emergency powers, the combination of the Right with Herriot defeated him.[68] On July 20 the
dollar was worth almost 50 francs in Paris.

Let Herriot then try or conclusively demonstrate the impotence of the
Left. The state coffers were empty, and to make assurance doubly sure
the Bank of France refused to lend itself to manipulations that might
have tided the Treasury over the awkward moment. Amid cries that
the government had juggled accounts to conceal the Treasury situation,
accompanied by ominous rumblings of popular discontent, Herriot was
dismissed by Parliament.

Yet the crisis was ridden with astonishing ease. The mere announcement on the morning of July 22 that a government of national union
was being constituted under the leadership of Poincaré,[69] who assumed
in addition the Finance portfolio, showed the extent to which the crisis
was psychological. There was magic in the very name Poincaré,
synonymous with sound finance and personal integrity. Within ten
days the franc was back to 41.50 to the dollar, thereafter to continue its
recovery until it reached 25 at the close of the year, a figure at which
it was to remain and eventually to be restored to gold parity.[70]

The period of financial trouble was the same during which the
Dawes Plan was put into effect and the Locarno agreements negotiated.
The connection may seem remote between the latter especially and the

---

[68] It is significant that Herriot, a Radical Socialist, voted — on broad
principles of policy — against the grant of emergency powers to a finance
minister, Caillaux, who was also a Radical Socialist.

[69] From the Radical Socialists (Herriot himself) to the Right all groups
participated, leaving out only the Socialists and the Communists. The
Chamber promptly granted Poincaré the emergency powers it had just refused
to Herriot.

[70] The ease with which Poincaré succeeded in restoring the financial
situation was due to the fundamental soundness of the French economy,
once the psychological factor of confidence had replaced that of fear. Even
Poincaré, despite his financial competence, only abandoned with reluctance
the unrealistic hope of restoring the franc to its prewar gold parity. Having
been stabilized *de facto* in December, 1926 the franc was redefined in terms
of gold at its new value in June, 1928. France thus paid for the war
through an 80 percent devaluation of her currency.

vagaries of the franc; Herriot, then Briand, as pointed out, were able to pursue with steadiness the new course of France's foreign policy.

Nevertheless, the troubled course of French finance had profound and lasting effects at home. The unity of the *Cartel* was broken through its inability to resolve the financial problem, to the point where many of its followers were alarmed. Poincaré earned the title of "savior of the franc" and correspondingly much prestige for himself and for the Right in general, in the same measure that discredit redounded to the Left. The episode, however, left behind it a trail of recrimination and bitterness: the Left had succeeded in frightening conservatives and moderates, holders of property in general, who would not forgive its irresponsible incompetence in money matters; the Left retorted with the charge that the will of the people had been thwarted by a conspiracy of the moneyed interests, the famous *mur d'argent*. [71]

A government for France made up of luminaries ranging over the major portion of the political spectrum and in which the brightest stars were Poincaré and Briand may seem a highly fragile combination. Domestic necessities alone made its existence possible; in face of the financial crisis and of the popular discontent to which it gave rise, deputies must for a time at least surrender their indulgence in pure or doctrinaire politics, characteristic of more normal times. Given the basic unwillingness of the moderate Left to espouse the views of its more radical allies, it had no other choice, in order to avoid disaster, than to support the "sounder" financial policies of the Right. Poincaré and this Right did not seek to push their advantage, however, beyond a certain point. The result may be called a compromise, a temporary truce, in which the outcome at the level of government, was not inaccurate expression of the will of the nation: the French people in their majority did not want their currency to collapse; in their majority again they did not favor a policy of blind intransigeance toward Germany. But the majorities that favored these two things were not the same, they merely overlapped, particularly in the Radical Socialist group. The team Poincaré-Briand was the expression of the compromise: the Left, or part of it, would tolerate its fiscal policies; the Right, or most of it, would tolerate Briand.

The result could of course be interpreted as subtle machiavellian calculation in France. Briand could go to Geneva and there present

---

[71] Actually, both sides were wrong. The failure of the Left was essentially the result of its inner differences which prevented its agreement on a policy that it had the votes to enforce in Parliament. More broadly, the financial troubles of France stemmed from the backwardness of economic thinking which caused the country to persist in approaching the problems of the postwar in terms of the no longer applicable political categories of pre 1914. This whole situation is well analyzed by François Goguel in *La politique des partis sous la Troisième République,* (Paris, 1946), pp. 192-205. Goguel traces to the events of 1925-1926 the bitter cleavage of French opinion that was to reappear with disastrous effects with the recurrence of economic difficulties during the nineteen thirties.

to the world the fair face of liberal, pacific France, while Paris would retain the substance of effective control over German impotence. This view is the counterpart of Stresemann's *finassieren*: [72] Germany would lull France with fair words as the price for the reality of more concrete advantage.

The issue is an interesting one that will probably remained unsolved [73] and that need not be debated here. Even if one assume reticence and mental reservations on either side, the fact remained of real alteration in the position and relations between the two countries and of undoubted relaxation in the prevailing climate of European politics. If this could be persisted in, the fears in France and hopes in Germany of the more intransigeant elements in either country might pass into the realm of oblivion.

However that may be, the effusions that had accompanied the formal admission of Germany into the League were followed within the week by the famous meeting of Thoiry which may be regarded as the apogee in the curve of Franco-German relations. Having succeeded in escaping the representatives of a prying press, Briand and Stresemann retreated to the French town of Thoiry, where in congenial surroundings and in the single company of an interpreter they spent the afternoon discussing the whole range and prospects of their countries' relations. By Stresemann's account [74] Briand was inclined to make the *grand geste*: the occupation of the Rhineland, the military control of Germany, the return of the Saar, were all considered; the slate in brief could be wiped clean. The real counterpart that Germany could offer lay in the realm of intangibles: genuine abandonment of aggressive intent. But clearly neither Briand nor Stresemann could seriously expect that this intangible — because intangible — could be offered to France, her Parliament or people, as valid compensation for the abandonment of concrete values. Germany must provide some ostensibly equally tangible *quid pro quo*.

This was in mid-September, 1926. Less than two months before there had been near financial panic in Paris, which Poincaré's name

---

[72] On September 25, 1926, just before Locarno, Stresemann wrote to the Kronprinz outlining the aims of German policy, which included revision of the Eastern frontier and the absorption of Austria; but it was first necessary to liberate Germany from the stranglehold of foreign occupation and, to that end, given Germany's current position of power, like Metternich in 1809, to *finassieren*. This letter of Stresemann's has been the basis of much debate as to his ultimate real motives and intentions. Apart from the linguistic question whether the German *finassieren* carries the same implications of deviousness as the French *finasser* from which it is derived, the mere fact that Stresemann was on terms of such intimacy with the Kronprinz as to select him for this particular confidence is natural ground for suspicion. On this point, see also n. 59.

[73] Even if, and when, French and German documentary information, hitherto unpublished, becomes available.

[74] The only first hand account available.

alone had arrested. The task remained of laying the solid bases of French financial rehabilitation. Germany, on her side, seemed to have successfully surmounted that hurdle and now enjoyed financial health; a possible "mobilization" [75] of her Reparation obligation might provide ready cash for France. From the French point of view, this might seem like exchange of the temporary for the permanent, but the severity of the financial crisis might make the operation palatable. Even so, Stresemann bargained closely, after which the German government initiated steps to implement a possible arrangement.

But, on the French side, Briand's conciliatory disposition, his readiness to turn a blind eye to small German violations of disarmament for instance, and to concentrate on the larger issues, was not too widely shared. Poincaré himself was after all Prime Minister and, what was more important, it soon appeared that the franc was in need of no further assistance. [76] By November it became clear that the grand scheme sketched out in the deceptively hopeful atmosphere of Thoiry was at least premature. Briand had to admit as much to Stresemann when they met again in Geneva in December.

The Ambiguity of Briand

The belief was widespread at this time that arms are in themselves a danger. Universal disarmament was the ultimate goal, admittedly dependent on security; clearly the goal was distant, but in the meantime the burden of armaments might be reduced. The total disarmament of Germany had been decreed ostensibly because Germany had been an aggressor, but also as a preliminary to the disarmament of others rather than as an end in itself. By 1926 such progress had been made in the relaxation of tensions that a first step was taken in the form of constituting a Preliminary Commission in May, preliminary to the eventual meeting of a disarmament conference. [77] Related to, but distinct from, the question of the reduction of armaments in general was the limited issue of the military control of Germany. Clearly, if there was cause to fear German intent, control of Germany was one important contribution to security, to French security in particular, but not to French security alone. The relaxed atmosphere of 1926, the tentative honeymoon of Thoiry, brought Germany an additional gain in the form of the termination of outside control. This implied a pretense,

---

[75] This meant realizing through open sale the principal of railway and industrial securities, the interest of which was earmarked for Reparation, and in turn depended on the readiness of private capital to purchase these securities.

[76] The massive and rapid return of expatriated French capital with the return of confidence soon provided France with ample funds; the vicious circle once broken, the reverse process operated with equal effectiveness.

[77] Germany was not yet a member of the League at this time but was invited to participate in the discussions which Russia, also not a member, likewise joined at the end of 1927.

the formal recognition that Germany had lived up to her obligations while evidence could be adduced that she had not. But this was precisely the sort of winking that Briand was willing to do, accepting at face value Stresemann's playing down of the harmless German fondness for parades and goose-stepping.

It may be granted that the actual extent of German armament at this time, whether or not it was within the narrow letter of the law, was not significant, and that Briand was justified in not adhering to the strictly legalistic view often characteristic of the French approach — provided the assumption on which he was proceeding were correct. The fact remained, of the significance of which the future alone could give adequate appraisal, that one more step was taken in the direction of weakening the French position; this was a corresponding step along the path of German restoration to full parity.

That this was Stresemann's goal there is no question, and with determination he pursued it. The great immediate aim of German policy was the complete liberation of the national territory from foreign occupation, important trump in allied, now mainly French, hands. It is at this point that there occurred that curious episode of the Kellogg-Briand Pact or Pact of Paris. This event need not detain us, yet warrants mention as an indication of the prevailing temper of the day. As the result of Franco-American negotiations initiated in 1927,[78] the whole world was invited to sign an undertaking to "renounce war as an instrument of national policy." The remarkable thing is that virtually all states, 57 in number, did append their signatures to the Pact of Paris.[79] Devoid of enforcing power, the Pact of Paris may also be said to have been largely devoid of meaning. Such in fact has been its fate and it is now only remembered, not as a meaningful contribution to the instauration of peace, but as a revealing expression of the passing aberration that the hope of the late twenties was.[80]

The ceremony of signature that took place in Paris on August 27, 1928 was the occasion for fine speeches, and truly widespread enthusiasm

---

[78] Begining with an innocuous gesture, intended to commemorate the entrance of the United States in the war in 1917, there followed a proposal made by Briand to Secretary of State Kellogg that France and the United States sign a pact mutually renouncing war. The American response was to propose a broadening of the pact to make it of universal application. After some negotiations, during the course of which Briand made it clear that the right of self-defense as well as the obligations deriving from League membership and from the Locarno agreements remained in effect, the text of the pact was agreed upon.

[79] The Soviet Union was at first suspicious, but after it had signed a similar declaration, the Litvinov Protocol, with its neighbors, in February, 1929, it too adhered to the Pact of Paris.

[80] The French and the Italian refusal to participate in a naval disarmament conference in June, 1927, the revival of Tunisian agitation by Italy, and many other facts could be cited as indicative of less than conciliatory tendencies at this same time, but the fashion of the day rather laid stress on Kellogg-Briand Pacts.

greeted the Pact. Looking at the recent past objectively, there was no denying that the record of the last three years, and especially since Locarno, presented an accumulation of decidedly encouraging signs.

Stresemann was in Paris for the occasion which he used to broach with Poincaré his current favorite desire, the final evacuation of the Rhineland: now that Germany was a member in good standing of the League, now that she had fulfilled past obligations and was fulfilling current ones, Reparation payments under the Dawes Plan, it seemed illogical that she should still be suffering the ignominy of foreign occupation, sign of implied distrust. Thus ran the German argument. The moral case had validity to which Briand might have responded; the legal argument was weak and Poincaré was strong on legality. Moreover, there had been a general election in France in 1928 which, understandably, had endorsed Poincaré for his accomplishment of salvaging the franc, just as four years earlier the French electorate had responded unfavorably to the government of the same Poincaré then associated with financial difficulties and increased taxation.

If the team Poincaré-Briand was continued, the influence of the former and of the Right in general could not but be strengthened by the result of the election. [81] Poincaré was not favorably inclined toward Stresemann's request, but there occurred and interesting repetition of the connection between financial matters and security reminiscent of the occasion, four years earlier, when Poincaré while still in control had allowed the bases to be laid for the evacuation of the Ruhr as a consequence of the financial settlement embodied in the Dawes Plan.

The Preparatory Commission for the disarmament conference had been sitting since mid-1926. The interminable and on the whole dreary debates that went on in its midst will not be considered here. [82] That they were inconclusive, if not futile, is shown with sufficient clarity by the fact that a disarmament conference did not meet until 1932, and then not as a result of sufficient or satisfactory preparation. What the preliminary discussions did conclusively establish was that they had to deal with irreconcilable approaches. In more restricted and more

---

[81] The election was a clear victory for the Right, taking this to mean all groups to the Right of the Radical Socialists, despite the fact that in the first balloting it received slightly less than 50 percent of the popular vote. This was the result of the operation of the electoral law and of inter-party arrangements for electoral purposes which have the effect of distorting representation. The most extreme discrepancy was in the case of the Communists who secured 14 seats out of more than 600 although they obtained 11.38 percent of the popular vote, a larger total than in 1924.

[82] The literature on the subject of disarmament is vast. The contemporary discussion may be followed in detail in the *Survey of International Affairs* for the appropriate years. For a summary of the entire subject we may refer to D. P. Myers, *World Disarmament, Its Problems and Prospects* (Boston, 1932) and to several works by John W. Wheeler-Bennett, in particular, *Disarmament and Security Since Locarno, 1925-1931* (New York, 1932) and *The Pipe Dream of Peace; The Story of the Collapse of Disarmament* (New York, 1935).

technical form, the old debate went on, going back to the drafting of the peace and of the Covenant, the core of which was which should have priority of disarmament or security. The French insistence that the former must come second seemed to belie to a degree the confidence often voiced by Briand that war had been forever banished. Yet even among the more trusting and conciliatory Left that view prevailed; as Painlevé, himself prominent member of that Left, put it, "a disarmed France would be a temptation, not an example." [83] The very inconclusiveness of the debate made its prolongation acceptable to those in France who had no trust in Germany and no faith in Geneva; it was better to let the discussion go on than to incur the onus of complete intractability: these were after all the days when the prestige of Geneva stood high and when the Roman maxim, *si vis pacem para bellum,* now again honored, stood in high disrepute.

In the last analysis, the French reluctance to relinquish the advantage conferred by the fact of unilateral German disarmament stemmed from French lack of confidence. The German claim voiced by Chancellor Müller, to equality of rights and to the evacuation of the Rhineland, logical consequence in German eyes of Locarno, Thoiry and the Pact of Paris, was answered by Briand at Geneva in a manner that Poincaré would not have disowned. [84]

This was no break, however. In September, France, Germany and Belgium signed an agreement preliminary to forthcoming negotiations with regard to Reparation and to the evacuation. Once more France was linking these two subjects instead of adhering to the more purely political connection between evacuation and security. In contrast with 1924, France was not in financial straits; she, like others, shared in the benefits of economic prosperity that covered the whole world at this time; her finances were sound, her budget in equilibrium, capital abundant, and the Treasury was accumulating a handsome surplus instead of having to beg advances from the Bank of France to meet its monthly obligations.

But there was another issue that had not been settled. Just as France had insisted in making a connection between her debts to her

---

[83] France could and did point to the substantial reduction of her military establishment. It was in 1928 that the term of military service was reduced to one year, though even this was qualified by being made subject to the prior recruiting of a career army of 105,000. There is all the difference in the world between reduction of armaments and general disarmament. Disarmed Germany took the effective (for debating purposes) position that it was up to others to bring their armaments down to the level of hers; this would create equality on which she put the stress. Failing disarmament by others she argued that she ought to be allowed to arm, to whatever was the common level.

[84] German insistence on the evacuation of the Rhineland was both persistent and pressing. It had been the subject of public statements on both sides of the Rhine, by President von Hindenburg himself and in the Reichstag on the German side, correspondingly in the French Chamber earlier during the year.

wartime associates and German payments to herself, so likewise with equal persistence her allies had declined to accept the validity of her contention. Not until 1926 did France make definite agreements with the United States and with Britain for the liquidation of her debts to them. Though implemented, these agreements were still waiting ratification by a French Parliament that was reluctant to commit the country to an obligation that would reach far into the future while no corresponding assurance existed of forthcoming German payments. [85] Leaving aside the question of commercialization of the German debt, broached by Briand in 1926, the smooth operation of the Dawes Plan in the favorable economic conditions of the day, made it seem both desirable and possible to place the German obligation on a basis similar to that of the interallied war debts. To be sure, France was not alone vis-à-vis Germany in these matters, but the fact that she was the recipient of the largest share of Reparation and *the* guardian of the Rhine made her the deciding factor, especially as Britain was more inclined to leniency than she. Out of this came a compromise, based on a *quid pro quo*, reminiscent of that which had brought about the evacuation of the Ruhr and the enactment of the Dawes Plan itself.

The negotiations that led to the formulation of the Young Plan and the detailed provisions of that scheme need not be retailed here. [86] It suffices to say that, as on the earlier occasion, experts appointed by the interested states elaborated the new scheme by June 1929. Their work was the basis of discussions at the Hague Conference in July, and, despite a minor flurry, [87] the Young Plan was accepted in August. For domestic French purposes, the new scheme, though sanctioning a substantial diminution of the original, and still officially unmodified, total of Reparation, had the advantage of realizability and definiteness, while establishing a *de facto* connection between war debts and Reparation through the concurrence of the twc sets of obligations. It was a French concession also to acquiesce in the substitution of the Bank of International Settlements in place of the Reparation Commission now to pass out of existence. Gradually, step by step, the French hold upon Germany was thus being relaxed.

---

[85] The funding agreements of 1926 provided for a schedule of payments that was to last until 1988, whereas no time limit had been set for the operation of the Dawes Plan. There was in addition the fact that France's commercial debt to the United States, amounting to $400,000,000, would fall due in 1929 unless the agreement which incorporated that debt into the wartime obligation was ratified.

[86] On the Young Plan we may refer to D. P. Myers. *The Reparation Settlement, 1930* (Boston, 1930) and to John W. Wheeler-Bennett and Hugh Latimer, *Information on the Reparation Settlement* (London, 1930).

[87] This was the result of certain objections on the part of the British Chancellor of the Exchequer, Philip Snowden. Snowden elected to express his views with more bluntness than tact, thereby creating a minor diplomatic incident with the French finance minister, Chéron.

But of greater significance in this process was the consent to the premature evacuation of the Rhineland, even though Poincaré's contention that the occupation constituted a guarantee of payment might be considered answered by the acceptance of the Young Plan. Whatever validity might be granted to Stresemann's claim that, in the circumstances of the day, the evidence of distrust that was the occupation was no longer warranted, to accede to the German wish, desirable as it might appear as a contribution to the restoration of normality, good relations, and confidence, implied on France's part the making of an assumption that was not wholeheartedly accepted, that of trust in future German intentions. To that extent, therefore, the French consent may be described as an act of French weakness. It was nevertheless not generally seen in that light abroad where the move was welcome; many thought it in fact overdue and belated. At any rate, once the formal ratifications of the Young Plan had been deposited in Paris, in May, 1930, the French government issued an official announcement that the evacuation of the third, and last, zone of occupation would begin immediately.

That doubt persisted in France is clearly shown by a decision the significance of which did not sufficiently appear at the time. It was in December, 1929 that the French Parliament voted the first appropriation for what came to be known as the Maginot Line, named after the war minister of the day who sponsored the proposal. The meaning of this eventually nefarious addition to security was profound and far reaching. The demilitarization of the Rhineland, guaranteed by both Versailles and Locarno, would not be affected by the final termination of the occupation. Nevertheless, France would no longer be physically present on the German portion of the Rhine; fortification of her own frontier might seem a reasonable substitute for the advantage now being surrendered, especially after the 1928 reduction of the term of military service. So it appeared to the French people, truly obsessed with their security, but equally devoted to the hope that they might avoid taking up arms again. How truly negative and pacific was the French temper was little understood abroad where talk of French militarism was still often heard.

But what is perhaps most surprising is that in France herself, self-appointed yet reluctant guardian of the existing order, the implications of the Maginot Line were little grasped. Two among these are especially relevant which may be put under the heads of military and political, respectively.

During the earlier part of the decade France had taken a progressive view of the military art. Her air force for a time was the largest and best, and the lessons of the tank seemed to have been learned to good purpose: in both these relatively new fields there was at least experiment which is the lifeblood of progress. But the record of the war itself had also made a deep impression, and the costly exaltation of the offensive, characteristic of 1914, registered in the holocaust of four years, had deeply impressed upon the military mind the economy of defensive strategy. Of this the Maginot Line was the supreme expression. The relative merits of offense and defense have had alternating attraction to the military mind. Behind the shelter of impregnable fortifications, France could continue to enjoy the fruits of victory, having found compensation for the long term deficiencies of her own power; she could even relax and forget that the last war was past and that new weapons of offense used as tools of a novel strategy might make a future conflict different in nature. Victory always contains the danger of a complacent, backward-looking confidence in the means that have procured it; such an approach was especially attractive to the French mind, genuinely fearful of German aggression, and hypnotized by that possibility, forever adding to the wall of defense, but little thinking that even for ultimately defensive purposes the initiative of offense might have to come from its side.

The political counterpart of the Maginot Line mentality was of even greater significance than the purely military. It might be pleasant and comforting to contemplate the addition of so many Polish, Czech, or other divisions to France's own, but the value of these, which could be considerable, derived from the prospect of France's engaging the larger part of the German forces. If France were to be content with preventing the invasion of her own territory, what could Polish divisions accomplish? The Franco-Polish, and other, alliances need not be in intent aggressive, but to exclude the possibility of French offensive action, should it come to the test, was largely to void them of their content. To be sure, the border fortifications could serve as bases from which an attack could be launched, but if used for this purpose they were but a misguided and expensive investment that would immobilize and divert a large part of the energy that should go into the offensive.

Polish thinking, for one, was far more realistic than French on this score. A French offensive in support of Poland was but logical strategy; for Poland to attack in support of a France content to sit in the shelter of her own defenses was to court defeat. It has been pointed out before that the Polish first interest in the French alliance was, quite naturally, the prospect of a French offensive *in support of Poland,* not the reverse. Of course it might be said, as many did in Britain even much later in the day, why seek involvement in Eastern Europe? But here it must be stressed that, by contrast with the British, the French view was the sounder that the hope of peace and security in the West, without an Eastern counterpart, was a dangerous and utopian fallacy. The phrase, indivisibility of peace, of later coinage, was no less true in 1930. France at this time had not yet renounced a European policy, but there were the seeds of inner inconsistency, hence weakness, in the simultaneous pursuit of the system forged after the war and the approach of which the Maginot Line was the symbol.

It was also symbolic, if wholly accidental, that the inauguration of the Maginot Line policy should coincide with the death of Stresemann.

Whatever may be thought about the controversial motivation of his policy, Stresemann had come to be associated with what may be described as the integration of Germany in Europe. To this end he had caused his country to make what it considered substantial sacrifices, such as the Reparation settlement and the formal acceptance of the Western frontier. But his efforts had not gone unrewarded; financial and military control by the victors had been removed from Germany; she was now a member in good standing of the League; dearest to his heart, the promise of the departure of the last foreign troops he had secured. In German eyes, to whatever part of the political spectrum they belonged, there was still much to do, for Germany still suffered from numerous disabilities. Which of these she might reasonably expect to be removed could be debated. Put in another way, Germany, any Germany, could be expected not to rest content until she had achieved full equality with others. But what then? Had the expansive force which had been hers before 1914, and in a broad sense lay at the root of the war, been spent, or merely been momentarily checked? In 1929 or 1930 there could be no clear answer to these questions that the future alone could resolve. In any case, the policy of Stresemann, in so far as it aimed at the removal of German disabilities, could not but be continued, whether the inner spirit that animated that policy be aggressive or peaceful.

The promise made to Stresemann, repeated after the formal ratification of the Young Plan, was duly kept. At the end of June, 1930 the last of the French troops departed from the German Rhine. That this should be cause for rejoicing in Germany, nothing could be more natural. But there were notes in the German rejoicing calculated to cause alarm among those followers in France of Briand's policy of conciliation, and not among them alone, whether in France or elsewhere. The point was made in Germany that the French concession, which, had it come in 1926, might have earned gratitude, was now felt as overdue and belated, and that it merely served to remind that much was still outstanding in the German account of grievances: the demilitarization clauses of Versailles and Locarno, the war guilt clause, the Saar, the frontiers of the East, etc. The undertone of threat that sometimes accompanied these reminders tended to put the final evacuation of the Rhineland in the light of a German victory that the weakness of others had been unable to prevent, mere prelude to further victories.

Even more concrete evidence of the German temper was forthcoming shortly. Among the welter of opinions that it is only natural to expect in a country of 65,000,000, where the word spoken and written was free, there was an unusually confused jumble of contradictions that went under the label of National Socialism. The leader of this group, one Adolf Hitler, frustrated would be artist of Austrian origin, had, during the war which he had welcomed as release, risen to the exalted rank of lance corporal in the German army. In 1923 in Munich he had succeeded in involving the outstanding wartime leader, General Ludendorff, in the ridicule that his attempted *Putsch* gained for him and his movement. The incident — it was no more than that at the time — earned Hitler a few months sojourn in Landsberg fortress, and this in turn provided him with leisure in which to set on paper his weird lucubrations. To those who had read *Mein Kampf,* the most apt comment seemed to be the French phrase, *ce n'est pas sérieux* (such trash is not to be taken seriously). Something that stood on the fringe of the lunatic fringe did not deserve attention on the part of sane and sober people. Apparently, this was the German verdict as well, for in the Reichstag of 1930 the Nazis stood represented by a membership of all of 12 deputies.

A general election was held in Germany in September, 1930. When the returns were in there were 107 Nazis in the new Reichstag. [88] What did this mean? Less than three months after the French departure from the Rhine, was this the measure of German appreciation? Inevitably, the question posed itself across the Rhine. Or was it passing German aberration, response to a momentary combination of circumstances? Certain it was that one of Hitler's battle horses had been and was the iniquity of the Versailles *diktat.* But then again, Hitler had said all sorts of things, made promises and threats galore — contradiction and falsehood were the least of his cares. Without anticipating a story the outcome of which is now known, it could be said that the end of the decade, the opening of which had seen the formal reestablishment of peace, found Europe and the world confronted with a multitude of problems that many had hoped had been or were by way of being liquidated.

On the French side, what had Briand accomplished? The sincerity of his desire for peace is not debatable fact, in which respect he was authentic representative of the national temper. But how best to preserve the peace? There were in France two antithetic schools of thought on that score. One that regarded Germany as unregenerate, waiting her chance for the renewal of aggression, logically concluded that any concessions made to Germany, any enhancement of her position and restoration of her power was ultimately a threat to peace. The other, more optimistic and humane, believed in the possible emergence of a peaceful Germany and would assist it by gentleness and trust. Either view might be warranted and constitute the basis for a policy; in combination, they stood to create mere confusion. Neither view commanded in France the clear allegiance of an unquestionable majority. Briand, the peaceful compromiser, hovered between them, making to Germany what concessions he could get ratified at home, holding on to what guarantees he felt he must retain. Understandable as this is, there

---

[88] The popular vote for the Nazis rose from 800,000 to 6,500,000. No doubt the great success of the Nazis was in large measure due to the impact of the economic crisis in Germany. The fact remains nevertheless that the Nazis stood for an aggressive foreign policy, and it is that aspect of their victory which is of significance in the context of this essay.

lay in it the ambiguity of a seemingly double-faced policy. One net result of it was undoubtedly the weakening of the French purpose to maintain the position of France and the order of Europe of which France, since the war, had been the chief defender and bulwark. The era of illusions was about to come to an end.

PART III

THE FALLACIES REVEALED

CHAPTER V

LES ANNÉES TOURNANTES *

1. EUROPE TEN YEARS AFTER THE WAR

The belief is naturally difficult of acceptance, while the process is in course of happening, that an age, a way of life, is dying, or even radically altering. The second half of the decade of the twenties offered much to support the belief, born of hope, that the great war unleashed by accident had been but passing interruption in the appointed course of European, and world, progress. Only in retrospect has it been made clear that the old was gone irretrievably, and that progress, if such it be, entails the instauration of a new set of forces and of values, perhaps existing in potential, but neither realized nor accepted before 1914.

The legacy of war was by no means wholly forgotten ten years after its end, but its wounds were in large measure healed. America was booming and though her influence on and relations with the outside world had been vastly enlarged, the fact had failed to permeate the national consciousness, content in the illusion that isolation was reality. On the other side of Europe, the novel experiment of the Soviets likewise seemed to proceed largely in isolation. As of old the Messiah, world revolution would some day come, but that day was unspecified, remote, and unpredictable; it might even be the result of the attraction of the example of the success of "socialism in one country"; meanwhile Russia's relations with the outside world may be described as normal, peaceful, and not very active. [1] There was still much to do at home in order to establish socialism in one country. As to the United States, they still adhered to that other fiction: for them the Soviet state in law did not exist.

---

* The heading of this chapter is taken from the title of a book by Henry Daniel-Rops, *Les années tournantes* (Paris, 1932), which might be translated as "The Hinge Years," because of its appropriateness as a characterization of the period of the turn from the decade of the twenties to the following decade.

[1] The Chinese situation during the middle twenties had attracted considerable Russian interest and interference. But with the success of Chiang Kai-Shek and his suppression of Communism, the Russian attitude toward China became one of relative passivity and non-interference.

To be sure, Europe was still beset by many problems, international no less than domestic. In Yugoslavia, for example, the use of arms in the Skupshtina betokened a less than perfect operation of democratic practice, and King Alexander had deemed it necessary to suspend the constitution of which his own authority took the place. But if the matrimonial vagaries of King Carol were intimately tied to the politics of Rumania, Czechoslovakia could be pointed to as definitely a success. Pilsudski ruled in Poland, but from behind the scenes and with a relatively light hand, while the new Austria showed signs of stable viability. Such troubles as there were in a section of Europe so violently shaken but a few years ago might, with a moderate dose of optimistic inclination, be looked upon as normal pains of growth and readjustment.

In Italy Fascism had restored order; what coercion there was seemed relatively mild, and if not all agreed that Mussolini was a great man, the stamp of official approval such as the British and American, gave the regime respectability. The Duce was given to speechmaking in the course of which he said many things; in 1928, for instance, he had extolled the virtues of revision of the settlements of peace — so long as this did not infringe on Italy's sacrosanct acquisitions. But to pronounce the platitude that treaties are not everlasting might be no more than harmless rhetoric, or possibly a gentle prod to France. For all the exaltation of the martial virtues, it seemed that Italy's international prestige had somewhat risen but that she was on the whole pursuing the traditional course of not immoderate enhancement of the national interest.

But most of all, the great dominant triumvirate of Britain, France, and Germany, under the guidance of the triumvirate of their foreign ministers, Chamberlain, Briand, and Stresemann, seemed to have traveled a fair distance toward a new stability. Germany had lost her 1914 bid for a place under the sun, meaning perhaps at least primacy in Europe; from the setback of her total defeat the road was long to recovery, but on that road she was definitely moving. Britain and France both had been diminished, to a degree that the deceiving fruits of victory concealed. At home, Britain was struggling with the impact of the demands of drastic readjustments in her economy; coal and textiles were sick, marring her landscape with the lasting sore of depressed areas; yet London had recovered much, if not all, of its primacy as the world's financial capital. With natural regret and some understandable grumbling, though on the whole with surprising good grace, the loss of place to the giant across the ocean was accepted by Britain.

France, too, had largely healed her wounds. The physical devastation of her land had been made good, and her finances, if managed with less care than Britain's, had with relative ease been restored to sound health. In both Britain and France the wish for peace was deep and strong at all levels: simple revulsion from the fact of war; also realization, often perhaps unconscious, that neither country could derive from renewed war any but further loss. This last consideration did not apply to Germany whose bid for dominance had come within measurable distance of success. Much depended therefore on the German mood, whether predominantly chastened or surly and resentful, hence ready for the opportunity of another adventure. It could be argued, and was, whether the most promising way of dealing with Germany was the French attitude of suspicious caution, whose concessions were slow, niggardly, and reluctant, forever qualified by distrust, or the British sense of fair play and sentimental trust in Saxon cousins, ready to grant concessions — especially so long as no risk was involved to its own interest or what it thought to be such.

The League of Nations had not proved the unquestioned and dependable preserver of the peace that some had hoped it would be, but the Genevan institution seemed to be taking root, though scepticism was still the attitude prevailing toward it in many quarters. Much sympathy was felt for it in Britain, with the qualification always that British commitments must not become either too extensive or rigid. France offered two highly contrasting approaches; one cold and scornful, mainly found among the Right, believer in *Realpolitik,* would, however, make use of the League for whatever advantage it could afford the French position. It was this view that fed outside suspicion of French declarations and motives. But the League also fitted well into the great stream of humanitarian tradition that flowed from the Enlightenment, through the Great Revolution, mainly into the parties of the Left. In Italy, Mussolini simply believed that the day had not come, if ever it would, of universal peace; the League was mere unrealistic Utopia and the suspicion that it was largely a convenient shield of respectability for the purposes of British and French power was strong in Italy no less than in Germany and in Russia. The German accession to Geneva, whatever the complex mixture of its motivation, could not but strengthen the League whose stock after Locarno had risen rapidly. To many smaller nations, the League seemed an unmixed blessing and hope.

Economic Illusions

But certainly one of the greatest, if not the single greatest, solvent of conflict and suspicion lay in the generally prosperous condition of the economy of the day. In 1925 German Reparation was put on a stable basis and the British pound went back to its prewar gold parity; the crisis of the franc in 1926 was easily surmounted. Although in varying degrees in different countries, the blessings of prosperity were generally visited throughout the world. Among the European nations they were particularly marked in Germany which underwent striking expansion. Outside Europe, the United States embarked upon a growth that seemed to dwarf their previous astonishing enough record. These were the days when reputable economists indulged in talk of the new economic era of unlimited growth, and the full garage slogan appeared for electoral purposes. The more lurid aspects of the era of bathtub gin that the experiment noble in purpose helped produce, and the resounding crash in which it ended, threw discredit upon a hope to which America clings anew after a quarter of a century has passed. [2] An analysis or discussion of the internal course of the American economy during the first postwar decade does not belong in this essay, but its relation to the outside world, especially its impact upon Europe, must be mentioned.

The catastrophic crash of the New York security market that occurred in October, 1929 was truly heard around the world. It was no isolated phenomenon, cause of America's and the world's economic crisis, but rather the explosive manifestation of tensions gradually accumulated. It serves nevertheless as adequate and convenient landmark for the initiation of a phenomenon that was world wide in its manifestations and effects. Among the fallacies under the shelter of which the world had for some years been functioning in apparent success, the economic stood revealed first.

One of the consequences of the war had been the abrupt reversal of the position of America from that of debtor to that of creditor country. Such a position had been Britain's, [3] among others, and in the course of time Britain's economy had come to operate on the basis of an adequate and seemingly durable equilibrium. Simplest expression of this condition was her devotion to free trade and recognition of the fact that an unfavorable balance of trade was the proper concomitant of the continued prosperity of her commerce. Similarly, America had been a debtor and the favorable balance of American trade was the device through which America's external obligations had been discharged.

The war having reversed America's position vis-à-vis Europe, to right the scales the balance of American trade with Europe should correspondingly have been reversed from being favorable to the opposite. Such elementary considerations were relatively little appreciated in post-1919 America; and even had they been the necessary measures that should have been their consequence would not have been easy of enactment in the free economy that was America's. [4] Infant industries grown to healthy giants might be able freely to compete with the outside world, but one of the early measures of the postwar period had been the raising of the American tariff wall. The answer to the question, how could the outside world, European countries in

---

[2] The current picture of the United States is characterized by an anxious hope that the present rate of expansion continue lest we meet both domestic and foreign catastrophe. The confident predictions of 1928 have become qualified hopes.

[3] Britain remained, on balance, a creditor country after the war, to a considerably reduced extent, however. Toward the United States, in particular, her position was reversed from creditor to debtor.

[4] The problem still persists and is still being dealt with through the device of loans and gifts which, in this context, may be regarded as a tax that the American people levy upon themselves for the purpose of subsidizing certain sectors of their economy.

particular, discharge their obligations to America, was basically the same as that to that other question of the day, how could Germany pay Reparation? In either case the debtor must contrive an adequate surplus of export trade. [5]

Even apart from genuine humanitarian considerations, America was desirous of economic recovery in war torn Europe: a prosperous Europe would be a better market for her goods. At the official level of policy decision, the suggestion of any connection between trade balances and payment of debt was viewed as heresy tinged with deficient morals; the comment of an American President, "they hired the money, didn't they?" with terse naïveté expressed that view. [6] The existence of a large debt owed by Europe to America, combined with America's efforts to enhance the favorable balance of her trade, was clearly, though not deliberately, calculated to compound difficulty in the domain of international finance.

But a debtor will have no difficulty in meeting his due payments if his creditor will advance him the wherewithal. Save as a possibly useful device of passing expediency, such an arrangement can clearly accomplish precisely nothing toward the ultimate discharge of a debt; it merely perpetuates it while also possibly shifting it. Yet this seeming absurdity, while concealed, was one of the bases of the international financial stability that the world thought to have achieved during the twenties. [7]

What happened, in simplest form, was this. Accumulating American capital, as capital normally will, sought profitable employment wherever it might seem available. Even apart from the investment in the American domestic development there was enough for use in opportunities abroad. A steady golden stream flowed out for some years from the United States that spread itself throughout the world. Not a little of it found its way to Europe, and of that a substantial proportion ended in Germany. Through the channel of Germany's payments to her own creditors, then of the payment by these of their American obligations, the golden stream in considerable part reverted to its source. There was no dollar gap or transfer problem.

This curious arrangement could of course be of indefinite duration, so long at least as its initial American spring would continue to be alive. For reasons mainly stemming from the domestic operation of

---

[5] The transfer of gold was obviously no solution to the discharge of obligations of the magnitude of those resulting from the war. To the extent that trade is free and currencies convertible, international debts may of course be discharged by multilateral rather than bilateral trade between debtor and creditor.

[6] The statement is attributed to President Coolidge. Whether authentic or apocryphal, it is apt expression of a prevailing view.

[7] The absurdity was, needless to say, not deliberately contrived, concealed as it was by the multiplicity of transactions, mainly of a private nature, involved in the outflow of American capital.

the American economy, [8] already before the sensational crash of October, 1929, the outward flow of American capital had begun to show signs of decreasing abundance. It soon dried up completely. That this new turn should have wide repercussions in retrospect surprises no one any longer. [9]

One of the unresolved difficulties that troubled the world's economy at large no less than the American was the relationship between the more flexible prices of raw materials and those more rigid of manufactured goods. To speak of overproduction at this point is to forget that the term is largely relative in meaning and that what rather counts is the relation between production and consumption; the problem is essentially of distribution, which means in turn such relationships as those between costs, wages, and services. Coming to Europe in particular, the distinction indicated earlier [10] still largely held between "inner", industrial, and "outer", essentially agricultural, Europe. By 1930, the fall of agricultural prices was creating serious strains in the latter, the repercussions of which were being felt farther and farther to the West. [11] Naturally, also, the decreased purchasing power of the producers of agricultural and raw materials had repercussions on the producers of manufactured products; if the wage structure of industry was more resistant to violent fluctuation than the open commodity market, decreased industrial production would translate itself into diminished employment. Mounting unemployment, agricultural and banking crises, were the manifestations of the world's economic illness, while the world's exchange of goods decreased in catastrophic fashion. Needless to say, decreased economic activity had the consequence of diminished revenues for the state at the very moment when the care of the army of unemployed industrial workers placed additional burdens on the national exchequer. [12]

A self-contained economy might isolate itself and be immune to the world wide disturbance; but in the lack of this asset concerted action at the international level would seem a more rewarding approach.

---

[8] The outburst of speculation that characterized the last stages of the American boom absorbed substantial amounts of capital. It must be seen, however, as sensational manifestation of the illness rather than itself cause of the collapse.

[9] It is impossible to lay too much stress on the extent to which a phenomenon, the retrospective analysis of which has made it simple to understand, went misunderstood and unperceived while it was taking place.

[10] See above, p. 23, n. 19.

[11] A chain of financing, at progressively higher rates of interest, led from London, through Germany, to Vienna which, despite the diminished position of Austria, had retained much of its role of financial capital of Eastern and Balkan Europe. In reverse, the effect of falling wheat prices, first felt in Bucharest or Budapest, would cause difficulties in Viennese banks, and from them back to Germany and to Britain.

[12] Countries like Britain and Germany, where social legislation was more advanced than in the United States or France, for example, were particularly affected by this factor.

There was much scurrying about of statesmen, financiers, and economists; their failure to produce any remedies itself served to intensity the
spreading sense of hopelessness. Instead of international cooperation,
the tendency was to seek individual salvation, be the consequences what
they might to others, thereby intensifying the vicious circle of declining
international exchanges. It may seem odd in retrospect that the reaction
of America, the great universal creditor, should have been to introduce
a new and higher tariff. France resorted to involved measures of
restriction, tariffs and quotas, in the endeavor to ward off the illness
that so affected other nations. [13] America was vast and wealthy and
France unusually self-contained for her dimensions; most nations did
not enjoy either of these advantages, but they too indulged in similar
restrictive practices.

Economic stress inevitably tends to intensify political, and this may
seem like a poor time to have thought of further relaxation of what
tensions still existed in Europe. And yet, and to repeat, internationally
concerted action was the most sensible approach to the common ail-
ment, and the very raising of the American tariff was in fact a strong
argument for Europe to act in unison. The impulse of the political
euphoria of the preceding years, though slowed down, was not yet
altogether spent. It was in 1930 that Briand, ever hopeful, produced
his *mémorandum sur l'organisation d'un régime d'union fédérale euro-
péenne.* [14] The scheme was no improvisation, but rather the result of
careful thought, a fitting climax and logical consequence of the spirit
of the Pact of Paris. When Briand had first broached the idea, Stresemann's response, though guarded, had not been unfavorable. But
within a month Stresemann was dead. While he himself could have
done little to stay the course of economic disintegration, his passing,
coming at the time that it did, nevertheless compounded the effects that
the loss of his personality represented.

Whatever sympathy there may have been in Britain for a genuine
composition of the Franco-German feud, Briand's proposal elicited in
that country less of enthusiasm than of suspicion. [15] Nor was suspicion
confined to Britain alone; even apart from the feeling, mainly prevalent among the defeated and the discontented nations, that this was

---

[13] France succeeded, or thought she had succeeded, for a time at least.
The better balanced French economy was more favorably situated than
most; but, even in the case of France, the illusion was of short duration,
and the depression, when it came, if never as severe as in Germany for
instance, proved uncommonly intractable.

[14] This was the result of the task with which Briand had been entrusted
as a consequence of his proposal made at the tenth Assembly of the League
in September, 1929.

[15] The persistence in Britain of the reluctance to participate too closely
in any scheme of European combination is an interesting phenomenon. Another world war has little modified this traditional British tendency, as shown
by the British reaction to such schemes as the Schuman Plan or the Common
Market.

but another version of a device to insure and perpetuate French "hegemony" in Europe, the sum total of the replies that came to Briand's memorandum is best described by the phrase "wet blanket." The proposal was stillborn; the position taken by such a periodical as *L'Europe nouvelle,* that the economic crisis was all the more reason for political action, eminently sane as it was, nevertheless amounted, in the circumstances of the deteriorating climate of the day, to putting the cart before the horse. [16]   Briand's proposal may be looked upon as the last flare up of the spirit of conciliation and reconciliation: without concerted French and German support there was clearly no sense in pursuing the idea.   After the German election of September, 1930, Germany was too wrapped up in her own domestic crisis; for her and for Europe the gathering storm must first blow over before the line of evolution that had been initiated could be continued or resumed. Meanwhile Europe must think in different terms, increasingly in the classical — some had hoped now outmoded — terms of power.

The year 1930 ended in an atmosphere of deepening gloom and confusion though not of complete despair. The worst had not yet come of economic decline which gave all indications of following an unaltered course, while the picture of politics gave ample cause for pessimistic expectations.   Hope still persisted none the less that the storm, if severe and even worsening, might still be passing storm and that the course of the immediately preceding years, prosperity and peace, seeming resumption of the pre-1914 direction, was the authentic line of Europe's evolution.   In retrospect, this may not seem unfair summation: the true significance and extent of the break that the First World War had been, for a brief time concealed by a combination of circumstances, was now to be fully revealed.   The fallacies of the prewar era were now to be disclosed, until it came to be fully accepted that, whatever the future may be, the world in any case is set upon new paths rather than seeking a return to a trail only temporarily lost. [17]   It might also be said that the years 1931-1932 were those during which the process of disassociation took place. The phrase *annus terribilis,* used to describe the year 1931, seems wholly appropriate. [18]

The Special Plight of Germany

Germany stood again at the center of the stage, and that in more senses than one. It has been indicated that the picture of German

[16] See *L'Europe nouvelle* throughout the year 1930, in particular the issues of January 4, May 24, June 21, July 5 and 19, September 6, 20 and 27, and October 4.

[17] In this connection, the contrast is revealing between the contemporary attitude toward the two world wars; the first largely appeared as accidental, temporary interruption, the second as an episode in a continuing process. In 1945 there was little talk and less expectation of merely returning to 1939. Significantly, the difference is symbolic between the persistent commemoration of the armistice of 1918 and the relative inattention to the armistices of 1945.

[18] *Survey of International Affairs, 1931* (London, 1932), p. vii.

prosperity and Germany's easy fulfilment of her obligations to others was in large measure due to the influx of foreign capital. Financial stringency in New York and in London, to a lesser extent in Switzerland and Holland, led to a demand for the return of some of this capital instead of its continued outward flow; simultaneously, the agricultural crisis in Eastern Europe created a financial stringency for German capital in so far as it had extended itself in that area. Germany was thus caught between two pressures, while, to make matters worse, her thriving export trade fell down to a calamitous degree.

The manifestations of this state of affairs were many, political no less than economic. The result of the election of the preceding September was not unrelated to an unemployment figure close to 5,000,000 in January, 1931: the growing pressure of the extremes, Nazi and Communist, if it had the effect of cementing the moderate coalition consisting mainly of the Center Party and the Social Democrats, under the leadership of Chancellor Brüning, [19] at the same time reduced the margin of this coalition to dangerous exiguity. More immediately, decreased economic activity, compounded by the burden of care of the unemployed, had budgetary repercussions, and the soundness of the currency seemed once more endangered. The announcement of the closing of the Viennese *Creditanstalt* [20] on May 11 created a profound shock throughout Central Europe and beyond.

The Dawes Plan of 1925 had provided for the possibility of German financial difficulties, but one of the prices for French acceptance of the Young Plan in 1929 had been the provision of an "unconditional" portion of Reparation payments. The simple question was, could Germany make payment? The crisis was fast coming to a head [21] and it was at once symbolic and appropriate that an appeal should issue from President von Hindenburg of Germany, the universal debtor, to President Hoover of the United States, the universal creditor, for immediate action.

President Hoover had been quite right in expressing the view a month earlier [22] that the world's current troubles were a legacy of the First World War, though his suggestion of disarmament for their cure betokened a less acute keenness of economic analysis. In any

---

[19] Brüning, of the Catholic Center Party, had become Chancellor in April, 1930.

[20] This and the contemporaneous attempt at Austro-German customs union will be dealt with presently.

[21] From the end of May there began a precipitate withdrawal of foreign funds from Germany. On June 12 the Reichsbank lost 200,000,000 marks in foreign exchange and the next day raised the discount rate from 5 to 7 percent. On June 5 President Hindenburg signed an emergency decree that combined increased taxation with cuts in government salaries and unemployment benefits. The visit of Brüning and Curtius to Britain at the beginning of June yielded no concrete results, for Britain was having financial difficulties of her own at the time.

[22] On May 4, addressing the International Chamber of Commerce.

case, he was not unprepared for action — there had been rounds of financial consultations and both Secretaries Mellon and Stimson were in, or about to go to, Europe — and with an eye also on the possible salvage of private loans, on June 20 he made the since famous proposal that bears his name: the Hoover moratorium advocated a one year suspension of all payments on intergovernmental debts.

The American initiative received widespread approval, markedly so in both Britain and Germany. But the French reaction was crucial. Two considerations gave it particular importance: first, France was the largest receiver of German Reparation; secondly, France, apparently immune at this stage to the impact of the economic crisis, was internationally in a very strong financial position. Paris was the haven of much capital that felt insecure elsewhere and short-term credits in foreign centers in French hands were also large.

Mr. Hoover is not open to the charge of undue French sympathy. Considering the circumstances and his own position, it would have been the part of tact at least to consult the French government prior to making his announcement. If the proposal had undoubted merit, [23] the fact was also true that France was called upon to make a sacrifice, and the manner in which the proposal was made gave color to the feeling that France's hand was being forced through her being placed in the invidious position where opposition would focus upon her the onus of being the chief obstacle to international recovery. Behind this lurked that other feeling — partly misunderstanding and in part correct — that Britain and America could perceive with ease and regard with sympathy what difficulties there were across the Rhine.

Without rehearsing the detail of negotiations initiated by the Hoover proposal of June 20, it will suffice to say that, though ungraciously, France finally gave her assent and the Hoover moratorium went into effect. The unfortunate proceedings doubtless robbed the Hoover proposal of much of its potential psychological value, although it may well be doubted that, had the French acceptance been accompanied by enthusiasm and good grace instead of reluctance, the Hoover moratorium would have stayed the course of the world's economic crisis. At all events there was ill-feeling, the aftermath of which, where America and France were concerned, was not long in appearing. [24] Even in the immediate the German crisis was not stemmed; it was on July 13 that the failure of the Darmstädter Bank was announced. One of the most profound effects of the German crisis was the political repercussions that it had. That there was an emergency in Germany was undoubted; the Weimar constitution in its wisdom had foreseen the possibility of emergencies, and article 48 of it provided for action

---

[23] It was in any case a palliative and a temporary measure designed to meet a supposedly passing emergency rather than deal with the fundamental problem of intergovernmental obligations.

[24] The French refusal to honor payment of the American debt after the expiration of the Hoover moratorium is touched upon below.

through the use of presidential power once the emergency had been proclaimed.

Such a device can have great merit, and there is nothing unusual in the power of ruling by decree being conferred upon a democratic government. The future alone would show that in the German case the use of the emergency provisions of the constitution was the initiation of a process that was to terminate in the final demise of the Weimar experiment. At the very least it was a danger signal, an indication of the fact that the democratic practice in Germany might lack the experience and roots that make possible such compromise as is essential to the conduct of government; it was measure of the inordinate stresses to which the young regime was subject. Rather than passing phase, government by presidential decree took on the guise of enduring device.

2. THE POWER OF GOLD

The stresses were indeed great that economic crisis placed on existing institutions everywhere. No better evidence of this than the British case can be given. It would be difficult to find a parallel for the respect and care with which British national finance has for a long time been handled. By dint of considerable sacrifice the pound in 1925 had been returned to its prewar parity. This decision, motivated by the desire to restore and maintain the prestige of the British currency, symbol of British financial reliability and soundness as well as valuable source of wealth that London drew from its recognized position as the world's financial capital — a position threatened by the recent rise of America — had cost the nation heavily by restricting the possibilities of its vital export trade. The depression added new strains to those existing. First, the rise in unemployment beyond calculations produced a drain upon the exchequer. On the issue of how to go about balancing the budget the Labor government of the day was divided and fell in August. [25] The coalition formed to deal with the emergency, despite assistance from New York and Paris, was unable to save the pound; on September 20, 1931 the Bank of England suspended gold payments while raising its rate from 4 ½ ot 6 percent; the pound thereafter had to find its level on the international currency market.

If the management of British finances continued sound after this, the event was none the less an historic one that shook the world's financial

---

[25] It was the issue of unemployment benefits that split the Labor party. Prime Minister MacDonald and his Chancellor of the Exchequer, Snowden, putting financial orthodoxy before social benefits, were opposed by the bulk of their own party. MacDonald resigned, to succeed himself as head of a "national" government. The ensuing election returned an overwhelming majority for the "national" coalition, in which, however, the Conservatives were far the largest component. The national government, still headed by MacDonald, continued in office, the opposition having dwindled to a much reduced Labor party, only a handful of whose members joined the coalition.

structure. [26] The contemporary announcement of unrest among the crews of the Atlantic fleet over the issue of lowered rates of pay accentuated the impression of impending doom. The kind of world which had really come to an end in 1914, but for a brief spell was thought to have come back to life, had to acknowledge its irrevocable demise, thereafter to embark upon uncharted seas.

Those in Geneva who were at this time still debating reports and proposals dealing with Briand's scheme of European union were more like shadows rehearsing a fantastic play than men of flesh and blood concerned with the meaningful reality of the moment. The center of gravity of international decisions had in fact drifted away from Geneva, where it seemed to have come to rest during the years of economic wellbeing accompanied by political relaxation. Economics was asserting its primacy; in the factories of the Ruhr, in the wheat fields of Eastern Europe, no less than in the great banking houses and the various national treasuries, lay the roots and the possible solution of the current economic ills.

Between them the United States and France had accumulated nearly 60 percent of the world's gold. The United States was plunged in deepening depression but, though little inclined to play overtly a major role in world politics, remained a source of great potential power. France, too, began to feel, though relatively mildly, the effects of the economic crisis. The surpluses which had accumulated for a time following the stabilization of the franc had by now been dissipated to make way for budgetary deficits. Financially, nevertheless, France remained a tower of seeming stability and strength among the ruins of crumbling economies. Money is power, and the circumstances of the time considerably enhanced the possibilities of French influence. In the spring of 1931 French loans went to France's Eastern allies, Poland, Rumania, Czechoslovakia and Yugoslavia. Would these be used to resolder the links that France's policy of leniency and conciliation since Locarno had to a degree loosened, would they allay the doubts suggested by the implications of possible withdrawal behind the Maginot Line? Would, in other words, the whole French system dedicated to the preservation of peace through strict adherence to the status quo reassert itself and be strengthened? In this respect the financial strength of France placed her in a far stronger, and a precisely reverse, position from that which had been hers at the very time, in the early twenties, when the French system was assuming shape. The use that France made — or failed to make — of her unexpected strength is highly worth examining. One major test arose from an unexpected quarter.

---

[26] Owing to the place of Britain in world trade, a large number of countries followed the British example and devalued their currencies along with the pound. These constituted the sterling bloc. The United States and most of the continental European countries remained on the gold standard, for the time being at least, constituting the gold bloc.

The Austro-German Customs Union

German diplomacy does not enjoy a wide reputation for deftness; it chose the year 1931 for one of the more clumsy manifestations of its aptitude. The treaties of 1919 with both Germany and Austria forbade the union of those countries save with the consent of the other signatories of the treaties. [27] The question of the *Anschluss* was therefore formally settled, but, even if only in academic terms, the possibility of it kept on being discussed. That Austria was Germanic no one sought to deny; there was much logic, especially of an economic nature, in arguing for the incorporation of the diminished Austria into the larger Reich; but then again there was a long historic tradition of difference between Berlin and Vienna which had been close allies for less than half a century. The strength of the Austrian desire for union was difficult of reliable assessment; also, it tended to vary with the changing circumstances, again largely economic, of the two countries. Among the major victors of the war, France and Italy, for simple reasons of national interest, were staunchly opposed to the *Anschluss*; for equally solid reasons, the Little Entente, especially Czechoslovakia, took a similar position.

It was therefore not without some surprise that, on March 21, the Powers received from German Foreign Minister Curtius the notification that an Austro-German customs union had been agreed upon in principle. That in the stress of the economic storm that was engulfing the whole world, little Austria should look for salvation, or at least for assistance, through integration in the larger body of the German economy can easily be understood, [28] but that Germany could hope to find a solution to *her* difficulties in the incorporation of the Austrian economy was open to some question. The statement that "the treaty is intended to initiate a reorganization of European economic conditions by regional agreements," extended into the contention that this was a step in the direction of Briand's European federation, was misplaced heavy-handed humor in view of the inevitable and obvious political implications of the move. [29] This, to be sure, was no formal *Anschluss*,

---

[27] The Austrian Reconstruction Protocol of 1922 had reiterated Austria's promise not to alienate her independence, specifying besides that she was to abstain from making with any state (read Germany) economic or financial arrangements that would compromise this independence.

[28] Dr. Schober, the Austrian Vice-Chancellor and Foreign Minister, had been to Paris a year earlier. From Briand he had received a sympathetic hearing but nothing more concrete than a promise of intercession with the Little Entente countries and reference to Briand's proposed European federation. The failure of effective relief through French action was one argument used by Schober as justification for the economic union with Germany.

[29] It was on March 3 that Briand, speaking in the French Chamber, had stated that any likelihood of the *Anschluss* had greatly diminished. The announcement of March 21 could not but cause him embarrassment as well as ridicule, hence was particularly inept in that context. Briand naturally

but it brought up at once inescapable recollections of the nineteenth century *Zollverein* and the subsequent course of German history. The carefully maintained secrecy of the negotiations lent color to the suspicion that there was full awareness of the political implications which were in fact the very ones intended, and this suspicion was not lessened by the tone of the German press which, though taken by surprise, in the main welcomed the announcement, but rather as a political success than for its ostensible motive. [30]

One result without doubt was accomplished; the French outcry was loud that greeted the news of March 21, news which tended to bolster the contention of those who claimed that trust in Germany was futile dangerous illusion, while correspondingly weakening the position of those, Briand among them, who placed their hope in precisely such a policy of trust. It seemed a poor way for Germany to go about initiating the cure of Europe's current ills. If, on the other hand, the German calculation was that a *fait accompli* would have the better of French, and other, opposition, a rude awakening was in the offing.

France, staunchly supported by Czechoslovakia, [31] from the outset took the position that the proposed customs union contravened existing obligations. After some exchanges, both diplomatic and public, among the various interested parties, it was agreed that the question would be considered by the Council of the League at the coming session in May, and the tension was further alleviated by an Austrian announcement that no further steps would be taken pending this test. At Geneva it was agreed to accept the British proposal to request the Permanent Court of International Justice to give an advisory opinion on the question whether the proposed Austro-German customs union was compatible with the provisions of the Treaty of St. Germain and those of the Protocol of 1922 on Austrian Reconstruction. Pending the court's advice no further action would be taken. [32]

But by the time this temporizing decision was agreed upon the scene had changed as well as the weapons with which the battle was being fought. Whether or not the announcement of the Austro-German customs union was intended to alleviate Austria's immediate difficulties, it certainly failed to have such an effect; it was on May 11, a few days

---

made the point, to the German ambassador, that if the scheme was intended to further his own plan it seemed odd that he should not have been informed of it. To argue at that level was clearly shadow boxing.

[30] In view of the domestic political situation of Germany, the interpretation did not seem unreasonable that the government had been seeking a foreign success to counteract its difficulties and as a foil to the loud Nazi charges of weakness in its foreign policy.

[31] Britain and a number of other states did not commit themselves at first. Britain especially endeavored to divert the dispute into a discussion of its legal aspects.

[32] This left unanswered the Franco-Czech contention that the political aspects of the question, as distinct from the purely juridical and economic, must equally be taken into account.

before the opening of the Geneva session that the failure of the Viennese *Creditanstalt* took place. It was in June that Germany's difficulties resulted in the institution of the above mentioned Hoover moratorium. If it should come to a financial battle, the pooling of German and Austrian distress seemed a poor weapon with which to enter the contest with French financial power. This power, to be sure, was looked upon with less than enthusiasm in London; in mid June the assistance that the Bank of England gave to the Austrian treasury foiled the French effort to trade French assistance for the price of Austria's abandonment of the customs union scheme. But Britain herself was entering a period of financial difficulties when for a time London was to seek the assistance of Paris.

Here was an unexpected turn of events. Nearly a decade earlier French military power had been counterbalanced by British (and to a point American) financial power; as a result, French monetary embarrassment had been an important factor in giving a large share to the Anglo-American voice in formulating the compromise of the Dawes Plan. Since that time the orientation of French policy, mainly under the guidance of Briand, had altered. But even though France had much reduced her military establishment she still retained an ample edge of superiority and the network of her alliances was still intact. For the moment at least the British financial weapon was reduced to impotence and those who would find assistance must now come to Paris where the supply of gold was ample. The opportunity was rare, and in all probability fleeting, of using the financial tool to political purpose. Would France rise to the occasion?

In the more narrow and immediate sense the power of gold could be used either in negative fashion to prevent such things as the Austro-German customs union, or to regain a measure of the relaxed controls over Germany. This, broadly speaking, may be said to have been the limited view of things taken by the French Right, dedicated to the proposition that the only effective fashion of dealing with the German problem was to hold Germany in continued subjection. More constructively, it would have been necessary to initiate bold and farseeing measures that could have lifted the whole economy of Europe out of its rut by breaking, among other things, the vicious circle of increasing restrictions that made worse for all the illness that each one was seeking alone, and to a point at the expense of others, to escape.

The negative aspects of French policy were the more conspicuously successful. It is no cause for surprise to find little French inclination to come to the rescue of an Austria toying with an economic *Anschluss*. The severe difficulties that the failure of the *Creditanstalt* initiated for Austria caused that country to appeal once more to the League for assistance in August. French gold was in a commanding position and the resistance of Foreign Minister Schober was finally overcome. The Permanent Court of International Justice had announced that its advisory opinion would be given on September 5. On September 3 Dr. Schober, speaking in Geneva, stated that, in view of the economic difficulties which had developed, the project of Austro-German customs union was being abandoned. [33] This, in combination with the unfavorable opinion of the Permanent Court, disposed of the issue, and French participation in measures for the financial relief of Austria was thereafter forthcoming. In passing, it may be worth noting that the opinion of the Court had the impressive backing of an 8 to 7 majority, a fact reminiscent of 5 to 4 decisions of the American Supreme Court and suggestive of the possibility that separation between the law and politics is not quite what some claim or wish that it would be. The American quip that the Supreme Court listens to the election returns may be recalled at this point. [34]

France, Germany and the United States

There were other evidences at this time of the power of French gold. Like neighboring Austria, Hungary too was faced with financial crisis; since London, her first choice, could be of little help at this juncture, of necessity she too must turn to Paris, the influence of whose wishes was clearly apparent in Count Bethlen's speech of August 5 and even more in the declarations of his successor Count Karolyi. [35] Even Soviet Russia, having encountered difficulties in the financing of her trade with Germany, gave signs of shifting her purchases to France, laying the bases for possibly more far reaching agreements. [36]

If the attempted Austro-German customs union had been for Austria the source of more hurt than assistance, the Hoover moratorium failed to be for Germany the restoring stimulus that was a large part of its intent. It was just after the final acceptance of the moratorium that the failure of the Darmstädter Bank gave a measure of the seriousness of the German financial crisis. The succession of collapses spreading from East to West in Europe made for embarrassment in London whose possibilities of initiative were thereby further hampered. Bitter as the

---

[33] This was confirmed by a corresponding announcement of Dr. Curtius in Germany.

[34] This is not to impugn the integrity of judges of the Permanent Court of International Justice or of the American Supreme Court, but merely to point to the fact that the interpretation of the law cannot at certain points help being political — indeed perhaps should not. It is of especial interest to note that the French, Italian, Polish, and Rumanian judges were part of the majority, while the German, British, and American judges took the opposite view.

[35] This was a setback to Italian policy which had been seeking to establish its influence among the ex-enemy states of Austria, Hungary, and Bulgaria.

[36] Soviet Russia at this time was bent upon domestic reconstruction more than upon the exploitation of opportunities for revolution that the economic crisis might provide. She also feared that French financial power might be used to extract from Germany political concessions that would make that country part of an anti-Soviet bourgeois bloc under French leadership; hence her desire to improve her relations with France and, as a corollary, even with Poland.

pill might be, Germany must accept the fact that if she was to be aided it was with France that she must deal directly.

Accordingly, the Austro-German scheme having been buried under the double weight of voluntary renunciation and of legal sanction, France's Prime Minister of the day, Laval, and her apparently permanent Foreign Minister, Briand, departed for Berlin at the end of September. The occasion took on historic significance from the fact that more than half a century had passed since French statesmen had visited officially the German capital, and, in view of the prevailing German temper, stringent precautions were taken by the German police services lest untoward incidents mar the event. It was possible to produce a crowd to wave French flags and cheer the visitors; the cry *Nie wieder Krieg!* had an authentic ring. Briand — *der alte,* as even older Hindenburg, impressed by the outward signs of his failing health, is said to have described him — was pleased, though not losing his sense of criticism or wit. Looking back to Thoiry, just five years earlier, the tables now were turned: it was France that was in a position to rescue the German financial structure. But Germany still entertained numerous grievances of an essentially political nature. A combination of financial aid with far reaching political concessions at this moment contained once more the possibility, and the possible assets, of a *grand geste*. It is idle to speculate whether it would have sufficed to stem the rising tide of German despair ; what German hopes were entertained on that score were bound to be deceived. Briand was old and ill, and also disillusioned, hampered besides by the increasing reticence of French opinion which recent trans-Rhenish developments could not but increase.

Brüning's expectations were more modest, not exceeding hopes of a substantial loan, but the mixed Franco-German commission that was organized toyed at least with prospects of a large nature: the possibility was even broached of a scheme that would have dwarfed by far the ill-timed proposal of the Austro-German customs union, that of a Franco-German one. There were those representatives of German industry who would not have been averse to the helpful (for the moment at least) intrusion of French capital in Germany. High hopes centered for a moment on the work of the Franco-German commission.

The French visit to Berlin was followed almost immediately by Laval's trip to Washington late in October. There was perhaps existent in some quarters in America, as in Britain, a tendency to look askance at France's current place of importance in the world's financial structure. However, facts are facts and must be recognized. In Washington, Laval was able to secure an American promise that there would be no repetition of such a performance as that of the manner in which the Hoover moratorium had been launched, and the *de facto* link between international debts (Reparation and the war debts to America) was acknowledged as well as what may be broadly described as the French right to financial leadership in Europe. In exchange, the flow of gold from New York to Paris was sharply brought to an end, but of American political commitments to the European *status quo* none were forthcoming. [37] The Hoover-Laval declaration of October 25 consisted on the whole of pious and in part irrelevant wishes, as on the subject of disarmament for instance. America and France, the two dominant financial powers of the moment, apart from their common devotion to gold, gave little indication of being possessed of constructive ideas of immediate applicability.

Coming back to Europe, so far reaching a scheme as a Franco-German customs union might, if realized, have shaken the whole continent out of the vicious circle of economic nationalism into which it was sinking ever more deeply. In the abstract, there was much to recommend the scheme and it was also true that the two economies were in considerable measure complementary; but, inevitably, when examined in the details of its more probable immediate consequences, considering the balance of trade between the two countries, it was clear that the likely effect at first would have been to export Germany's difficulties, unemployment for one, to France. On the French side, the project did not go beyond exploring the possibility, capable of extension into political ramifications, of French participation in German industry. It was not long before it was apparent that the Franco-German commission would produce no results of appreciable consequence.

To sum it up briefly and bluntly, the root of the difficulty lay in the limitations of the French economy which, if it enjoyed the advantage of a considerable degree of self-containment and internal balance, was ill-equipped to face the competition of the outer world, especially the German. Some of the same drawbacks intervened when it came to the problem of Danubia, or more broadly Central and Eastern Europe. France might make loans to her smaller allies, even to Hungary or Austria, but in the long term France could provide no satisfactory outlet for these essentially agricultural economies whose natural connection was with industrial Germany. Economically, there is much logic in the old German dream of *Mitteleuropa,* but precisely therein lay one of Europe's major dilemmas, in the fact that German ambition has overflowed into political implications which have been the source of opposition to its designs.

To the problem of mid Europe France was not blind. Barring its mere integration into the German economy, some sort of reconstruction of the Habsburg domain, in its useful economic aspects, was often

---

[37] The idea that the "injustices" of the peace, especially where Germany was concerned, and of which France was the chief upholder, should be redressed had wide currency in America at this time. The French visit to America was the occasion for a somewhat sensational interview given to representatives of the press by the then Chairman of the Senate Committee on Foreign Relations, Senator Borah. Senator Borah, doubtless depending then as later on his own sources of information, held views as definite as strong on the score of how the peace settlements should be revised, even though the precision of his knowledge stood somewhat exposed in the course of the questioning to which he was submitted.

contemplated. While vigorously opposing the Austro-German customs union in 1931, France had also submitted a "constructive memorandum" alongside her critique. But this, and other "constructive" proposals, hinged in the main on the easing of the protectionist policies of the newly formed states. Such eminently sane suggestions ran into the factor of the jealous nationalism of these new states; France did not see her way to risking the displeasure of her own Eastern allies by exerting pressure on them to see the light of reason. [38] The various Danubian schemes came to nothing.

If the sudden rise of France to a position of unwonted eminence in the world's financial councils was viewed with a somewhat jaundiced eye in Britain and America, apart from the pettier aspects of resentment at intrusion, there were some valid bases for the American and British feeling, especially the latter. Paris lacked the qualifications that background and experience had long provided London in her role of world financial capital. [39] Moreover, the power of French gold was but momentary reflection of accidental and transitory circumstances. France's seeming immunity to the impact of the world crisis was about to come to an end. The second half of 1931, albeit still in a mild way, saw depression creeping into France; the budget showed a notable deficit. Thus it happened that whatever opportunity there was — such as it may have been — to use economic and financial advantage for ends of far reaching results, not only was shortlived, but also was allowed to pass unused either for European reconstruction or even in the more limited domain of Franco-German relations.

What in the circumstances can only be described as a deep-rooted vice or failure of the French body politic to rise to the occasion is aptly summarized in the words of François Goguel:

> The inability of the French public mind as a whole to give lasting support to a coherent policy toward Germany had thus combined with the illusions entertained in France on the score of the strength that the country derived from its financial prosperity; the diplomatic action of the Paris government had as a consequence been so hampered that it had not known how to take advantage of circumstances either to resume against the Reich an energetic policy of military hegemony, or to attempt with it a concrete collaboration, economic in the first place, but which could have been lasting by approaching the political issues, and by being extended to the other European states struck by the crisis. [40]

---

[38] Italy might have been expected to play an important role in this area, but, in large part for political reasons again and because of the limitations of Italian resources, what happened was that Central Europe became an area of contest between French and Italian influences, the latter achieving some success among the ex-enemies, Austria, Hungary, and Bulgaria. Italy's leadership of this "league of malcontents" accomplished no more than negative results.

[39] On this point, reference may be made again to Francis Delaisi, *La bataille de l'or,* cited earlier.

[40] Goguel, *op. cit.,* p. 313.

3. FRANCE AT HOME

Even apart from the passing opportunity furnished by economic conditions, France still continued to be the keystone of the political structure of Europe. The direction and aims of her policy remained therefore of prime importance, and since their roots lay in the operation and conditions of the French people as a whole the circumstances of the French milieu assumed significance far beyond the confines of France alone. The permanence of Briand at the foreign office was to a degree misleading: what Briand did or could do in 1931 or 1932 was quite different from what he could attempt in 1926.

Until 1932

The election of 1928 in the atmosphere of economic wellbeing and against the background of restoration of the soundness of the currency had, not surprisingly, endorsed Poincaré and his National Union. The very conditions of the success had further weakened the allegiance to the government, at no time enthusiastic, of the Radical Socialist group. [41] The party congress of Angers was the occasion for a vote of censure that resulted in the resignation of the Radical Socialist ministers. It might be taken as an indication of the fact that France had returned to "normalcy" — or else that she was living in a world of make believe — that the ostensible issue should have been the now largely superseded one of laïcité. [42]

Poincaré was able to continue without the Radicals, and the result was a return to the more normal operation and divisions of French politics. Poincaré was no longer young; the growing strain of office caused him to resign in July, 1929, when he had to undergo a serious operation, and the occasion marked the end of his long career in French politics. Whatever may be thought of his personal character and of the merits of his policies, he had done honorable service to the nation and to the Republic, in the annals of which he remains one of the dominant figures.

The passing of Poincaré was in a sense the passing of an era. Briand took over his succession, retaining the foreign office as usual; but there was in this an anomaly, for Briand was fundamentally a man of the Left whose support alone had made it possible to pursue

---

[41] The relative success of the Socialists, who had remained in clear opposition, caused the Radical Socialists to feel that their normal position on the Left would be electorally more profitable. The factor of personal rivalry was likewise of importance; thus, Caillaux, one of the party's luminaries and outstanding financial experts, found it difficult to forgive Poincaré his success in an attempt where he himself had failed. Though conservative enough, Caillaux found himself in alliance with the younger, more doctrinaire and radical, as well as politically ambitious, elements of the party.
[42] Specifically, an incidental provision introduced by Poincaré that would have facilitated the recruitment in France of certain religious orders.

his foreign policy. It was a combination of the Center-Left that over-
threw him as soon as Parliament reopened in the autumn. The outcome
was clarification; after some intricate manoeuvring, [43] Tardieu succeeded
in forming a government of moderate, or Center-Right orientation.
Tardieu and Laval dominate the remaining period of the existing
legislature. [44] They represented the advent of new blood in the direction
of the state, men whose conditioning background of political experience
consisted of more recent happenings and issues than those of the turn
of the century. It was not so much a break as a transition, however, and
Briand whose prestige at home and abroad was, by this time, so great
continued in his customary post.

Tardieu had been Clemenceau's right-hand man in the making of
the peace. Wealth and intelligence he both possessed in more than
usual measure, but the expectations founded on the latter quality were
on the whole to be deceived, the flaw residing in deficiency of character.
Fine words he used to expound attractive sounding programs of domestic
renovation, but in practice he proved noisy and brash rather than
constructive. The handsome 19,000,000,000 franc surplus, accumulated
during the fat years under the careful husbanding of Poincaré's stewardship, soon began to be dissipated; much of it went to the satisfaction
of scattered individual interests instead of being used for large schemes
that might have bolstered the French economy, of whose immunity to
crisis Tardieu preferred to boast instead. His abrupt manner was ill-
devised to make his progress smooth, either with jealous politicians or
with his peers abroad. Defeated once in February, 1930, he continued
as his own successor until the end of the year when the Senate intervened, as it does on rare occasions in France, to overthrow his government. [45]

A short interim, which again confirmed the impossibility of organizing a working Left majority, brought Laval to the Prime Ministership.
Laval had not been born to wealth, and the uncouthness of his origins
he never wholly shed; the dubious tinge of his teeth, his fingernails, and
his inevitable white necktie became legendary, while his features would
not have jarred in a rogues' gallery. Like many a successful French
politician, Laval had gradually evolved from the vociferous proclaiming
of slogans of the extreme Left to what was by this time generally

---

[43] President Doumergue entrusted Daladier of the Left wing of the
Radical Socialist party with the task of forming a cabinet. Doumergue's calculation, which proved correct, was that the inability of the Left to organize
a viable coalition would thereby stand exposed.

[44] A good contemporary summary of the work of the 1928-1932 legislature
may be found in *L'Europe nouvelle*, March 26, 1932.

[45] The delicate balance — or confusion — of the French parliamentary
scene may be judged from the debate on foreign policy in November. This
resulted in support of the government by the Right which had attacked
Briand's policy, while the Left which was favorable to it voted against the
government, a clear illustration of the distorting intrusion of domestic, and
generally petty and personal, quarrels into more important issues.

regarded as a conservative orientation; his private fortunes had not suffered in the process. If a code less than rigid had served him, his skill and shrewdness could not be denied. Attached to no particular grouping, he had accomplished the not inconsiderable feat of having retained amicable connections in nearly every quarter. Realistic, pragmatic, and unprincipled, Laval was *par excellence* the agile contriver of *combinazioni*. The cloudy atmosphere of petty personal and partisan politics, the limited concern for temporary accommodation, were eminently suited to his skills; not larger policy of long term implication or the perceptive appreciation of the significance of fundamental principle, even in politics, not excluding French politics. Under the guidance of so mean a star France existed through the year 1931, unable to make up her mind with clarity, letting pass unexploited what opportunities circumstances brought to her door. This has been indicated before, and, to repeat, the connection is important between these domestic conditions and the failure of clear and resolute leadership, a failure that boded ill for the future in view of the responsibilities of France in Europe.

Briand was still Foreign Minister, but his influence was fast declining along with his failing health. His prestige and long service led him to think that the prize of the presidency of France might be his; the office carries little power, but the prestige of it might seem apt crowning to his long and distinguished career. Accordingly, he let his name be put forward in the election of May, 1931; his defeat by the relatively colorless Doumer was a heavy blow to Briand and seemed to confirm the impression that the interpretation of egalitarianism in the Third Republic was tantamount to placing a high premium on lack of distinction. [46]

Briand's prestige at home naturally suffered from this setback. If he chose to stay on at the Quai d'Orsay, the influence of Laval was increasingly permeating all aspects of French policy. When the two went to Berlin in September, Briand could still be witty, but his role was one of effacement; there was no French response to the German cries of *Retten Sie uns!* Laval went alone to Washington, and when Briand presided in Paris over the meeting of the League called to deal with the Manchurian affair, [47] gasping for breath between painfully uttered sentences, he was truly a pathetic figure. Briand retained his clarity and fully understood that his dream of peace through recon-

---

[46] The presidential election of 1931 was the occasion for some of the more sordid manœuvres of French politics, Briand's defeat being brought about in part by the activity of some of his cabinet colleagues, among them Laval and Tardieu. To a degree, there was in this poetic justice, and Briand may have been reminded of his own role in denying Clemenceau the prize of the French presidency in 1919.

[47] The meeting was held in Paris on account of Briand's state of health which prevented his going to Geneva. The Manchurian crisis, which is not dealt with in this essay, result of the Japanese aggression in Manchuria, was the first of a series of major failures of the League which marked the beginning of the end for that institution.

ciliation, if ever it were to come true, must wait for better days. Already he had spoken of casting off his burden and exchanging it for the pilgrim's staff. It was in a sense fitting that he should be displaced: in January, 1932, Laval took over his office. [48] Two months later Briand died; his passing was symbolic of an age and of a hope which in effect he had outlived.

As the time approached for the general election, the picture of French politics was that of traditional normality. Since the dissolution of Poincaré's National Union, France had been governed by the moderate Right. The fast accumulating clouds of the foreign situation had made no great impression on the electorate; distrust of Germany had tended to increase, but the extravagant talk of the wilder elements in that country, precisely because of its extravagance, could not be taken seriously by a people strongly biased by the faith in reason that was so large a component of its tradition. The threats contained in the explosive possibilities of economic crisis, mass unemployment, in Germany and elsewhere, went largely not understood in a country rather devoted to the complacent contemplation of what it thought its own immunity to the world's ills; if there had been, by 1932, economic deterioration in France, the extent of it was still comparatively very mild.

Nevertheless, the Right was now on the defensive instead of being able to capitalize, as four years earlier, on the concrete achievement of currency stabilization and prosperous finance. The result of the first balloting marked accordingly a resumption of the "normal" *sinistrisme* of French elections; in the context of the very great stability of French voting habits, the small shift that occurred could be rated a definite victory for the Left. [49] The effects of this victory in terms of parliamentary representation were magnified by the recurrence of the alliance between Radical Socialists and Socialists in the second balloting.

The Election and the Legislature of 1932

The four year period from 1932 to 1936 which contains the life of the new French legislature also contains the kernel and climax of the story of the entire long armistice. At the beginning of it the French system in Europe was still essentially intact, in the sense at least that its mechanism was largely unimpaired and capable of functioning, if

---

[48] The occasion of the Cabinet reshuffle was the death of Maginot. The state of Briand's health was the pretext for his ouster. Laval himself was overthrown in February, to be succeeded once more by Tardieu whose tenure filled the gap until the general election that took place in May.

[49] Just before the election President Doumer had been assassinated by a Russian. The groundless effort by the Right to capitalize on this incident, in a manner somewhat reminiscent of the Zinoviev letter incident in the British election of 1925, failed to impress the French electorate, but the Communists suffered a setback by comparison with 1928.

only the prime mover should decide to give it the necessary impulse; at the end of it the machine had been tested and failed to operate; though still in being, its existence was purely theoretical and formal and it was henceforth safe to proceed to the piecemeal dismantling of its individual parts. The story of how this came to pass, which will be the theme of the rest of this essay, is intimately dependent upon the story of the inner operation of this central core of the system, the whole complex that the name France encompasses. Needless to say, the passage and the perspective of time make analysis — or autopsy — easier and give the story a clarity that its contemporary unfolding lacked. Even before 1936, however, the inability of France to act abroad and to resolve her quandaries at home, related and interacting aspects of the malady of France, did not go unperceived to many acute observers, both in France and outside. The danger grew gradually, if fairly rapidly, and during the earlier part at least of the four year period the illusion of normality could still continue to prevail.

The Radical Socialists had emerged from the election as the largest group in Parliament; Herriot was consequently given the task of forming the new government, which he did in June, taking himself, as eight years earlier, both the Prime Ministership and the foreign affairs port-folio. Herriot represented the more conservative orientation of Radical Socialism; moreover, the passage of eight years and his experience of 1924 had left a mark on him: [50] for the soundness of finance he had developed considerable respect. In addition, he felt real concern for the security and for the state of defenses of his country. [51] Despite the electoral alliance with the Socialists, on both these scores substantial differences existed. Under the leadership of the humane and cultured, but also starry-eyed and doctrinaire, Léon Blum, the Socialists in France were the one group that adhered with conviction to the view still widely popular in some other countries that the road to security and peace lay through disarmament. As to their cure for a declining economy, they saw it in increased governmental intervention and expenditure rather than in the orthodox approach that laid first stress on balanced budgets. If greater revenue were needed, such devices as a capital levy always stood in reserve in the Socialist armory.

In the knowledge that the Socialists would not share ministerial responsibility, the team that Herriot assembled was an attempt to secure support from the moderate Center; it therefore did not represent

---

[50] Herriot's own account of this period, as given in his recollections, *Jadis, D'une guerre à l'autre, 1914-1936* (Paris, 1952), understandably a defense of his actions, suffers unfortunately from the twin faults of glibness and super-ficiality.

[51] Though generally favorable to a broad policy of reconciliation, Herriot preferred the international to the bilateral or regional approach. The failure of the Geneva Protocol, which he and MacDonald had eleborated in 1924, deeply disappointed him, and Locarno he only accepted as a second best and with definite reservations.

any substantial deviation from those that had just preceded it in office. The attempt had very limited success that did not reach beyond some individual acquiescence, and, as a consequence of this, Herriot could only maintain himself so long as the Socialists would suffer him to stay. The results of this uncertain equilibrium appeared immediately.

Herriot wanted a balanced budget, but a firm stand on this issue would have caused his downfall. He chose the weaker course of letting the Chamber whittle its provisions on the plea that some steps at least were being taken on the path of financial soundness. By itself, such an act held no fatal implications; France certainly could, without disaster, stand another deficit. What gave it more than ordinary significance were the circumstances of the time. Reynaud's warning during the electoral campaign that a victory of the Left would endanger the soundness of the currency may have seemed a questionable and needlessly alarmist piece of tactics; but if the crisis were to last and deepen, as was in fact to be the case in France, a financial policy of undirected compromise and drift might indeed lead to precisely that result. If the Left was united on the broad plane of principle and ideology, the first test of the budget fairly raised the question of its ability to deal coherently with economic and financial crisis. [52]

It may perhaps seem curious that another simultaneous event should have failed to arouse a more marked reaction than it did in French opinion. The Hoover moratorium of 1931 was to last one year. Already in January, Chancellor Brüning had given warning of Germany's inability to resume the Young Plan payments upon the expiration of the moratorium. Considering the energy spent in the attempt to collect German Reparation and the bitterness generated by that issue, the lack of notice that Brüning's announcement received is surprising, even though the idea had made considerable progress that the whole matter of intergovernmental obligations deriving from the war had better be abandoned as a bad job. [53] Almost unobtrusively, and with a minimum of debate and delay, the Lausanne conference in July, 1932 wrote finis to the chapter of German Reparation. [54]

---

[52] This is not to say that the measures that would commend themselves to the support of the opposition would have had better results, as the test was eventually to show. Therein precisely lay the weakness of the French structure, in the inability to override a collection of specific interests for the ultimate general good of all.

[53] To some extent also the fact was of significance that financial interests, in France as elsewhere, were by this time anxious to safeguard the German payment of interest on the "commercialized" Young Plan bonds held in private hands; this payment would be more likely to be forthcoming if Germany were free of the payments directly due other governments. Thus, one classical French source of opposition to leniency toward Germany found itself shifting to agreement with instead of opposition to the international, especially the Anglo-American, position.

[54] In final settlement of Reparation, Germany remained liable for the payment of a lump sum of $750,000,000, a payment which in the end was never made.

This may well be regarded as a constructive achievement, the final recognition of reality, but one aspect of the problem had been left out of the arrangement. Despite the precedent of the Hoover moratorium itself and despite the widespread expectation of all concerned directly with the problem of Reparation, the United States had never consented to the formal linking of that issue with that of the allied wartime debts. The matter could no longer be avoided when the time came for the resumption of payments to America, which fell due in December, 1932. A great debate took place in the French Parliament. As an issue between America and France the status of the matter was as clear as was the unlikelihood of agreement. At the legal level, America's position was simple and unassailable, resting on the letter of a contract. But this, in French eyes, only made it the more in the nature of compounding insult with injury, especially after the cavalier manner in which America had dealt with French interest in the matter of the moratorium. On the score of the moral validity of the American claim French opinion was well-nigh unanimous. But, however harsh and unreasonable Uncle Shylock might be, the bald repudiation of a contract was not a step to be taken lightly by a nation that set so much store by the sanctity of written obligations. Emotion in the end prevailed, and the French Parliament declined to honor France's obligation.

The immediate consequence of this act was the fall of the government; Herriot took a firm position in favor of meeting the December 15 payment, and in one of the best speeches of his long career took his stand on the broad ground of international morality and of the deeper long term value of American friendship and goodwill for France. [55] Actually, Herriot was rather glad than sorry to shed the cares of office at this point. In face of the inability of the Left to produce and sustain a more coherent policy, he was not reluctant to avoid the embarrassments that he saw looming in the future. The American debt debate furnished him the occasion for a graceful exit while his personal prestige, both at home and abroad, was enhanced by the manner of it.

If the issue, in absolute terms, was of far less importance than many other current ones, whatever may be thought of the merits of the French case — in justice and in fairness they may be granted strong — for France the move was a mistaken one. The natural irritation that it produced in America was but one aspect of the isolation in which France was placing herself while it weakened her moral position if and when it should come to resort for herself to the argument of the sanctity of international obligations.

---

[55] The French attempt to maintain a common front with Britain in the matter of the American debt failed. Financially, Britain was in far greater straits than France at this time and the British view of the moral aspects of the matter was generally similar to the French. But Britain did not see her way to breaking her word and incurring American displeasure. It was not long, however, before she too, under the pressure of necessity and in face of American intransigeance, resorted to the plea of impossibility in continuing to meet her obligation.

4. THE RE-EMERGENCE OF GERMANY

This was a particularly poor time to take such a position, for throughout the year that was closing the situation across the Rhine had been one of steady deterioration. But before returning to the crucial aspect of the affairs of Europe that the course of German events constituted, and for the sake of completeness, another important development of the year 1932 must be mentioned.

The Final Failure of Disarmament

The use of the adjective important may be questioned when referring to the subject of disarmament in 1932. In retrospect, it is quite clear that, in the circumstances, the debate was both unrealistic and futile, as even the contemporary course of discussions revealed. These discussions nevertheless absorbed much of the energy and time of the chancelleries of Europe. The question therefore must be mentioned but it will be sufficient to outline its development in briefest fashion.

Ever since 1926 the Preparatory Commission for the Disarmament Conference had been conducting its leisurely debates, examining reports, estimates and comparisons. The essentials of the discussion have been indicated before: [56] in briefest form the theses, disarm and you will be secure, to which forever came the answer, we shall disarm as soon as we feel secure, were locked in irreconcilable opposition; the changing versions of this fundamental difference, the weary proliferation of schemes, will not be used to burden this presentation. [57] Finally, in February, 1932, the Disarmament Conference opened its sessions in Geneva. Considering on the one hand the record of divergence in the Preparatory Commission, and on the other the already vastly altered atmosphere of 1932 by comparison with that of a few years before, it may seem strange that the conference should be called at all. In fact, the negative consideration of the reluctance to face the implications of the open admission of failure was not alien to the decision to have the meeting take place: peoples' hopes were still high despite the steady deterioration of the international atmosphere.

It fell to Tardieu to submit the French scheme that went under his name. In view of his long and consistent record, where in word and by pen Tardieu had always stressed the danger and the duplicity of German machinations, amenability to compromise, let alone surrender, was hardly to be expected from him. The Tardieu plan was not exactly what might have been expected — or feared; bypassing more timid suggestions for the reduction or control of limited aspects of armaments, Tardieu proposed from the outset the creation of an international army to insure the security of Europe. The plan received in British quarters

---

[56] See above, pp. 181-82.
[57] The references cited in Chapter IV, note 82, may be mentioned again at this point.

the reception that might be expected, and this predictable outcome was probably not alien to Tardieu's calculations: in the abstract and for debating purposes there was merit in the proposal; the virtual certainty of its rejection would leave things as they stood, among them France's position unimpaired. On a later occasion, when Litvinov blandly proposed in Geneva the simple universal abolition of armed forces, the feeling was widespread that his intent was largely to embarrass others; much of the same reaction greeted the Tardieu plan regarded by some as a manoeuvre that did not even have the merit of subtlety. Whether or not Tardieu was disappointed, in any case nothing came of his plan which soon joined others in the dusty files of abortive proposals; on droned the debate for a time, repeating the often heard exchanges of the Preparatory Commission. Adjournment was the only alternative to a public and outright acknowledgment of failure, but not until an American proposal [58] in June, of which France and her allies were the chief opponents, served to confirm the view of those who felt that France's main concern was to maintain the *status quo* of her military preponderance.

After Tardieu, France had again a government of the Left from which might be expected greater sympathy for the reduction of armaments. But, allowing for a certain difference of emphasis between Right and Left, the French position on the score of armaments was largely a national matter. The slogan, security, arbitration, disarmament, still expressed the proper sequence in Herriot's mind, as it had in 1924. The passage of time had done little to increase his readiness to place trust in Germany; on the contrary, he was much impressed by the bulky dossier on German rearmament complied by French intelligence. [59] In addition, the fast developing events in Germany during the second half of 1932 were a source of profound disillusion to one who had cherished the hope that democracy might in time strike its roots in the Reich.

The universal approach to the problem through the agency of the League Herriot found more congenial than that of regional, or worse, bilateral arrangements. When the Disarmament Conference resumed its sessions, it was Paul-Boncour who presented in November a new plan which was predicated on the earmarking of national contingents for the purpose of enforcing League decisions. [60] From the standpoint

---

[58] President Hoover, again stressing the connection between armament expenditures and economic bad times, proposed through the American representative the abolition of certain weapons and a one-third reduction of standing armies. Both Germany and the Soviet Union approved the American proposal.

[59] An exhaustive discussion of German rearmament during this period may be found in the recently published dissertation of Georges Castellan, *Le réarmement clandestin du Reich 1930-1935* (Paris, 1954).

[60] The French plan was an elaborate one. A good exposition and discussion of its features may be found in *L'Europe nouvelle*, November 19, 1932.

of results accomplished, the Herriot-Paul-Boncour plan did little better than Tardieu's. Of possibly greater significance than this proliferation of plans aimed at reducing armaments was the fact that in September Germany announced her withdrawal from the conference.

While Germany had shared in the discussions, the fact of her own lack of arms inevitably made her position a special one on the sidelines of the debate. The problem was for her first of all to achieve a condition where the specific issue of what arms and how much of each would be lifted from the domain of abstraction. The German memorandum of September, focused on the demand for what had been for long the chief German desideratum, *Gleichberechtigung,* equality of rights with others. Failing the granting of this preliminary condition, Germany would decline longer to participate in the futile game of unending procrastination which the disarmament discussion had become. The German action was a warning: what if Germany should take it upon herself to rearm? Would France, would her allies, would any one, then take up arms to stifle in the embryo the clear danger that such a step would constitute? The issue did not yet arise, and the dilemma that the German withdrawal presented was met by others with evasion in which Germany was, for the time at least, willing to participate. A declaration in December that recognized in principle Germany's right to equality brought her return to the Disarmament Conference. What the meaning of this declaration was time alone could tell. It could, if shortly implemented, be one more step along the road, the beginning of which may be placed at Locarno, of complete German rehabilitation; but it might equally be possible further to prolong the six year old discussion.

The End of the Weimar Republic

The German action of September, apart from the overwhelming support that the claim to *Gleichberechtigung* would command at any time from the German people, was not unrelated to the uncertain domestic conditions of the Reich. The last year in the life of the Weimar Republic was a troubled one. The end of the term of office of President von Hindenburg gave rise to a situation which, had it not been so full of serious implications, would have been fit for humorous treatment. Generally deceiving the expectations of both his initial supporters and opponents, the aging Marshal had loyally served the Republic rather than play the role of Trojan horse that many had predicted. His personal prestige unimpaired, despite his age, he was now induced to be a candidate for his own succession, but in the novel guise this time of standard bearer of the forces broadly speaking of the Left that wanted to preserve the Republic. The election he won, though by a narrow margin; [61] it was perhaps fitting that the Republic

---

[61] Owing largely to the Communist refusal to join the Republican forces and the consequent insistence on running a Communist candidate, von Hindenburg failed to obtain the absolute mapority necessary for election on the

should be saved by the embodiment of the old imperial order, for by comparison with the rising tide of unreason, the Wilhelmine Reich may well be regarded as eminently sane and reasonable, but the judgment was shrewd that "despite the personal success of the octogenarian Marshal Germany will soon have no choice between the experiment of Hitler and civil war." [62] Chancellor Brüning, sober and even austere to the point of lacking color, was eminently a representative of sanity; in face of the growing difficulty of his task he had to yield place in June to von Papen, the Presidential choice, a choice that some would regard as one more illustration of the limitations of the political understanding of the military mind.

It is sometimes useful to look to the animal kingdom for models of the traits that best characterize a man; in the case of von Papen the fox and the snake readily come to mind as symbols. It is undoubtedly some indication of the man's abilities and character that he has been able to survive personally unscathed through the various regimes that have held sway in Germany. [63] Well connected with both blood and wealth, even outside of Germany, this rather irresponsible intriguer had won the confidence of Hindenburg. In an attempt to resolve the stalemate of impotence that was characteristic of the existing Reichstag an election was held in July; it brought the Nazis to their peak of parliamentary strength with 230 representatives, a success never hitherto achieved by any German party. The Communists also made gains. [64] Here were two groups calculated to remind one that *les extrêmes se touchent*; for all their mutual hatred, Nazis and Communists had this in common that they would with satisfaction contemplate the demise of Weimar. Their combined strength and negative cooperation in sabotaging the proper operation of the system raised indeed the question whether they might not in fact destroy it, and that according to the very laws of its own constitution. The Italian precedent of ten years earlier became relevant at this point when another democracy had meekly surrendered and constitutionally signed its own death warrant; the difference now being that in the German case Nazis and Communists combined, or possibly Nazis alone, might soon reach a majority of numbers, whereas in 1922 there were a mere thirty-five Fascists in the Italian Parliament. Far seemed the days of making the world safe for democracy; the question rather was, how safe is democracy in Germany, or perhaps, how much longer is it safe?

July also witnessed the driving of another nail in the coffin of German democracy, the suspension of the Prussian government super-

---

first balloting. It should be pointed out that the issue was no longer that of Republic versus monarchical restoration, but rather of the preservation of the Weimar Republic against the threat of the Nazis.

[62] *L'Europe nouvelle*, April 16, 1932.

[63] Deeply involved as he was in Nazi diplomacy, his postwar trial has resulted in his exoneration.

[64] They obtained 89 seats in the Reichstag with 14.5 percent of the popular vote.

seded by von Papen's assumption of the post of *Reichskommissar* for that largest of German states. No less significant than this act itself was the meekness with which the existing legally constituted government of Prussia allowed itself to be evicted. [65] How could Germany be governed in the circumstances save by continued resort to the Presidential prerogative? And so it was. But the very fact of the too prolonged use of the emergency provisions of the constitution also raised the question of the adequacy of that instrument. It was indeed a part of von Papen's program to effect reforms in the constitution. Once more, in November, the weary German people were called to the ballot boxes; the division of their views had changed little, though some found comfort in the fact that the steadily ascending curve of Nazi success was deflected by the mild setback that they suffered. [66] It is always a temptation in politics to seek to draw the sting of uncomfortable opposition by associating it to the responsibilities of power. Von Papen's fondness for involved intrigue would be especially responsive to this approach, and Hitler was offered the vice-Chancellorship, which, after some qualms of inner searching, he refused.

Von Papen yielded place to General von Schleicher, who became Chancellor on December 4. The feeling was strong, both in Germany and outside, that the crisis had been overcome, that the Nazi danger was on the wane, that a strong man was at last in control who would at least maintain the country in the paths of order and legality. His reception abroad was definitely favorable.

The convulsions of the German body politic found no reflection in the position of Germany on the international scene; this position instead had tended to improve. The greater assertiveness that the demand for equal rights in armament entailed, pushed to the point of withdrawal from the Disarmament Conference, has been mentioned; but more than this, the international climate was rather favorable to Germany than the opposite. By contrast, one may speak to a point of French isolation.

Herriot had been sound in pointing to the inopportunity of antagonizing American feeling in the matter of the issue of war debts, even though America, unusually absorbed in the contemplation of her deepening domestic ills, was little minded to take an interest in the affairs of Europe. [67] But France had also parted company from Britain

---

[65] It may be regarded as an interesting, if misplaced, manifestation of German law abidingness that the reaction of the Prussian government to illegality was to appeal to the Supreme Court. With consistency, von Papen simply ignored that body's verdict at the end of October.

[66] The popular vote for the Nazis fell from 37.4 percent to 33.1 percent and their Reichstag membership from 230 to 196. By contrast, the Communists improved their strength from 89 to 100 deputies, the popular vote for them rising from 14.5 to 16.9 percent.

[67] Save in so far as there was some feeling that the European crisis had had and was having repercussions on the American economy.

in the matter of the American debt. In both countries, America and Britain, the tendency was to look away from the less pleasant aspects of the German scene; Nazi and other excesses, in so far as they were at all acknowledged — and had not people learned the wisdom of discounting the propaganda of atrocity tales? — were seen as the understandable reaction of a proud people downtrodden and browbeaten. Who but the French in their pathological obsession of fear (to take the kinder view of their actions) were responsible for this German behavior? Similar views, in varying degrees, had not a little currency among neutrals, in large measure permeated by the liberal *Zeitgeist* of the postwar, which had with more emotion than reason recoiled from the wartime exaggerations about German war guilt. [68] The Russian and the Italian views of things tended to be less emotional than the Anglo-Saxon; they had in common an opposition to the existing system, born in the former of the fear of a coalition of capitalist states, in the latter of the dislike of having been robbed of the asset of the balance of power. For both, a restoration of this balance, a division of Europe into at least two camps, had seemingly obvious advantages. Support of Germany to counterbalance the French predominance of power, after all still existing, had understandable appeal. [69] France still had her allies and it is perhaps an exaggeration to speak of France's isolation at this point, but these smaller allies had their own problems, the main focus of which was not Germany in all cases; [70] in addition to which, in view of the current importance of the condition of their economies, the fact was of significance that, save for the loans she granted them, France had been able to do little to provide the needed outlets for the production of their fields. [71]

The international situation of Europe at this time is best described as fluid. By contrast with 1931 which had brought in full force the

---

[68] The role of the school of revisionist historians which, outside of Germany herself, prospered most vigorously in the English-speaking countries, in creating an even more false climate and impression than the one it set out to redress would make an interesting study in itself. After a second World War, when the German role has been somewhat clearer, the revisionists of the post First World War are being revised in turn, until it is difficult to escape the feeling that many historians, in so far as they elect to deal with contemporary matters, are also not immune to the influence of election returns — or their international equivalent.

[69] This tendency was manifested for instance in the disarmament discussions when the American proposal in June, 1932 had received German, Russian, and (qualified) Italian support. Russia, for her part, was not averse to hedging as shown by her contacts with France.

[70] Yugoslavia was more concerned with Italy, and Rumania with Russia, which last was also of considerable concern to Poland.

[71] There was much discussion of the problem of agricultural Europe during 1932. Tardieu himself came forward with a Danubian Plan. This, like other French schemes, was hampered on the one side by the French insistence on divorcing the economic from the political aspects of the problem and on the other by opposition, largely for political reasons, from such quarters as Italy.

stunning impact of economic and financial crisis, the year 1932 marked a pause, if not recovery. The world somehow continued to exist, no major wars had broken out; [72] the structure of relations that had taken shape after the war was still in operation. The malcontents, if louder and bolder in the expression of their discontent, were still possessed of insufficient power: Germany, for all that she had been making some useful preparations, was still essentially deprived of arms; Italy by herself lacked the strength for the effective leadership of challenge; the Soviet Union was more concerned with the vast domestic programs that her directors had but recently launched, and with the negative desire to pursue her experiment free of external interference rather than with the urge of missionary zeal set on world revolution.

Much depended therefore on the quality of a leadership that France still had it in her power to assert. Power attracts support quite as much as it breeds opposition: Poland might to a degree grumble and feel that higher consideration was her due, even by her great French ally; but Poland also had clear views on both the German and the Russian dangers; these were the deep realities of her existence, far overriding in importance any real or imagined slights that her prestige might suffer. Poland could be counted upon to remain loyal to the French alliance, provided only that she entertained no doubts on the score of the French willingness to uphold the existing system. It has already been mentioned that the basic similarity of interest that underlay the Franco-Polish and other similar connections was a very strong cement; but also that the burden and responsibility of leadership were in large measure French.

The German problem therefore stood at the center of the situation. Short of a genuine German acceptance of the ways of democracy and of peace — a prospect surrounded by at least some doubts in 1932 — the continued enforcement of German impotence was the best guarantee of the continuance of peace; if German power were restored, then, even apart from any likelihood of German aggressive intent, some readjustment in the relations among European states would become unavoidable. The troubled political scene of 1932 Germany was but reflection of the deeper currents that ran through a society wrenched from the earlier security of its familiar moorings. The instauration of Weimar had been no violent revolution; the parties that were the bulwarks of the Republic, Catholic Center and Social Democrats, were long familiar in the Kaiser's days, but the structure of German society had been brutally

---

[72] Important and fraught with long term consequences as they were, the events in the Far East had relatively little direct repercussion in Europe, save perhaps in seriously weakening the League. But, even in that respect, some comfort was derived in pro-League quarters from the consideration that Manchuria was far away, that the United States and the Soviet Union, two of the Powers most vitally concerned in that part of the world, were not members of the League, which was essentially a European institution. The test of this optimistic fallacy was to come four years later in connection with the Abyssinian affair.

shaken by such events as the great inflation. There was in Germany a great reservoir of unfocused discontent combined with frustrated hope. Granted good times, the existing tensions might conceivably have gradually resolved themselves into a pattern of stability; the advent of crisis, particularly severe in Germany, not surprisingly brought to the surface these tensions. The German people did not have the long, slow, peaceful record of experience that the British had had in learning the practice of the art of self-government; they had not in the hard way as the French learned the lesson of the costs and risks of arbitrary rule, with the consequence of building up as in France perhaps a blind, but also a useful, resistance to encroachment by the executive power.

Imperial Germany, it might be said, had irresponsibly brought them to grief. But their defeat was too unique an experience against which stood a long record wherein the main associations were order, prosperity, and respected power. After 1815 it was not long in France before the Napoleonic star was ascendant, for all that France, unlike Germany, had had a chance to plant at home a Jacobin tradition. It is not necessary to have recourse to German fantasies of race in order to perceive the attraction of the strong state and the leader, to the people of Germany. The record of the war itself lent credit to the comfortingly complacent myth that defeat must have been the operation of accident and trickery. The voices that evoked the glory of the past, that promised to redress the wrongs inflicted by the crafty foreigner, found ready audience. How else could it have been?

Yet from what may be regarded a natural enough phenomenon in the German reaction to crisis, what conclusions to draw? The hadsome figure on horseback that had been general Boulanger in the eighties seemed for a time to have captured the popular imagination of France. Boulanger quickly evaporated. The picture of the Viennese would be painter, whose lip bore the hallmark of a famous comedian, seemed fitter object for the cartoonist's pen, even though the phrase *le ridicule tue* has no wide German currency. The patent trash of his lucubrations was clearly not the stuff of the sober business of governing the state. The response he evoked was mob appeal, but fickle is the mob; more sober men would know how to annex, tame, or divert, if they could not destroy, this fleeting aberration. Solid, conservative men, leaders in business, in politics, and in the army, thought so in Germany; the prospect did not seem improbable outside.

There were early voices of caution and there have been many retrospective analyses of the Nazi aberration of Germany, but the prevailing tone of the first years of the decade was rather one of unbelieving, if at times qualified by suspicion, scepticism. Had not the Nazis suffered a setback in the last 1932 election? Von Schleicher would know how to deal with the situation. The reaction abroad to his assumption of the German Chancellorship was generally a favorable one of hope.

Of the obscure murky intrigues that went on behind the scenes of German politics during the last months of 1932 and the first of 1933 the result alone need be mentioned here. The forthright German General von Schleicher, the Catholic nobleman von Papen, the exalted patriot Hitler could perhaps be better described by less attractive adjectives; between them they contrived the unexpected result that another stalwart, forthright, patriotic, honorable, and doubtless well-intentioned, man, President von Hindenburg, just recently reelected bulwark of the Republic, appointed Adolf Hitler Chancellor of Germany.

The early domestic record of the Nazi regime is too well known to warrant repetition. Briefly, it may be said to have duplicated the earlier Fascist one, with the difference that with a greater sense of urgency, with German thoroughness and ruthlessness, while some would say Italians are possessed of the opposite qualities, what Mussolini did in amateurish fashion in the course of four years, Hitler accomplished far more effectively in the space of the same number of months. Reichstag fire, Göring antics, Göbbels oratory and manoeuvres, elections, [73] outlawry of opposition, these were details by comparison with the main result accomplished. *Gleichschaltung* was the slogan; Germans must shed their divisions to replace them by common purpose, first for the liquidation of the current emergency, then for the greatness of the Reich, incidentally destined to thousand-year duration. This Hitler would accomplish, but clearly only if not hampered by the everlasting fetters of an impotent bickering Parliament. The Reichstag agreed: following the model of the Italian Parliament in 1922, another democracy, acting in accordance with the laws of its proper operation, signed its own death warrant in March, 1933.

5. THE WAVE OF THE FUTURE

What the significance of this act would be the future alone could reveal. That future is now known and it is not unfair to say that this was the emergence of something truly new. The similarities between Italian Fascism and more aptly named German National Socialism were patent from the beginning; but Russian Communism was generally thought of as the very antithesis of both. The large common element

[73] The election of March 5, 1933 was a highly interesting one and particularly significant in that it may be regarded as the last free consultation of the German people before the war. The democratic parties held their own in this election, both in terms of popular vote and of parliamentary representation; the Social Democrats received 7,000,000 and the Center 5,500,000 votes. The Communists lost 1,000,000 votes and their representation decreased form 100 to 81 members. The Nazis and the Nationalists joined forces for purposes of the election and between them obtained a majority of Reichstag seats, 340 out of 647. But while the Nationalist vote remained essentially unchanged, the Nazis made enormous strides, obtaining 17,000,000 votes; this represented an increase of some 5,500,000 over the preceding election.

of the three systems, that the word totalitarian expresses best, went for many years unperceived, at least by the popular consciousness. But that element has in the long term the greater significance, for all three systems are manifestations of a failure, best measured by the recoil from the wartime slogan, "to make the world safe for democracy." The nineteenth century democratic wave, after a misleading postwar surge, had begun to recede: rooted in the economic and political liberalism of the West, where it had slowly grown and matured, the democratic concept had been favorable indeed to the rising of the masses; but increasingly as one moved away from the Atlantic shore the rising had taken place in conditions that differed from the West European. Mass man having risen, clamoring for his rights, yet incapable of dealing with crisis through the ordely process of a British parliamentarianism, the totalitarian solution was *one* relatively simple response to the problem of how to keep society and the state functioning in conditions of order.

This is not saying that totalitarianism in the abstract is preferable, but merely to point out the fact of adaptation and response to circumstances. Therein lay the strength of these trans-Rhenish and transalpine systems that mere defeat in war has done little by itself to destroy. For good or ill, mostly for ill, the live forces of the day no longer seemed to reside in the stable, relatively contented, sluggish democracies of the West. [74]

The responsibilities assumed by the modern state, or foisted upon it, under all climates, are vastly different from what they were but yesterday. Not alone for the preservation of domestic order and the protection from outside aggression do men now look to the state, but rather more for the insurance of at least tolerable conditions of physical existence. When the delicate and intricate machinery of modern economy grinds to a halt or merely falters, to speak to the unemployed masses of the long term automatically regulating effect of supply and demand, of the "normal" alternating cycle of prosperity and depression, to

---

[74] This certainly applies to the period of the thirties, but the most significant development since then has been the course of the United States in two respects. First, the astonishingly successful operation of the American economy which has belied most forecasts; second, the no less remarkable reversal in the assumption by America of a role of leadership in world affairs; in neither respect can the adjective sluggish by any stretch of the imagination be used to describe America's performance. The consequence of this is that the issue has been more clearly joined at the present time, the United States and the Soviet Union representing the two poles of opposition. In view of the democratic nature of the American milieu, much hinges therefore on the continued successful operation of the American economy under its present form of modified capitalism and on the continued willingness of the American electorate to accept the responsibilities of power.

stress the merits of the laboriously slow process of education, is apt
for them to take the guise of insult compounded with the injury that the
individual feels is no fault of his own, as in fact it is not.   State
subsidies and doles are palliatives at best which for that matter an
impoverished state can ill afford. Broadly speaking, it might perhaps
be said that Russia, Italy, and Germany, to speak of major European
states alone, were, under the pressure of circumstances, groping for
solutions that the mere imitation of Britain, America, and France did
not seem to provide.

The fundamental revolution of our time was taking place beyond
the Rhine and the Alps. If Napoleon's dictum is true that a revolution
is an idea that has found bayonets, the central problem of the early
thirties was whether Germany would secure these bayonets — or their
more up-to-date equivalent, airplanes and tanks. The situation placed
an enormous responsibility upon France, so far prime keeper of the
order of Europe. Britain was of little assistance. Unable to perceive
how fundamentally she was in the same position as France vis-à-vis
the challengers of the existing order, Britain still thought in narrow
classical commercial terms; a revival of the German economy, be it
under Nazi auspices, was a desirable result, which in addition would
be of assistance to the improvement of Britain's own economy. Ideas,
especially abstract ideas in the domain of politics, must never be taken
too seriously, certainly by contrast with the concrete reality of trade.
Compounding this supposedly hard headed approach with the misguided sentimentality of well-intentioned fairness, German grievances,
so loudly voiced by Hitler, were in large measure either condoned in
Britain or viewed with sympathetic toleration. It was rather France
that had been the obstacle to the restoration of genuine peace, and in
so far as there was understanding of the French outlook it was the
sympathy one grants the sufferer of pathological obsession. At best
with gentleness, Britain would press on France the desirability of
further concessions.

America was of even less use than Britain. The suggestion that
America might have a common stake with Britain and France in the
preservation of the existing order would generally at this time have
evoked reactions ranging between resentment and disbelief. America
was very much wrapped up in her own economic crisis and at the end
of 1932 indulging with perhaps even more than customary gusto in the
antics of a presidential election. The slogan of more prosperous days,
"we planned it that way," came home to roost, and the long period of
postwar Republican rule came to an end. President Franklin Roosevelt
took office almost at the same time as Chancellor Hitler and, interestingly, the period of rule of the two men was destined to be almost
identical. They were to be the great opposing leaders in the great
drama of the following decade, but, if sound and brave words about
the virtues of international cooperation issued from Washington, the
new administration in effect showed itself to be dedicated to American

recovery somewhat regardless of the consequences to others. [75]   In so far as Nazi policies and rantings registered in America, the response was highly unsympathetic; but the mere suggestion of growing danger in Europe was added argument for not being naïvely sucked again into foreign quarrels, be their merits what they might.   The inescapable position of influence and power that was America's was by the American people understood not at all.   Their representatives, from whom greater perceptiveness might have been expected, reflected their mood with regrettable accuracy.

British and American neutrality, sympathy to a point, was clearly useful to the German effort to rehabilitate German power.   Just as it was wholly natural that France should stress action through collective agencies — to avoid her own isolation — so likewise it was the obvious tactics for Germany to try to deal with others on the basis of a bilateral approach — to avoid dealing with a coalition; what alliances or coalitions existed should therefore first be disrupted.   There was not in existence at this time any Anglo-Franco-American, or Atlantic as we should call it now, coalition.   If the basic community of interest among the three existed, the English-speaking part of the combination failed to perceive it; one need only consider how fantastic it would have been at this time for any one in responsible office in either Washington or London to proclaim that "our frontier is on the Rhine." [76]

France could hardly be deaf and insensitive to what was being said and felt across the Channel and beyond the Atlantic.   The British and American share of responsibility for the course of events that culminated in a new Armageddon is not light.   But granting this, the fact remains that France was the advanced bulwark, or first line of defense, of the existing system.   Taking a broad and long term view, it may be fair to say that the burden was too great a one for French power to carry, that the existing system was too divergent from existing reality, hence must sometime, somehow, be altered to take proper account of this reality. True as this is, the explanation is in a sense too simple.   If others had no special claim on France to keep order and peace for them, France too was of the system, in a sense its prime beneficiary, and she had responsibility to herself.

---

[75] The London Economic Conference met in 1933 as the result of American initiative, and one of its chief aims was the stabilization of currencies.   It was in large measure rendered futile by the simultaneous American decision to embark on currency manipulation at home.

[76] There were individual exceptions of which Sir Winston Churchill, who early grasped the nature of the Nazi danger and the desirability of close Anglo-French cooperation and of the support of French armed force, is the most outstanding.   But Churchill was a voice crying in the wilderness, and it is a measure of the British temper of the time that his warnings should have been one of the very arguments for his being looked upon as a brilliant, but also erratic and not dependable, not to say dangerous, guide of policy.

It is the purpose of the last chapter of this essay not only to look into the passing of the old system, but to observe the manner in which France surrendered her leadership, and worse, with it her own defense and safety. Once this was done, by 1936, the story thereafter to the formal outbreak of hostilities may be regarded largely as a postscript, the logical if not inevitable unfolding of consequences contained in germ in this French surrender.

Chapter VI

THE ABDICATION OF FRANCE

A considerable space of time will have to elapse before the proper place of Adolf Hitler in the roster of historic figures can be assessed with any reasonable confidence, or the role of the episode of Nazi Germany in finally encompassing the destruction of a world and of a way of life can be measured with any accuracy. From the German people Hitler had received the mandate to lift them out of their despondency. The man had faith, a faith that was in essence simple if hard to understand by those who thought that the course of twentieth century civilization was set along the path of essentially rational endeavor: the German people — no awkward questions to be asked that would pin the concept to precise definition — were possessed of superior endowment; their superiority entitled them to special rights, among them that to rule and organize inferior specimens of human kind.

The concept of superior race or chosen people was neither new nor original with the Germans; it is in fact rather common and ancient. But what was new about Nazi Germany was the assertion of the right to use force to make true the contention and carry into effect its utmost implications, be they the physical annihilation of others. So preposterous a fantasy, just because it was so preposterous, carried little conviction to reasonable minds, many of whom refused to acknowledge its possibility long after evidence had irrefutably accumulated that it was the actual policy of an existing state: the widespread disbelief of American troops until they physically entered Dachaus and Belsens is on record. This very scepticism was for long a valuable Nazi asset.

More concretely and immediately, Hitlerian rantings could not — again in the eyes of some people — form the basis of practicable policy. But in Hitler fanaticism was compounded with, and concealed by, much shrewdness. A clear program was set: before Germany could proceed to enforce world encompassing claims, she must have power; in order to have power, she must rid herself of the fetters that limited her freedom to create that power. The fetters in simplest form bore the name Treaty, better *Diktat,* of Versailles; they were maintained by the system, the French system, that had grown out of the peace settlements. The destruction of Versailles and of the French system was therefore the first preliminary aim of Nazi policy.

The method chosen of achieving this end was the only one possible: a frontal attack on the system would likely have revivified its vigor; therefore at first allay suspicion, capitalize upon existing differences, such as the Anglo-French, extract concessions through a skilful alternation of seeming reasonableness and threats, all the while appealing to the sense of fairness in others, meanwhile building up strength until the time was ripe for open challenge; not least, capitalize upon the fact that the democracies, not excluding the French, mainstay of the existing system, were truly peaceful, hence could safely be provoked to considerable lengths before they would react — if ever, or at least too late.

That Hitler was nightmare to France needs no explaining; but even in France the precise nature of happenings beyond the Rhine was wrapped in the baffling confusion of mystery. At most those who had always claimed that confidence in Germany was a chimera thought themselves justified. Yet the 30th of January to a degree brought some relief in France: the wilder expectations were belied; Germany had made no challenging gesture that called for the necessity of clear and immediate decision. There was time to think about the future, which meant in turn that French attention could remain largely focused on domestic concerns, pursuing the mean and uninspired game of divisive politics,[1] while the German experiment would unfold itself to give clearer indication of its true content and direction.

1. ITALY AND THE BALANCE OF POWER

But if France was at first largely passive, the advent of Hitler in Germany at the very least posed for Europe a very large question mark. So far, in this entire story, little mention of Italy has been made. This has been for the simple reason that, in the existing structure of Europe, the Italian role could not be an important one, owing to the limitations and the relative degree of Italian power. Britain, France, and Germany have overwhelmingly filled the picture up to this point. This was about to change. As ever, the Italian role can become significant, in fact disproportionate to the true relative measure of Italian power, when opportunity presents itself of altering the scales of fairly even balance.

No sudden accretion of power came to Italy at the beginning of 1933, but Mussolini, for all his bluster and bombast, for all that he has been with justice described as Sawdust Caesar, was devoid of neither intelligence nor of political sensitivity. For that matter he did no more

---

[1] After the fall of Herriot on the issue of the American debt, a brief interim during which Paul-Boncour filled the Prime Ministership and the foreign office was followed at the end of January by the formation of the first Daladier Cabinet, in which Paul-Boncour continued as Foreign Minister.

than continue to operate in the stream of the classical tradition of Italian foreign policy. To be sure, there was some favorable prejudice on his part toward German Nazism from the fact of the similarity between the new German ideology and the earlier Italian version of the same product. Besides, imitation is flattering. The relative sanity of Italian practice made easy the discount of wilder Nazi talk while turning a blind eye to the childish aspect of racial fantasies. Mistaken on this score like Britain, though not like Britain hampered by the immixture of sentiment in politics, Mussolini could analyze the European scene in simple and crude terms of power. A diminution of the French position, a corresponding increase of the German, seemed for Italy a desirable end. Beginning from this simple premise, of classical conception, Mussolini thought the occasion ripe to launch a new initiative. If the attempt ended in failure — at this time at least — it was nevertheless fraught with significance as measure of the fact that it was thought already possible to challenge the existing structure.

The occasion out of which grew, indirectly at least, the Italian initiative was the perennial of disarmament. To talk disarmament in 1933 may seem in retrospect wholly unrealistic; in fact it was. But two considerations must be borne in mind. One, the general state of opinion which, especially in the English-speaking countries, with a persistance amounting sometimes to blind faith, still put the cart of disarmament before the horse of security, while at the same time exaggerating the beneficial effects for an economy in crisis that would result from the reduction of armament expenditures. The other, of greater genuine relevance, stemmed from the fact of the new German regime which put a premium on the ending of tergiversation by facing all with a dilemma: either Germany would rearm with the consent of others, or else these must be prepared to take forcible action to prevent her rearming should she decide to take the law into her own hands. Clearly, no one could advocate a policy of letting her rearm *in defiance* of the verdict of others.

Here also, in the development of German policy, as in the case of Italy, there was consistency. The demand for *Gleichberechtigung* antedated the advent of Hitler; it had led to Germany's withdrawal from the disarmament discussions in September, 1932; when she returned to them in December, her claim had been recognized in principle "within a system that insures the security of all nations." This was the familiar language of diplomatic evasion, but it must fairly soon be clarified. The "constructive" French plan submitted by Herriot and Paul-Boncour in November was the concrete proposal under discussion at the moment of Hitler's advent in Germany. The details of technical discussions are secondary to the fact that more than ever France was bent on security first while Germany put equality foremost. [2] But what if Germany

---

[2] A German decree of February 24 allowing the enrolment of the S.A. (Nazi Brown Shirts or *Sturm Abteilungen*) and the *Stahlhelm* as auxiliary police naturally increased French fears and suspicion. The same applied

should violate the disarmament clauses of the peace? Clearly, nothing could be worse than failure to act in that event, a failure which would then be tantamount to putting a premium on illegality and force; the possibility of granting under pressure what had been refused to a more patient and reasonable German approach had also little to commend it. France had no doubt the physical means of suppression, and resolute action on her part would have commanded the support of her smaller allies; but such action would have placed her in a very invidious positions in the inevitable debate that would have ensued at Geneva around such issues as the applicability of the Locarno guarantee. British opinion at this time was to a large degree sympathetic to the German claim. [8]

The League or the Concert of Europe

The impasse into which the disarmament discussion had drifted had in it the danger of developments more serious than continued procrastination or renewed adjournment. In their anxiety to prevent the awkwardness of an open break, the British ministers, Ramsay MacDonald and Sir John Simon, arrived in Geneva at the beginning of March bearers of a new plan. This is where Italy came in.

As on many past occasions there was a good deal in common between the Italian and the British view: both were basically favorable to the restoration of full German equality, and not only in the limited field of arms. But where British opinion was deeply impregnated with the *mystique* of pacifism and the belief in the inherent evil of armaments, Fascism was not hampered by such limitations. Mussolini would grant that universal peace might be an attractive utopia of some distant future, but for him the concept did not correspond to any living reality of the moment: reality consisted of the world of states, as usual engaged in competition; arms and the use of force were not so much abstractly good or evil as the expression of the world that was and for long would continue to be. Geneva and all that it stood for, peace, democracy, christian love, represented at best misguided sentiment, of no validity in politics; at worst a useful but disingenuous tool that served the wealthy, "have" nations to wrap with the cloak of morality the preservation of their interests. Mussolini's espousal of revisionism, definitely voiced since 1928, may be regarded as the Fascist moral equivalent of the French insistence on the sanctity of treaties, of the British devotion to the respect for law.

---

to the occupation of the old army barracks at Kehl in the demilitarized zone; in this last case direct French pressure on Germany procured the immediate Nazi evacuation of Kehl. Both happenings pointed in the direction of preparation for unilateral German action in the event of failure to grant her demand for equality.

[8] For an analysis of the temper of British opinion, see *The History of the London Times*, vol. IV, pp. 881 ff.

In Fascist eyes, the trouble with the disarmament discussions, and the reason for their futility, was the simple one that they were conducted on a plane that did not have contact with the facts of the international situation, the true reality of which was power. The Italian approach was therefore simple, clear, and "realistic." Accept the fact of power first and from that then proceed to make adjustments: this done, the debate on disarmament would largely lose its meaning, in fact it would even be possible to come to some meaningful understanding for the limitation of arms that would have hope of being valid because freely consented to by all. Even the stalemated disarmament discussion might thereby thus be saved. [4]

In concrete terms, the air should first be cleared of false pretense: the foggy ideology of Geneva, the denial of the German claim to equal rights, the corresponding French attempt to maintain hegemony in Europe. Britain in the Italian view was a lesser problem, for her devotion to high moral purpose interfered little with a clear perception and pursuit of real and immediate interest. There were, in actual fact, four great European Powers, Britain, France, Germany and Italy — Russia was not European. [5] Between them they possessed the means, hence should, leaving aside the empty fiction of the equality of all nations, openly accept the responsibility for the organization of Europe. This could for the long term, though incidentally, be better guarantee of peace for all than the existing artificial structure; assuming "reasonable" aims of all, differences could be "reasonably " compromised. Even more, should one member of the ruling quadrumvirate display inordinate ambition, the effect would probably be its restraint within the inner circle of power by the automatic combination of the other members. This last consideration was highly relevant to the professed French fear of Germany: if they objected to French hegemony so-called, Britain and Italy had no interest or desire merely to replace it by German; France could therefore be assured of their support in the event of unwarranted German claims, let alone German aggression.

Such an approach is not to be lightly dismissed, or out of hand condemned on moral grounds alone. It did of course run counter to the whole spirit of that other experiment noble in purpose that was the League of Nations. The League was predicated on the assumption

---

[4] On the origin and initial motivation of the Four Power Pact, See the article by F. Jacomoni. "Il Patto a quattro" in *Rivista di studi politici internazionali,* Jan.-Mar., 1951.

[5] The omission of Russia is an interesting one. Despite the ideological difference between them, relations between Fascist Italy and Communist Russia were rather good than the opposite. Although it would be anticipating history to credit Mussolini with a clear perception of the Russian position of power that the Second World War was to produce, the fact remains that it was to take little more than a decade to bring about the emergence of the United States and of the Soviet Union as Powers in a class by themselves, putting the four European Powers of 1933 in an entirely different category.

— clearly denial of the facts, yet possibly of value like the one under-lying domestic democratic practice that leads to the simple rule of one man one vote — of the equality of nations large and small. If the French wish for safety was understandable, how long could deference to it be expected to keep Europe divided into unequal camps, victors and vanquished, armed and disarmed? France did not want hegemony *per se,* she merely claimed that she must enforce discrimination until a universal system could safely take its place. She was prolific of schemes for putting teeth into the League. Others who criticized her and doubted the authenticity of her contention — especially America and Britain where peace loving well-intentioned opinion was strong — might incidentally have tried the experiment of taking her at her professed word; this would of course have meant committing their own vast power to the upholding of the ideal of peace through the League.

But the fact was that all attempts to provide the League with effective power had so far failed, however one may wish to apportion the res-ponsibility for their failure, and the result was an indefinite perpetua-tion of a system patently based on inequality and discrimination, hence source of stress and invitation to challenge. If the ideal could not be attained, there might be value in being content with less perfect, more modest, ambition which, better suited to human limitations, would also have better prospect of practical effectiveness. The concept of a four Power directorate of Europe could be regarded a mere formalization of the old fashioned Concert of Europe, or even the post-Napoleonic Holy Alliance. From the standpoint of high Wilsonian hopes, of the prospect of hitching the battered wagon of the community of nations to the star of universal, lasting peace, this was a sad comedown. Yet, for all its shortcomings, the Concert of Europe had not served Europe ill during the century that ended in 1914. Why pretend that the League was universal when neither America nor Russia were among its members; why insist on its world encompassing function when Japan had just successfully defied its verdict? [6] Let Europe, if she could, be content with the organization of her own peace.

In retrospect, again, it may be said that the valid criticism of the Italian proposal lay not so much along the line of arguing that it injured the League. If the Concert of Europe had functioned with success during the nineteenth century, if what conflicts had occured had been of relatively brief duration and very circumscribed in scope, this result stemmed from the prior condition of a large area of consent in regard to the proper aims and functioning of power, reasonableness if one will. It is this condition that no longer existed: the aims of Nazi Germany

---

[6] It could well be argued that the Manchurian affair, as it had developed, with Japanese aggression successful *in spite of* League condemnation, re-presented a situation worse than the old fashioned power bargains. From the point of view of the victim itself, China in this case, there is little to be said for encouraging its resistance to aggression through an unjustified reliance on assistance which in the end remains purely verbal.

were not limited; [7] they were not circumscribed by any element of reason or of fairness, unless one grant the Nazi premise of German superiority with the consequences that Nazis drew from that premise.

Mussolini's Four Power Pact

The germ of the idea was present in a speech of Mussolini in 1932, on the occasion of the tenth anniversary of the advent of Fascism. Events since that speech, the advent of Hitler to power and the disarmament stalemate in Geneva, made the time seem propitious for putting it in concrete terms. Mussolini chose the occasion of the visit of the British ministers to Geneva for the purpose of keeping alive the disarmament discussion to invite them to Rome. What he suggested to them was both simple and brief, contained in six short articles, first draft of the Four Power treaty. The gist of it was this: the four Great Powers of Europe, Britain, France, Germany and Italy, would, jointly and on a basis of equality among them, insure the maintenance of Europe's peace.

This naturally implied the elimination of German disabilities and grievances. Germany would gradually achieve equality, and stress was put on article 19 of the League Covenant which provided for the revision of existing treaties. The four Powers would in common "induce" the acceptance by others of their decisions, and mention was also made of readjustments in the colonial field. It is of interest that the reaction of the British ministers was immediately favorable; they undertook to take up the proposal in Paris, where they did not encounter the opposition that might have been expected. [8]

For the forces that might have been expected to oppose the four Power proposal were considerable. Apart from the fact that the pact was essentially a denial of what the League stood for, hence would arouse suspicion in any pro-League quarters, there were two, distinct but closely related, logical sources of distrust. First, and generally, any revisionism could only be at the expense of the victors of the war; if there was no suggestion of tampering with the frontiers of France, the same was not the case where Poland and the Little Entente were concerned. The prospect of peace being preserved through joint pressure of the big four to "induce" others to accept their decisions inevitably

---

[7] The same might be said of the aims of Russian Communism, with the important qualification that they were very long term aims, rooted in an interpretation of history that did not call for Russian aggression at any particular time. The chief anxiety of the Soviet Union at this time was essentially defensive, and the preservation of peace seemed to it the more desirable condition. As to Italian Fascism, for all its common elements with Nazism, it was still at this time in what may be regarded as the stage of reasonableness.

[8] The greatest hesitancy came at first from Germany where it was feared that concessions to her might be too slow in being granted.

recalled the numerous past instances where the price of agreement among the Great Powers had been furnished by the smaller ones. From the point of view of the peace and good of Europe as a whole this might indeed be preferable to the outcome of Sarajevo, but such a view could hardly be expected to commend itself to the prospective victims. A loud and clear outcry was immediately forthcoming from the Little Entente. [9]

Secondly, and more concretely, the new dispensation was clearly also the denial of the system of alliances through which these countries were linked to France; it was in fact intended as a substitute for the French system. [10] For France herself the question posed itself thus: what guarantees of her security would she obtain to take the place of those that she possessed through the existing superiority of her arms and her alliances? If one took the position that the German demand for equal rights could not much longer be deferred, how effective would be the good will of Britain and of Italy in the event of need, or perhaps at what point would it become effective? One thing was certain, those countries would press upon France many concessions, among them probably the abandonment of her allies. Moreover, the Italian case became very weak at this point, for there was every reason to expect that Italy would soon resort to the exploitation of the restored European balance, in cruder terms to the gentle game of blackmail, for her own national advantage. Since there was little that could be offered her by Germany, France would be the logical objet of her demands. [11] The risks seemed far too great, and French acceptance of the Italian scheme too much in the nature of exchanging the substance for the shadow of security.

Voices were naturally raised in France to point out these things: advocates of *Realpolitik* of the Right, pro-Leaguers of the Left, though for entirely different reasons, could join in criticizing Mussolini's scheme. The outside pressure of the Little Entente, Polish and Belgian remonstrations, could hardly be ignored. Britain herself had second thoughts: she, too, held hostages to revision, the former German colonies for instance. In the end nothing came of the Italian scheme; for purposes of face saving, a Four Power Pact was initialed in Rome in June, but it was an instrument largely devoid of meaning, since it reaffirmed the *status quo* preserving clauses of the Covenant and

---

[9] For purposes of greater effectiveness the Little Entente had just reorganized itself, having set up in February a Permanent Council of its foreign ministers.

[10] "The Anglo-Roman system offers a premium to destroyers. It sanctions a regression, a return to the pure mechanism of brute force, an extinction of hope." Editorial in *L'Europe nouvelle*, March 25, 1933.

[11] It should be remembered that Italy had never abandoned the contention that she had not received from France the "adequate" colonial compensation provided for in the Treaty of London of 1915.

stressed that revision could indeed occur, but *only* in accordance with established procedures. [12]

The whole episode might be regarded as passing incident, an exercise in the normal routine of chancelleries; it was in fact soon largely forgotten. Yet its significance was considerable and its implications went deep, and it may also be regarded as an exercise in testing the existing relationships of power. Fascism, for all the mildness and reasonableness of its performance in action so far, did represent the dynamic of change by contrast with the reticent static of conservation; its support of Nazi Germany was in that context both natural and logical. But Italy alone had too little power and Germany so far had none in actual existence. Without the clear support of Britain there was no possibility of successful challenge of the power residing in the French system, so long at least as that power did not of its own accord choose to yield. Thus, the attempted challenge, if it had failed, stood as a warning, while the fact that the initial French reaction had been much less vigorous and clear than that of France's allies was calculated to raise doubts on their part. As in the case of Locarno, doubts lingered in Warsaw for instance about the reliability of French purpose. It was time for France to mend her fences, or at least to indulge in some clear thinking; the barometer of international politics was set to "change," a policy of drift risked being overtaken by events, the course of which might be much harder to control.

Yet drift was all that the weary shadow boxing of the disarmament debate that went on in Geneva, uninterrupted by the negotiations attending the Four Power Pact, represented. That story can be dealt with very briefly. In an effort to break the stalemate into which the discussion of the Herriot-Paul-Boncour plan had bogged down, Macdonald came forward in March with a more concrete scheme, the main feature of which was the setting at 200,000 of the standing armies of France, Germany, Italy and Poland. [13]

Though the German reaction was critical, in one of his early public pronouncements, on May 17, Hitler indicated his willingness to accept the principle of the MacDonald plan. Hitler's speech was generally regarded as conciliatory by foreign opinion; actually it may be viewed as one of the early steps in the game of cat and mouse that he played with such mastery and success for so long. The recipe, when analyzed in retrospect, was of the simplest: first create a *fait accompli,* be it

---

[12] The work of emasculation of the Four Power Pact was largely done by French diplomacy; instead of frontal opposition or refusal, France proposed alternative formulas which became the bases of discussion and were essentially embodied in the final draft.

[13] Germany was to achieve effective equality gradually over five years, and a permanent disarmament commission of control would be established. In addition there were provisions for the gradual elimination of military aviation and the banning of bombing, and a naval conference was to meet in 1935.

special legislation, repudiation of a treaty, later, seizure of territory; then, while opinion was still stunned and shocked by the boldness of the move, give it an excuse for failing to take counteraction by proclaiming in tones of utmost earnest and sincerity that the latest coup — incidentally forced by the unreasonable dilatoriness of others in granting some essentially reasonable German claim — was the last one, and that henceforth Germany had no further demands to make. [14] At this time, Hitler, still deprived of power, found it useful to cultivate the climate of confidence. On a note of relative optimism the disarmament discussions were adjourned from June to October.

When they resumed, it soon appeared that nothing had been settled: France now insisted on the prior establishment of effective controls of supervision before any German rearmament could be allowed. There was point to von Neurath's complaint that the earlier basis of agreement had been shifted, but Germany found herself without support at this point. [15] Cutting for good the Gordian knot, on October 14 Hitler sent a telegram to Henderson, president of the Disarmament Conference, announcing Germany's withdrawal from the discussions. Five days later, the further announcement was made that Germany withdrew from membership in the League as well.

Here was at last clarification: Germany would now take the law into her own hands. Her act did not of course by itself alter the existing structure of the European system; whatever instruments existed, Versailles, Locarno, and others were neither breached nor repudiated, though it might indeed be expected that their validity would soon be overtly challenged. [16] More than ever, France in particular was now faced with the necessity of making clear decisions; legalistic discussion would no longer suffice: either she must accept for Germany the lifting of restrictions, and on that basis possibly come with her to an understanding, or else she must be prepared to enforce the rights that the existing law made hers.

---

[14] This technique was particularly effective with British opinion, obsessed by the "injustices" that the peace had dealt Germany. The climax of it came with Munich, when the essential "reasonableness" of Germany's Sudeten claim was eagerly accepted in order to cling to the hope that "peace in our time" had truly been secured on the basis of Hitler's promises to Chamberlain.

[15] This was in part the result of her own activity during the summer. To a degree, outside opinion had been antagonized by the manifestations of the racial policy of the Reich (the complaint of Silesian Jews was before the League) and there had been in particular an Anglo-French rapprochement in the matter of disarmament procedure.

[16] German rearmament was in fact going on and had been for some time, though not yet at an alarming pace. On this point, see above, p. 218. n. 59. A German plebiscite on November 12 gave the not surprising result of 95 percent endorsement of the government's action in withdrawing from the Disarmament Conference and from the League.

2. The Confusion of France

But the totality of the French scene presented a picture that was one of anything but unity and resolution. Such a condition might not have mattered in a different place or at another time; it was less dangerous to others and in many respects more attractive, certainly more human and humane, than that of the strength derived from the dreary uniformity of willing or enforced consent across the Rhine. But France at this time was still the country that stood at the center of the power system of Europe and was its most important prop. The fact that this state of affairs placed upon French power a burden out of proportion to its capacity made all the greater the responsibility of France; divided counsels were a luxury that she could not afford, and the inaction to which irresolution led was to prove fatal, to France herself of course, but to the whole structure of Europe as well.

The roots and manifestations of French divisiveness are naturally to be observed in the domestic scene of France. That scene during the years from 1932 to 1936, those coinciding with the life of the legislature elected in the former one, would warrant a book by itself. No more than passing indications can be given here, but reference to them is essential for an understanding of events, which when their ripe fruit fell were on the whole received with unbelieving wonder by a world that had been inattentive to the process of erosion of its structure. France moreover, like Britain and America, operates in her politics under the democratic dispensation, a fact which lends added importance to the diversity of currents of opinion reflected in the end in governmental councils and decisions of policy — or the avoidance of decision.

The Depression in France

If diversity of opinion is one of the manifestations of freedom, hence worth quite a high price, some of the floundering that took place in France at this time loses in attractiveness what it may gain in plausibility. The seeming French immunity to the distress that most of the world was enduring was temporary delay rather than basic difference; in so far as there was pride in it, it was foolish pride, manifestation of deficient quality of economic understanding.

By 1933 it could no longer be said that the economy of France was operating at a normal level, let alone a prosperous one. The British devaluation of 1931 had been a severe blow which was countered by protective rather than by parallel measures: the device of quotas was peculiarly, if not exclusively, French. [17] In so far as the aim was to

---

[17] The initial attempt to impose duty surtaxes to compensate for the effect of cheapened currencies having led to international complications, quotas were resorted to in an effort to prevent an overlarge influx of goods from countries with devalued currencies.

protect the French market, it was successfully achieved; the result was also to maintain high the level of French prices, to deprive the French consumer of the benefit of lower prices, and to impede the sale of French products abroad. Producing interests were strong enough in France to obtain legislation favorable to their immediate ends. [18] The attempt to fix the price of wheat by legislation, measure of the political strength of agricultural interests in France, was such a dismal failure that it soon had to be abandoned. [19]

In 1933, America embarked on a new course with the advent of the Democratic administration of Franklin Roosevelt. Whatever the ultimate verdict on the quality of the economic thought of that administration, of its flexible willingness to experiment there can be little question. Impressed at once by the catastrophic decline of prices, especially raw material and agricultural prices, and by the dangers of uncoordinated currency manipulations, America indulged in the seemingly contradictory operations of promoting a Word Economic Conference in London, to be largely devoted to the subject of currency stabilization, and at the same time devaluing the dollar. In America too domestic necessity, or what is thought such, receives priority.

Independently of the merits of this (to others) starling performance, the fact of the devaluation of the dollar was obviously important to all. France by this time was coping with financial difficulties, natural consequences of the condition of her economy. Already for some time, the treasury surplus of the late twenties had been dissipated to give way to accumulating budgetary deficits. Gone was the day, short lived and passing, when gold had flown to France and when, as late as 1931, its accumulation in Paris had given France political possibilities of which she had failed to take advantage. The movement of gold began to be reversed in 1932 and by the end of 1933 was reaching disquieting proportions. [20]

How meet the economic and financial crises? Especially after the American action in respect to the dollar, with the gold bloc reduced to exigous dimensions, much could be said for bringing the franc in line with other major currencies. A few isolated individuals, such men as Paul Reynaud, adequately aware of the functioning of international economy and finance, understood and considered the possibility of currency manipulation done in the right manner and at the proper time. They had few followers in France where instead the overwhelming mass of opinion, at all levels of competence, remained blindly attached to the

---

[18] This might be compared to the raising of the American tariff in 1930, but American economic policy in other respects underwent a marked change with the inauguration of a new administration in 1933, whereas France continued on the path of traditional orthodoxy.

[19] The legislation was so contrived that, while failing to procure the wheat growers the legal price, it prevented a corresponding fall in the price of bread.

[20] 5,000,000,000 francs were lost during the last quarter of 1933.

preservation of the franc. The experience of the postwar devaluation had firmly anchored in the French mind the association of it with nothing but loss and swindle.

Nor did Keynesian ideas of massive governmental intervention, pump priming the economy, advocating the merit of deficits in times of low economic activity, such as found wide and sympathetic hearing in New Deal America, find much response in France; much devotion was professed instead to the virtues of a balanced budget. This was the problem that had confronted the Left upon its assumption of power eight years earlier and brought about its downfall. His fingers burned on that occasion, Herriot yielded power with little reluctance in December, 1932. But in other respects the situation was now wholly different from that of 1924, for France was caught in a crisis the control of which was largely outside her hands instead of being about to enter the era of expanding prosperity characteristic of the second half of the twenties. Barring such radical measures as a capital levy, that only few advocated in any event, the time seemed not propitious for increased taxation.

Reduced expenditures were the alternative, and the financial policy of France, now and for some years to come, was generally one of deflation. But cutting government expenditures always comes hard in politics, particularly for the Left, a substantial portion of whose clientele consisted of those very government employees destined to be the victims of financial soundness. [21] The result was hedging compromise that combined the timidity of deflation with the disadvantage of unbalanced budgets, while French prices were on the whole maintained, to find themselves out of line with those of the rest of the world. The stagnation of the French economy was destined to continue during the rest of the decade.

These indecisions of the government majority of the Left lay at the root of ministerial crises that merely furnished evidence of persisting impotence. After the fall of Herriot in December, Paul-Boncour lasted through the following January; Daladier, his successor, managed to survive during the major part of 1933, when Sarraut followed him for a month, then Chautemps for two more. When Daladier appeared once more at the head of the government at the end of January, 1934 the scene was set for more far reaching crisis.

The Malaise of France and the Impact of Foreign Ideologies

For a profound malaise was at work in the body politic and social of France. Daladier, Sarraut, Chautemps were all members of the Radical Socialist party. This may be regarded as in a sense both

---

[21] The class of governmental employees was very large in France, considering that it included such categories as the communication workers (post office, telegraph and telephone) and the whole educational system. The railway system and utilities had not yet been nationalized at this time.

appropriate and symbolic of the condition of France in the thirties. The Radical Socialists were the nearest embodiment existing of the dominant tone and quality of the Third Republic; to a considerable degree they harked back to the values and issues of pre-1914 — the religious quarrel for instance — now largely superseded and displaced in their importance by the stress of changed economic conditions. The Radical Socialists were apt representatives of the basic conservatism, backwardness if one will, of a nation to which much of the modern world appeared as an unpleasant, insufficiently understood, burden. The principles of 1789, the Rights of Man, were valid values that in some respects more than ever needed defending, but the defense of them must be in terms of the conditions of the modern world. The apprehension of these came but slowly and gave rise to internal stresses in the Radical Socialist group. The proceedings of the Radical Congress held at Vichy in October reflected these divergences [22] as well as the rivalry between the old and the new leadership that centered around the personalities of Herriot and Daladier. Neither provided effective or adequate leadership.

The crisis of the Socialist party, the other bulwark of the Left, was far more serious and severe, for it amounted to a growing cleavage between the rank and file, the *militants,* and the parliamentary group; [23] within the latter the temptation was strong to share in the actual responsibility of government. The leader, Léon Blum, in some respects better suited to the debate of abstract principle or literary issues than to rough politics, yet managed to hold the party together: with reservations and reluctance it supported the Radical ministries though allowing them on occasion to fall and be replaced by indistinguishable new combinations. There was considerable rethinking in the Socialist fold on the score of the suitability of time-worn slogans and interpretations to circumstances the unforeseen novelty of which it was increasingly less easy to ignore. If the French structure, political and social, seemed remarkably unaffected by the aftermath of the war, the same was clearly not the case across the Rhine and beyond the Alps, where the very name National Socialism betokened an approach that was new as well as confused. Some impact from this was felt in the ranks of French Socialism where one finds a Déat willing to deal with Hitler, a Marquet not unsympathetic to Mussolini. [24] Some of this may be credited to personal idiosyncrasy or ambition; the schism of the neo-Socialist group in 1933, though in practical terms of politics of minor importance at the time, was none the less symbolic of confused stirrings and divided counsels among the followers of Marx in France.

---

[22] See *L'Europe nouvelle,* Oct. 14, 1933.

[23] This was the result of the electoral system of France. The massive support of Socialism was to be found in limited areas, such as the mining region of the North, but, as a result of electoral combinations, many Socialist deputies were elected with the support of more conservative Radical votes.

[24] Both Déat and Marquet had a chance to put these early propensities to effective use during the episode of the Vichy regime.

Fascists and Nazis, especially the latter, were ostensibly anti-Marxist with enthusiasm, even if not averse in practice to stealing some leaves from the Marxist book. But the role of Moscow, Rome of the Communist faith, was a turbid one. Especially until the actual advent of Hitler to power, and for all the enthusiasm with which Nazis would break German Communist skulls, Russian Communism, too literally believing its own Bible, focused on that aspect of Nazism which stressed its eagerness to destroy Weimar. Since, in effect, the demise of the Weimar Republic, in the Communist book again, would be a step on the road to world revolution, that consummation could be contemplated with equanimity in Moscow; the result was that the German Communists, refusing to cooperate with the defenders of the Weimar Republic, in practice served the Nazi purpose. Without considering the little known details of the murky and tortuous record of the Kremlin's, [25] or the Commintern's, policy before, during and after 1933, its operation could not but add to the confusion of the French scene.

If some aspects of Russian policy may seem detrimental to the success of its appeal in France, compensating factors were favorable to it. The obvious inability to deal with economic crisis had the logical consequence of turning men's attention to other available nostrums. These were the days of technocrats, but their particular approach, so widely discussed in the United States, commanded relatively little attention in France. If it came to planning and directing the economy, the Russian example had a longer standing claim to attention. The fact that Russia was wrapped in considerable mystery and was relatively inaccessible to outsiders served to increase in many minds the aura of prestige surrounding five year plans, the accomplishments of which, on order or on hand, received far more attention and publicity than the fate of Ukrainian kulaks and the horrors of widespread policy-induced starvation.

Communism has never recoiled from violence, in which respect it differed from much of the Left. It is among this Left, particularly in the Socialist fold, that the recoil from the horrors of war translated itself into the attraction of pacifism. [26] For a long time the refusal to fight was encouraged by Communists in France: it could serve to weaken the morale of the French army, prime tool of the capitalist state most responsible for the preservation of the order that the Soviets regarded as inimical to themselves. This was to work in fertile ground,

---

[25] As a state among states, and for immediate purposes, the Soviet Union had adopted a policy of hedging. Having decided to place greater stress on internal development, "socialism in one country," than on world revolution — not abandoned indeed but put off to some indefinite future — Stalin was cultivating relations with the various capitalist states: in 1929 a non-aggression pact had been concluded with France, but even the advent of Hitler did not prevent a renewal of the Russo-German treaty of 1926.

[26] The vogue of pacifism was by no means a peculiarly French phenomenon; it was in fact much deeper in Britain for example, as witnessed by the curious episode of the Oxford Oath.

for the tradition of anti-militarism has old and respectable roots in France, traceable long before 1914.

There is point to registering also — a phenomenon that would warrant a study of its own — the influence of the system of education, especially at the elementary level. In overwhelming measure the French *instituteur* was a devotee of the Left, often doctrinaire and not seldom of the extreme variety. [27] The freedom, or licence, characteristic of the French milieu, did little to impede the inculcation of his doctrine. The struggle that might seem out of date between *instituteur* and *curé*, rallying foci of antagonistic factions, was still characteristic of the life of many a French village.

The divisions, uncertainties and unresolved confusion of what may be broadly described as the French Left [28] were of particular significance since the Left, or a part of it, was in power. Greater unity might be looked for on the Right, yet this was not the case. The Right might be consistently in favor of sound finance and a forceful policy toward Germany, but at this time not a little division prevailed among its ranks as well. In matters economic and financial French business and financial interests may be described not so much as conservative as unenlightened; [29] by contrast with their American counterpart for instance, who are conservative enough in terms of political categories, their reluctance to expand, take risks, try novel methods, is a striking phenomenon. The devotion to sound state finance goes unaccompanied by willingness to bear the burden of direct taxation. In matters of foreign policy the French Right reacted in the manner that might be expected, and to it the advent of Hitler was proof that it had been correct in its estimate of France's eastern neighbor.

But the discontent and malaise of which the failure of leadership was at once cause and effect found reflection in the Right as well as in the Left. It was no novelty for French conservatives to claim that

---

[27] To a degree, this was a legacy of the older fight to establish the Republic securely. Its defenders had a perfectly correct appreciation of the importance of capturing the mind of the young, and the tradition of anti-militarism and anti-clericalism, so important in their own makeup and experience, thus tended to perpetuate itself. The impact of this republican indoctrination was much less considerable at the upper levels of society and of education. Mention might be made at this point of the very considerable influence of the teacher-philosopher Alain, to an analysis of whom a special issue of *La Nouvelle Revue Française* has recently been dedicated, *Hommage à Alain* (Paris, 1952).

[28] The broad division between Right and Left is a convenient one and has validity; a better characterization of the basic cleavage is implied in the terminology of François Goguel, *parti de l'Ordre* and *parti du Mouvement*. In the actual practice of politics, shading is more delicate and one could well speak of Right, Center, and Left. Nevertheless, and especially for electoral purposes, the basic cleavage between Right and Left, Order and Movement (or change) tends to reassert itself.

[29] There are naturally qualifications to this, but the generalization is valid as descriptive of the prevaling tone. That is one of the reasons for the very different quality of relations between labor and capital in France on the one hand, in America and Britain on the other.

the Republic was incompetent: present conditions were simply one
more proof of the fact. This did not mean a renascence of royalism,
irretrievably dead, though the *Action française,* from the quality of
intellect that it gathered, carried an influence wider than the insignificant
number of its adherents would indicate. But the stress on the values
of order and authority by contrast with the looseness of the libertarian
republic could be asserted with seemingly renewed justification. One
need not be pro-German or pro-Italian, quite possibly in fact the
opposite, to argue that from the point of view of their own respective
national advantages Mussolini and Hitler were on the right path. The
very danger they represented to France was argument for the strengthening of France, and this could best be done by emphasizing order,
authority and discipline, the older values, as was being done across the
Rhine and the Alps, instead of entrusting the country's safety to the
inconclusive gabble of the *Palais Bourbon.* Anti-parliamentarianism,
again no novelty, tended to reappear in France, as usual mainly recruited from the ranks of the Right.

Here again there was old precedent to draw upon in France, where
ligues have repeatedly appeared upon the scene. Without harking back
to the wars of religion or the Fronde, the *Ligue des Patriotes* had been
contemporaneous with Déroulède and Boulanger, and even during the
twenties a rather feeble essay of the same nature was that of the
Jeunesses patriotes. The *ligues* of the thirties were of greater significance. A *ligue* in France is not a political party, rather a movement
for the purpose of arousing opinion and pressing for some action; it
is a symptom of dissatisfaction with the operation of the body politic.
This is the time when *Jeunesses patriotes, Solidarité française,* and
Croix-de-feu were making their greatest impression. The last named,
under the leadership of Colonel de la Rocque, achieved the greatest
fame.

De la Rocque had some points in common with General Boulanger.
A military man, for all the scorn he poured on the chatterers in Parliament, his most significant assets were personality and talk; of ca-
pability for action little evidence was ever forthcoming form him. In
fact, the threat that the *Croix-de-feu* and their compeers constituted to
the existing institutions was never very serious, though their very existence
and the noise that they made unduly magnified the danger. This was
particularly the case where the Left was concerned, and the later phenomenon of the Popular Front was at least in part the creation of
its imagined fears. Program and methods of the *Croix-de-feu* were
none the less revealing; the charge that their general tendency was
Fascist on the whole is warranted, provided one remember that they
were also patriotic French. Recruited on the Right, they had nevertheless awareness of the social problem: they wanted national unity
and recognition of the workers' interest, though frowning on the divisive
methods of the class struggle, but beyond this little precision was to be
found in their specifications. As to their action, though it never passed
the stage of rehearsal, it showed at least awareness of modern methods:

the importance of propaganda, salesmanship, they understood as well as the use of posters, the striking value of large rallies gathered together with efficiency and expedition. The significance of the *ligues* was mainly as symbol of the dissatisfaction that pervaded the country. Their recruits naturally tended to be among the young.

If the structure of France had shown remarkable imperviousness to change, the impact of war had been profound on the generation which had come of age just before, during, and immediately after its occurrence. The ranks of this youth had been decimated, with the result, incalculable of precise calculation, of leaving great gaps in the personnel that would normally have been rising to leadership during the decade of the thirties. The consequences of the fact that France is normally a gerontocracy were thereby accentuated, but there was much soul searching and thinking among the younger survivors of the war.

The carriers and originators of ideas are ever relatively few in numbers, but their role is always considerable, particularly in a country like France where the intellect rates high standing. It would be relevant at this point to examine the state of French culture as a whole. This would take us along fascinating bypaths but also into fields too broad for adequate consideration in this treatment. This may be said: if there was relative decline in the French standing in at least some fields of scientific endeavor, and if reliable assessment of the quality of artistic and literary accomplishment must await further passage of time, there was no lessened restlessness, vigor, and interest in the discussion of ideas. The younger war generation, now approaching the time for the filling of places of responsibility and leadership, had not been unaware of a changing world. [30] The result of this intense activity and searching, conducted in the main by men of good will and honesty of purpose, was in the final reckoning added division, and through division contribution to ultimate disaster. No coherent basis of agreement emerged from the turmoil of discussion, and by the early thirties the recognition was already dawning on the searchers that their efforts were futile ; [31] they went from there on their increasingly divergent ways, some of them eventually landing in the most unexpected places. [32]

---

[30] The result of this activity is best reflected in literary production, and one of its most valuable manifestations is the proliferation of reviews and magazines, many of them short lived, of the period. The *Nouvelle Revue Française* and *Esprit* are outstanding, but more transitory creations such as *L'Ordre nouveau, Plans, La Troisième Force*, Bergery's *La Flèche*, among a host of others, deserve citation. Many of the writers were *engagés* long before that post-Second World War term came into use, witness men like Montherlant, Drieu la Rochelle, Gide, Bernanos, Giraudoux, to take some names at random. Among a considerable literature, relevant to this point, may be cited the collection of essays published by Daniel-Rops, *Les années tournantes* (Paris, 1932).

[31] See, for instance, an interesting analysis in *L'Europe nouvelle*, Sept. 2, 1933, under the title, "Une génération en quête de discipline; de l'inquiétude à la décision."

[32] The line of development is easy to trace that led some of these men, e.g., Montherlant, Drieu la Rochelle, in the camp of collaboration with the Nazis after the collapse of 1940. But it would be altogether misleading

The most significant aspect of this state of affairs was the ultimate sterility of its outcome. If the French mind, collectively, displayed no diminution of its agility and liveliness, it failed nevertheless to produce solutions that attracted widespread and enthusiastic adherence within its own milieu. As in Britain in some respects, the prevailing climate of a system that was too old, successful, and tired, seemed inimical to the easy acceptance of bold innovation. Certain it is that neither France nor Britain at this time offered a picture of leadership in political ideas that would attract imitation by others. Such leadership, however for other reasons unattractive, came from elsewhere. Both Germany and Russia were the homes of ideas, or ideologies, which, whatever else may be said about them, were lacking in neither vigor, determination, nor self-confidence.

The label "made in Germany" tends to arouse in France suspicion; yet there were those in France, as already mentioned, who could see good in the Nazi stress on authority; they came from a variety of quarters. The stagnant state of the economy, that timid measures of hesitant orthodoxy failed to revive, was a natural boost to nostrums from Moscow, whose extensively publicized experiment of five year plans attracted wide attention. [33] The appeal of economic promise to unemployed and partially employed needs little explaining, but among intellectuals, mainly of the Left, there was not a little eyeing with sympathy of the Soviet experiment. This was by no means the case in France alone; those were the days when Soviet stock was high among those everywhere who thought of the Liberal label as being rightfully their own; in France there was to a greater degree perhaps the feeling of despair in the ability of the existing system to deal with current ills. [34]

To a degree, though only to a degree, there occurred in France the same phenomenon that has occured in other times and places, most recently and fatally in neighboring Germany. The extreme Left, the Communists, and some elements of the traditionally conservative Right joined in berating and belittling the ineffectiveness of the parliamentary

---

to charge them with active and conscious pro-Germanism at this time. On the score of French opinion in regard to Germany two useful books may be cited: Jean-Marie Carré, *Les écrivains français et le mirage allemand* (Paris, 1947), and Charles Micaud, *The French Right and Nazi Germany, 1933-1939: a study of public opinion* (Durham, N.C., 1943).

[33] For all the dearth of accurate knowledge about conditions in the Soviet Union, the inauguration of the five year plans in 1928 undeniably launched it on the path to becoming a major industrial state.

[34] The experiment of the American New Deal attracted less attention in France. Apart from the fact that France is not possessed of the resources of America, there was the added consideration that America was still floundering in deep depression, and the philosophy of the New Deal, if one may use such a phrase, was wrapped in not a little confusion. Also, the American action at the time of the London Economic Conference hardly served to enhance American prestige and influence. In America, too, for that matter, there was not a little sympathetic interest in the Soviet experiment and in the idea of economic planning on the part of New Dealers and Liberals generally.

institution. This was an inauspicious moment for Parliament to furnish concrete grounds for the charges brought against it.

The 6th of February 1934

To the American reader, a measure of corruption in politics, more specifically the improper use of the privilege of political power to shield financial malfeasance, should be neither startling nor difficult to understand. Such imperfections, resulting from the deficient supervision of human failings, call for redress but are not generally considered adequate warrant for advocating the overthrow of the system of government. The leaders of the Third Republic have on the whole been honorable men, but there exists a twilight zone where at a third or fourth remove contact becomes established with some of the less savory manipulators of the underworld of finance. The record of the Third Republic is studded with a series of politico-financial scandals, of which the Panama affair of the nineties is perhaps the best known. Another such affair was to break at this time; the confused circumstances of the moment and the accumulated tensions of the French milieu were destined to give it importance and significance, both immediate and actual, as well as symbolic, to an unusual degree.

Alexander Stavisky was one of many Central European Jews to whom the leniency of French practice had furnished opportunities once established in France. The details of his activity need not detain us; it will suffice to say that his large scale financial legerdemain came to light late in 1933. [35] The fact, now publicly revealed, that his manipulations could hardly have occurred without the connivance of the mayor of Bayonne, who was in addition a Radical Socialist deputy, and that a long record of familiarity with the police had neither interfered with Stavisky's personal freedom nor with his ability to pursue the course of his operations, had in it the makings of a succulent scandal most suitable to exploitation by the press. So it was, and the Stavisky revelations were big headlines at the beginning of 1934. The affair was not devoid of musical comedy elements, fit objects for the wit of *chansonniers,* but when the missing Stavisky was found by the police in Chamonix with a bullet through his head, large sections of the public were willing to believe that he had been "suicided" in an effort to put an end to a widening circle of implications.

These were indeed far reaching: [36] they were the bases of wild charges in the Chamber where anti-semitism and xenophobia were

---

[35] The specific occasion was the failure to redeem municipal bonds of the city of Bayonne, the proceeds of which had been appropriated by Stavisky. This was only the last and most sensational of a series of financial misdeeds.

[36] One of Stavisky's lawyers had been the brother of Prime Minister Chautemps.

mixed with attacks on Radical freemasonry in corrupt control of Parliament. Some of these charges were echoed outside the walls of the *Palais Bourbon*; the streets of Paris resounded to the cry *à bas les voleurs*! taken up with gusto by *Camelots* and parading hotheads, sometimes abetted by well-intentioned, outraged, but uninformed citizens. Toward this agitation the police was markedly lenient, a fact interpreted by some as indication of the personal predilections of their chief, Jean Chiappe.

The tradition is old in France, especially in Paris, of political street agitation, and by now the affair had developed into an all out contest between Right and Left, the former sensing an opportunity, the latter suspecting an unwarranted exploitation of this same opportunity, and for that reason tending to rally to the defense of the existing government. However, after some hesitation, judging the situation untenable, Chautemps resigned. But no basic change of control ensued; the new Prime Minister, Daladier once more, was personally unimpeachable but still represented Radical leadership. His Cabinet was due to appear before the Chamber on February 6.

The choice of Daladier was not of the most fortunate, largely for reasons of his personality. He set about cleaning the mess that he had inherited, but one of his first moves, the dismissal of Chiappe, merely served to aggravate the tension both within and outside Parliament; rumours and accusations were freely passed that a coup was being contemplated by the government, [37] and street agitation increased rather than abated. While the deputies were in session on the afternoon of the 6th of February, demonstrators mainly recruited from such organizations as the *Jeunesses patriotes* and the *Solidarité Française*, as well as from those of ex-servicemen, were by prearrangement gathering across the Seine in the Place de la Concorde. The normal addition of the merely idle and curious and of homecoming office workers helped to fill the vast square with a large mob. As will happen at times on such occasions, an insufficient cordon of police, barring access to the bridge and the Chamber, yielded to the enervating strain of persistent provocation and baiting and finally resorted to the use of arms. A few people were killed and some others injured, and the cry of the mob changed from *voleurs!* to *assassins!* Again, later at night, there were a few more casualties.

---

[37] The ambitious and energetic Frot was charged with this intention as well as with being the real driving force behind Daladier. Daladier's dismissal of Chiappe, taken by Chiappe as well as by opinion, to be in the nature of a reprimand, had in it an element of ambiguity since he was offered the Residency of Morocco.

Daladier was also guilty of a markedly deficient sense of humor. The performance of Shakespeare's *Coriolanus* at the *Comédie Française* during January had been used as the occasion for anti-democratic demonstrations. The director of the *Comédie Française* was dismissed and replaced by, of all people, the head of the *Sûreté Générale*.

No one had quite planned it that way, but the accident of circumstances gave them a new and unexpected turn. There is no evidence whatever that the demonstrators had any plan beyond the venting of their displeasure against the corrupt representatives in the Chamber; the later charge that this was a Fascist plot has no more foundation than the fantastic accusation that the government deliberately ordered patriotic Frenchmen to be massacred. The episode was a passing outburst of fever in the body politic, but the consequences of it, now that blood had been spilt, were considerable, both in their immediate concrete sequel and in symbolic terms.

However wild and unfounded the reciprocal charges, these were freely made and they received considerable credence. In order to perceive its true significance, the episode must be set against the background of the historic French tradition of Parisian revolutions on the one hand, of the restlessness of Europe as a whole on the other. As to the first aspect, there was considerable exacerbation and a marked sharpening of the political and social cleavage of France. The Left, alarmed, recalled other occasions when the Republic had been threatened by the agitation of the street and proceeded to close its ranks, endeavoring to forget and minimize its own internecine quarrels. The 6th of February may be regarded as the catalytic act that finally precipitated the birth of the Popular Front; [38] on the opposite side of the political fence, the possibilities appeared to some, though only after the event, that were contained in the occasion. [39]

The government was in a quandary and its counsels divided. Needless to say, opinion and the press were highly agitated and gave vent to violent partisan feeling. In the end, Daladier, not a resolute man despite his reputation, yielded to the moderate advice which took the position that, apart from rights and wrongs, his continued tenure of office would tend to exacerbate existing divisions when what the country needed was cohesion and calm. Daladier resigned and the crisis was resolved by an appeal to the neutral personality of ex-President Doumergue, who agreed to come out of his retirement and organized a union ministry of sorts.

---

[38] Here also the element of irony is not absent, for among the most enthusiastic promoters of the Popular Front were the Communists. They even claimed credit for having organized anti-Fascist demonstrations on the 6th of February when the simple truth was that they, like others were caught totally unprepared by the turn of events to the extent that Communist ex-servicemen were part of the demonstrating mob on the Place de la Concorde. Credit must be given the French Communist leadership, however, for its alertness in recognizing the possibilities of exploiting the situation.

[39] Interestingly enough, the *Croix-de-Feu*, best known of those groups with Fascist tendencies, did not participate in the rioting of February 6. They had gathered on the left bank of the river, on the opposite side of the *Palais Bourbon* from the Place de la Concorde. Their intervention was feared, and might indeed have brought the mob into the Chamber, but they remained inactive, and certainly Colonel de la Rocque had made no preparations aiming at a political coup.

Outwardly, the constitutional crisis, if there had been one, was surmounted in classical fashion, and the whole episode would not have received the space given it here did it not mark a turning point in this story. Elderly, easygoing *papa* Doumergue represented a conservative devotion to the old Republic, but as a man Doumergue was not a replica of either Clemenceau or Poincaré. The cleavage of opinion, of which the events just recounted were a manifestation, was not healed. Even though there had been no master mind or master plan behind the 6th of February, the feeling rankled in the Left that the Right had with success made use of the weapon of the Street to rob it in Parliament of its rightful control. [40] It is *after* the 6th of February and not before that the *Croix-de-feu* and other Rightist groups knew their best days and that, correspondingly, the Left closed ranks in the Popular Front; but the results of this in politics were not clearly sanctioned until another general election two years later.

Meanwhile, division and confusion continued to increase, a condition to which the international situation contributed. Traditionally, the Right has asserted a prior claim to the monopoly of patriotic feeling; it also represented the interests of property. Its predilection in matters economic and financial was for what were regarded as orthodox methods, sound money, balanced budgets, and deflation; this was the way to make France strong in the face of external danger, not least the German. There was no Russian danger, militarily, but the persistence — in France the accentuation — of economic crisis gave weight to the Russian danger, ideologically. The Nazis proved themselves skilled salesmen, both at home and abroad, in presenting themselves as the saviors of civilization against the Red peril. The French Right was not pro-German, but the charge that it could contemplate with equanimity, even with sympathy, some aspects at least of the Nazi contention, if often exaggerated, is not devoid of foundation. Specific cases might be mentioned of individual Frenchmen who went a very long distance in convincing themselves, and even trying to convince their fellow countrymen, that Hitler was at bottom a reasonable man with whom one could come to an understanding. [41] They are revealing and significant, but chiefly of the fact that confusion was penetrating the traditionally nationalistic Right.

---

[40] As pointed out before, while the broad distinction between Right and Left is valid, in actual practice the orientation of the government tends to be settled by the decision of what may be loosely called the Center. This group, in which the tendency to climb on the band-wagon is strong, or enough of it, will throw its weight on one side or the other, thereby deciding the color of the government. This makes at once for ministerial instability and for continuity of policy.

[41] An early example is the case of his interview with Hitler published by Fernand de Brinon in the *Matin* in November, 1933. De Brinon had been, and continued to be, a consistent Germanophile. Yet it is interesting to consider that the article was published with the approval of Daladier, a fact which may be cited as an illustration of the confusion prevailing in France.

On the opposite side of the political fence, it was on the Left that traditionally one found the international outlook. It was that Left which had supported Briand's policy of reconciliation with Germany, and even to a point accepted the explanation that the Nazi phenomenon was at least in part due to the failure to treat with greater generosity the Germany of Weimar. To the French Left, Nazism could not but be anathema; once Moscow had become convinced that Nazi Germany meant real danger, and accordingly issued new instructions to its followers abroad, the whole French Left to its farthest extreme could once again pick up with unanimity and conviction the patriotic component of the old Jacobin tradition. One might see here a comedy of errors, for rather than become united on the common national ground, Frenchmen were effectively confused and divided by contending interpretations of the national interest, the while throwing increasingly bitter accusations at each other, ranging the length of treasonable bent. [42] The expression is old in France *travailler pour le roi de Prusse,* though *faire les affaires du Tsar* has never gained currency. In this division of feelings and counsels must be seen added manifestation of the fact, previously mentioned, that the active forces of the time came not from the Western democracies, France for one, but from beyond the Rhine and the farther Vistula.

These complicated, sometimes petty, internecine quarrels had consequences far beyond the range of the local, or even merely French, complex in which they occurred; that is the reason why the internal condition and climate of France has been considered at some length. For the system of power relationships under which Europe had functioned for more than a decade was the French system. If, outwardly, the system still existed, forces were rising to question its validity and effectiveness; this last named attribute largely depended on the conditions of the French milieu. Not only its physical conditions, the state of its economy, finances and armed forces, but quite as much upon its moral and psychological state. In other words, what would French policy be in the troubled and fast altering state of Europe?

---

[42] Of actual treasonableness there may have been a certain amount, then and later, but that aspect of the matter is secondary and relatively insignificant by comparison with the much more fundamental, because deeper rooted, factor of divided confusion in the body politic as a whole, and within the separate sections of it. The case of the Radical Socialists is especially significant; that party was traditionally tne most authentic representative of the middle-of-the-road Third Republic which it had played a very large role in shaping and directing. Its natural instinct and affiliation lay with the Left, but in many respects it was attracted to conservative practice; the stresses to which circumstances subjected it were reflected in inner divisions and a resulting loss of influence. After the 1936 election it had to yield place to the Socialists as the core of Left leadership.

3. CAN FRANCE MAINTAIN THE STATUS QUO?

The indications of unrest and questioning were not lacking. Two may be cited as good illustrations of the state of things, which had their centers in Vienna and Warsaw, respectively. Events in Germany could not but have important repercussions in Austria, where their impact had divergent effects. Needless to say, there were Nazis in Austria; their connection with their German compeers and the record of German intrigues and interference need not detain us here. From the internal Austrian point of view the question was: would Austria preserve her independence and what forces would work to that end? Austrian Socialists, especially in view of the treatment meted Socialists across the German border, could be counted on to show little enthusiasm for their own destruction, which is what an *Anschluss* would have meant. However, by 1934, under the leadership of Chancellor Dollfuss, Austria's was in effect a semi-dictatorial regime with marked conservative and clerical leanings. Chancellor Dollfuss was dedicated to the preservation of his country's independence, but some of his supporters, specifically the *Heimwehr*, [43] were equally dedicated to the suppression of the Socialist influence. They had their way; but not until, after persistent provocation, the alarmed Socialists resorted to the use of arms in their defense. For a few days, around mid-February, there was virtual civil war in Austria. [44] Socialism was thoroughly defeated and Chancellor Dollfuss was confirmed in power, now free to mold his Austria along the lines of his own Christian predilection and of the Mussolinian corporative model. [45] Also, on February 17, a joint declaration was issued by Britain, France, and Italy reasserting their support of Austria's independence. In the nature of a warning to Germany, the precise value of this somewhat platitudinous declaration was uncertain.

Austrian events were a warning, both of existing tensions at the heart of Europe [46] and of possible German attempts at altering the *status*

---

[43] The *Heimwehr*, led by Prince von Starhemberg, was the element in Austria closest to Italian Fascism. It worked in close alliance with Fascism and was commonly credited with receiving subsidies from Italy. Since May, 1932 it had been part of the government coalition. For the story of Austrian events at this time we may refer to the *Survey of International Affairs, 1934* and to the exhaustive work of Charles A. Gulick, *Austria from Habsburg to Hitler* (Berkeley and Los Angeles, 1948).

[44] This was quite a different affair from the accidentally precipitated violence in Paris; the fighting was organized and severe and lasted several days, and the casualties — in the hundreds — were correspondingly higher. Not until the regular armed forces of the government, using artillery, had been brought into play, did the Socialists surrender.

[45] For the sake of preserving Austria's independent existence and their own the Austrian Socialists were willing to tolerate the Dollfuss regime in exchange for a modicum of parliamentary operation. Naturally, their support would be difficult to enlist after they had been ruthlessly suppressed.

[46] Dollfuss's internal policies were, to a point, an attempted response to the economic difficulties of the country.

quo. But if an eventual *Anschluss* with Austria tended to be taken for granted in Germany, rather more bitter feeling was associated there with the Polish frontier. Rabid nationalists that they were, the Nazis could expatiate with authentic enthusiasm on that subject. All the more surprising therefore that the world should be apprised, in January, 1934, of the signature of a non-aggression pact between Poland and Germany. This meant no alteration in the German, or the Nazi, view of things; it was mere temporary expedient, fitting well into the Nazi mode of operation which consisted in allaying suspicion, dividing potential enemies, and avoiding momentarily fruitless disputes; [47] as such, the Nazi motivation was easy enough to understand.

But the Polish behavior may seem more difficult of explanation. If the leaders of the Polish Republic, Pilsudski for example, would not be unduly exercised or shocked at the suppression of freedom that Nazism stood for, neither were they Nazis themselves nor naïve believers in German words and good intentions, whether Nazi or other. Poland had been since 1921, for good and simple reasons, allied with France. What the Polish action expressed was therefore mainly a lack of confidence in the reliability of the French alliance; not a changing of sides — the French alliance was not abandoned — but doubts. This Polish action, mistaken though it may have been in retrospect, must be regarded in the context of a succession of developments in France: Locarno treaties, Maginot Line, the current state of France, this last perhaps the most important, which give it a certain plausibility. The Nazi pact was for Poland mere momentary reinsurance and hedging. [48]

It was less than two weeks after the signing of the Nazi-Polish Pact that there was rioting in Paris. Small as the matter was *per se* the event was impressive; it gave added point to Polish, and other, suspicion that the purpose of France might be weakening. Call it evidence of a decadent democracy as some would, the fact remained that at the very heart and traditional home of democracy on the continent, the place which for so long had furnished inspiration and leadership to those in Europe who labored for its spread, there was some question-

---

[47] Such an agreement would have been difficult of enactment under the Weimar regime, owing to the intensity of feeling of an opinion then free to express itself. This touches upon the crucial issue of the advantage that totalitarian systems enjoy over free ones in the conduct of their foreign policy. The Nazi-Soviet Pact of 1939 was a larger edition of the same type of operation.

[48] The problem of Poland was at best not simple, and one can sympathize with her dilemma. Caught between Germany and Russia, a temporary lessening of tension on the German side could commend itself as momentarily useful. Another aspect of the matter was the Polish suspicion that France might return to the pre-1914 connection with Russia as insurance against Germany. If it came to a choice of evils, the Russian has traditionally loomed larger and worse than the German in Polish eyes. One can also understand the Polish feeling that, under no circumstances, be it as allies or liberators, must Russian armies be allowed to enter Poland. The Russian record, past and present, confirms the difficulty of getting the Russians out of Poland once they have come in, under whatever guise.

ing of the central democratic institution, Parliament. Could it be that the rising tide of unfreedom had reached such heights that even France might no longer be safe for democracy? Should that be so, what use could France so rended be in terms of power?

The significance of the Nazi-Polish Pact was not misunderstood in France. Hitler could with skill exploit its propaganda value, and this he did not fail to do; here was concrete evidence of Germany's will to peace and tangible proof that she was willing to make a positive contribution to its preservation. In France it was rather felt that this was but a move in a much larger plan, no less than the destruction of the French system. But the domestic turmoil culminating in the events of the 6th of February naturally filled at the moment the French political horizon.

The Foreign Policy of Barthou

The aftermath of these events, where the government was concerned, was the above mentioned formation of a ministry under Doumergue. To a degree, this was a triumph for the Right. Doumergue, a neutral personality, had achieved a degree of popularity through the homely paternal pose that he had adopted during his tenure of the presidency of the Republic. An old Radical and freemason, his leanings were definitely conservative in matters of domestic policy. The Socialists refused him their collaboration, and the effects of the electoral victory of 1932 were largely undone. Despite the seeming emergency, the new government was not truly one of national union as had been Poincaré's in 1926.

Doumergue's foreign minister was Louis Barthou, whom we have met before. Barthou belonged to the same generation as both Doumergue and Poincaré, and in matters of foreign policy very definitely to the Poincaré school of thought. Able, cultured and peppery, he might be expected, with the support of Tardieu, [49] who had also joined the government as Minister of State, to make an effort to put back France's policy on the path from which Briand and the Left had diverted it for so many years. This is in fact what he endeavored to accomplish: his policy was simply that of restoring to its full meaning and effectiveness the original postwar French system of alliances, while possibly enlarging the scope of that system. Such a policy may be described as at once clear and sensible. But circumstances had vastly altered during the last decade. Apart from the domestic state of France, there was the

---

[49] Tardieu, Clemenceau's trusted lieutenant, also an able and highly intelligent man, represented as much as any one in France the tendency to distrust Germany. But, in addition to too great an attachment to the good things of life, Tardieu had begun to lose a sense of proportion and drifted more and more into a position of irresponsibility, as his outpourings in the press increasingly witnessed in this and the following period. Tardieu's book, *L'Heure de la décision* (Paris, 1934) may be cited at this point.

general unrest prevailing throughout Europe; most specifically, there was Hitler's Germany, vastly different in 1934 from the Germany desperately striving to liberate the Ruhr.

This is the background against which Barthou had to direct the conduct of French foreign policy; his attempt has considerable significance. His immediate attention was engaged by the perennial of disarmament, a tale fast approaching its end. After the withdrawal of Germany from the disarmament discussions and from the League, direct negotiations with her had none the less continued. A French plan was presented to Hitler in November, which the German answer to it in December seemed to make a promising basis of negotiation. [50] However, France insisted on the prior return of Germany to Geneva, which Germany in turn would not entertain until agreement on the matter of her rearmament had been achieved. [51] The French reply of February 14 was more intransigeant in tone, reflecting the French reaction to the Nazi-Polish Pact as well as the new orientation of the government issued from the events of February 6.

A British effort at mediation at this point was destined to failure. [52] After much debate, the French government, in a note of April 17, refusing to sanction German rearmament, which for that matter had been initiated and therefore in a sense rendered negotiations useless, asserted that "France would henceforth insure her security by her own means." This last phrase was the heart of the matter, and the French note may be said definitely to have written finis to the discussion of disarmament. [53]

Much has been said on the score of the French note of April 17. No doubt, in diplomatic terms, it was a clumsy move, for it put upon France the onus of responsibility for failure, a situation that the Nazis knew how to exploit to the full. But it is well to distinguish between shadow and substance. German rearmament at this time was already under way; the real issue was therefore how to deal with it. Since no one

---

[50] Once the central issue of the existence of a German army was accepted by France, the implementation of the details of its organization and dimensions might be expected to be not impossible of compromise.

[51] Quite apart from the nature and intentions of the Nazi regime, there was point to the German feeling that to rejoin the League and the Disarmament Conference might serve the cause of unending procrastination. At the same time, the shift from Genevan to direct negotiations represented a German tactical success.

[52] Anthony Eden, who held the position of Lord Privy Seal at this time, went on a tour of the chief European capitals. He obtained a qualified agreement in Berlin and acceptance in Rome, with the result of putting the matter up to France.

[53] The French Cabinet was divided on this issue. Barthou, like the French Ambassador in Berlin, François-Poncet, favored continuing the negotiations, while Doumergue and Tardieu advocated the intransigeant attitude that was adopted. They seem to have been motivated by belief in the instability of the Nazi regime, and this cleavage in French opinion at the governmental level is itself significant.

proposed to take action to enforce the provisions of Versailles, it was merely realistic to acknowledge an existing fact. Britain was prepared for this, and the preceding exchanges seemed to indicate that France was ready to do likewise. From this point on the question was: what value was there, if any, in a German agreement to voluntary limitation? The argument that any future breach by Germany of her new obligations would have placed her in the position of law breaker cannot be given too much weight; that she already was at this time, and the result of any future breaches would depend wholly upon the reaction of others to the breach. [54] Allowing that this was 1934 and that the precise nature of ultimate German intentions was unknown, the traditional French distrust of German promises had in this case large warrant. The French note, if tactically not skilful, does not have the importance sometimes attributed to it; to a point, it may even be said to have served the purpose of clarification: German rearmament, henceforth, if openly acknowledged, would be an unmistakable breach of existing law; whether open or secret, it behooved France — and others — to "insure their security by their own means." [55]

To a point France did this by seeing to the strengthening of her own military establishment, [56] but more important was the task of diplomacy. Barthou's policy had two aims, already stated: to confirm and restore the existing alliances; to enlarge their scope. April found him in Warsaw. The warmth of the personal reception that was given him was pleasing, but official discussions were less reassuring. [57] Polish reticence was in part due to scepticism on the score of the validity of the French connection, but the Russian question was also part of it.

---

[54] Conceivably, British opinion could have been aroused to resist such a breach, whereas it was on the whole sympathetic to German breaches of the "iniquitous" clauses of Versailles; on the other hand, a rearmed Germany would be in a far stronger position to assert and enforce any new claims that she might fancy.

[55] The suggestion appearing in the *Popolo d'Italia* of May 13 of putting a stop to German rearmament through preventive war need not be taken too seriously. It would have had point in the context of a regime like the German, but in the context of the British and French milieus it was wholly unrealistic.

[56] Reductions in the military budget, adopted in the spring of 1933, were canceled before the end of the year, and the Doumergue government was responsible for a program of expansion of aviation and of strengthening the defenses of the Maginot Line. This last aspect of it emphasized the defensive outlook of French policy, open on that score to the criticism previously indicated.

[57] Popular feeling was more pro-French than that of the government, especially of the Foreign Minister, Colonel Beck. This last, considering himself to have been slighted in Paris, thought to return the slight by failing to meet Barthou at the station upon his arrival in Warsaw. Too much should not be made of personal idiosyncracies and views though these play at times an important role. On these events the recollections of the French Ambassador in Warsaw, Jules Laroche, *La Pologne de Pilsudski, Souvenirs d'une ambassade, 1926-1935* (Paris, 1953) and those of Comte Jean Szembek, *Journal 1933-1939* (Paris, 1952) are both useful.

The Russian Card

This is not the place to enter into a discussion of the details of Soviet foreign policy over the years. [58] Like Germany, Soviet Russia had been dedicated to expounding and opposing the iniquities of the French system. The advent of Hitler in Germany in 1933, coming after the successful Japanese action in Manchuria in 1931, was to the Soviets food for second thoughts. There had been a period of ambiguity and readjustment during which German Communists could in effect assist in the destruction of the Weimar Republic while Russia was at the same time seeking the reinsurance of a series of non-aggression pacts. [59] More and more, abandoning the stress on world revolution, Russia began to discover the virtues of peace, in fact of peace maintained through preservation of the *status quo,* meaning by this that she feared being the object of possible attack from quarters other than the wicked capitalist coalition led by France. The voicing of such sentiments could not but be pleasing to French ears; the French Chamber gave a unanimous vote of approval to a Franco-Soviet non-aggression pact on May 18, 1933. The pre-1914 Franco-Russian alliance had been the clear result of common fear of German aggressive intent.

To Barthou such memories were congenial. However, there could hardly be a question of simply exchanging a Russian alliance for those then in existence; Russia for that matter no longer had a common frontier with Germany. The solution of the problem was found in what came to be known as a "Locarno of the East." Briefly, the scheme was this: a defensive alliance involving the Soviet Union, Germany, Poland, Czechoslovakia, Finland, Estonia, and Latvia would, after the Locarno model, put under the guarantee of all the frontiers between these various countries. [60] While Franco-Russian negotiations were proceeding satisfactorily, more difficulty was encountered in two quarters: in Germany and among France's East European allies. Barthou, resuming his role of diplomatic travelling salesman, went East again, in June, this time to Bucharest and Belgrade. The results of this diplomatic activity may be summed up as follows. On May 5 a Russo-Polish protocol extended for ten years the non-aggression pact of 1932, but Poland was to remain cool to the idea of an Eastern Locarno. On June

---

[58] A convenient brief summary may be found in the *Survey of International Affairs, 1934;* Michael T. Florinsky's *World Revolution and the U.S.S.R.* (New York, 1933), despite the date of its publication, remains a valuable analysis.

[59] During 1932 non-aggression treaties were signed with Finland, Poland, Latvia, Estonia, and France.

[60] Immediate military assistance was to be provided in the event of aggression, and the membership was to remain open to other states, such as France. There was to be, in addition, a Franco-Soviet treaty of mutual assistance and a declaration that these instruments were compatible with the League, hence the corollary of Russian admission to Geneva.

9, both Czechoslovakia and Rumania resumed formal relations with the Soviet Union. [61]

The Eastern Locarno proposal was submitted to Germany in July. It will suffice to say that two months later Germany definitely turned it down. Whatever her professed reasons (Nazi Germany could not envisage for herself the possibility of having to give Communist Russia assistance), the fact was that it did not suit the German book to enter into arrangements of this nature, and that the conclusion of bilateral agreements was preferred by her. Increasingly as France — and Russia — insisted on the virtues of *collective security* and on the indivisibility of peace, Germany was dedicated all the more to exploring the possibilities of the divisibility of her potential opponents — or future victims.

An Eastern Locarno without Germany was still possible, would in fact have the virtue that it might take on the color of an anti-German coalition. But without Polish participation the scheme could have no meaning. Poland under no circumstances would entertain the prospect of granting free passage to either German or Russian armies, be they ostensibly coming to her own assistance; her abstention therefore prevented the success of the scheme. What was left of this particular suggestion was, from the French point of view, of questionable value: an improvement in Russo-Czech and Russo-Rumanian relations was little compensation for the deteriorating quality of the Franco-Polish alliance. Poland had hitherto been the single most substantial counter in the French system.

There was another legacy of this diplomatic activity, reflection of the uncertain state of the relationships of European states. The consequences of it were for a time subtantial; properly dealt with, they might have led eventually to results quite other than those that did occur. France and Russia may be said to have stood at opposite poles in politics, prime exponents respectively of systems and philosophies agreed upon their mutual irreconcilability and dedicated to their mutual destruction. Passing time and changing circumstances had altered this. For France, the fixed point of the German danger, a danger made more real by the prospect of impending German rearmament, had brought even Barthou to contemplate with favor the possibility of a renewed Russian connection.

The conservative outlook is perhaps more inclined to a dispassionate approach to the facts of power, and this, combined with the general "softness" of the Liberal Left where the Soviet Union was concerned, had the possibility of making a renewal of the Franco-Russian connection a truly national policy for France. On the Russian side, the passage of the years likewise had caused world revolution, if not to be aban-

---

[61] The problem of Russo-Rumanian relations was particularly difficult of solution owing to the Bessarabian issue. A non-aggression pact in 1932 failed of acceptance at the eleventh hour owing to Rumanian recalcitrance, and this situation even held up for a time the conclusion of the Franco-Soviet Pact.

doned, to be put at least temporarily on ice. That was one of the meanings of Stalin's triumph over his rival Trotzky. More and more the Soviet state was resuming the position and role of a state among states and falling back into the normal channels of diplomacy. The series of agreements just mentioned may be seen as evidence of this.

This changing atmosphere was the background of the proposal for an Eastern Locarno. Simultaneously, Franco-Russian exchanges and contacts were increasing. [62] The atmosphere of the time made it imperative, for France especially, to take the League into her calculations. Two dates may be juxtaposed: on September 12 Germany signified her rejection of the Eastern Locarno proposal; on the 18th the Assembly of the League of Nations, by a vote of 39 out of 42, voted the admission to membership of the Soviet Union, for whom as was but logical, a permanent seat was created on the Council. [63] Now that the Eastern Locarno proposal, following the German and Polish refusals, was for the moment at least dead, the achievement of a more limited direct Franco-Russian agreement could be pursued, which would, following current usage, appear in the guise of bolstering the peace preserving purpose of the League. The contrast between earlier pronouncements issuing from Moscow and those that began to be forthcoming from the Kremlin, professing to recognize the virtues of what had always been the French contention that peace would best be maintained through preservation of the *status quo,* a little later the more specific acknowledgment of the value of the French military establishment, while in Geneva Litvinov became the ardent advocate of collective security, are not devoid of a touch of humor; they were reflections of the changed Russian view of the international scene. [64]

Out of this state of things a Franco-Russian Pact eventually was born, but not until other concurrent developments had introduced some complicating elements. These must be mentioned briefly. Barthou's efforts to revitalize the existing alliances, and his endeavors to establish a Russian connection, were equally understandable policies. But he had failed to reconcile them through an Eastern Locarno, with the consequence of introducing an element of possible weakness in the French system. Poland had elected to follow the German rather than the French lead in the matter of security in Eastern Europe. In a different quarter a not wholly incomparable situation was to develop.

---

[62] French military circles were favorable to an alliance, and there were contacts in Paris between the Russian military attaché and the French General Staff headed by General Weygand. Also, in January, 1934, a Franco-Soviet commercial agreement was signed.

[63] This is not to say that the admission of the Soviet Union to the League was exclusively contrived by France or that it took place solely because of the failure of the Eastern Locarno arrangement, but the role of French diplomacy remains none the less paramount.

[64] In keeping with the changing policy of the Kremlin, Communist parties everywhere began to shift their positions from blanket opposition to cooperation with other "peace loving" elements of the Left. It is this change which eventually resulted in the formation of Popular Fronts.

Italian Possibilities

It has been pointed out that Franco-Italian differences were small in substance, hence at that level easily adjustable, but deeper on the score of basic outlook and interests, hence less amenable to compromise in that respect. France could do little fundamentally to alter the general position of Italy; through her alliances, especially the Yugoslav, she rather appeared in the guise of stumbling block to the spread of Italian influence in Central Europe. Out of this had come into existence the ineffective League of malcontents. What really counted at this point were Germany's intentions toward Danubia, her natural preserve as much as Italy's, and quite as much the Italian view of these German intentions. These last were uncertain, but at the very least called for caution.

For all the preconceptions that ideological sympathy might induce, the events of February, 1934 in Austria could be turned to good account by Italy. The suppression of Austrian Socialism called for no tears from Mussolini, but the result of it must not be Nazi control of Austria. Increased dependence on Italy was the logical way for Dollfuss to strengthen his own authoritarian policy while maintaining the independence of the country. Italy's hold on Austria was thus tightened, and the Rome Protocols of March, 1934 were expression of this outcome. [65]

German developments were calculated to inculcate doubts abroad both about the nature of German intentions and about the solidity of the new regime. But in the end the bloody events of June in Germany rather served to consolidate the hold of Hitler on the country. [66]   It

---

[65] There were three instruments: a consultative pact between the three countries (Italy, Austria, and Hungary) in which they undertook "to concert together on all the problems which particularly interest them and also on those of a general character"; a second protocol looking to the development of their economic relations; and an Italo-Austrian agreement providing for the immediate conclusion (before May 15) of a new Austro-Italian commercial treaty. This last instrument was intended to help maintain Austria's independence by alleviating the country's economic difficulties.

All in all, there was considerable political content in the Rome Protocols, initially thought to be primarily economic in their scope. This caused a certain amount of concern on the part of the Little Entente, but there had also been a tendency to rapprochement with Italy with the conclusion of Italo-Yugoslav and Italo-Rumanian commercial agreements at the beginning of January, 1934. To a degree, this activity may also be regarded as a continuation of the Franco-Italian rivalry in Central Europe; France was responsible for a plan, originated by Tardieu, for the assistance of Central Europe through the organization of a loose form of federation, a plan which found no favor with Italy.

[66] The internal struggle for control of the Nazi party culminated in the ruthless purge of one faction. In retrospect, this event makes clear that the control of such a system as the Nazi is not necessarily weakened by dissent when there is willingness to deal with such dissent with complete ruthlessness. The same phenomenon has occurred in Soviet Russia where it may be said that purges have been a part of the normal operation of

was not long in fact — less than a month after the purge — before the Nazis thought to test the international situation. The attempted coup in Vienna, on July 25, was accompanied by the murder of Chancellor Dollfuss but failed of its purpose of the seizure of power in Austria. [67] For all that Germany adopted a "correct" attitude and denied immixture in Austria's national affairs, the episode and its significance were clear. All that need be retained of it at this point is the clarity and determination of the Italian reaction, far more vigorous than the French. [68]

This, too, is understandable: if Italy could view with a sympathetic eye the restoration of a German power that would balance the French, she, like Britain, wanted balance, not another hegemony, especially one that showed signs of such aggressiveness in its makeup. Also, for all his toying with revisionism, Mussolini had always made it clear that the concept could have no applicability to Italy, whose frontiers were sacred. With the unanimity of which Fascism had made it capable, the Italian press expressed itself in no uncertain terms on the score of the nature of Nazism and the German nation. Mussolini at this time had a correct estimate of the facts of power and soundly adhered to the traditional Italian policy of which the defense of the independence of Austria had, since the war, been one of the cardinal tenets.

Here was a clear and specific interest that Italy had in common with France. Just as Barthou had shown interest in the possibility of a Russian connection, so likewise his outlook toward Italy was of a similar nature. Nazi activity seemed to play into his hands. But, as in the case of Russia, where Poland was the obstacle, so in the case of Italy, Yugoslav fears and the Franco-Yugoslav alliance could be a stumbling block. Barthou had been to Belgrade in June, and the possibility of an Italo-Yugoslav rapprochement was the logical object of his efforts. It was in fact arranged that King Alexander pay a visit to France in the autumn, which, while being outward notice of the solidity of the existing connection, would offer an opportunity for extended political discussions.

But unexpected accidents sometimes distort the course of history, if only for a time. While riding through Marseilles, where King Alexander had landed on the 9th of October, both the King and Barthou were assassinated. The murder was the deed of Croat malcontents who, in the tradition of 1914 Sarajevo, thought terrorism the way to give

the system. Such a condition, understandably, is difficult to grasp by people living in a condition of freedom, who tend to misread the fact of a purge as a measure of the strength of the opposition, hence of the lack of solidity of the system.

[67] For a detailed discussion of these events we may refer to the same sources as in note 43.

[68] Mussolini's despatch of Italian forces to the Brenner was unequivocal notification to Germany and understood by her as such. For all her surreptitious rearmament, Germany was not yet in a position to face hostilities, even with Italy alone. France naturally was opposed to the *Anschluss*, but, unlike Italy, was content with verbal remonstrances.

expression to their feelings and to further the realization of their ends.[69] There were in fact several points of resemblance between the events leading to Sarajevo and those that had their climax in Marseilles twenty years later. In the present instance three countries were involved in complicated intrigues and in assistance furnished to the Croatian malcontents, Italy, Germany and Hungary, three revisionist states. The precise share of their involvement [70] need not concern us here, where only the impact of the assassination on the larger framework of Europe need be considered.

In the limited field of Franco-Yugoslav relations, the demise of King Alexander and Barthou doubtless was a setback. The King's successor in Belgrade, Regent Prince Paul, showed sympathy for an orientation of Yugoslav policy in the direction of a rapprochement with Germany. This tendency had significance far beyond the limited reaches of merely Yugoslav policy; it was both symbol and reflection of two things. The first, which might be labeled ideological, derived from the fact that Nazi methods of government might easily appear in Yugoslavia more suitable than those of the Western democracies; by its very existence the Nazi regime thus constituted an important pole of attraction, and not in Yugoslavia alone. The second, not unrelated to the first, is that this shift may be regarded as an expression of doubts on the reliability and effectiveness of French power. There was thus a common point in the behavior of both Poland and Yugoslavia when it came to the operation of the French system.

Barthou's attempts in this direction may therefore be regarded as failures, though conceivably, had he not died, the unfolding of the tale might have been different. But there were other factors in his policy that were more serious elements of weakness. The attempt to revive the existing alliances was a wholly natural one. The effort to secure the assistance of Russia was likewise understandable, and the Eastern

---

[69] The source of Croatian discontent lay in the internal operation of the Yugoslav state. For all that the formation of the Kingdom of the Serbs, Croats and Slovenes had been a voluntary act, there were substantial differences between Serbs and Croats. But the circumstances of the time of the formation of the union, mainly the fact that Serbia had been in existence as an independent entity, led to the organization of the new state around the existing core of Serbian institutions and administration. The Croats, who regarded themselves as more "civilized" than the Serbs and were in fact more culturally advanced, not unnaturally resented what appeared to them as the treatment of a conquered people. Feeling was strong for at least a measure of autonomy, and in its extreme forms went the length of advocating separatism. This state of affairs had led King Alexander in 1929 to suspend the constitution and to install a virtual dictatorship, mainly in an effort to preserve the integrity of the state. But this action inevitably put an added premium on secret agitation and terrorist tactics.

[70] Sufficient evidence is for that matter lacking. The incident did not lead to the international complications that were feared for a time, and the weakest of the three, Hungary, alone was the object of formal reprimands. Cf. J.-B. Duroselle, *Histoire diplomatique de 1919 à nos jours* (Paris, 1953), p. 216.

Locarno proposal the logical corollary of the desire to avoid the dilemma, either Russia or Poland. But in the face of Poland's recalcitrance, the dilemma could not be avoided and there was danger of its ending in neither Russia nor Poland if the effort was persisted in in defiance of unalterable fact. For reasons that have been indicated before we must take an even dimmer view of the prospects for the long term of securing Italian adherence to the French camp.

To have friends is desirable, but the value of mere numbers is questionable when this implies friends that among themselves may be unable to agree. If the judgment seems too strong that, during his last brief passage in office, Barthou contrived "to make a mark upon international history which seemed certain to endure and likely to prove unfortunate", [71] a more appropriate, if highly picturesque, characterization, is this: "The wild beasts whom the French *virtuoso* was proposing to drive in double harness were not even carnivores of the same species. He was undertaking to yoke a Russian vulture to a Polish eagle, and a Lion of Saint Mark to a Yugoslav unicorn; and nothing short of success in this pair of *tours de force* would entitle him to receive the victor's crown." [72]

4. THE RETURN TO THE POLITICS OF PURE POWER

Enter Laval

The succession of Barthou at the French foreign office therefore took on particular significance; in the existing state of flux characteristic of the relationships of Europe, a state induced by the combined impact of economic crisis and the uncertainty attaching to the future course of the Nazi phenomenon, it no longer sufficed to rest on established positions and drift along past lines of policy. What for that matter were the directing lines of French policy? Barthou had been fertile of schemes, old and new, in fact too many schemes pursued at once. His death did not involve a complete ministerial reshuffle. The Doumergue Cabinet remained unchanged, save that Pierre Laval filled in it Barthou's vacated place. [73]

Laval we have already met; his essentially opportunistic outlook had found no cause for alteration. The events of another decade, the role played by this man during the days of France's sorrow, his willingness to work with the Nazi conqueror, the ultimate defeat of Nazism and downfall of Vichy, have brought his name into most thorough disrepute. That the man was unprincipled, little capable of response to the motivation of ideal, did not need the evidence of subsequent events to establish; yet these events and the error of his judgments

---

[71] *Survey of International Affairs, 1934,* p. 387.
[72] *Ibid.,* p. 350
[73] The Doumergue government, mainly for internal reasons, did not last long after this. It fell in November, and Flandin became Prime Minister, Laval remaining, however, in charge of foreign policy.

ending in failure and ignominious death have tended to cast an undue reflection on his direction of affairs in 1935. From October 1934 to January 1936 Laval was France's Foreign Minister; in the context of the circumstances of the time Laval was no villainous traitor; according to his lights and predilections he, like his predecessors, labored to promote the security of the entity whose relations to others were in his care. That the result of his activity was unsatisfactory may be regarded as expression of two things: the limitations of his competence, the nature of the French complex during this period. [74] Both of these warrant examination.

Ostensibly, there was no change of orientation in the policies that had been pursued by Barthou: the effort to secure the Russian as well as the Italian connection was continued. But in reality there was a difference. It is a commonplace to stress at present the similarities in fundamentals between the Soviet and the Nazi regimes; times were different twenty years ago when all that called itself liberal felt increasing revulsion for Nazi deeds but, overlooking not dissimilar ones in the Soviet domain, focused with sympathy in varying degrees on the professed ultimate aims of the Soviet experiment. This earlier outlook has left a lasting stamp on the appraisal of Laval's activity. For Laval was little responsive to idealism or ideology; the nature of the regimes that held sway in France's immediate neighbors left him indifferent; he was in fact quite capable from his own point of view of appreciating the greater facility of government without the fetters of a free parliament and press. In brief, Laval was predisposed in favor of direct agreement with these neighbors.

Where Germany was concerned, the discussion of disarmament may be regarded as having been closed since the French note of April. [75] There was one outstanding issue, however, said Hitler, between France and Germany, namely the Saar. The least that can be said is that Laval greatly facilitated the settlement of the issue. France apparently made little effort to use the means of pressure she possessed, allowing free scope instead to Nazi propaganda and pressure in the Saar, and the plebiscite held on January 13, 1935 produced a 90 percent vote in favor

---

[74] This is not meant as defense of Laval and his policies which, even by the purely pragmatic test of effectiveness, must be judged failures, but, especially in view of the circumstances of his subsequent career, it is essential to guard against the tendency to read into 1935, and to judge 1935 by, the standards that the unfolding of the events of another decade caused to become the prevailing ones. It is no more than natural that the bitterness aroused by defeat and occupation and by the role of Laval during the occupation should color estimates of Laval's earlier activity, certainly in France, but outside of France also. This is all the more reason for caution in appraising 1935.

[75] See above, p. 257. This note, while in effect putting an end to the discussion, did not result in the formal disbandment of the Disarmament Conference. However, its continued discussions until 1935 were so futile and conducted *in vacuo* that it seems warranted not to register them in this essay. To all intents and purposes the rearmament race was under way, albeit relatively slowly at first.

of the Saar's return to Germany. [76] This might be said: if the outcome was foregone and inevitable, it was perhaps as well to reduce to a minimum any legalistic bickering over the reaching of it. Was not this, for once, applying the advice so often given France by her well-meaning friends across the Channel and the Atlantic, rather than evidence that Laval was crudely pro-German? At any rate, the Saar duly returned to her German allegiance on March 1, and Hitler, though essentially a humorless man, solemnly declared that Germany had no outstanding claims remaining against France.

For all this, Laval was not averse to seeking reinsurance against the German danger. As mentioned before, he continued along the lines of his predecessor, but with this difference that he seems to have set greater store by the Italian, rather than the Russian, alliance. It was partly because Laval was set on making the Italian connection that France made every effort to play down the aftermath of the double assassination of Marseilles: it would be awkward to delve with too much thoroughness into the possible extent of Italian involvement in the activities of Croatian terrorists. [77] These efforts were successful, and once it was clear that no major complications were going to ensue, Laval was free actively to resume the course of his Italian policy to which Mussolini had been responsive. [78]

He was in Rome during the opening days of 1935. Negotiations were not protracted, and on January 7 the public announcement was made of complete agreement between the two countries. Ostensibly, the nature of the agreement was this. In Europe, France and Italy declared their common devotion to the continued preservation of Austrian independence; outside of Europe, they liquidated the petty but long standing quarrel arising from the Italian contention that France had not fulfilled the promises of colonial compensations contained in the Treaty of London of April, 1915, which had brought Italy into the war. Agreement was now reached on the meaning of "adequate," which

---

[76] The plebiscite was held in accordance with and in fulfilment of the provisions of the Treaty of Versailles, after attempts at a direct Franco-German understanding had failed. There was no question of the Saar's German character, but it was thought that the nature of the Nazi regime might cause enough Saarlanders, Catholics and Socialists, to opt for the continuation of the *status quo* instead of the return to Germany — the third possibility, incorporation into France, was never a serious one. The Nazis brought into play their full apparatus of propaganda and threats, but, apart form the effects of the latter, impossible of measurement, there is reason to regard the outcome of the plebiscite as essentially the expression of the simple fact of the Germanness of the Saar. The best treatment of the plebiscite is Sarah Wambaugh, *The Saar Plebiscite* (Cambridge, Mass., 1940).

[77] Those who were captured were tried in France at Aix-en-Provence, but the proceedings of the trial were circumscribed so as to raise a minimum of international complications, while the proceedings at Geneva endeavored to pour oil on the troubled waters of the relations between Yugoslavia on one side and Italy and Hungary on the other.

[78] In a speech at Milan on October 6, Mussolini had voiced the warm hope that an understanding with France would materialize.

qualified compensations in that treaty, and Mussolini declared that all outstanding issues had been settled. [79]

The Laval-Mussolini agreement was destined to have enormous consequences, far exceeding any probable expectations on the part of its makers. The story of the making of it and the precise nature of what passed in Rome will in all likelihood remain forever wrapped in a measure of mystery. [80] Two things were immediately clear. The interest in the preservation of Austria was a genuine common interest, hence, barring unforeseen developments, could be regarded as the lasting and authentic basis of a common Franco-Italian policy; neither had to pay the other a price for the acceptance of this view. But in the colonial field more questions were raised than answered by the agreement. In brief, why should Italy, with her bargaining position enhanced through the resurgence of Germany, now choose to be content with such small change? Enlargement of the "collection of deserts" that her imperial activity had so far been, hardly seemed a satisfactory answer, especially as she herself was making a concession in Tunis.

The answer, to a point, was simple. Mussolini had obtained from Laval the promise of French *désistement,* a free hand, where Abyssinia was concerned, though the precise meaning of *désistement* [81] is what was to give rise very shortly to disagreement and recrimination. At all events it appeared for the moment that Italy had been enlisted in the French camp, and this might be regarded as a considerable achievement, subject to the qualification, however, that the assumptions on which her decision was made were valid and the implications of it capable of fulfilment.

---

[79] France ceded to Italy some 114.000 square kilometers of desert south of Libya, a small strip of French Somaliland, and the strategic islet of Doumeirah at the southern entrance of the Red Sea. Italy was also to receive 34.000 shares in the French-owned Jibuti-Addis Ababa railway, but on her side acquiesced to the gradual ending of the special status of Italians in Tunisia between 1945 and 1965.

[80] These constitute a fascinating bit of history on which so far we have some evidence from the participants and some second-hand evidence from close associates of theirs. The simplest explanation, quite plausible though not necessarily correct, is that there was genuine misunderstanding on both sides. The most relevant testimony, in addition to Laval's own statements, is contained in P.E. Flandin, *Politique française, 1919-1940* (Paris, 1947) and J. Paul-Boncour, *Entre deux guerres*, vol. III, *Sur les chemins de la défaite, 1935-1940* (Paris, 1946). For a discussion of the evidence we may refer to the author's, *Italy from Napoleon to Mussolini* (New York, 1950) and to the close analysis in L.B. Namier, *Europe in Decay* (London, 1950), as well as to G. Salvemini, *Prelude to World War II* (New York, 1954).

[81] That is the point on which conclusive evidence is not available and will probably never be. Laval ever insisted that the free hand he had granted Mussolini was meant in economic terms, and that Italian penetration must be short of war. That Italy had designs on Abyssinia did not need subsequent disclosures for proof; it was in December, 1934 that the frontier incident of Wal Wal was the occasion for opening a dispute with Abyssinia, but this in turn did not reveal the precise nature and extent of Italian intentions.

Laval was neither a stupid nor a naïve man, though limited by his insensitivity to values other than the immediate and material, and also by the range of his knowledge, his lack of culture, as the charge was often put in France. That where Germany was concerned he did not have Barthou's single minded determination of suspicious purpose may be granted. With Germany, Nazi Germany or any other Germany, Laval would deal. But to repeat, this was not tantamount to treacherous intent as much as to erroneous appraisal; with Italy meanwhile he had contrived a *combinazione* highly congenial to his temper, and Italy could be used as a counter in the game of bargaining with Germany.

The Formal Rearmament of Germany

A momentary relaxation had followed the Saar plebiscite. Anglo-French negotiations were under way centering around mutual assistance arrangements and the elaboration of a Western Air Pact. Hitler had made a conciliatory speech on March 1 and Sir John Simon was due in Berlin to discuss matters with him. However, given the German uncertainty, in both Britain and France measures were taken to strengthen the military establishments. [82] It is at this point that, having withdrawn to Berchtesgaden to commune with his inspiration, as often on the eve of important decisions, the Führer emerged to inform the French Ambassador, François-Poncet, that he had just promulgated a law reintroducing conscription in Germany, in preparation to the organization of an army of 36 divisions. [83] As justification for his action he gave the failure to reach agreement on the subject of rearmament and the increasing armament of others.

Here was a clear and simple act. The treaty of peace, specifically the provisions of article 160, [84] was blatantly violated. No clearer legal basis for action could exist. But what action? There have been those who subsequently have judged France remiss for failure to take forcible action at this time. There is little doubt that what there was so far of German military force in being could hardly have opposed even serious resistance to a military move by France. One may even assume that such a move, after it had achieved its purpose, [85] would not have been disapproved by countries like Russia or Poland, and that Italy would

---

[82] A British White Book was issued on March 4 in London which justified increased military expenditures on the ground of German rearmament. In France, the Chamber voted on March 15 the reinstitution of the two year term of military service in order to compensate for the deficiency of manpower that would result in the next few years from the deficiency of births during the First World War years.

[83] The admission had been made a few days earlier in Germany of the existence of an air force.

[84] This article specified the limit of seven infantry divisions and of a personnel not to exceed 100,000 men for the German army.

[85] What the precise effect of any such action would have been in Germany is a matter for speculation, but that it could have achieved the primary purpose of enforcing the disarmament provisions of the Treaty of Versailles does not seem open to debate.

not have judged detrimental to her Abyssinian purpose to find other European states entangled in a distracting issue.

But what of Britain? There can be little question that for some time, whether at the official or at the popular level, Britain had become reconciled to the acceptance of the rearmament of Germany. The Nazi technique might be awkward and brutal, but, fundamentally, Britain was no longer minded to enforce the provisions of the peace that sanctioned German inferiority. There was in fact not a little of the feeling that the German decision had the merit of cutting the Gordian knot of disarmament, of clearing the atmosphere of false pretense, and that it created a sounder basis for future meaningful agreement. [86] *Pro forma* the British government could do no other than protest the clear unilateral violation of a treaty, but there is more significance in the decision to proceed with the proposed visit of the British ministers to Berlin.

If France could find no support, but rather disapproval, in Britain for any overt action — reoccupation of the Rhineland for instance — it is also legitimate to assume that Britain would not have prevented such action on France's part. The decision therefore rested with France; but the France of 1935 was no longer led by either Clemenceau or Poincaré. The argument sometimes derived from the state of organization of the French army must be rated essentially pretext; the lack of will is more important. Due recognition must be granted the psychological perception of the Führer and the combination of boldness and skill that motivated his decision. Reluctance to carry forever the burden of vigilance that the policy of holding Germany in a condition of impotence entailed caused many to lend an at least tentatively hopeful ear to the Hitlerian assertion that no more was wanted than the removal of discrimination. Just how heavy would be the burden of single handed action and why incur the onus of being the perpetual obstacle to peace based on equality rather than on discrimination and force? The German contention that for the long term — fifteen years had already passed since the end of the war — Germany must recover the rank of accepted and respected equal carried substantial moral weight.

These hesitation were reflected at the level of governmental decisions in France; the consequence of them was to confine the French response to the diplomatic level. Italy, like Britain, had issued a protest, and on March 23 representatives of the three Powers agreed in Paris on the form that their action should take: the British, John Simon and Anthony Eden, would explore the situation in Berlin, whence they would go to Moscow, stopping at Prague and Warsaw on their way. This exploration done the three Powers would examine the situation in Stresa.

---

[86] Reference may be made to the *History of the* [London] *Times,* cited previously. A very useful source, as well as a convenient one, is the publication of the French Foreign Office, *Bulletin périodique de la presse,* of which the foreign section, *Bulletin de la presse étrangère,* analyzes the foreign press by countries. This survey was issued at irregular intervals, covering periods ranging from about three to eight weeks.

The platitudes that made up the communiqué issued after the Anglo-German conversations in Berlin suggested that little common ground existed, [87] and if the atmosphere was warmer in Moscow, the views of Colonel Beck in Warsaw showed a surprising degree of identity with those expressed in Berlin. The record of the Stresa meeting from April 11 to 14 can only be described as astonishing. For Italy there were two distinct issues of significance at the moment: the European situation was one, but her own future course in Abyssinia was of greater immediate moment to her. [88] Yet, strange as it may seem, and hardly credible were it not in fact true, European matters alone were considered at Stresa.

Mussolini had properly appraised the situation in advance. The statement that "the result will be a communiqué which will represent a least common denominator between the Powers and which therefore — short of surprises — can only be of a general or consultative character — "consultation" being the last resource of indecision in the face of reality," which appeared in the *Popolo d'Italia* of April 11 is a perfectly correct summary of what had happened when the meeting closed. [89] There were no surprises, either in the form of intruding the Abyssinian question or of Britain taking a firm position where Germany was concerned. Thus, France, despite her efforts, failed to obtain anything more substantial than a condemnation of German methods, an agreement to consult in the event of further breaches by her, but not a definite commitment that Britain and Italy would resort to economic and financial sanctions — let alone military ones — and the prospect of more talk and pious resolutions at Geneva when an Extraordinary Session of the Council would take up the matter.

This is precisely what happened. After much debate, on April 17, the Council by a vote of 13 out of 15 members [90] passed the Anglo-Franco-Italian resolution that had the boldness to condemn Germany by name for her action of March 16. The value of moral condemnation of this sort, in the failure of willingness to go beyond the use of words, is highly questionable; one effect that it had was to irritate German opinion while solidifying it in support of Hitler, a doubtful gain. That all were not blind to the drift of the general situation is shown by the impossibility of finding a neutral to act as *rapporteur* for the resolution: if France herself was now content with words why should anyone else incur the risks of future German displeasure?

---

[87] A fact confirmed by Sir John Simon's statement in Commons on April 9.

[88] Military preparations had been under way for some time and the sending of troops and matériel to Eritrea and Italian Somaliland was currently going on.

[89] Quoted in the *Survey for International Affairs, 1935*, p. 157. The article was credited to Mussolini's own hand.

[90] Germany was no longer represented in the Council and Denmark abstained.

Within a month of the open German challenge the balance sheet was this: Germany had in substance scored a notable success; if so minded, she could proceed to ask for more. Given her current temper, it might be said that the moral condemnation that she had incurred, for all its emptiness, was notice that it behooved her to make her power effective before she could achieve moral equality as well. In the default of action, Italy could feel reassured that things would for the time remain quiescent in her rear — in Europe — and therefore concentrate on the pursuit of her Ethiopian scheme. No less important, the failure to mention Abyssinia at Stresa, the insistence on limiting the Council resolution to the maintenance of peace *in Europe,* and the marked British reaction of discomfort at the mention of the word "sanctions", could well be taken by her as advance confirmation of whatever interpretation she might choose of Laval's free hand in Abyssinia. [91]

The Stresa Front, so-called, was but the flimsiest of structures. The clearest achievement at the time of its making was Germany's successful breach of a treaty. What mattered were two things: German intentions was one; for the rest, the position that Britain and Italy would take in the event of further German action. On the score of these last two countries, this also was clear: Italy had, and probably for some time would have, other, extra-European preoccupations; Britain had evinced as great a fear as ever of undertaking any definite future commitments. The real fact was that Britain was essentially reconciled to the prospect of German rearmament. Britain did not want a war or a renewal of the German threat; but with astonishing lack of perception, under the guise of reasonableness, fairness, and sensible practicality, she was embarking upon as sorry a misreading of the future as is recorded in her annals. [92] For the sake of ultimately desirable results — the restoration of German equality — Britain was prepared to overlook both the nature of Nazism and its methods.

This view is confirmed by a relatively minor but significant episode which, because of its repercussions, is worth mentioning. It was during the visit of Sir John Simon and Anthony Eden to Berlin in March that Hitler had advanced the claim to a naval establishment bearing a ratio

---

[91] The Council resolution stated that "this [Germany's] unilateral action, by introducing a new disturbing element into the international situation, must necessarily appear to be a threat to European security," and later spoke again of "the maintenance of peace in Europe," During the course of the ensuing discussion, Litvinov supported the resolution with enthusiasm, but pointed to the possible implications of the qualification *in Europe.* He was rebuffed by Sir John Simon, whom Laval and Baron Aloisi, the Italian delegate, both supported.

It must be remembered that this was the very moment when the Ethiopian delegate failed in his attempt to obtain action from the Council in the matter of the Italo-Ethiopian dispute which had been before it.

[92] There were voices of dissent in Britain, Churchill's and Vansittart's for instance, but they were generally dismissed as those of prejudiced or unbalanced advocates. What is more astonishing is rather the degree of unanimity in British opinion at all levels.

of 35 percent to the British. Granted the premise of both the inevitability and the legitimacy of German rearmament, this proposal had the earmarks of Hitler's skill: it could be taken as evidence that Germany acknowledged the mistake of the Kaiser in embarking on naval competition with Britain. To make the story brief, it will suffice to say that, on June 18, an Anglo-German agreement was signed that gave sanction to the German wish. Doubtless the point had merit that if Germany was bent on rearming in any event, there was value in her voluntary consent to limitation; the question might be raised, however, of the value of German promises and whether in the event of their breach Britain proposed to adopt the legalistic French position so often criticized by her. But more significant was the French reaction to the announcement, one of combined anger and dismay. [93] From the French point of view what mattered was not so much the precise terms of the agreement as the fact that Britain was placing the seal of her approval on that most heinous of all crimes, revision of treaties without the consent of their signatories; France, too, had signed the Treaty of Versailles now with levity modified, and the timing of this incident could not have been worse chosen. [94] If it were true that in face of an assertive — not yet to say aggressive — Germany, Britain and France had the same fundamental stake in preservation, that for that purpose each was in equal need of the other, for either to drive a wedge between them must seem like irresponsible frivolity. The impact of this episode was far greater and more disastrous than the relatively secondary fact of a degree of German naval rearmament.

The Franco-Soviet Pact

If, as far as the value of the British connection was concerned, German rearmament, whether through the Stresa aftermath or the naval agreement, had resulted in a definite setback, there was another asset for France to draw upon in Europe. Barthou himself had initiated a return to a new version of the pre-1914 Franco-Russian connection, a tendency to which, especially in view of the failure of the Eastern Locarno proposal, the Soviet government was not unresponsive.

For some years the Soviet Union had been hedging. Already in 1932 she had signed a non-aggression pact with France. [95] This had

---

[93] The French government had received on the 12th a British memorandum notifying it of the tenor of the impending Anglo-German agreement. The French reply, making the points that might be expected in no uncertain terms, had no effect on the British decision to proceed with the agreement. One of the curious elements in this episode is the British surprise at the intensity of the French reaction; another is the agreement that the 35 percent ratio did not apply to submarines. This last caused not a little surprise in Britain herself.

[94] Its bearing on the Abyssinian *imbroglio* will be mentioned later.

[95] The agreement pledged either party not to join a coalition directed against the other and to renounce interference in the domestic affairs of the other.

not meant a total reorientation of Soviet policy, for the prior German connection was by no means undone, not even after the accession of Hitler to power in 1933. The Kremlin was in fact very slow in abandoning the doctrinaire belief that anything detrimental to bourgeois capitalist democracy anywhere was a good, but the nature of the Nazi regime and its treatment of German Communists, for all that Hitler insisted that their fate was a purely domestic German question, was inescapable ground for second thoughts. Under these circumstances the Franco-Russian rapprochement could prosper.

Despite the fact that the French Chamber had expressed itself in favor of the Russian connection by the impressive vote of 520 to 0 as early as May, 1933 — a vote that may be viewed as a response to events across the Rhine — negotiations were somewhat protracted. Barthou pursued the scheme of an Eastern Locarno, and his successor, Laval, was personally cooler to the Soviets and more interested in the furtherance of his Italian policy. This in itself was cause for a degree of suspicion on the Soviet side, but the time that saw the conclusion of the Laval-Mussolini agreement also witnessed an exchange of verbal bouquets between France and the Soviet Union. The German action of March 16 opened a new chapter in the story of armament while Germany definitely turned down the Eastern Locarno suggestion. The announcement of the imminent signature of a Franco-Soviet Pact was made at the beginning of April, on the eve of the Stresa meeting, and the pact finally was signed in Paris on May 2, 1935 by Laval and the Soviet Ambassador, Potemkine.

The Franco-Soviet Treaty of Mutual Assistance [96] in the main conformed to French wishes. While Russia was interested in the Far Eastern no less than in the European situation, France did not wish to be diverted in the former quarter; the treaty accordingly provided for either state coming to the immediate assistance of the other in the event of unprovoked aggression by a European state (article 2); in the event of danger of aggression, they would consult with a view to accelerating the operation of article 10 of the Covenant (article 1). Should either party be the victim of aggression by a European state, whether a member of the League or not, and should the Council of the League decree sanctions, the other party would lend all assistance (article 3). Even in the event of the Council failing to reach a unanimous decision the provision of immediate assistance would be operative.

However, "immediate" was not synonymous with *déclenchement automatique,* for an appended protocol went on to explain that the two parties would seek to procure a speedy decision by the Council, adding that "should the Council, nevertheless, for some reason, make no recommendation or fail to reach a unanimous decision, effect shall never-

---

[96] The text of it may be found in *Documents of International Affairs, 1935,* pp. 116-19.

theless be given to the obligationg to render assistance." [97] By way of further assurance to France, the protocol also stated that the provisions of the agreement were not to go into effect in a way that would be inconsistent with existing treaty obligations of the parties and that would make them in turn liable to the operation of sanctions against them. [98] The Franco-Soviet treaty was supplemented by a similar Soviet-Czech agreement which, however, contained the qualification that the provisions of mutual assistance, in the event of aggression, would become operative only if France came to the assistance of the attacked country.

Like its predecessor of the eighteen nineties, the Franco-Soviet pact was born of a common interest the name of which was German danger; it is a good measure of the evolving state of the relationships among European states. The dominant new fact was the resurgence of Germany, specifically her rearmament, which, though for some time initiated, was still incomplete but could be assumed to place Germany within measurable distance of being able to assert in the councils of Europe a voice commensurate with her power. Such a condition would in many respects be sounder, certainly less artificial, than that hitherto prevailing when Germany had been shackled in impotence. If, in view of the subsequent record, there may be reason to regret that German impotence was not continued, the fact remains that for the longer term the dominance of Europe by a system of Powers centering around the French constituted an anomaly. The French system was a makeshift, a temporary arrangement; in the failure to substitute for it an effective security system based on the League, the return of both Russia and Germany to the councils of Europe on a basis of equality constituted a more normal, even in a sense a fundamentally sounder, state of affairs. The question was how to operate the new system.

The situation was neither unfamiliar nor unprecedented; it was merely the condition of pre-1914, the situation of the days before the League had come into existence. The return to "normality" and balance is the aspect of it which made it acceptable to British reasonableness and to Italian realism alike. The consequences of this return to what, in the context of the past, was a more "normal" situation was undoubtedly a blow to the prestige of Geneva and could not but mean a lessening of the importance of the French role in Europe.

However, the League was still not dead, nor was French power destroyed. This last, specifically the French army, was in fact still generally regarded as the most solid reality of the day. The pure re-

---

[97] Clearly, there was an element of ambiguity in this attempt to define the meaning of "immediate." It was this provision that formed the basis of the German contention that the Franco-Soviet Pact was not compatible with the Locarno treaties.

[98] What this meant was that France reasserted the validity of Locarno. By implication, therefore, in the event of a German attack against Russia French action might be subordinated to the decision of the Locarno guarantors, Britain and Italy.

lationship of power was therefore more than ever the crucial factor of the future. Having declined to assert itself in the test, French power must therefore reexamine the scene. The Franco-Soviet treaty was one answer, undoubtedly a strengthening of the French position, as was likewise presumably the Franco-Italian agreement. But for this there were compensating losses. Both these relationships, the Franco-Russian and the Franco-Italian, were in the nature of associations of equals, in which either partner could have an equal voice, by contrast with the earlier French alliances, characteristic of the French system.

These other alliances were by no means abandoned — this was still a transitional stage of readjustment in the relationships of power — but rather continued unaltered. Ostensibly at least, for their status and significance could not remain unaltered in the flux of changing circumstances: the Czech connection was not only confirmed, in a sense it was even strengthened, but the case was other with Poland, as Laval had occasion to discover on the occasion of his passage through Warsaw. [99] Nor was the League wholly abandoned: France had procured the couching of the language of the Soviet Pact in terms that set it in the framework of her League obligations as well as of Locarno. [100] France in a sense therefore was still consistently adhering to the policy of collecting guarantees and of seeking assistance for her security from whatever quarters it might be forthcoming; but, to repeat, the stress had shifted to the relationship of power, especially among Great Powers. [101]

---

[99] Following the signature of the Franco-Soviet Pact, Laval paid a visit to Moscow, on May 13-15, where he was greeted with cordiality. He stopped in Warsaw on his return and found the Poles, Colonel Beck in particular, highly exercised at the prospect of Russian troops entering Poland in the event of a Franco-German conflict. Despite the fact that the Franco-Soviet Pact still envisaged the possibility of an Eastern Locarno, Poland was adamant on this score, and the net result of the Franco-Soviet agreement was to weaken the Franco-Polish connection while strengthening that between Germany and Poland.

Marshal Pilsudski died just at this time and his funeral in Cracow, which was attended by Laval, was the occasion of a conversation between him and Göring, present for the same occasion. On Laval's visit and the state of Franco-Polish relations some useful light is thrown by the memoirs of the French Ambassador, Jules Laroche, cited before.

[100] This in fact was one of the sources of ambiguity, hence of weakness, of the Franco-Soviet Pact, for the meaning of "immediate" and of "aid and assistance" remained subject to interpretation. The clause in the Soviet-Czech Pact subordinating the operation of that pact to French action reflects the same reticence.

[101] Of the German position little need be said. Germany had obviously achieved a great victory; now that she was going to be rearmed, it was reasonable to assume that it would be a mere matter of time before she would remove whatever other disabilities still remained from the treaty of peace. For the record, Germany presented a memorandum on May 25 to the French government — as well as to the British, Italian and Belgian — — wherein she took the position that the Franco-Soviet Pact, specifically the first article of the explanatory protocol, was incompatible with the Treaty of Locarno which she, however, refrained from denouncing.

If the League was not dead it had certainly fallen on evil days; the least that could be said of it is that it seemed powerless against the drift toward the reassertion of the politics of power. [102] Yet this need by no means be tantamount to the immediate failure of peace. But in view of the fact that peace had hitherto been maintained through the French system, although that system was undergoing alteration and the role and position of France were undergoing corresponding diminution, that role and position still remained of capital importance.

France undertook some things — reintroduction of the two year term of military service, additional credits for her fortifications — in the limited field of strengthening her own physical position, just as Britain began to look to some rebuilding of her naval power; these things, however, were of relatively secondary importance, certainly so by comparison with the more elusive imponderable that the word "will" best describes. Would France be willing to meet the test of decision if the necessity arose? Her failure to respond, save with words, to the German challenge of March 16 augured ill on that score; yet in a way, the Franco-Soviet Pact was an answer that opened new possibilities.

That answer had very wide support in France and might provide the ground on which the national will could unite. Once Stalin had discovered, and publicly acknowledged, the virtues of French arms, French Communists could become patriotic. The French Jacobin tradition could supply them with ready material both for action and words; more concretely and immediately, they ceased their opposition to the extension of the term of military service and to measures of rearmament in general. This was precisely the sort of thing that the conservative Right, those dubbed militarists by the outside, had always been clamoring for. The French military themselves, for their part, were rather enthusiastic than the opposite about the prospective asset of innumerable Russian divisions. The Right could evoke memories of the old Tsarist alliance and its usefulness to France while the Left focused on the rosier aspects of the Soviet experiment.

Such as it was, the unity that was thereby produced was but momentary and passing. Two sets of circumstances, related but distinct, cne deeply rooted in the French complex itself, the other fortuitous and accidental, at this very moment combined to reduce to ineffective confusion the functioning of France as a unit of power in Europe. Con-

---

[102] The Manchurian affair of 1931 does not fall within the compass of this essay, but inevitably the successful aggression of Japan had impaired the prestige of Geneva. There was some point to the contention that, in the circumstances, more specifically in the absence of the United States and the Soviet Union from the League, the Manchurian affair was not a fair test; that the League was essentially a European institution that might still prove its effectiveness and competence in an issue where European Powers alone were involved. The withdrawal of Germany and the failure of the Disarmament Conference were additional blows to the League, compensated however by the accession of the Soviet Union, whose spokesman, Litvinov, became the most eloquent exponent of the virtues of *collective* security.

sidering how crucially important the position of France still was at this time, considering as well the manner and the circumstances of her action — rather her failure of action — the final section of this tale can aptly be described as the abdication of France.

5. THE ABDICATION OF FRANCE

The Domestic Uncertainties of France

The events of the 6th of February have been mentioned and their significance as indication of the malaise pervading the French body politic. Their immediate aftermath, at the level of government, had been the formation of the Doumergue ministry, a broad coalition, and an abatement of the political fever; many deputies had been frightened and for a time were willing to hold their pettier quarrels in abeyance. Inevitably, Doumergue reminded one of Poincaré of eight years earlier; he too, an elder statesman, ex-President of the Republic, was meant to symbolize national union and appeasement; welcomed by the Right, he was accepted, or at least tolerated, by an appreciable segment of the Left. But the difficulties with which he was confronted were fundamentally more serious than those which had faced Poincaré, not to mention the fact that, in terms of personal stature and competence, Doumergue was no Poincaré.

In addition to what might be regarded as the normal internal divisions, characteristic of the French milieu, the country was by now fully involved in the tensions arising from difficulties of an economic nature. As on other occasions, the failure of the Left to agree on economic and financial measures had led to its downfall and to the substitution of a more clearly marked conservative orientation in the seat of the governement. Apart from the appeasement of political passions, the single most concrete and urgent task that faced the new government was the care of the national economy. But Doumergue also felt — in which many in France agreed — that economic troubles derived in part at least from political management; from this view derived the stress on the necessity of reform in the operation of the political mechanism of France, *la réforme de l'Etat,* as the phrase went. In concrete terms, this meant stronger assertion of the rights of the executive, the power of dissolution of the Chamber for instance.

For a time France had seemed immune to the impact of the economic distress that had engulfed the world, and this had been cause for foolish self-congratulation. As late as 1932, France was the holder of 27 percent of the world's gold, a higher proportion than in 1914; when the British pound, subsequently the dollar, had been devalued, the franc did not follow suit. But the British and the American devaluations, if they served to arrest the fall of prices, were not followed by any marked increase in them; French prices, still in terms of gold, must therefore automatically be relatively higher, or else they must fall nominally in order to maintain their level in relation to world prices. International trade does not have in the French economy the place that it holds in the British; nevertheless, France could not be immune to the impact of the British and American actions: the French effort to immunize the French economy from the effects of a world wide phenomenon, the resort to various forms of protective devices, could not arrest the decline of French economic activity.

If the depression never reached in France the severity and the depths that engulfed America or Germany, its effects were marked none the less. During 1933 there was a considerable loss of gold, while declining state revenues resulted in budgetary deficit. Unemployment was not severe, trifling in fact by comparison with its dimensions across the Rhine, but the official figures — some 250,000 in 1933 — fail to convey a proper picture of its impact: partial employment was widespread and, even more, the psychological factor of the fear of unemployment. These manifestations of economic ill-health, relatively mild as they were, only registered with gradualness on the popular consciousness, but the events of February 6, though primarily political in their significance, were an awakening and a shock to all sectors of the national life; some of the same psychological loss of confidence as in 1924 and 1926 was beginning to reappear.

The task of economic and financial restoration was therefore the most immediate and pressing. The problem was approached along lines of classical orthodoxy, and, in view of the political divergences that blocked financial action, parliament granted the government limited powers to rule by decree. Some reductions were effected in state expenditures, but the impact of other events — German rearmament in particular, already surreptitiously under way — served to undo the effects of economy: the operating budget for 1934 showed a deficit of nearly 9,000,000,000 francs. [103]

In the French financial thinking of the time, one point was fixed: the franc must not be devalued. Agreement on this was virtually unanimous, and the voice of Paul Reynaud, who advocated emulation of the Anglo-American example of devaluation, is conspicuous for its isolation. The finance minister of the day, Germain-Martin, with all the prestige (in France substantial) that an academic position conferred upon him, was applauded for what was considered to have been a successful puncturing of the fallacies of Reynaud's arguments. [104] The

---

[103] There was a temporary return of confidence and inflow of gold after March, 1934, but it did not last beyond that year.

[104] The possibility of devaluation, accompanied by proper manipulations that would prevent a rise in prices equivalent to the depreciation of the currency, was generally considered rank heresy, despite the existing example of other countries. Reynaud, then and later, has been conspicuous for the soundness of his forecasts. For a variety of reasons, though esteemed and respected for his intellect, Reynaud has never commanded either widespread or enthusiastic support in France.

balance sheet of the Doumergue administration in this field was therefore negative, and the position of the French economy continued to
deteriorate during its tenure while the beginnings of recovery were
visible abroad. [105]

It was partly because of this situation, tangled as it became with
the issue of *réforme de l'Etat,* that Doumergue was overthrown in November, 1934. [106] Flandin who succeeded him was essentially a middle-
cf-the-roader; the constitutional issue, bitter source of division, he
would not pursue. But in the field of economics and finance his policy
is best summed up as drift. Since there was no recovery in France, if
anything slow aggravation of illness, the financial straits of the state
could not be alleviated. They, too, tended to worsen, and as borrowing
was becoming more difficult, the device of advances from the Bank
of France to the state was again resorted to. Inevitably, this put the
Bank, as in 1924, in a position to exert pressure on the government. [107]

Reluctantly, Flandin asked for powers of government by decree.
They were refused, the government fell, and the familiar ritual was
once more enacted. It is not rare in France that a Cabinet crisis has
to occur before the Chamber will accept the view that there are no
alternatives, save perhaps even less palatable or likely ones, to the
proposals it has just rejected. [108] When, after some difficult negotiations, Laval succeeded in forming a government, the Chamber granted
him in financial matters the powers that it had just refused Flandin.

The most thoroughgoing essay at deflation ensued. The franc was
to be maintained, but costs and prices, in government and elsewhere,
must be pushed back — ten percent was the figure. Salaries, pensions,
rents, even interest on government securities, all were impartially

---

[105] The figure of unemployment increased by over 150,000 during the
year.

[106] Doumergue introduced in France the Rooseveltian technique of the
fireside chat. The fact itself was disliked in the parliamentary milieu, inclined
to read into it one aspect of Doumergue's design to strengthen the Executive.
One such radio address at the beginning of November, while Parliament was
in recess, announced his intention to ask that body when it reconvened the
vote of credits for the first quarter of 1935, so that budgetary discussions
would not stand in the way of those of constitutional reform. This was
widely interpreted as a step preliminary to the dissolution of the Chamber.
Using the pretext of the breach of constitutional etiquette involved in Doumergue's failure to consult the Cabinet prior to his public announcement,
the Radical ministers withdrew from the government whose resignation automatically ensued.

[107] Specifically, there was the matter of a large amount of government
bonds due to mature on June 15, hence the problem of their redemption.
The Bank was dedicated to financial soundness, meaning a balanced budget.

[108] If this may fairly be regarded as a shortcoming in the operation of
the French political system, criticism of the system should proceed with
caution. For all the awkwardness involved, the fact remains that the system
has functioned. Ordinarily, short of unusual circumstances of stress, it may
be said that the waste of time, effort, and efficiency is not too high a price
for the sake of higher values implicit in the preservation of a democratic
system.

reduced. Such an attempt had in it a note of desperation, and more of naïveté in the quality of thinking that stood behind it than of correct appraisal of economic possibility. It will suffice to register its failure, a failure which, just because the effort was so drastic, could not but by itself leave matters worse than they had been before. France seemed hopelessly shackled in the coils of an insoluble economic dilemma.

Flandin had been an authentic middle-of-the-roader, and his government may be regarded as covering an even broader range than that of his predecessor Doumergue; the loss of control by the Left that was the outcome of the 6th of February was not retrieved. Though there had been some relaxation of political tensions, two potentially troublesome facts remained in the background: the resentment of the Left at its loss of control; the failure of economic improvement. Political divisions, passions and suspicions were therefore held in suspense rather than genuinely appeased. The period of Laval's Prime Ministership, form June, 1935 to January, 1936, assumes considerable significance, no less on the domestic than on the foreign plane; the two were destined for that matter to become inextricably and hopelessly entangled at this very time.

At the domestic level, in the domain of economy and finance, the failure of Laval has been mentioned. The value of the franc was indeed maintained, but despite the drastic deflation French prices were neither substantially reduced, hence brought into nearer alignment with external ones, nor was the budget balanced; a deficit of over 10,000,000,000 francs in a budget of some 50,000,000,000 was the balance sheet for the year. As to economic activity in general, not only did it fail to improve, but unemployment rather continued to increase. [109] Discontent and loss of confidence were natural attendants of prolonged economic stagnation; the German action in March could not but further shake confidence, and the Belgian decision later in the year to devalue the currency and abandon the gold bloc, while Italy and Poland introduced exchange restrictions, tended to put the issue of the fate of the franc not so much in the form: can it be saved? as: how long can its value be maintained?

Conditions such as these are fertile gound for political stress and for suspicion, partly warranted, but in large measure also feeding upon itself. The net result, at all events, was, if not disintegration, at least a profound cleavage in the French body politic. Laval himself was little loved or respected, yet his mastery of the art of retaining contacts in all quarters had brought him to the position that he held; broadly speaking, he was more acceptable to the Right than to the Left, whose suspicion his accession to power increased. The occasion of the na-

---

[109] It stood at some 440,000 at the end of the year and it is figured that 40 percent of workers in enterprises employing more than 100 persons were affected by either total unemployment or short work. Cf. Goguel, *op. cit.*, p. 341.

tional holiday, July 14, 1935, both in fact and symbolically, brought out to a nicety the divisions of France.

The day was fair and eminently suitable for the traditional military display that a deliberate effort was made to render impressive, part answer to the questions raised by the rearmament of Germany now openly proclaimed. But more significant perhaps than the display of military strength was the fact that Paris witnessed on that day two separate and distinct ceremonies. At the Arc de Triomphe, war veterans, service organizations, but most of all the *Croix-de-Feu* and kindred *ligues,* marched in rather impressive formation. At the opposite end of the city, from the Bastille, a far larger if less disciplined mass of people proceeded to march on the boulevards. The workers of Paris carried French as well as Red flags, but rather more of the latter; they sang the *Marseillaise* and the *Internationale,* but the latter was rather more audible; the marchers were in the main adherents of the Socialist and Communist parties, but the presence of Daladier and some other Radical Socialists was widely noticed and loudly cheered. The day went off quietly enough; no incidents occurred; but the rival cries of *Vive la Rocque! La France aux Français!* and *Les Soviets partout!* that answered each other at the opposite ends of the city were adequate expression of ominous divergence.

The divergence, taking the nation as a whole, was perhaps less profound than this makes it appear. This very sane appraisal may be quoted:

> Who knows at bottom a corner of our country knows that in it man is a complex being, desirous of justice but concerned with his interests, opposed to privilege though seeking it for himself, wishing reforms but fearful of disorder. Fanatics will never give him satisfaction for long. The real test will not be that between the two hostile blocs, however powerful they may appear, but rather will take place in the middle opinion, which will vouchsafe or withhold victory to the one or the other according to the tendency that will prevail in it. That is why on the side of the ligues as well as on that of the Popular Front, the fundamental preoccupation should not be so much the increase of their numbers or the elaboration of a technique of the coup d'état, but the bringing of the opponent to make those mistakes that will turn average opinion against him. [110]

France had not gone either Fascist or Communist. But France was subject to a deep malaise for which there seemed to be no cure or alleviation. To the extent that this was due to the deficient quality of the management of her own economic practice, the possibility of cure may be regarded as having lain within her own power. But this was also the country that had, with less enthusiasm than reluctance, and largely from inescapable necessity, undertaken to build and sustain

---

[110] Article entitled "Pour le 14 Juillet: vérités aux gauches," by Fabre-Luce in *L'Europe nouvelle,* July 13, 1935. There is an excellent series of articles in *L'Europe nouvelle* during this period.

an organization that would insure the functioning of Europe as a whole. Already in 1935 France was no longer *the* power in Europe; larger things in fact, associated with contending ideologies that had possibilities of applications unlimited, were ever more intruding on the scene. France was in process of evolving from the position of initiator, guide, director of European policy, to that of being the object of pressures from the outside. The old structure of Europe was however still formally in existence; but in one sense the whole story might be summed up by saying that France, the essential tool of the preservation of the international order of Europe, was not adequate to the task, as there had been every reason to believe, from the very beginning, that for the longer term she could not be.

As a whole, the French people would much rather have cultivated their garden in peace, inefficiently as they might do it. But the fact that France was such an essential piece of Europe ruled out for her the possibility of mere withdrawal. The outside pressure of rival ideologies was inevitably echoed in France. The echoing was louder than the actual impact, but appearance can have greater reality than substance sometimes has. The French people became profoundly and bitterly divided, each side focusing ever more on the other (French) side, feeding its fears from its interpretation of the intentions of its opponents. There was no dearth of outward manifestations on which these fears could thrive. It was just at the time of the governmental crisis that substituted Laval for Flandin that the *ligues,* especially the *Croix-de-Feu* and their leader Colonel de la Rocque, asserted themselves in impressive fashion. Their methods and techniques were calculated to cause the cry Fascist to be raised against them. [111]

The great popular manifestation of the 14th of July had been the answer of the Left; its participants swore to remain united in order "to give bread to the workers, work to the young and peace to the world," in other words, to fight the economic crisis (more specifically the government's program of deflation) as well as the rising tide of Fascism (more concretely, to seek the dissolution of the *ligues*). The bulk of those who had participated in the occasion were Socialists or Communists; this was the outcome of the cooperation between the two

---

[111] The model of Fascist, and even more Nazi, techniques, rallies, parades, military organization, was not lost on them. As modern up-to-date advertising techniques, the effectiveness of these methods can hardly be denied. However, by themselves, they are little more than advertising, and the real question is what do they advertise? It is equally undeniable that there was a marked dearth of clear thought in the leadership of the ligues, and not a little well-meant and high-minded, if befuddled, old fashioned idealistic patriotism among their adherents. This, of course, does not invalidate the fact that they were potentially effective tools that might fall under the control of clearer-minded individuals or forces that might use them to their own ends; to that extent the fears of the Left had point.

There is not a little similarity in terms of personality between Colonel de la Rocque and General Boulanger of fifty years earlier: a misleadingly attractive personal façade with little that was solid behind.

parties, of which the earlier formation of a *Comité national de Rassemblement populaire* was the concrete manifestation. The Communist-Socialist rapprochement [112] had also born concrete fruit in the municipal elections of the spring in the customary form of electoral combinations; the success of the Communists, especially notable in the *ceinture rouge* (red belt) of the industrial suburbs of Paris, had in turn given body to the fears of the Right. Both Communists and *ligueurs* were making progress during 1935, each group magnifying the fears of the other while both together contributed to the increasingly sharp division of the nation.

The Radical Socialists, a party of moderation at heart, were placed by these events in a quandary. The general ideology of the Left appealed to them, and Daladier had joined the Socialists and Communists on the 14th of July; [113] but of constructive economic ideas they were largely deficient and, albeit with reluctance, they tolerated Laval; his lack of success in this field, however, made his appeal increasingly less potent. The party congress in the autumn finally decided that the party as a whole should cast its lot with the rest of the Left by joining the *Rassemblement populaire,* increasingly described already for some time as the Popular Front, which the Radical Socialist decision may be said to have brought into formal existence. [114]

The Foreign Uncertainties of France: The Abyssinian Imbroglio

The sharpest focus of the bitter quarrels and divisions of France was domestic, but the impact on them of the outside was inescapable. Not only in the form of French Fascists, or presumed such, versus French Communists, but as luck would have it in the form of a major, though until a short time before wholly unforeseen and unexpected, international complication. Within France, the effect of the Abyssinian imbroglio was to make confusion worse confounded and to raise the bitterness and recriminations of her divisions to further heights of weakening disintegration.

---

[112] This cooperation was made possible by the changed attitude of the Communists. The Kremlin had drawn the lesson of its mistaken tactics in Germany and resolved to avoid a repetition of the Nazi success elsewhere by ordering Communist parties to cooperate with other forces of the Left, more broadly with all those who opposed Fascism. As usual in such arrangements, the Communists' vigor and singleness of purpose tended to give them a leading and disproportionate share in the direction of the Popular Fronts that they joined. This domestic policy of the French Communists was the logical counterpart of the Franco-Soviet Pact on the international plane.

[113] Daladier had remained embittered by the sequel of the 6th of February. The epithet *fusilleur,* commonly used by the Right in referring to him, rankled and made him readier to join their opponents.

[114] This decision of the Radical Socialist congress was tantamount to the death warrant of the Laval government since the reunited Left had a majority in Parliament. The Radical ministers lingered on for a time, however, and only resigned in mid-January, in connection with further developments in the Abyssinian affair.

The record of the Abyssinian affair must, even at this distance, fill one with wonder. Where the three chief European participants are concerned, Britain, France, and Italy, it reminds one that they whom the Gods would destroy they first make mad; seen from across the Rhine, this record correspondingly could supply strong argument for the old German motto *Gott mit uns*.

Much ink has flowed out of this episode, the retelling of which would be idle; [115] those aspects of it only which have relevance to the present tale will be retained. The fundamental fact is simply this: Italy wanted to expand her influence over Abyssinia. In the context of earlier days, such an attempt would have been viewed as a local manifestation of the imperialism of Europe, the record of which was writ large over the whole African continent. Italy had in fact made an earlier essay at Abyssinian conquest, [116] and one of Mussolini's motives was to erase the shame of Adowa. As such, an Italian conquest of Abyssinia would be in precisely the same category as a French establishment in Morocco or a British in Egypt; one may even readily grant that, on balance, the Italian control would have brought to the backward country the benefits of more advanced civilization. This is essentially the light in which the matter was viewed in Italy, and to this day is viewed with a surprising degree of unanimity. [117]

Some other facts are equally clear and simple. Both Italy and Abyssinia were members of the League. When a dispute developed between them, the Abyssinian appeal to the League was as logical as it was inevitable. Nor is there need to waste time on purposely involved technicalities: Abyssinia *was* the object of Italian aggression. What else was the League for, if not for the purpose of successively preventing, then punishing, aggression? The skeptical contention that it was peculiar to have discovered the sins of imperialism at the particular point of time when some states — read Britain and France — were in possession of vast empires while others with as good a claim if not

---

[115] The literature dealing with the Abyssinian episode is abundant but of very mixed quality. By way of general references the following may be cited. The *Survey of International Affairs, 1935,* vol. II (London, 1936) remains fundamental; to it may be added another publication of the Royal Institute of International Affairs, *International Sanctions* (London, 1938); also, André Mandelstam, *Le conflit italo-éthiopien devant la Société des Nations* (Paris, 1937). On the Italian side may be cited Raffaele Ciasca, *Storia coloniale dell'Italia contemporanea* (Milan, 1940) and Corrado Zoli, *La conquista dell' Impero* (Bologna, 1937). Of especial relevance to the treatment of his essay are P. Vaucher and P.H. Siriex, *L'opinion britannique, la Société des Nations et la guerre italo-éthiopienne* (Paris, 1936) and Gaetano Salvemini, *Prelude to World War II* (New York, 1954).

[116] In 1896. But the defeat of Adowa caused Italy to abandon the attempt at the time.

[117] Fascism may have gone in Italy but it is interesting, if perhaps distressing, to observe the extent of the inability in that country to acknowledge the foundations of the objections to the Abyssinian undertaking. More than any other perhaps, the Abyssinian episode was a national, rather than a purely Fascist, affair during the entire period of Fascist rule.

a better did not enjoy such benefits, carried in Italy considerable conviction — understandably so — yet in the case was beside the point. [118]

One more preliminary aspect of the matter should be mentioned. There is considerable validity in the contention that such an institution as the League could only have meaning and hopes of successful operation if it was an organization of states that had reached at least a roughly comparable stage of political development, states capable, as the phrase goes, of the responsible discharge of their international obligations. The fiction, therefore, that a backward state is fit for membership, while it may have some uses, is also fraught with dangers. Whether Abyssinia had reached such a suitable stage of development could at least be debated. [119] However, as of 1935, in fact as well as in law, Abyssinia was a member in good standing of the League.

Italy's Abyssinian plans had been in the making for quite some time; they had behind them for that matter the record of a tradition going back half a century. Mussolini's estimate of the international situation was sound that made him judge the time propitious for the launching of his adventure. Having attended to military preparations, he then proceeded with the diplomatic. This was the real sense of the agreement concluded between himself and Laval at the beginning of 1935. This has been mentioned, as well as the surprising failure to discuss the Abyssinian problem at the Stresa meeting in April of that year.

In the circumstances, the position of France was obviously crucial. Allowing for the uncertainty that surrounds the precise nature and content of the Laval-Mussolini exchanges, this may be said: Laval was indifferent to the fate of Abyssinia; he put little stock in the League, and he was bent on securing the Italian connection. If one takes the extreme view of *Realpolitik,* wholly dismissing the League, and thinks in terms of pure power, a case could be made in logic from the French point of view for cementing a coalition that would include Britain, Russia and Italy — the First World War alliance. In that context, the case of Abyssinia could appear as one that it would not be beyond the skill of diplomacy to deal with while giving satisfaction to the Italian wish.

---

[118] In the last resort it became necessary to fall back on the argument that the world of 1935 was different from — presumably better than — that of pre-1914, when there was no League of Nations. This argument is not to be dismissed with flippancy, for, whatever the shortcoming of the League, the fact remains that it represented an essay and a beginning in the direction of instituting the rule of law in the relations among nations. At the same time, in view of these shortcomings, most particularly the failure to prevent the successful Japanese aggression in Manchuria, it is easy to see how, from the Italian point of view, such an argument appeared as little more than a manifestation of British and French cant.

[119] Much was made of this point in Italy, and the question had in fact been raised at the time of Abyssinia's admission to the League in 1923. The supreme irony lay in the fact that, in 1923, Italy had supported the acceptance of Abyssinia while it was Britain that had expressed doubts.

At best, the situation in Geneva was awkward. After the failure of the initial attempt at arbitration of the Wal-Wal incident of December 1934, specific starting point of the story, the record is the tortuous one that may be summed as a succession of attempts to contrive a peaceful solution that would be acceptable to Italy. [120] But Mussolini proved less than accommodating and his resort to overt military action in October faced all with the inescapable fact of aggression. Unable to conceal or deny evidence that was so blatant, the League had no choice but to register the fact and thence proceed to the imposition of sanctions against Italy.

But what sanctions? The real issue was whether they would reach the point of military action; the peculiar result had been achieved where the possibility had to be contemplated of war in Europe between Italy on one side and inevitably on the other Britain and France, a curious way to deal with the German danger.

This last was, in French eyes, the only one that really counted. Of actual French interest in Ethiopia there was relatively little; [121] of greater substance was the British stake, deriving from the water supply of the Blue Nile that issued from Lake Tsana in Ethiopian territory. [122] The mere defense of British imperial interest presented no necessarily insuperable obstacle, and Britain had not in the past been unfriendly to Italian expansion in East Africa, which she had even at times encouraged.

A combination of circumstances, however, led Britain at this point to become the champion of the League. [123] Hitherto it had been France who, in Geneva, had argued in favor of a stronger League; nothing could be more full of irony and awkwardness than to have Britain now become converted to such a view of things at the very moment when France, through Laval, was desperately trying to hold back the

---

[120] These may be followed in detail in the *Survey of International Affairs,* 1935, vol. II, *Italy and Abyssinia,* devoted exclusively to the Abyssinian affair.

[121] The small possession of French Somaliland, or Jibuti, had had little value from the time that France had abandoned the grandiose scheme of incorporating Abyssinia in a vast empire that would have spanned the whole width of the African continent from East to West. It had strategic value as a station on the way to the Far East and was also the terminal of the French-owned Jibuti-Addis Ababa railway. From the Italian point of view, French interest and activity in that region was more in the nature of pin-pricks than of a real interest. This is well brought out in such a book as Francesco Salata, *Il nodo di Gibuti* (Milan, 1939).

[122] A tripartite Anglo-Franco-Italian agreement of 1906, aftermath of the Italian failure of the preceding decade, had defined the interests of the three Powers in Abyssinia. An Anglo-Italian agreement of 1925, despite Abyssinia's membership in the League at the time, was largely blocked by Abyssinian objections sustained by French support.

[123] It was in June, 1935 that were published the results of the famous Peace Ballot, which showed British opinion to be overwhelmingly in favor of what may be described as a strong League policy, even to the point of resorting to military measures.

League. [124] Had circumstances been other, the somewhat sudden British conversion would have been welcome in France; as it was, it could not help but be highly suspect. It could be, and was, explained as mere devotion to the defense of British interest: just as France thought primarily of the League as providing possible additional assistance against a German danger, so likewise Britain, now that a substantial imperial interest was at stake — control of the Red Sea route to the East — would like the assistance of others in the form of collective League action. This might be understandable, but must appear at once naïve and callous: it was in March that Britain had shown herself willing to condone in reality German rearmament; it was in June that she had taken the further step of giving her unilateral sanction to the naval rearmament of Germany.

There were many in France who had little use for Laval and his Italian machinations, but even among those few responded to the consideration that here was an opportunity to bind Britain securely to support of the League and collective security as a valuable precedent for future occasion. Opinion was widely and violently divided in France on the merits of Mussolini's enterprise; it was essentially united in viewing the possibility of a conflict with Italy as sheer folly. But, seen from Britain, especially in the eyes of the well meaning opinion that had just expressed its devotion to the League, the French behavior was merely one of inconsistent and selfish duplicity: France was behaving badly, showing callousness where anything but her security, her obsession with the German danger — an unreasonable obsession to boot — was concerned. Feeling at the popular level ran high on both sides of the Channel fed by the easy recourse to moral judgment. It might be pointed out that if France, through Laval, had manoeuvred herself into an awkward situation, the popular British expectation of France, especially in the persistent refusal to assume firm responsibilities on the Rhine, also seems somewhat less than reasonable.

Complications did not end at this point. The British government selected this time for holding a general election in which the Abyssinian *imbroglio* specifically, more broadly the question of the League in general, was a central issue. Ostensibly, the government of Britain was still that of the National coalition that had emerged from the crisis of 1931; in fact, it was a Conservative government. Even in Britain, politics is politics, and, in view of the results of the recent Peace Ballot, much was made of devotion to the League as the foundation of British foreign policy. When subsequently asked why this had been done, Prime Minister Baldwin is credited with the retort that without it the election could not have been won. Not without justification, some rather harsh judgments have been passed on this episode.

---

[124] France, especially in view of her past record, could hardly refuse to recognize the Italian aggression, but even then Laval may be said to have lived up to his end of his bargain with Mussolini by using every effort to limit the range of sanctions and to minimize their effect.

The results of the election were certainly satisfactory to Mr. Baldwin: he had won it. Yet this made things all the more awkward. With a view to liquidating the Abyssinian *imbroglio* as best might be, Laval and Britain's Foreign Secretary, Samuel Hoare, at the beginning of December elaborated the famous scheme that bears their joint names. The plan, under the fiction of an "exchange of territories" would have handed over some two-thirds of Abyssinia to Italy while giving her a virtual protectorate over the rest. Here was old time diplomacy at work. In terms of *Realpolitik,* the scheme had merits: the real issues lay in Europe, not in East Africa; in terms of ethics, the word fraud best characterizes it. Whether the urbane skill of British reasonableness would have been equal to the task of "selling" the scheme to Parliament and public opinion must remain an interesting speculation. Clearly, Sir Samuel must have thought so, and the subsequent picture of the innocent Britisher taken in by the wiles of his unprincipled, unscrupulous French counterpart can at best evoke a skeptical smile.

But in any event, the operation must be handled with care. However, a *coup de théâtre* intervened at this point that upset all the nice calculations. An indiscretion in the French press, as early as December 9, made public the essential lines of the Hoare-Laval project. [125] The reaction of British opinion was both instantaneous and intense, on the

---

[125] The source of the indiscretion is credited to the well known French journalists Pertinax (Marcel Géraud) and Geneviève Tabouis who sent their information from London. Their indiscretion was made with the calculated intention of wrecking the scheme; not however because of its abstract or ethical merits, but because of their feeling that Laval's Italian policy was unsound, which last judgment was correct. Cf. Geneviève Tabouis, *They called me Cassandra* (New York, 1942).

To these events and their sequel may be traced much of Laval's intense hatred of Britain, with the subsequent consequences that this feeling had. It may be pointed out that, in the particular matter under discussion, there is little to choose between Hoare and Laval. Sir Samuel had to withdraw from the political scene for a time, but Laval was the convenient scapegoat for British moral indignation, and Laval's resentment is altogether understandable. The subsequent fate of the two men gives food for interesting reflections. Sir Samuel Hoare soon returned to office and continued as a respected member of British society, political and other; Laval ended in dishonor and was shot following a questionable trial after the war. As private characters the two men were very different; as politicians rather less so. In the last resort, Laval was shot and dishonored not for private peculations, but as the price of his political acts.

The story does not end here, however, for these events left traces and repercussions in the relations between the two countries. In this connection mention is appropriate of Professor Salvemini's analysis of the Ethiopian episode in his *Prelude to World War II.* Professor Salvemini, no lover of either Mussolini or Laval, has nevertheless come to feel that the popular contemporary view of the respective roles of Britain and France in the whole affair is incorrect and that the larger share of the blame belongs to the British, ostensible defenders of the League though they seemed to be at the time. To this writer that judgment seems on the whole warranted. Mention may also be made of Sir Samuel Hoare's recollections, Viscount Templewood, *Nine Troubled Years* (London, 1954).

score of morality, as much as if not more than on the score of national interest. After some awkward explanations Sir Samuel relinquished his office. The French reaction was less intense and more realistic: however unpleasantly and awkwardly, and be it at the sacrifice of some principle, the Abyssinian affair should be liquidated. Laval, too, had to give explanations that were awkward, but for the moment his government survived.

The sequel for Abyssinia was brief. The Hoare-Laval plan had appeal for Mussolini, but the British explosion eliminated it as a possible solution. While discussion of intensified sanctions proceeded in Geneva, the war in Abyssinia went on; to the surprise of many, once Marshal Badoglio had been put in charge of operations, its course became successful and speedy. In May the Italians entered Addis Ababa, and the outright annexation of the whole country was proclaimed by Italy, while Mussolini raised the stature of King Victor Emmanuel by setting the imperial crown on top of his royal one. Clearly, the League could take no further action at this point. On July 4 sanctions against Italy were lifted, thereby giving implicit recognition to the *fait accompli* and to the success of brutal aggression. The Duce could, and did, boast that Italy had successfully defeated the combination of sixty nations. The claim was not unpleasing to Italian ears.

The consequences of the episode were very great. To all intents and purposes the League of Nations as an effective agency that any one could trust for his protection was now dead. It would be idle and beyond the scope of this discussion to essay an assessment of the share of responsibility for its outcome. That Italy was the prime mover is clear beyond debate. For France to have adopted a policy of clear and determined support of the League, whatever the consequences, would have been consistent with her former professions; it would have been an act of courage deserving of admiration and praise, that British opinion doubtless would have granted in full measure. Whether in view of the British reticence in regard to the making of future commitments and the readiness of British opinion to perceive the justification of German deeds and claims it would have been an act of wisdom rather than a quixotic gesture, there is solid reason to doubt.

However that may be, the demise of the League served to restore with greater clarity the pure relationships of power as the dominant factor of the European scene. But in that context also the Abyssinian episode had consequences that were profound. The core of European stability remained in British and French power, possibly assisted by Russian. [126] The Hoare-Laval proposal may be taken as an indication that the governments of Baldwin and Laval had no unbridgeable divergence in their philosophies and methods. However, Britain and

---

[126] The Soviet line of policy had been to support the League and collective security. Russia had little difficulty in appreciating the possibilities of *Realpolitik*, but, inevitably, the course of the Abyssinian affair introduced an element of uncertainty as to the true intentions of French and British policy.

France are both democracies wherein opinion is both free and vocal and may not, beyond a certain point, be ignored. Baldwin had had to sacrifice his Foreign Secretary to the indignant surge of opinion in Britain. One clear legacy of the *imbroglio* was a deep cleavage and not a little bitterness between British and French opinions. This might pass, but for the moment made more difficult the acceptance and operation of a common policy.

Italy had been Laval's own special card. But whether Mussolini had the better of him or was by him misled, Laval was callous and insensitive to the imponderable of a well-intentioned opinion. His reported envy of Mussolini who could govern without the fetters of a free Parliament and press is accurate measure of his inclination. His own home opinion did not rise in indignation as the British did, but Laval did not long survive the failure of his scheme. [127] Worst of all, the result of his too involved machinations was a renewed estrangement between Italy and France. With deliberate intent, during the unfolding of the Abyssinian adventure, Italian opinion had been roused to a high pitch of resentment against both France and Britain.

And yet it might be argued that, on balance, Laval had served Mussolini well; and Mussolini was far freer in directing Italian policy than any French or British government in their corresponding domains. From the standpoint of power politics and relationships Mussolini in fact made a very sane statement when he declared, once Abyssinia had been conquered, that Italy was now a satisfied Power. But he, too, had been made mad, perhaps by the very degree of a success that exceeded all planned expectations. Instead of drawing from his statement the sound corollary that he now ought to join the ranks of the Powers of conservation in order to preserve the peace and the structure of Europe, along with the fruits of his aggression, he was soon to embark on further, to himself and to others, ultimately fatal adventures. [128]

---

[127] His very skilful defense of his foreign policy at the end of December won him a vote of confidence by a small majority, but the desertion of the Radical Socialists caused him to resign in January without even meeting again the test of the Chamber.

[128] It makes for interesting speculation to consider what the course of events might have been had Italy chosen the path of peace and conservation instead of embarking on further adventures. The least that can be said is that, in the shifting relationship of power that was evolving, Italian power had an opportunity to exert very considerable influence in altering the balance, specifically in making secure the emergence of Germany to the point where that country felt it safe to launch upon overt aggression. That success caused Mussolini to lose his former sense of proportion is the most likely explanation, and the megalomania that characterizes Italian policy subsequent to the Abyssinian episode can aptly be described as the Fable of the Bull and the Frog.

6. THE END OF THE FRENCH SYSTEM

Nazi Germany understood the operation of power and *Realpolitik,* more congenial to its outlook than the "mystical nonsense" about universal peace. The German reaction to the Hoare-Laval plan is enlightening; the strong dislike evinced for it was logical enough: it merely reflected the fear that, should the scheme succeed, it might be prelude to the effective restoration of the Stresa front. If both Hitler and Mussolini understood and appreciated power, the tortuous operation of the British and French democratic milieus was to them source of puzzlement that even led them to suspect involved and dark machinations that in reality did not exist. Both had respect, however, for French power in being, more narrowly for the French military power still enjoying at this time the aura of prestige that the First World War had bestowed upon it. It was sound reasoning for both to feel that if the structure of Europe was to be altered in a fundamental manner, the central core of that structure must first be isolated, preliminary to the breaking of the structure. The implications of this operation Hitler understood and could face; Mussolini, to his own greatest hurt, sadly misunderstood them.

France, to a point, played into their hands. The technical aspects of France's management of her armed forces and her military policy are an important item in this story, [129] but in the last analysis the basic tone and temper of the French complex is of greater significance, and for that reason must be stressed.

The advent of Laval to the Prime Ministership had inaugurated the most thoroughgoing attempt to enact a policy of deflation, from which no benefits ensued, but rather a further decline of economic activity. It may seem surprising, in the circumstances, that this same period should have witnessed a minimum of labor unrest. The superficial quiet was misleading, for if strikes were few, pent up discontent was mounting, building up in fact for an explosion. The Communist role becomes important at this point, for the changed outlook of the Kremlin had the effect of causing the French Communists to adopt the tactics of collaboration with other elements of the French Left, thereby tending to restore the unity of the French working class whose divisions had been one of the causes of its ineffective weakness.

As between France and Russia, the pre-1914 relationship was in some ways reversed. Instead of the Tsar being reluctant to make a connection with radical, republican, godless France, all that there was

---

[129] It was in France that a young officer, Charles de Gaulle by name, wrote a book, *Vers l'armée de métier,* published in 1934, that was both interesting and important. In it de Gaulle showed a clear grasp of modern technical developments, from which he stressed the necessity of mechanization and of an army built around a corps of technicians. De Gaulle's ideas, as it turned out, had great success among the German military who adopted and perfected them. In France, de Gaulle had no success; he ran into two

in France of conservative, *bien pensant,* propertied interests, [130] now looked askance at radical Moscow. Any Franco-Russian connection must therefore contain elements of weakness deriving from the reciprocity of suspicion. Yet in both cases, before 1914 and now, there was the simple element of common interest stemming from common danger, the German. The Communists in France had espoused the cause of French armament.

But at the level of economic and social relations, differences persisted between Right and Left, were becoming in fact intensified and exacerbated. The result of the municipal elections of the spring of 1935, as mentioned before, was such that each side could feed its fears on the successes of the other. Into this situation the Abyssinian crisis intruded with the effect of catalytic agent. The Left was ideologically anti-Fascist and generally pro-League; Mussolini's Ethiopian aggression gave clear and simple focus to its stand. The Right, supposedly more "realistic," tended to focus on the danger of "unrealistic" adventures into which it thought France's strength stood in danger of being diverted away from Europe. The Right was not pro-German, but much of it manoeuvred itself into becoming pro-Italian. It is in connection with the Abyssinian episode that one can trace a marked shift of orientation in the French Right; [131] the neatest expression of this was the somewhat later slogan, Rather Hitler than Blum! [132] In addition to which, the French in general, Left or Right, had little real stomach for military adventures, while the behavior of Britain was largely unsatisfactory to all. [133] The confusion of France was a marvel to see.

The government of Britain, apart from the traditional reluctance toward Eastern European embroilments, was somewhat less than enthusiastic about a close Franco-Russian connection, despite the

difficulties. On the one hand opposition from those in control of military policy: it was none other than Marshal Pétain, revered legacy of the First World War, who expressed scepticism of the value of the tank; on the other hand, at the political level, the idea of an *armée de métier* aroused instinctive opposition because of its possible political implications. Here also Paul Reynaud stands out as a well-nigh solitary exception; as in the case of financial policy, Reynaud spoke with prophetic lucidity, specifically endorsing de Gaulle's ideas, both in Parliament and outside, but found no response.

[130] With some qualifications in the peasantry, among some of whom the revolutionary tradition of Left voting persists to a remarkable degree.

[131] Cf. Charles Micaud, *The French Right and Nazi Germany,* cited above.

[132] This must be interpreted with caution and not literally as an expression of the intensity of anti-Communist rather than of pro-Nazi feeling, and also because the prospect of Hitler's coming was largely in the nature of a figure of speech. The significance of such an expression may best be understood, in the American milieu, by recalling some of the statements made about and the feelings aroused in certain quarters by "that man in the White House."

[133] The reticence of the Left on the score of sanctions, especially military sanctions, must be noted. Even Blum, for all his attachment to the League, wrote that the Admiralty had got out of hand when naval units of the British fleet were sent to the Mediterranean.

formal blessing it had bestowed upon the Franco-Soviet Pact, and there
were those in France who felt that, in the last resort, the British connection was the most essential. Such a view would appeal to middle-of-
the-roaders, many in the Radical Socialist group for example, for all
that they were formally, and liked to think of themselves as being, of
the Left. It was in fact shortly after the incident of the Hoare-Laval
proposal that the Radical Socialist ministers quit Laval's government
and brought about its downfall.

The succession went to Sarraut, a middle-of-the-roader among
middle-of-the-roaders, staunch reliable Radical Socialist Republican of
pre-1914 vintage, not a man of unusual stature or extraordinary
personal strength, while Flandin took the Foreign Office. The Sarraut
ministry was in fact little more than a caretaker government, for a
general election was shortly to take place, pending which little could
be expected of marked significance in terms of policy. The stage was
set for the last act of our story.

The Remilitarization of the Rhineland

The Franco-Soviet Pact, it will be remembered, had been signed
on May 2, 1935. It had evoked strong condemnation in Germany, but
the speech of Hitler before the Reichstag on May 21 had been taken
as conciliatory rather than the opposite; in it the Führer had asserted
his respect for all commitments, in particular Locarno, freely assumed
by Germany. [134]   The rest of the year saw the unfolding of the Abyssinian imbroglio which naturally held the center of the European stage.
Germany needed time to proceed with her rearmament, and the embroil-
ment into which the other Locarno signatories had become entangled
she could contemplate with equal shares of equanimity and satisfaction.
In addition, Laval seemed in no undue hurry to procure ratification
of the Franco-Soviet Pact. The matter was in fact only brought up
as one of the last acts of his administration, in January, 1936. The
Sarraut government laid the treaty before the Chamber which passed
the bill for its ratification on February 27; it received a comfortable
majority though not the unanimous approval of the preceding year —
the vote was 353 to 164 — and final ratification by the Senate was
foregone. [135]   Debate in that body was scheduled to begin on March 12.
The various dates in this tale are significant.

---

[134] The door to future objections was left open, however, by the qualification that this attitude was conditional upon that of others in regard to
the Locarno Pact.

[135] It is at this point (on February 28) that there occurred the minor
sensation of the publication in the French newspaper *Paris-Midi* of an interview given by Hitler to the French publicist Bertrand de Jouvenel. With
seemingly complete forthrightness Hitler conveyed an appeal for a Franco-
German rapprochement. The fact that the interview had been granted a
week earlier and that its publication was withheld until the 28th has been
the source of not a little comment and speculation.

On March 2, the French Ambassador, François-Poncet, on instructions

For some time the German press had been discussing with increasing acerbity the theme of the incompatibility of the two instruments, Locarno and the Franco-Soviet Pact, while on the French side there was open discussion of the possibility of a German move in the demilitarized zone of the Rhineland. Speculation on that score was abruptly ended on March 7. Having consulted his advisers and found divided counsels among them, Hitler settled the issue between himself and his intuition. Three things happened almost simultaneously on the 7th of March. The ambassadors of the Locarno Powers, summoned to the Wilhelmstrasse, were handed a memorandum; immediately thereafter, this memorandum was read by Hitler to the Reichstag summoned to meet at noon. The world was thus apprised of the third event in course of taking place, the entry into the demilitarized zone of regular formations of the German armed forces. Almost simultaneously the Paris noon press came out featuring the headline, *Les troupes allemandes entrent en Rhénanie*.

It was a tense moment on both aides of the Rhine. The first instinctive popular reaction in France was that trouble had come that would be met by some action. But Hitler's intuition had given him sound counsel. The memorandum [136] presented to the Locarno powers was not devoid of skill. The heart of it, giving justification for the German move, lay in these words:

> The German government have continually emphasized ... their readiness to observe and fulfill all the obligations arising from the Rhine Pact [Locarno] as long as the other contracting parties were ready on their side to maintain the pact. This obvious and essential condition can no longer be regarded as being fulfilled by France.

The claim, clearly asserted, that the Franco-Soviet Pact constitued a breach by France of her Locarno obligations was followed by an offer to proceed to new negotiations leading to what might be described as a revised version of Locarno. The principal proposed bases of negotiations were

1. The creation of similiar demilitarized zones on both sides of the frontiers of Germany with France and with Belgium;
2. The conclusion of a twenty-five year non-aggression pact between the three countries; this pact, like Locarno, to be under British and Italian guarantee.

In addition, Germany proposed the conclusion with the states bordering her on the East of pacts similar to the one she had concluded with Poland in 1934; she also suggested that, now that her reason for having left Geneva (failure to grant her equality of armaments) had been removed, she could rejoin the League.

---

from his government, had an interview with Hitler and von Neurath to inquire about the bases of this rapprochement and was told that specific German proposals would be forthcoming shortly.

[136] Text in *Documents on International Affairs, 1936*, pp. 41-5.

The objection may occur at once that it was peculiar to announce in the same breath the repudiation of one obligation and the offer to assume another. What faith could be reposed in German promises when Germany was the sole judge of their continued validity? This was indeed the weak point in the German case which did not escape the French and, in general, their continental allies. The issue of the compatibility of the Franco-Soviet Pact and Locarno could be argued, for all that both Britain and Italy, guarantors of Locarno, had already answered the query in the affirmative; in no event could it be seriously maintained, however, that the German interpretation of law was alone valid. [137]

But the presentation of the German case was mainly directed to outside, more particularly to British, opinion. [138] The British reaction at the level of both government and opinion was, to say the least, interesting ; unlike the case of Abyssinia, at the time of the Hoare-Laval proposal, the two were now largely in agreement; what exceptions there were, were largely in the nature of voices crying in the wilderness. [139] British opinion had shown considerable devotion to the ideal of peace; more recently great enthusiasm for the League as the chief and best peace preserving agency. It was Britain, not France, who in Geneva had been the main promoter of sanctions. Here was a clear violation of the Locarno treaty, to say nothing of Versailles, both of which bore the signature of Britain.

This, Britain could do no less than acknowledge, but the conclusion in this case was not that action should be taken at once under the provisions of Locarno; it was rather that negotiations should be undertaken, essentially on the basis of the German offer. In retrospect, this seeming willingness to trust the destroyer of trust himself at the very moment he was performing his act of destruction may seem like aberration. It was; but it is at this point necessary to recall the state of British opinion in the year 1936.

Both Foreign Secretary Eden and the London *Times* delivered Germany a moral lecture on the subject of the respect due one's obligations and on the proper manner to set about changing these when desired; but from this both went on to a curiously optimistic acceptance of the

---

[137] Actually, such was in effect and to a large extent the Nazi view, in so far as any concept of legality was at all retained. The feeling ran deep in Nazi mentality that was given blunt expression by Gauleiter Wagner speaking in Munich on March 14: "What Hitler did on March 7, benefited the German people. Anything that benefits the German people is right; anything that harms the German people is wrong." Cited by Alexander Werth, *The Twilight of France 1933-1940* (New York, 1942), p. 70.

[138] As to Italy, although Mussolini had not yet committed himself to Hitler, in view of the circumstances of the moment, there was every reason to expect that Italy would show little inclination for taking forcible action against Germany.

[139] Churchill's own account of this whole episode may be found in *The Gathering Storm* (London, 1948), chapter XI.

fait accompli; as the *Times* concluded in its editorial of March 9, "it is the moment, not to despair, but to rebuild."[140] The simple fact was that, with a surprising degree of unanimity, British opinion was ready to accept as basically and morally sound Hitler's justification of the German action, just as with equal fervor, it saw a moral wrong where it came to the Italian conquest of Abyssinia. Law, in the last analysis, must indeed rest on moral foundation; yet to alter the standard of the applicability of existing law, however good the intention, and in the process to remain blind to the reality of the operation of power can, and did, have unexpected results. In its manifestations, though not necessarily in its conscious intent, much of British opinion was in effect pro-German. It would be difficult to argue that, even in 1936, between Mussolini and Hitler, the latter stood for the higher standard of ethics.

However that may be, seen from across the Channel, the British reaction had the earmarks of confused thinking. Even to those in France who had felt embarrassed at the invidious role that France had played in the Abyssinian affair, the Rhine was more important: on that score feeling was nearly unanimous. That Britain should grow exercised about distant Abyssinia yet remain essentially unmoved by events on the Rhine was rather more than understanding could encompass. But if the French view of things was clearer than the British, French action was no more effective or adequate. To a degree indeed the British reaction may be regarded as having been a source of restraint and discouragement for France. But, true as this may be, it cannot be considered as sufficient or valid justification for the French failure to respond to the German challenge.

France had effective power of her own that, in the last resort, she could have used alone; she need not be, unless she so elected, a mere dependent whose foreign policy Britain could decide for her. Nor for that matter would she have been alone. From Russia at this time she would have had at least approval, and from her other allies, even quite possibly from Poland, active support, had things come to the point of active hostilities with Germany. There was power enough available to face any contingency with confidence, to say nothing of the fact that, had it come to war, even Britain, though probably delivering herself of pious lecturing, would by the mere necessity of her own safety not have been able to allow an improbable German success. And this is taking the worst possibility into consideration, for the probability was rather considerable that a determined show of strength would have sufficed to cause a German renunciation.

If France failed to react, on this, the last opportunity granted her to act and give leadership to Europe, the reasons for this failure are to be found in the country itself and its condition. What has been said before

---

140 This episode may be followed in the *Bulletin périodique de la presse* (presse anglaise: du 21 février au 25 mars 1936). For the [London] *Times* in particular, the *History of the Times,* vol. IV, Part II, pp. 898 ff. is of considerable interest.

of the domestic state of France here becomes paramount. The Sarraut government had limited authority until the nearing day, in May, when the French people would go to the polls; this people was at this time divided and confused, broken up into factions the focus of whose pre-occupations was in the main other French factions; to the extent that external events and ideologies had an impact on the French body politic they had served to exaggerate and exacerbate its internecine differences.

When the Sarraut Cabinet met, twice during the day, to consider the events of March 7 it, too, found divergence within itself; [141] the presence of the French military leaders did not help crystallize opinion, but rather furnished an opportunity for the shifting of responsibility between them and the government. That the German move called for an answer was obvious. But what answer? Some of the ministers favored the taking of immediate action; others preferred delay and consultation. As to the military, who had had long warning of the coming reoccupa-tion, they were averse to taking risks, meaning anything less than full mobilization; the responsibility for such a decision was not theirs but the government's. But such an operation would be costly and en-danger the franc, to the intangibility of which all were equally dedi-cated.

The probable reaction of other Powers, Britain especially, to any French decision naturally loomed large. Consultation with the British Ambassador had brought counsels of caution. To the greatest relief of Britain, among others, the French government, apart from taking some relatively unimportant military precautions, decided to confine itself to consultation. [142] The entry of the German forces into the de-militarized zone was the clearest violation of both Locarno and Ver-sailles, instruments of equal validity in law, whatever the German feelings about them might be; but the view was taken that this was

---

[141] An important source bearing on these events is the *Rapport de la Commission chargée d'enquêter sur les événements survenus en France de 1933 à 1945* (Paris, no date). This consists of two volumes summarizing the findings of the commission (the *Rapport* proper) and eight volumes of hearings (*témoignages*). This investigation, initiated in 1947, is not free from bias and, naturally, the witnesses, comprising a large number of the leading political personalities of the period under investigation, are chiefly concerned with justifying themselves. The publication contains nevertheless a wealth of valuable information in the form of personal testimony as well as of statistics on the condition of the French armed forces.

Also, P. E. Flandin, *Politique française 1919-1940*, Paul-Boncour, *Entre deux guerres*, vol. III, both cited above, and André François-Poncet, *Souve-nirs d'une ambassade à Berlin, Septembre 1931 - Octobre 1938* (Paris, 1946).

[142] There was little danger at this stage of a German attack on the French frontier, hence manning the border fortifications was a largely mean-ingless gesture. On March 8 Prime Minister Sarraut delivered a radio address in the course of which he spoke brave sounding words about not tolerating the menace of German guns over Strasbourg. As a preliminary to concrete action they might have been appropriate; in default of such action they were both empty and foolish.

not a "flagrant" violation of Locarno that would justify immediate French action. Once the French will to act had shown itself deficient, the ambiguity of Locarno had full scope.

The various French participants in this episode all have made excellent cases for the positions that they took and for their failure to take effective action. Valid and understandable as their individual positions may be, nothing can alter the fact that the initial decision not to respond in kind to the German action was the crucial one. The sequel is of relatively secondary importance. Specifically, the Council of the League was seized of the question; of course it condemned Germany — what else could it do? But what really counted was the fact that Germany was allowed to retain the fruits of her unilateral violation of one more obligation, thereby ridding herself of her last significant disability. Hitler's intuition was proved correct once more; his gamble had succeeded, and, inevitably, this success enormously enhanced both his self-confidence and his prestige at home no less than abroad.

Formally, little was changed in the structure of European pacts and treaties; Locarno, the French alliances, the Franco-Soviet Pact were still extant. But they were little more than scraps of paper: the spirit of Locarno certainly was dead; it had been in fact for some time, as Mussolini quite correctly had observed some years before. No less important than the spirit of Locarno, more important in fact since that spirit was dead, the French will, mainspring of the system of Europe, gave evidence, if not of total demise, at least of such deficiency that none could be expected longer to place reliance upon it. At this moment France was still mistress of her choice; that choice was abdication.

France Surrenders Leadership to Britain

It took three more years for the full meaning of the consequences of the French abdication to unfold. Yet the final outcome, if logical, was not inevitable. A new situation was created in Europe by the emergence of Germany to a position of armed equality with others. The French system was dead, a fact of which the Belgian decision in October to return to the pre-1914 status of neutrality was clear recognition. Yet Europe had long and successfully functioned before 1914 without Leagues and Locarnos. France, if she no longer "controlled" Europe, was still one of the important Powers of Europe, albeit only one. It might even be said that the artificiality of the French system could not in any case have endured forever, denial as it was of the true facts of power, and that the return of both Russia and Germany to places of influence commensurate with their potential, provided a sounder basis for the reorganization of Europe. They were many in Britain who felt that, however unfortunate and awkward Hitlerian methods might be, the removal of German disabilities was basically sound and desirable: in that interpretation the remilitarization of the Rhineland was not so much suitable cause for indignation, let alone retaliation, as an opportunity to rebuild on more solid foundations.

If that were so, for the moment at least forgetting Leagues and ideologies, considerations of power and power equilibrium must become paramount. There were now three great forces in Europe. In the East stood the vast Soviet state; a resurgent Germany in the center; Britain and France stood in the West, basically dedicated to the same interest of conservation. Italy would stand on the fence as usual in such a situation, no initiator of policy herself, save in the event that special circumstances might give her power the opportunity to tip the scales.

The abdication of France was reflection of her weakness, that stemmed in turn as much at least from the internal divisions and stresses of the French complex as from inherent deficiencies of her physical means. The French perception of the whole European scene was at this time on the whole clearer than the British, and one result of French weakness was the conclusion that, in the last analysis, the British connection was *the* single most essential. The conclusion was sound. The question was how to maintain the union of the two.

The Rhineland coup of March 7 came on the eve of the French general election. That election was fought with considerable bitterness. The impact of economic stress, the total failure of the government to introduce measures that would revive the stagnant national economy, the outworn and stubborn dedication to the preservation of the currency, in combination with the developments of the international situation, specifically the Abyssinian affair, all these complicated by the intrusion of alien ideologies, had gone to give a sharpness more than usual to the ordinary cleavages of French opinion. For purposes of the election the Left had rallied as on earlier occasion in order to save the Republic from the threat — in large measure imagined — of the French Fascist Right. This Right in turn viewed the Popular Front as Communist controlled and saw in it the threat — also largely imagined — of *les Soviets partout*.

The Popular Front was indeed anti-Fascist and the Communists were active in it. Much of its concern, however, was with the more limited and concrete issue of the well-founded grievances of the working people of France; the *deux cents familles,* current version of the earlier *mur d'argent,* and the Bank of France were the villains, made blacker by their supposed Fascist sympathies. When the dust of electoral battle had settled and the ballots were counted it appeared that the Popular Front had won the election. A government headed by Léon Blum, leader of the Socialist party, and supported by the Radical Socialists on one side and the Communists on the other took over in June from Sarraut.

There was high elation on the Left: the people at last had come into their own; they were going to rejuvenate and revitalize the country in the best tradition of militant, patriotic jacobinism. France stood indeed in need of reform and rejuvenation, especially at the level of her economic and social institutions; the stress on that aspect of things was wholly sound. The impatient workers of France, eager for the enactment of the millennium, somewhat embarrassed a government wholly sympathetic to their cause by confronting the country with an epidemic of strikes, in which the somewhat novel technique of the sit-down — reminiscent of the 1920 Italian occupation of the factories — was widely used. Meanwhile the government embarked upon the enactment of a program of social reforms not unlike those of the American New Deal, and like the latter in America long overdue in France. Sound and progressive as this was, the economic implications of such measures — the first impact of social benefits is apt to be higher costs — showed that the advent of the Popular Front was not accompanied by an improvement of the economic thinking characteristic of the preceding years. It fell to the government of Blum, apologetically rather than out of conviction, at last to devalue the franc in September — at the wrong time and in the wrong way as was correctly said, for the French economy failed to revive under its guidance.

Basically, the stress on economic and social problems was warranted. But, more immediately, the effect was to confirm the fears of those who had equated the advent of the Popular Front with that of revolution. If the electoral victory of the Popular Front had been decisive and impressive, it was so in terms of parliamentary representation rather than of votes in the country at large. The shift of opinion at the popular level was far from overwhelming; the advent of the Popular Front meant not reconciliation in France, but greater bitterness than ever. The stress of the Left on matters primarily domestic was understandable enough, in a sense even inevitable, for it may be regarded as but the natural manifestation of the normal operation of the democratic system of France. But France is in and of Europe, in a way that even Britain is not, and she cannot afford to withdraw in isolation while attending to the redressing of the deficiencies of her domestic scene.

France cannot live without a foreign policy, and in 1936 foreign developments had greater importance than ever. What has been called the abdication of March created a vacuum and the need for readjustment of the relationships of Europe. Apart from the general ideological antipathy to Fascism in all its forms, the Popular Front did not introduce fresh ideas in the domain of foreign policy. It continued to cling to the necessity of the British connection, but from a correct premise drew a false conclusion. For all the domestic stress and confusion, France as a nation among nations still had considerable power that was held in high regard by all. That power was as necessary to Britain for *her* defense as the asset of British power was necessary to French security. Here was the soundest basis for an intimate association of equals, founded on the basic identity of their essentially defensive interest vis-à-vis the outside.

In simplest form it may be said that the asset of her position France simply threw away. Within a month of the coming to power of the Popular Front, the government of France was faced with a major and awkward decision as a consequence of the outbreak of civil war in next door Spain. Military coups in Spain were no novelty and their effect usually had spent itself wholly within the confines of that country, essentially removed from the main stream of the affairs of Europe. But this occasion was different. Since the preceding spring Spain had been governed by a Popular Front combination somewhat similar to that which now held power in France. Those who attempted a coup in July were not only the representatives of the normal conservative forces of Spain, operating through the army, they had connections in and very soon concrete assistance from Fascist Italy and Nazi Germany, especially the former. That is what turned the Spanish civil war into the much larger test of rival ideologies on one hand, into a contest between the Fascist states and the Western democracies — perhaps one should say France — on the other.

Of this contest one episode alone, at its very beginning, will be retained. On combined grounds of ideological sympathy and national interest, it might have been expected that the Popular Front government of France, especially once the initial military coup in Spain had failed of complete success and had degenerated into open civil war, would have used its influence to insure the victory of the existing government of Spain. True, French opinion was bitterly divided and feeling ran very high in France over the Spanish war; the desire not to exacerbate these divisions further, the fear of transplanting into France the quarrel of Spain, is understandable, if perhaps another instance of timidity. In view of the international implications of the Spanish war the desirability of close cooperation with Britain was more than ever essential.

The government of Britain at this time felt no overwhelming reluctance toward a change of regime in Spain, and in general it may be said that Britain, government as well as opinion, was largely and truly neutral in the Spanish dispute — perhaps the only country genuinely so in Europe. French and British policy continued to act in unison in Spain through a very simple device. It was the government of Léon Blum that proposed the policy of nonintervention in Spain and the installation in London of a committee to supervise nonintervention. This pious fraud served the purpose of preserving Anglo-French unity, but the fact that it came from the Popular Front government of France gives it special significance. Having abdicated in March, France took the next logical step: appropriately it might be said in a sense, she totally surrendered leadership to Britain.

The events of mid 1936, across the Rhine and beyond the Pyrenees, mark the close of this story. For the better part of two decades Europe had been held together under the sign of a system that had been called the French system. How this system had come into existence, and how it functioned, has been the essence on this tale. The initial, inherent and unavoidable vices that lay in the French system from the very time of its inception have been indicated. What the last part of this story has shown is the transformation of that system into something the shape of which was not yet clear in 1936. That the French system was in some ways unsound from its inception, for the reason primarily that it was based on a relationship of power that could not last indefinitely, has been stressed repeatedly. The peculiar form that the change would eventually take was not predictable at first. The fact that France is a democracy, in more specific terms the problem of operating an effective foreign policy in a democratic milieu, had resulted in the unexpected answer of abdication and surrender.

From this point on the field was open wide; what leadership there was came from others: Britain, Germany, the Soviet Union, later on the United States, became the chief protagonists in the record of a society, a world, a way of life that fundamentally had come to an end with the outbreak of the first great conflict that the pistol shots of Sarajevo had set in train. These other Powers, whether in combination or singly, have so far not succeeded in organizing a system that can by any standards be called stable. Whatever their ultimate outcome may be, the revolutions of our time are not yet ended.

PART IV

EPILOGUE

ANOTHER TWENTY YEARS OF CRISIS

1. THE CONSEQUENCES OF FRANCE'S ABDICATION

By mid 1936 France had, of her own accord, surrendered the burden that she had assumed after the end of the war of being the mainstay of the structure of Europe. The fact that the French system was an artificial creation, in the sense that it had been the outcome and expression of passing and accidental circumstances and did not correspond to the long term realities of the relationships of power; expressed in other words, the fact that France had undertaken the burden while possessed of the fundamentally negative outlook of defense, lies at the root of France's abdication.

Without France, the French system was obviously devoid of meaning. Something else must therefore take its place, possibly of course sheer anarchy. But in any event the relationships of power became paramount, especially since the League, too, was dead and may therefore be properly left out of further calculations. The Mussolinian proposal of 1933, embodied in the Four Power Pact, was, in theory at least, one solution. But it had failed.

With the formation of the Rome-Berlin Axis in October, 1936 there were, as already mentioned, three major forces in Europe: the Soviet state, the Axis, the Western democracies of Britain and France. These last two countries tended to work in increasingly close unity, a unity however that was purchased at the price of virtually complete French surrender to British leadership. The French instinct was sound that had always desired a close union with Britain, but much of our story

---

Note. — The essential purpose of this entire essay has been accomplished once we have come to the point of France's abdication and her surrender of leadership in Europe. However, whether she would or no, France remained after 1936, and continues to be, one important segment of Europe. This epilogue is therefore intended to bring the story up to date through the quarter of a century that has elapsed since the abdication of France. The story is not a happy one, but what is most significant from the point of view of the main theme of this essay, it is *another* story, one in which France is one of many actors and for the most part not even a major one. This epilogue is therefore no more than a brief summary and survey without any intention at either detail, completeness, or thoroughness, wholly different in scope from the rest of this treatment. Thus, no attempt is made to document this section or to give references, or to appraise the extensive and growing literature that deals with it.

has been taken up with the reasons that prevented the realization of this wish. Now that it was being realized, the fact of union might assume greater importance than the details of its operation: be the leadership primarily British or French, or the result of joint decision, community of purpose and of action was the essential fact. Unfortunately, for Britain and for France, and for much else as well, their common tragedy and that of Europe may be summed up in the statement that the failure of French will was followed by a failure of British understanding.

The British reaction to the remilitarization of the Rhineland, stemming as it did in large measure from the British sense of reasonableness and fairness that saw in the occasion an opportunity to rebuild instead of a clear threat, was also based on a total failure to appreciate the nature of Nazi Germany, from whom it expected fairness and reasonableness comparable to its own. In the face of accumulating evidence, persistent hope turned into wilful blindness.

France of course was at liberty to accept or reject such leadership as came from Britain, but the interesting thing is that the failure of 1936 was not retrieved by her thereafter. If the steadily deteriorating situation placed a higher premium than ever on the value of the British connection, France never made a serious effort to assert a place of equality in the making of decisions for the partnership. This in turn was due to the fact that France failed to put her own house in order.

Some things she did. The government, as much as the military themselves and sometimes more than they, set about reconstructing and enlarging the country's military edifice. Neither appropriations nor results were lacking, and the tales of deficiencies in French matériel when the test came in 1940 are in large measure legend. Save in the air where this deficiency was patent, the French army was substantially equipped in 1940. In the use and management of this equipment and in the quality of leadership lay the real flaws. In the mid thirties, Marshal Pétain, full of years and prestige, stood high in the military hierarchy of France. Pétain and other French military leaders thought little of the possibilities, so assiduously explored across the Rhine, of the airplane and the tank.

The retrograde quality of military thinking had its counterpart in the economic domain. The same Reynaud, whose thinking in both fields was up-to-date and clear, continued to iterate his Cassandra-like warnings; his role bears some resemblance to the contemporary one of Churchill in Britain: both men were granted brilliance; both remained voices crying in the wilderness surrounded by not a little suspicion.

The government of Léon Blum assumed the double burden of social reform and rearmament. But French economic activity failed to revive and the devaluation of the franc, when it at last became inevitable, proved little more effective in restoring economic health than the preceding attempts at deflation had been. The outcome in the end was a dreary repetition of the familiar cycle: as in the case of the Left victories of 1924 and 1932, that of 1936 was followed by a disintegration of the successful coalition under the impact of the ineffectiveness of its financial management. Nor were political passions appeased. France had abdicated her leadership, but she was doing even more; she was not even playing a role commensurate with her true power. The price of all this was continued slavish surrender to the initiative of Britain.

The active force of change in the European scene as a whole lay most of all in Germany, secondarily in Italy. British suspicion of Soviet intentions was not without foundation, but Russian interest at this time, as interpreted in Moscow, was also on the side of peace and conservation. In terms of *Realpolitik* British policy could have striven to accomplish either one of to things: to organize such overhelming force as the Axis could not have hoped successfully to meet, in other words close co-operation with Russia, enlarging and giving real meaning to the hesitant Franco-Soviet connection; or else seek to divert German ambitions to the East, and should it come to open conflict be in a position with France of either arbitrator or *tertius gaudens,* letting Germany and the Soviets exhaust each other; then, if need be, throw their weight at the appropriate time on the suitable side in order to procure the outcome desirable to themselves. In such crude terms as these, this policy could doubtless not have been presented to an opinion that meant well and had just discovered the merits of the League; yet it would have been but a continuation of Britain's traditional policy of continental equilibrium and *divide et impera.*

Britain chose to do neither. It may be granted that the spectacle of Russian domestic developments, the succession of curious trials and purges from which a startled world was asked to believe that much of the Soviet leadership, in particular what remained of the early associates of Lenin in establishing Bolshevism in Russia, was tainted with the crime of treason, was ill calculated to inspire confidence or trust either in Soviet motives or in the value of the Soviet military establishment; it is likewise true that, for all the excesses of Nazi aberration and brutality, often denied or doubted for that matter, the whole German complex seemed a more congenial and understandable one than the Russian. The fact remains that the leaders of Britain wholly misread the European picture.

Stanley Baldwin, from June, 1935 to May, 1937, Neville Chamberlain thereafter, were the British Prime Ministers. In the foreign field at least neither man can be said to have had outstanding competence. The case of the latter, who held office during the last period of the disintegration of peace, is especially relevant and enlightening. An honorable British gentleman, he may be said to have been a most authentic representative of his country's opinion and temper; therein precisely lay his failing, a fact which again raises the question of the operation of foreign policy in a democratic milieu. Chamberlain's failing lay not in his intentions; rather in his presumption of competence in a field where it was wholly deficient. With complete success he guided Britain, and others with her, on the path of disaster.

The name of Chamberlain has come to be associated with the word appeasement, quite rightly so, yet in a way unfairly. *Per se,* appeasement carries connotations that are on the whole favorable, though it is always well to realize that there are certain beasts to whom the taste of blood has merely the effect of inducing a demand for more. Not in appeasement as such, like peace itself desirable in the abstract, but in the fallacious assumptions that stood behind the attempted appeasement lie the proper grounds of criticism of British policy.

Civil war had been raging in Spain since the summer of 1936. Britain, as mentioned, was the only authentic neutral in that contest which roused to high pitch ideological passions elsewhere. To isolate the conflict through the abstention of all was an eminently sound recommendation. But Italy and Germany would not abstain; non-intervention became a fiction and a fraud. Even a fiction can have value and a fraud may be pious; but in effect non-intervention was no more than a shield behind which Italy and Germany could proceed unmolested. Russia, too, intervened, though in relatively moderate fashion, and substantial surreptitious assistance went to the Spanish government from sympathetic elements in France. This, however, was not comparable to the massive Fascist intervention and served little purpose other than to prolong the agony of Spain.

Britain was essentially willing to pay the price of Spain, apparently oblivious to the fact that it was time to think in terms of strategy, that French arms were still the chief bulwark of peace and order on the Continent, and that France was quite simply being militarily encircled. Britain indeed seems to have entertained the possibility of disrupting the Axis. Again, in the abstract, such a policy was defensible had it not, too, been founded on erroneous assumption. The methods used were such as to produce results precisely the opposite of those intended. What could the Italian government make of a situation where its ambassador in London reported a meeting with the British Prime Minister and his Foreign Secretary during which the former had taken sides with the Italian envoy against the latter? Some years ago Mussolini had ranted about the rotten corpse of liberty and decadent democracy. This might be dismissed as mere rhetoric. But was it? One may understand the frog being deluded into thinking that it might yet achieve the dimensions of the bull. Why should Mussolini and Hitler sever their partnership when it was paying such handsome dividends?

Thieves are said to abide by a code of honor of their own. When, in the spring of 1938, Hitler decided that the time had come for effecting the *Anschluss,* he may have shown little regard for this code of honor of thieves, but he also once more showed the shrewdness of correct understanding. No Italian divisions appeared on the Brenner, as four years earlier; Mussolini instead greeted the event with a smile — albeit a forced one — and declarations of approval. France utterly failed to react, while in Britain the acceptance went far of the German claim to the fundamental legitimacy of the union. Needless to say, without French support, the Little Entente did not take any action.

The significance of the *Anschluss* was very considerable. It did not lie in the limited asset of the addition of the physical resources of Austria to those of the Reich, but in the broader political implications for Europe as a whole. Weakened by her adventures in Abyssinia and Spain, deeply committed in the latter still, at odds with France and Britain, Italy at the moment had no assets with which to bargain: her position in the Axis had altered from that of partner to hostage. Possibly, she might still have rejoined the Stresa combination; but she, more accurately Mussolini, elected to throw all caution to the winds and use her influence to further a total and grandiose destruction of the existing order of Europe. Within barely more than a year, in May, 1939, she cemented her ties with Germany in the grandliloquently named Pact of Steel.

Apart from the limited, though by no means negligible, strategic significance of the union of Austria with Germany, this was added confirmation of the French abdication in Europe. For one thing, it was the first instance of German expansion beyond the borders of the Reich, the first clear challenge to the territorial arrangements embodied in the settlements of peace. If the view were to be accepted that Central Europe was the proper field for German expansion, the states within that area would find it desirable to come to terms as best they could with the new force that would, in one form or another, dominate the whole region. A Pandora's box had been opened: the tacit acceptance of the validity of the German claim to Austria inevitably enhanced the prospects of Hungarian revisionism; Poland, or at least the directors of her policy, tried to comfort themselves with the contemplation of their ten year pact with Germany and with the consideration that German ambition had, for the moment at least, turned southward. As to the possibility of any equilibrium being established between the two members of the Axis, Italy had already become too feeble a reed, whose influence the *Anschluss* itself had further devalued.

The initiative of policy for Europe as a whole had passed to German hands which used it with combined ruthlessness and skill. For Europe as a whole again, France had been the central core of resistance to change; the structure of connections that France had forged was in process of being tested and broken, with an eye to the isolation of France on the continent. Within the smaller compass of the Central European scene, Czechoslovakia had a comparable role of being the kernel of resistance to change; she was the logical candidate for the next German move.

It was not long in coming. For the benefit of those benighted optimists who would rather put faith in any scrap of paper of even evanescent verbal statement rather than acknowledge the true state of things, Hitler had been profuse of reassurances to the Czechs at the time of the *Anschluss*. It was to take all of six months before Czechoslovakia met her fate.

In view of the dimensions of the real stakes — the domination of Europe — the issue of the Sudeten minority might almost be dismissed as what is colloquially called a red herring. Yet a most convenient herring it was, especially when it came to dealing with British opinion. There is every reason to believe that when Prime Minister Chamberlain alighted from his plane on his return from Munich and waved yet another scrap of paper wherein over his signature and Hitler's was contained the promise of peace in our time, to a degree at once overwhelming and distressing, he was the authentic representative of the well-intentioned but wishful-thinking British opinion of the day.

The Munich episode is one that has given rise to much feeling and to the flow of quantities of ink; more than any other single episode it is the one responsible for the unfavorable overtones that have come to be the predominant, and unjust, associations with the term appeasement. The great excitement was due to the drama of the circumstances that went with the occasion; to a considerable extent it was not warranted. For Munich was after all but a logical step in a sequence. What really mattered were such considerations as these: was there reason to believe that Germany would rest content — in other words was appeasable — with the control of Central Europe? If so, the price paid for peace might not be called unreasonable.

If the contrary view is adopted, then a balance sheet must be struck between losses and gains. Would Britain and France find themselves in a more favorable position to wage war at a later date than in October, 1938? Time they did purchase at Munich; the price they paid was not only the loss of the Czech military asset, but the handing over of the Czech resources and strategic position to Germany. What mattered most of all perhaps was the view that one took of the Russian enigma, in two respects: politically, would Russia live up to her commitments, specifically would she abide by the terms of her treaties with Czechoslovakia and France? Militarily, what was the value of the Russian asset for purposes of war? The Soviets were excluded at Munich, which may be regarded as the unforeseen implementation of the Mussolinian proposal of 1933; that they should regard their exclusion as other than an affront and solid grounds for suspicion could hardly be expected; the new international guarantee of the rump of Czechoslovakia that emerged from Munich was hardly calculated to impress them.

Soviet suspicion and dislike could be dismissed, however, if the intention was to divert Germany into a collision with Russia, provided only that such an outcome could be successfully contrived. These are the basic criteria that should be used in appraising what was done at Munich, not the rights and wrongs of the Sudeten question, not Hitler's rantings, or abstractions about the merits of appeasement *per se*.

Nevertheless, if Munich may be viewed as but logical consequence of the developments that came before it, the fact that it brought out these consequences in the full light of day warrants the symbolic place of importance that has come to surround the name. Abject is a strong word, yet it seems apt in describing the French role at Munich. Daladier does not seem to have shared the fond illusions of his British colleague, but in the circumstances felt that once again France could not dissociate herself from Britain; France was reaping the fruits of her surrender of 1936. In the last analysis, she, not Britain, had a formal alliance with Czechoslovakia that she could not describe as a far away country about which she knew little. Yet the whole leadership in this affair, not only in the last stages at Godesberg and Munich, but from the time, shortly after the *Anschluss,* when it became clear that Czechoslovakia was the next point where German pressure would exert itself, was exclusively British, with France following in *abject* acquiescence. What France did in effect do at Munich was to let publicly be known what in fact she had done in 1936. The price of such behavior is not alone loss of prestige and standing abroad, but to a point uneasy conscience and loss of self respect. However much explained in terms of special circumstances, the successive behavior of France over Abyssinia, the Rhine, Spain, and Czechoslovakia does not make an attractive picture. Why should others have more faith in France than France had in herself?

This was playing into the hands of all the forces of destruction of the existing order, more specifically it was playing the Nazi game. To Britain, the result was not wholly unsatisfactory: she had the French connection wholly on her own terms, while Chamberlain's astonishing self-confidence did not recoil from continuing a leadership so successfully headed toward disaster.

From the standpoint of any realistic appraisal, the maiming of Czechoslovakia in October, 1938 and her destruction as an effective force must be tantamount to the acceptance of German hegemony in Central Europe. In that context, to balk at German rule in Prague was little more than legalistic formalism, refusal to accept the implied consequences of one's actions. Yet it was precisely the appearance of the Germans in Prague that induced a strong reaction in Britain. This reaction of high indignation was highly unconvincing and suspect to many; it was in fact tantamount to changing the rules of the game that Britain had apparently been willing to play. The subsequent precipitate guarantee of Poland, given at first without consent or consultation of that country, could only be a puzzling gesture that was widely misunderstood, in any case not the simple warning that it was intended to be.

Therein lay at once the weakness and the strength of Britain. As indicated earlier, Chamberlain was the authentic representative of his country's opinion, and, from the standpoint of the proper functioning of a democratic system, suitable leader of it. Well beyond the eleventh hour British democracy refused to be aroused and to recognize for what it was the nature of the regime that had become established across the Rhine. No better illustration can be given than the course of events of 1939 of the basic difficulty arising from fundamentally diverse outlooks, antagonistic ideologies. In the last analysis, Berlin and Moscow spoke the same language, which was not the language of London and Paris. Little wonder that when London approached Moscow, with hesitation and reluctance to boot, it met profound suspicion. The Nazi-Soviet Pact was the outcome of it all, and of that step the consequence was war within ten days. Here was tragedy in the most authentic sense: Armageddon again brought about in large measure, or at least not prevented, by the inability to procure understanding of those so deeply dedicated to the avoidance of its repetition.

The role of France in the last months of peace continued negative and passive. September 1939 found a British people essentially united. By contrast, there were those in France who could raise the cry, why die for Danzig? There was point to the question, for Danzig was not the real issue. And if the real issue was the larger one of the basic order of Europe, as it was indeed, was Danzig a better issue to have chosen than Czechoslovakia a year earlier or the Rhineland in 1936? The case could well be debated. But time for debate was no longer. Those consistent appeasers in France who would have yielded in the matter of Danzig, who accepted the implications of German control of Central Europe contained in earlier happenings, could not at this point control the policy of Britain, to whose leadership France had slavishly surrendered. Significantly, the first declaration of war against the Reich emanated from Britain; France's came a few hours later.

If one takes a broad view of the matter, the recurrence of war a mere twenty years after the end of the first cataclysm meant this. As a consequence of the combination of specific circumstances and of the failure to understand the extent to which the nineteenth century world was altered, an attempt had been made after 1919 to reorganize Europe on a basis that did not correspond to ultimate reality, be it the long term relationships of power, the nature of economic development, or the broad phenomenon of the rising of the masses. The rise of new ideologies in control of large states, in one form or another totalitarian, the world economic crisis, the inadequate French system, were all manifestations of the failure to provide satisfactory solutions to the problems of the postwar period. But the world, and Europe in particular, were still organized in the framework of sovereign states, the operation of whose relationships of power it has been one of the purposes of this essay to analyze.

The inadequacies of the French system had been fully revealed by 1936. The organization of Europe had failed, and its chief prop, France herself, had in effect surrendered and renounced the role that she had, with more reluctance than elation, undertaken to play. Russia and Germany were back, or about to be back, in the category of effective Powers, while the problem of Danubia had not been resolved. Since the French system was gone something must take its place that would more accurately reflect the true relationships of power. Whether the three main forces, the Soviets, the Axis and the Anglo-French combination, might have succeeded in effecting the transition in peace is idle speculation; the fact is they did not. The historic record is barren of illustrations of major readjustments of power taking place by peaceful means. That is the true significance of the renewed outbreak of war in 1939; in that context, the landmarks of the story since 1936, Spain, Munich, Prague and Danzig, sink into secondary significance, outward manifestations of the malady of Europe, clumsy and ineffective essays at reorganization.

War it must be therefore, meaning another essay to effect the readjustments that the First World War had failed to realize. The essay was destined to provide some important clarifications, but not the closing of the chapter: we are still in the midst of the confused transition the tale of which opens with Sarajevo. Of the story of the war some aspects only will be retained in this closing chapter.

2. THE SECOND WORLD WAR

The initial stages of the conflict offered some curious features, as if, despite the formal outbreak of hostilities, the world were still reluctant to accept in full the implications of the situation. Whether or not the Nazi state was impelled by the inner necessities of its nature, or more narrowly by the domestic state of things, to take the initiative of hostilities, it may be said in retrospect that the German bid for power was not mere senseless gamble. The swift destruction of Poland was testimony to the effectiveness of German arms; Russia collected a share of the spoils as the price of her acquiescence, while Communists abroad generally behaved as loyal allies of the Nazis.

But in the West nothing happened at first. Eight months of "phoney war" were cause to wonder whether some new accommodation might not be forthcoming. However, following a demonstration of Anglo-French ineffectiveness in Scandinavia in April, the main attack upon the West was launched in May. The core of power in the West, as in 1914, was the French army, an instrument generally held in high esteem. The German plan of campaign in 1940 was basically the same as in 1914: turning the French defenses through the Low Countries; this time Holland was invaded as well as Belgium. The French army, assisted by a relatively small but well organized British force, was large and, save in the air, not deficient in equipment. But its leadership, unlike the German, had failed to recognize the possibilities of the new tools of war. The result was disaster, and that with such speed that incredulous observers everywhere found it difficult to adjust themselves to the pace of events. By mid June the mighty French war machine had been irretrievably broken and German forces were roaming at will through the length and breadth of a country stunned and disorganized at all levels of its existence.

A decision of rare import faced the French government. The fundamental question to be answered was whether the war was truly lost or whether there was any ground for hope that its fortunes might yet turn. The case could be debated, and the French government of the day was divided. That the military power of France was destroyed was not debatable; the Soviet Union was acting as a loyal member of the Nazi-Soviet partnership, and America was primarily concerned with the avoidance of involvement. That left Britain alone. Britain evinced no inclination to come to terms with Nazi Germany, but for defeated France the question was, could Britain by herself, or even if she had the use of the French fleet and the French empire, ultimately defeat Germany, now essentially in control of the resources of the continent of Europe? Would not Britain herself be defeated or perhaps shortly come to terms while she still had power to bargain?

The French collapse had the effect of bringing out with clarity the place that France had filled; the magnitude of the chasm that her disappearance revealed was brought in the full view of all, and the extent to which the whole structure of Europe, and even much outside of Europe, rested upon the oft-berated power that had been the French. Outside of Britain the view was widely held that Germany had in effect won the war, and that, at best, Britain might effect some not too onerous compromise; on the basis of dispassionate appraisal of the existing evidence there was more solid ground for such a view of things than for the opposite. That such a view should have prevailed in France can be neither cause for surprise nor evidence of treacherous intent. Heroic gestures are admired and one respects the individual who gives his life in defense of a cause, be it a hopeless one. But it is not the primary function of government to make heroic gestures; rather to preserve the nation and protect the people under the most favorable terms that circumstances will allow, be the price humiliating and bitter.

In their distress, the people of France in their overwhelming mass, stunned as they were, above all wanted a termination of their plight. They turned for leadership to the ancient but respected figure of Pétain. Pétain sued for an armistice which was shortly granted; Hitler could do a jig and erase Germany's shame in the very identical setting of Rethondes where in 1918 she too had acknowledged defeat. Beyond this, the Pétain government obtained from the French Parliament the warrant of its own demise. The Third Republic was dead, and in Vichy where the government sat, Pétain, Head of the State, could proceed with the experiment of restoring the supposedly traditional virtues, the pursuit of whose path France had presumably abandoned, thereby coming to grief. The picture was neither inspiring nor pretty; the sordid chaos of disaster seldom is. This may be said perhaps: those were ill-qualified to pass judgment who had in the preceding years so often berated the oppressive operation of French power and even done their best to diminish that power; nor those who had judged harshly the rotten "decadence" of France: French power could now do no harm, and Vichy professed devotion to the restoration of the moral health of France.

By contrast, the picture of Britain was the inspiring one of heroic endeavor to which the voice of Winston Churchill gave both picturesque and dramatic expression. It was he who, farseeing, at the time of Munich had stated that "England has been offered a choice between war and shame. She has chosen shame and she will get war." Just come to the Prime Ministership, it was his lot to fight the war and to retrieve the shame. Here also perhaps this may be said: had the heroism of Britain been in the end of no avail — as many at the time judged that it could not be — the world would have largely forgotten, even more than it has, the magnificence of the British performance. We, the free peoples, may be thankful that the combined effects of Britain's heroic determination and of a series of circumstances, among them German miscalculations and blunders, proved incorrect the cooler appraisal that pointed to defeat.

Airplanes and tanks will not be stopped by gestures, however noble these may be. Power in its crudest form, weapons, must now decide the day. French power had been destroyed and France as a result could henceforth play no very significant role in the struggle. The purely military role of France in the war was in fact negligible, certainly by comparison with that of the other chief contestants. Yet, as the war instead of ending became prolonged and spread until nearly the whole world was involved, the place of France retained significance. In Vichy, Laval rather than Pétain was the director of decisions. Of the demise of the Republic Laval had been one of the architects; ideological attachment to principle or liberty the man had none. Yet as a guide of the French state a policy he had. His dislike of Britain was deep, stemming from earlier experiences; the feeling had not a little support in France, fed in part by the contemplation of the humiliating contrast between the behavior and place of the two countries, in part by memories of interwar relations; in extreme form, the phrase, Britain is willing to fight to the last Frenchman, expresses it.

Laval's basic assumption that Germany had won the war, if not unreasonable, proved false. On that assumption, however, France must adjust herself to the new condition of Europe. Pending the day when the assumption would be verified she still had some assets to use: she had the considerable resources of her economy that Germany naturally wanted to use; she had not surrendered her fleet that she might always, if too hard pressed, turn over to the allies; and she might do likewise with those parts of the empire, mainly North Africa, that had not under the flag of Free France raised by de Gaulle in London already joined the anti-German coalition. Within the limited possibilities of German-dominated Europe, France was thus in a position to hold some balance vis-à-vis Italy for instance; from the German viewpoint there was some question which was of greater value, the assets of defeated France or those of allied Italy. In the picture of the larger contest, France hedged, refusing to make formal peace, yet collaborating with Germany to a point. The operation of such a policy has little of nobility, and less of attractiveness, in it, yet can still be described as defense of the national interest. As a consequence, and to a degree, France was treated with some circumspection by Germany, while the allies, especially America, indulged in their Vichy gamble.

At the same time, the Free French movement, relatively small as its material contribution was (the imperial asset had decided importance) kept alive the possibility that France could at least formally be counted in the ranks of the allied coalition. The judgment is credited to Laval in the early days of Vichy that "unless England is defeated promptly we shall all be criminals." This represents an eminently sound appraisal, and it was therefore fitting, in the larger and poetic sense rather than in the narrow legal, that Laval should in the end be shot for treason. As time passed, the war spread, and German victory began to appear increasingly remote if not doubtful, the forces of resistance in France, as elsewhere in Europe, began to take heart.

The discipline of Commmunism may fairly be described as admirably inhuman. When, in June, 1941, Hitler decided to emulate Napoleon in his Russian campaign, he also went back to the more congenial role, in the Communist book, of Facist beast. Communists outside the Soviet Union had, with minor exceptions, accepted the Nazi-Soviet Pact of 1939. They had behaved thereafter as loyal German allies, using their best endeavors to sabotage the French war effort. Their success had surpassed the wildest expectations and they were now to pay the price of the mistaken wisdom that derives from too rigid adherence to doctrine. Yet the price they paid without flinching: the Communists in France became resisters; they became in fact the staunchest single backbone and asset of the Resistance movement in which their role was large, effective, and eminently creditable. In doing this they also laid the bases for the future perpetuation of the confusion of France.

Just as the Channel moat, as in the past, had been the salvation of England, so likewise the traditional assets of dimensions and climate prevented the destruction of Russia. America was still meantime debating what amounted to the issue of whether she was part of this planet or not. Pearl Harbor decided the matter for her. America was unprepared but her resources were huge; granted the protective safety of two oceans, she had been able to afford the luxury of unreadiness and could now, relatively undisturbed, proceed to forge the weapons of victory for all. As in the First World War Germany was confronted with a virtual world coalition; before the might of it, she and her one significant ally, Japan, went down. The tide turned late in 1942 with the almost simultaneous occurrence of three events: Stalingrad, El Alamein, and the allied landings in French North Africa. The story from that time on was one of virtually unbroken allied progress, culminating in the grand *Götterdämmerung* in Germany.

The securing by the allies of French North Africa to a point further decreased the importance of France, for it deprived her of the bargaining asset that Vichy's control of it constituted. When metropolitan France was at last liberated in 1944, the actual French contribution to the liberation, if useful, was none the less more symbolic than real, in terms at least of the proportion of effective French power compared to American and British that went into the task. It was not long after the French collapse in 1940 that Marshal Smuts had delivered himself of the opinion that "France is gone in our day and perhaps for many a day." Yet as it began to be clear that the final triumph of allied arms was no more than a matter of time, the urgency became ever more pressing for the making of plans for the future, the reconstruction that must come after the negative purpose of defeating the German bid for power had been achieved. One of the questions among many was that of the future place and role of France.

3. SINCE 1945: FRANCE IN EUROPE TODAY

The situation in 1945 presented certain similarities with that of 1918, but also very substantial differences. Much stress has been placed in the whole course of this discussion upon the false appearence of the relationships of power that the First World War had produced; this has been shown to have been one of the basic reasons for the failure of 1919 and the return to war. In respect to the distribution of power as it existed in 1945 things were much sounder than in 1919. One of the chief effects of the war itself had been the clear emergence of the United States and the Soviet Union to positions of power that dwarfed all others; both were among the victors and in a position to enforce their will, not only at the moment of victory and pending the restoration of more normal conditions, but for a period of indefinite duration. Britain was a full member of the victorious coalition; she certainly had made an ample contribution to victory and, in moral terms, her record was unique and outstanding. But if she had redeemed the mistakes of her own prewar policy, the instinct that caused her to put such a high price on the preservation of peace had been sound, only the method faulty. Just as for France in the first war, the cost of victory had been too high for Britain which emerged from it injured, impoverished, and diminished, while the growth of American power had in effect been substantially accelerated and enhanced by the war.

Whatever may be thought of the overall record of Nazi Germany — and on that score there would seem to be little room for divergence — the military performance of Germany could not but command high respect. Nevertheless, the second German bid for power in a quarter of a century, like the first one, had failed, and in far more disastrous fashion than the first: the sacred fatherland this time had not remained immune to the facts of war and invasion which had instead been visited with full effect upon the length and breadth of German soil. Whatever the impact of this might be, then and later, upon the attitude and feelings of the German nation, especially in view of the novel techniques and instruments to which the war itself had given rise, it did not seem probable that Germany could by herself, in any predictable future, achieve again a place of the first rank. The state of power relationships therefore was after the Second World War sounder than it had been after the first.

But it has also been shown that, if the basic unsoundness of the arrangements that derived from the false position of power in which France was placed by the circumstances that followed the first war was a major cause of the failure of peace, matters were aggravated as a consequence of the disintegration of the first wartime coalition: America had withdrawn into her shell and Britain had begun to think of means to counterbalance what she looked upon as the too great power of France. In this respect the post Second World War situation presented some similarity with the first. The precipitate dismantling of the American war machine, essentially a manifestation of the operation of the democratic process in America, certainly was calculated to convey to others — though not to that end intended — that America was about to repeat the withdrawal that followed the first war. It makes for an interesting and disturbing speculation to consider what might have been the consequences of this American performance but for the lucky accident of the temporary American monopoly of atomic weapons.

For the Second World War alliance was highly different from that of the first. The First World War coalition soon fell apart, and we have traced the disastrous effects of Anglo-French difference during the interval between the wars. But important as these differences were the fact remains that Britain, America, and France basically spoke the same political language. The Soviet Union now did not speak the same language as the Western democracies; the grand alliance had *no other* binder besides the common German peril; this was now gone. Whatever alterations the future may bring in the course and shape of the Soviet state, after thirty years of existence it was still dedicated to the fundamentals of its initial ideology. The period of peaceful co-existence had been but temporary delay in the appointed course of evolution; what the effects of indefinite prolongation of it might have been is idle speculation. The war itself fitted well into the Marxist book: capitalist states, as predicted, had fallen out among themselves, thereby providing a novel opportunity for schemes of world dimensions, only temporarily put on ice when world revolution had failed to materialize after the First World War.

There were no means for dealing with America herself, but her seeming withdrawal was an invitation to take action elsewhere. Europe lay prostrate and powerless and much of Asia was seething with ferment. America — and Britain — had acquiesced in a vast extension of direct Soviet control into Europe; in the rest of it, especially in France and Italy, Communists might infiltrate their influence and magnify it to eventual control: their record in the wartime resistance was a ready made opportunity. With the demise of Vichy and the instauration of General de Gaulle's provisional government in France, the Communists participated in the coalition that governed France and that continued for a time after the resignation of de Gaulle and the adoption of a new constitution for the Fourth Republic; the period from 1945 to 1947, when the Communists were finally ejected from the government in France, was a highly delicate one. If the Communists could establish themselves in control of France by means of ostensibly peaceful infiltration, the whole continent of Europe, like a ripe fruit, would fall into the Kremlin's lap.

Simultaneously, great efforts were made to take advantage of the diminution of Britain. There was no appreciable Communist group in Britain, but the difficulties of the Empire, especially in Asia, could be exploited. Here also, Moscow could capitalize on the authentic desire for independence of subject peoples, for whom America felt not a little sympathy. Britain's wartime Prime Minister, Winston Churchill, had an essentially correct understanding of the situation as he had had of the Nazi danger long before 1939. But Britain, too, is a democracy; in Britain, as in America, at the popular level, the Russians enjoyed a very considerable degree of goodwill from the fact of the alliance and from the quality of their wartime performance. It was in the very midst of international negotiations, at Potsdam, that the British people gave the Labour Party its first clear mandate to govern.

But if Russian calculations, like Nazi before 1939, were based on hard headed realistic analysis, they too were fettered by the limitations of their understanding of the operation of the Western democratic milieu. Briefly, the Russians like the Nazis may be said to have overplayed their hand, until they managed to convince would be friends of the impossibility of fair collaboration. Britain had never gone the length of America in reducing her wartime establishment; she was holding the outpost of Greece against the machinations of Communist intrigue. But Britain's resources were badly strained; in 1947 she made it known to America that she would be unable longer to continue to sustain the cost of that particular undertaking. In the midst of some doubt and confusion, President Truman obtained from Congress an appropriation for the immediate assistance of both Greece and Turkey.

The proclamation of the so-called Truman Doctrine may be regarded as the signal for the joining of the issue. Since then, in one form or another, but with at bottom only secondary variations, America's policy has been one that the word containment, current version of the *cordon sanitaire*, best describes. The detailed and specific manifestations of it, Berlin blockade and air lift, Korean intervention, need not be discussed at this point.

But one aspect of American policy must retain our attention in closing this tale: the recreation of effective strength in Europe, in that part of Europe at least not under the direct rule of the Kremlin, the hold of which was becoming increasingly stringent in all aspects of the life of Moscow's satellites. The war had wrought immense havoc in Europe, and America's contribution to her reconstruction had been substantial, generous, and prompt. The recuperative capacity of Europe also proved to be considerable. To make a long story short, it may be said that the combination of her own efforts with American assistance succeeded in solving the problem of Europe's economic reconstruction. But the clear drawing of the line of cleavage between the Soviet Union and the United States gave added importance to the prize of Europe. Outside of the United States, free Europe remains the greatest reservoir of industrial production and skills. All free Europe that is, for her individual members had in relative terms become so diminished that their collectivity alone could have hopes of playing a role of power comparable to that of the two superpowers.

Free Europe as a whole had had enough of war. But whether to defend herself against the Russian menace, or to avoid being merely sucked in as passive object in the contest between America and Russia, to be able in other words effectively to play the role of Third Force, joint action, some form of integration of Europe, seemed desirable. Since there is fundamentally no fear of aggression as between Europe and America, America espoused the cause of the integration of Europe and threw her influence behind those native elements in Europe which, seeing nothing but final disaster for all in the perpetuation of age-old intra-European quarrels, also advocated union. *Unite or Perish* ran the title of a book by Paul Reynaud.

But at this point old issues reappear and the relationships of the power triumvirate of Britain, France, and Germany, as before 1939, intrudes upon the scene. Pre-1939 French fears of Germany, both her power and her purpose, may be said to have been proved justified. That much Britain would grant and recognize the similarity of British and French interest; but Britain did not feel herself sufficiently diminished to become merely one member of an integrated Europe, while integration confined to the continent aroused in her quite as much suspicion as enthusiasm. Britain declined to take the leadership of a united Europe.

Thus the old problem of the Franco-German relationship once more looms large. The estimates of the extent of French power in 1939, legacy of the first war, had proved sadly mistaken; yet the picture was now overdrawn in reverse, legacy that it was of the French wartime performance in the second. French and German power were both after the war reduced to nonexistence; but potential remained. Allowing that the German potential is larger than the French, by reasons of geography, numbers, and resources, France remains unavoidably an important portion of Europe. The nature of Germany's wartime record moreover had had the effect that much of the 1919 French contention was now granted by the United States and Britain. France was thus granted guarantees as well as membership in the circle of Great Powers. But, clearly also, this membership was largely one of courtesy by contrast with the 1919 position. Fictions can be of use though they also contain the danger inherent in the distortion of existing fact. Formally, France was in the position of being one of the Powers controlling the fate of Germany; in effect, she was largely dependent. Her awareness of dependence, the memory of the humiliation of 1940, and the consciousness of current impotence, understandably made her unusually sensitive; already during the war, what seemed at times absurd grandiloquence, delusions of grandeur, and personal cantankerouness, on the part of General de Gaulle, which often irritated his allies, was in reality an effort to keep alive the future claim of France to a position of importance. The granting to her by others of a position that did not correspond to her existing power gave her the means of exerting at least momentarily disproportionate influence.

Yet for the longer term that influence, however diminished, could not but remain substantial. In simplest terms, to organize Europe without France does not seem a realistic undertaking. But would it be possible to make France the central piece in the organization of Europe? At this point further complications intervened. The outbreak of war in Korea in the summer of 1950 caused the United States to proceed beyond the general recovery of Europe to the stress on the prompt reconstruction of effective military power in Europe. That power at the time was very small, for stress, quite rightly, had been on economic reconstruction. The American aim, focused on the Russian danger, was the recreation of a number of German divisions.

Not in France alone did the prospect of German rearmament pose a painful dilemma. Yet France could not afford mere negation; the solution, for the moment, was found in the French proposal of the creation of an integrated European army in which German contingents would be merged with others, reminiscent in some respects of French proposals of twenty years before. Under the renewed pressure of danger, would Europe succeed in laying the bases for her integration, this time beginning at the military level? There was in France considerable support for the prospect of integration, though not at the military level at first. The proposal of Foreign Minister Schuman which was to lead to the organization of the European Coal and Steel Community may be regarded as a French attempt to reassert French leadership in Europe, though in a wholly different form and by means other than in 1919 of the mere maintenance of superior force.

The question may therefore be said to have been: was France equal to this task of leadership? And this question raised in turn the same question that was paramount during the interval between the wars: the nature, mode of operation, and effectiveness of the whole complex that is France. Two aspects of the matter must be considered at this point, which in broad terms may be labeled the physical and the moral.

The Second World War did not mean for France a bloodletting of the same magnitude as the first, though casualties arising from all sources were by no means negligible. But the physical destruction was greater in the total than on the earlier occasion; it was not sensationally concentrated in a limited area but spread throughout the land. In addition, the dislocation of the whole economy was thorough; German exactions during the occupation had been very large, and the burden of debt was enormous. The difficulties of the prewar period, both economic and financial, therefore reappeared, but they were greatly magnified in intensity. For France, as for other countries of Europe, the immediate postwar period was a dreary passage, but, especially after 1947, progress was both substantial and rapid. However, in the management of finance the same contrast appeared with Britain as during the interwar period; the result was budgetary deficits, inflation, devaluation, and the failure to reach a stable equilibrium in France.

Matters were complicated by the political impact of the war, which may be said in this respect to have greatly accelerated the trend begun in the thirties and of which the Popular Front was the clearest expression. As in Britain again, the state found it necessary to assume vastly increased responsibilities for the welfare of the people. Though less widely known than the British, the French program of social services is of a similar nature. The phenomenon is world wide for that matter; the advent of the welfare state is nothing but the extension of a long term trend, the rising of the masses coming into their own. Not only were social services vastly extended, but likewise the direct control of the state over a large section of industry; as in Britain, the immediate postwar period witnessed in France a rash of nationalizations.

This is not the place to debate the merits and shortcomings of the welfare state, a question which for that matter is becoming increasingly academic. More important than the issue of the abstract merits of free enterprise may be that of the quality of management of resources under whatever dispensation or system. In this respect the French has been deficient. Some excellent, even remarkable, accomplishments have taken place in France, the development of water power resources for instance, or the restoration of transportation, but the situation as a whole raised the question whether France had not undertaken more than her resources could bear. The simultaneous attempt to restore the physical damage of war, to institute a large program of social services, and to implement another ambitious program of industrial renovation and expansion, to which have been added the burdens of war in Indochina and then the reconstruction of military force at home, taken all together amount, in simplest form, to an impossible problem of financial arithmetic. There have been those in France, M. Mendès-France prominent among them, who for some time have claimed that France must cut her cloak to suit her cloth, in other words must choose which of her various undertakings she can afford to pursue, and just how much of each she can manage with prospects of success.

The potential resources of France remain considerable, and it has been shown that one of her prewar weaknesses lay in the operation of her body politic. That is the second, or moral if one will, aspect of her problem. After the demise of Vichy the question assumed therefore unusual significance of the shape that the political reconstruction of France would assume. It might have been expected that the shock of war, defeat, and occupation would have at least jarred the old mold into different shape. General de Gaulle, when he came back to France in 1944, stood as the symbol of a united nation; he enjoyed vast prestige and, as head of the provisional government, was possessed of considerable power. The traditional French suspicion of the man on horseback is deep and strong; Vichy if anything had confirmed its soundness. But in the fluid and confused aftermath of war and liberation the possibility existed of institutional reform. What the story would have been had General de Gaulle used his power to effect substantial transformations is futile surmise; the fact is that, whether mistakenly or wisely, he proved himself a respecter of the democratic tradition and practice and voluntarily surrendered his power.

France gave herself a new constitution that launched the Fourth Republic on its course. The instrument evoked passive rather than enthusiastic acceptance, and the Fourth Republic has been a close replica of the Third, to the point that the quip was made, even while it lasted, that the Fourth Republic was already dead and had been succeeded by the Third. Some added mechanical complications were introduced which served better the purpose of making the functioning of institutions more cumbrous and creaky rather than enhancing control by the people. General de Gaulle, ill suited to the normal game of politics, launched a movement, the *Rassemblement du Peuple Français*, intended as the name indicates to produce unity in the nation. The movement failed of its purpose; though disclaiming the characterization of political party, it became in fact largely that and its representatives in Parliament became increasingly integrated into the old time functioning of French politics.

Another novel constellation in the political firmament of France was the *Mouvement Républicain Populaire*. This group, of Catholic inspiration, is in the tradition of Christian Socialism, more familiar in Central Europe. It represents an effort to integrate the values of the Catholic tradition with the social realities of the modern world and fits into the tradition of which the papacy has at times made itself the exponent. French Catholicism continues, more than ever perhaps, to be a very vigorous growth, not so much in the sense of increased church attendance as because of the quality of intellect in its service. But this phenomenon, full of interest as it is, has limited political significance. The M.R.P. has a core whose social thought and policy are definitely progressive, not to say radical, but the great boom that it enjoyed immediately after the war was in considerable measure the result of the fact that much that was suspect because of its wartime support of Vichy thought to find shelter in the fold of the M.R.P. The party therefore does not provide so much a common ground for unity as an uneasy compromise. Its role has been important as the pivot of postwar coalitions, but in effect it was torn by internal divergences and found it difficult to compete with the clearer appeal of the traditional Right and Left.

The Extreme Left, the Communists, greatly benefited from the war. Their record in the Resistance gave them a seemingly authentic claim to the representation of the national interest, especially by contrast with the uninspired (to use the kindest epithet) role of the traditionally nationalistic Right during the Vichy episode. More important, however, was the response of a very large section of the French electorate to the basic failure of France to put her economic house in order. In this respect there was mere continuation of the trend of the thirties, going back to the Popular Front, but with the aggravation of conditions inevitably brought on by the war. It might be put this way: all shades of political persuasion, ranging from the Extreme Right to the Socialists, have had their day and their chance and all have failed; the result has been a deep sense of futility and despair, which, combined with the traditional appeal of the Left, just because it is Left, has produced the very large and stable Communist vote, nearly 30 percent of the total, in postwar France. It is often said, and with justice, that the Communist vote in France is in large measure a negative vote of protest. The contrast is significant between a stable Communist vote of about 5,000,000 and a steadily dwindling circulation of *L'Humanité,* the official organ of the party, until it sank to not much above the 100,000 figure. French Communists, like other Frenchmen, are free to exercise their choice of literature, and this freedom they do exercise.

But the most significant result of it all was that the effect of the war and its aftermath was not to produce unity in the French body politic. On the contrary, there was further fragmentation of the political spectrum, until the French National Assembly stood divided into six main groups of roughly comparable size. Not only this, but on many issues these groups stood divided within themselves; many questions of social policy for instance would command Communist and Socialist support as well as that of a section of the M.R.P. and of the Gaullist membership. There is much to be said for diversity in many aspects of human endeavor; it is a manifestation of freedom, and freedom in France remained very great. But the question arises whether this luxury France can afford; the stalemate in the field of political action has been indicated as one of the sources of strength of the extremes. Beyond a certain point the fact has to be faced that, precious as the value of free dissent may be, without independent existence freedom to differ can have little meaning. For more than four long years after 1940 the independent life of France did not exist.

That episode itself, as pointed out, in fact served to complicate divisions. During the days of Vichy there were unquestionable resisters just as there were outright collaborators. Both groups were minorities; the mass of the French people, as any people in such circumstances, sought to survive as best they could, bowing under the storm, accepting inescapable necessity. As a consequence, individual records are far from clear and the lines become hazy that separate collaborators from resisters, with a great opportunist core in between.

The hopes of political renovation were deceived, and the surprising, some would say distressing, thing is the extent to which the political life of France fell back into old grooves. The cause of this phenomenon lay in the fundamentals of the economic and social organization of France, of which her political structure and functioning are the reflection. That structure has shown remarkable imperviousness to change and justifies the seeming paradox that the difficulty in France arises

less from governmental instability than from a too stable rigidity that
the word ossification has sometimes been used to describe in less
attractive fashion. It is enlightening in this respect to contrast the
French and the American milieus for instance, where another seeming
paradox appears: France with a very large Communist vote and a
tradition of political radicalism appears as the essentially conservative
entity; America, afraid of largely non existent Communists lurking in
every corner, is the progressive one. Solid Republican business men
so devoted to free enterprise are highly radical in their outlook by
comparison with their French counterpart. M. Mendès-France is wholly
right in feeling that all mechanical arrangements have secondary importance to the fundamental necessity of economic renovation; a large
French military establishment unsupported by a sound economic structure
would give but a dangerously misleading illusion of strength, actually
might be a source of weakness through being too severe a drain on
the economy.

These things are no secret in France where there is no dearth of
intelligent people who perceive them with clarity and would essentially
agree with the foregoing analysis. Perhaps there is a certain source
of weakness in what is sometimes called the analytical quality of the
French mind — French mind meaning the product of historic tradition
as molded by a system of intellectual training: all too often a Frenchman will feel that, having analyzed and understood with clarity a
situation, the task has been completed and no further responsibility is
involved; decision with a view to action seems much less interesting
than speculation and analysis. Not a few have withdrawn into the
passivity of indifference, giving ground to the perennial charge of
decadence, while others have gone over to Communism, largely from the
feeling that nothing short of the upheaval that the advent of Communism
would produce would suffice to break the stifling mold of seemingly
unbreakable institutions and ways.

Yet there are those who retain confidence and hope, mainly from
the emergence of a new generation. Earlier in this essay the fact has
been pointed out of the consequence of the holocaust of the First World
War in the ranks of the potential leaders of the thirties. As the result
of the great gap the older leadership tended to be unusually prolonged,
and more than ever France became a gerontocracy. To a degree the
mere passage of time is remedying this situation; the remnants of the
First World War generation are inevitably fast disappearing, and a new
generation is rising that has not suffered the same decimation as its
elders, conditioned by the interwar rather than by pre-1914. In addition,
an interesting phenomenon has taken place in France. The usual postwar occurence of a spurt in the rate of births has been sustained in
France until the country has achieved one of the highest birth rates
among the Western nations. Whatever the reasons for this — social
policy perhaps, as some think — the fact is peculiarly striking in view
cf the very long and unique French record of stability of numbers. To
be sure, an annual increase of some 300,000 to 400,000, even if sustained,

will take a long time to alter the proportion of French numbers to others, and mere numbers no longer have in our industrial age the importance they had in the days of the man with the rifle as the basic unit of armies. But long before this happens, if it should happen, the age composition of the French people will undergo marked alteration. The combination of this fact with the coming of a new generation into the positions of leadership might, before long, have considerable consequences.

But, clearly, this is speculation and in any case would take time. Here and now France exists as she is, and being what she is the problem is for her to find her proper place in the community of nations. The fact that only a few years ago the place of France was so large and that as late as 1940 so much was expected of her very understandably makes readjustment all the more difficult and painful. Just because others had expected of her more than it was, under any circumstances, reasonable to expect, France is entitled to consideration and patience, from those especially who earlier declined to make a commensurate contribution to the common purpose of preserving the peace, meaning primarily America and Britain.

Whatever delusions of grandeur may have been entertained in France after the First World War — and they were not characteristic of the dominant temper — have effectively been laid to rest by the second. A measure of understandable discouragement in fact took their place and there are not a few in France who view the world of states as an unpleasant place, and the problems of the relationships of power as an unattractive game from which they would well be out. Circumstances being what they are, the great contest between organization and freedom, of which contending ideologies are the expression, has taken the more limited and concrete form of the contest between the two great centers of organized power of which the United States and the Soviet Union are the respective embodiments. All her tradition tends to put France in the camp of the former, yet there are those in France, as elsewhere, who would wish the quarrel away and put it in the simple form, a plague on both your houses. In France particularly, the feeling is strong that she has been too long the advanced sentinel of freedom; no nation can think of itself as expendable and resents others viewing it as such.

All this is understandable enough, even deserving of respect and sympathy; yet it is fundamentally wishful thinking that is beside the point. The mere facts of the physical totality that is France, if nothing else, preclude her suddenly shifting into the position that for some time has been Switzerland's or Sweden's; France constitutes too great and valuable an asset, standing at too important a crossroads; whether she would or no, she cannot escape the mainstream of contemporary issues and stresses.

In some respects the present position of France is reminiscent of that of twenty years ago. Then, too, the French people as a whole made an attempt to escape their responsibilities; they concentrated on their internecine quarrels and when confronted with the test of outside pressures — Nazi action at the time — they sought to dodge it through inaction. Failing other adequate leadership to take the place of their own, it was not long before the outcome was disaster, for them as well as for others. France to be sure stands in an exposed position — though the developments of the techniques of destruction are altering the significance of that fact — but if others have no special call on her to bear the burden of insuring *their* protection, the reverse is equally true. That line of argument, sometimes indulged in, is wholly barren and merely conducive to pointless emotional recrimination. France in the last analysis bears a responsibility to herself.

Yet not to herself alone, for though she no longer holds the central and crucial position that was hers twenty years ago, her decisions, or failure of decisions, cannot but have considerable effects on much of Europe and beyond that continent as well. So far she has failed to decide and there has been at times, especially in America, impatience with her tergiversations and difficulties, from the feeling that it was equally impossible to do with as to do without France. American impatience and annoyance is also wholly understandable; its effects and manifestations, at the official level, have, with occasional exceptions, been kept under control.

Two important decisions have taken place in France, the effects of which reached much beyond her borders. In the Far East, in Indochina, partly through faulty management after the war, France became involved in hostilities with the native forces desiring independence, increasingly entangled with and supported by outside Communist assistance. That war, conducted with complete lack of conviction and enthusiasm where the bulk of the French people were concerned, to the point that regular army recruits could not be used for it, was a huge drain on French resources that France could not afford, and absorbed a large part of the assistance given by America to France for her recovery at home. M. Mendès-France had for some time been one of the few men engaged in politics who had had the courage to proclaim that the costly and hopeless undertaking should be liquidated, and that the later this was done the more difficult extrication would be. It was one of the first acts of his administration, after he became Prime Minister in June, 1954, to negotiate an armistice in Indochina. Considering the unfavorable military position, he obtained unexpectedly favorable terms. Indochina will remain a problem, like Korea, but a problem for the whole free world and for America in particular; it is on balance a gain that France has shed a responsibility that she could ill afford to carry.

Another significant decision that has recently come from France concerns the reconstruction of military force in Europe, more specifically in Germany. It was a French plan, formulated as early as 1950, that became, with subsequent modifications, the basis of the European Defense Community. But the rearmament of Germany, in whatever form and however controlled, understandably aroused mixed reactions in France. For a long time, successive French governments, though professedly favoring the scheme, did not see their way to submitting it to the parliamentary test. It was again Mendès-France who undertook to put an end to this procrastination; the result was rejection of the plan in August, 1954. The subsequent dismay, especially American, was perhaps premature, for alternative solutions were immediately forthcoming.

It is out of the problems of empire that an unexpected turn has taken place. Mendès-France had succeeded in liquidating the Indochinese imbroglio; he also laid the bases for the peaceful transition of the Tunisian and Moroccan protectorates to independence, thereby inaugurating a possibly fruitful new line of imperial policy. For it was becoming clear that the reorganization attempted after the war in the form of the French Union was not an adequate solution to the changing conditions of the dependent world. However, Mendès-France did not long survive these accomplishments, falling victim to the play of customary politics and to the limitations of a somewhat intransigeant personality.

He had served the useful purpose of effecting a difficult transition, but had no time to launch a program of more fundamental reforms of the French domestic milieu. However, North African affairs again intruded in the form, this time, of rebellion in Algeria, that was launched in November, 1954. Algeria is no protectorate, but constitutionally part of France herself. If the prospect of service in Algeria commanded little enthusiasm from the bulk of young French conscripts, Algeria was not Indochina; it is too close to France, and it also contains a substantial French population. Of the dreary tale, unresolved at this writing, it will suffice to say that Algeria increasingly absorbed the French army, correspondingly withdrawn from Europe, and that increasingly also the Algerian question had repercussions in France herself. There was not a little discontent in the army, whose leaders smarted under the lengthening record of humiliations, and also, not altogether without reason, felt that the armed forces to a degree at least were victims of irresponsible political behavior at home.

The accumulating tension finally reached breaking point when, in May, 1958, the possibility of a military coup in France became a real threat. The outcome was rather surprising. Faced with a serious challenge, the leaders of the Fourth Republic essentially decided on surrender; with not a little skill, they navigated through a difficult passage which led to the assumption of the Prime Ministership by General de Gaulle.

Thus the Fifth Republic was born, for de Gaulle would only govern on his own terms, and one of the first tasks of the new government was the drafting of a new constitution that vests considerable power in the executive. The reform of the state, favorite theme of twenty years ago, had at last been effected, and de Gaulle became President.

The Fourth Republic died unmourned, and there is no denying that the political management of France had run into an impasse. But it is also well to consider that history may take not too severe a view of the difficult period. During the thirteen years of its duration, and under the appearence of everlasting stalemate and confusion, much had been done, most important two things. Not only had the economic recovery of France been successfully accomplished, but the hope could be entertained that the French economy might finally emerge from the rut of stagnation that had characterized it before the war; behind the façade of political disorder, a whole group of younger men, of whom Jean Monnet is the best known representative, quietly labored to renovate the ways of French industry and to bring the whole economy in line with those of more progressive nations. Should the attempt, still in process, prove successful, it will have truly revolutionary impact. A price was paid for this in the form of inflation; French finances, again, have not been managed like British.

One reason for the paying of this price lies in the same political legacy of the past, that prevented the adoption of certain measures. And this touches upon the other significant accomplishment of the Fourth Republic. There could be no question in France of disfranchising between a quarter and a third of the electorate that consistently voted for the Communist Party, a party thoroughly subservient to the dictates of the Kremlin. Nor was this ever suggested or attempted, though the Communists were with skill evicted from participation in the government in 1947. Thus it may be said that the Fourth Republic, essentially with success, conducted an operation, in the economic domain comparable to the Russian, but without the resort to Muscovite methods of suppression. Here also a price had to be paid, the normal game of French politics.

But that price was in the end too high, and the inability to deal with the imperial problem brought down the Fourth Republic at last. It must be left to history to unfold, then to appraise, the record of the newly born Fifth Republic, but something must be said of the present situation.

The most significant aspect of the Fifth Republic so far has been its identification with one man; the present government of France *is* General de Gaulle. And in this very fact many, in France and abroad, perceive a weakness and a danger, for a man is not a system. The best that may be hoped is that his power and prestige may serve to introduce modifications in the political system of France that may prove of lasting and stable value. If France has cause to fear a strong executive, neither is it inevitably foregone that history is fated forever to repeat itself — the institution of a strong executive had served America well — but this is clearly a matter for the future to reveal.

When he came to the Presidency of France, General de Gaulle had already achieved an established position in the annals of his country from the role that he had played during the Second World War. In-

evitably a controversial figure, he is all the more so from fitting ill into
the normal categories of politics and politicians, primarily a military
man thrust by events into a political role.   The gibes of a former
American President rather revealed limited comprehension and perhaps
dubious taste; Churchill made a sounder appraisal.

Two things should be mentioned about the Fifth Republic and de
Gaulle, aspects of his fundamental desire to restore France to a position
of respect and power.   They may be placed under the heads of imperial
and European.   There is not a little irony in the fact that, considering
the forces that secured his advent to power, de Gaulle should have
thrown the French empire — community, or union as one will — into a
state of total constitutional turmoil.   What the outcome may be, we do
not know, but a stalemate has been broken, in place of which a fluid
condition has been created.   The personal reception given de Gaulle in
overseas territories, not excluding Algeria, by the native populations,
is, to say the least, a highly interesting phenomenon.

Considering likewise de Gaulle's own past record, it is of equal
interest to contemplate the close cooperation between himself and
Chancellor Adenauer of the German Federal Republic.   The story of
Franco-German relations is a continuing one, but it is taking place in
a novel context.   One interesting aspect of it, on the French side, is
a different temper from that which prevailed after the First World War.
Though no love may be lost and doubts persist, there is in France a
far greater willingness to accept the view that the solution of force is,
for the long term, an unfruitful one.   There can be no question this
time of the extent of Germany's defeat; but the French defeat of 1940
is a more substantial reality than the formal acceptance of France in the
ranks of the victors.   Equality in defeat may create a more favorable
climate than the false and transitory relationship of power that the
First World War had established; the unquestionable demotion of both
French and German power vis-à-vis the rest of the world works to the
same effect.   Of the sincerity of Adenauer's repudiation of the works
of Nazism there is no reason to doubt, any more than there is of de
Gaulle's patriotic devotion.   Perhaps de Gaulle's greatest political asset
lies in his refusal to abide by the traditional laws of French politics,
as his ten year retirement would seem to indicate.   Legacy of the past
though he may be, imbued with the concept of French grandeur to a
degree that some have called pathological, he has certain qualities of
flexibility and open-mindedness that may enable him to face the new
world with fresh ideas; he it was after all who showed these same
qualities in his own chosen military field a quarter of a century ago.

The future of Franco-German relations is full of uncertainties, and
the present importance of two men may itself constitute a risk, to say
nothing of the fact that the Frenchman is no longer in his prime while
the German is definitely ancient.   These two men, however, represent
not themselves alone, but deeper forces that exist in their respective
countries; it is upon the real depth and strength of these forces that the

future course of Franco-German relations depends. Nor should one be blind to the fact that the possibilities of deviation from the path of cooperation are numerous. Even the present formal position of France constitutes an advantage, and it is not hard to conceive of Adenauer playing a role in Germany comparable to that of Stresemann in paving the way for the restoration of German power. Thus, much depends upon the temper of the German people as well, a temper which for that matter may alter under the impact of unforeseen circumstances. The German military record is both impressive and disturbing, but it is worth considering that it is not so very long ago that the French people themselves graduated in sufficient numbers from the appeal of military glory. Should an era of Franco-German cooperation materialize, the possibilities of it would be enormous, ranging all the way to a federal Europe, for the combined power of the two countries would constitute a very large focus of attraction for the rest of the Continent.

Likewise the imperial domain remains full of uncertainties. Close economic cooperation between North Africa and not only France but all of Western Europe, especially after the discovery of large sources of energy in the Sahara, is a most logical solution on which the most glowing prospects can be built. But nationalism is not a rational force, though both real and potent.

In the French case, much depends upon the ability of the whole complex that is France in adapting itself to the changed circumstances of a fast changing world, different from anything previously known in the history of man. Substantial alterations in economic practice could not but go hand in hand with profound social repercussions. It might be said in fact that the fundamental roots of the problem are sociological and cultural. French society in its fundamentals has been of a highly conservative cast, for all the radicalism of thought that thrives in its midst. The very quality of French culture is in some ways an obstacle to change; the fundamental tone of that culture, to put it in somewhat simplified form, remains mathematical and literary, in a world where physical and natural science and technology have become the dominant molders of change. There was point in Mendès-France's observation that it was many years since a Nobel prize in the sciences had gone to France. To a considerable degree, unconsciously or consciously, many representatives and carriers of French culture are fearful of the novel face of things, of which, in their different ways, yet with a surprising degree of common ground, America and Russia are the outstanding expressions. Their fears that many values are threatened by the trends of the modern world are wholly justified; in that context it is quite understandable, in a sense appropriate, that in France should be heard the harshest words about America; for, among Western states, France is the most recalcitrant to the new influences and values which America does in fact represent. America often exalts the value of individualism; this devotion is usually genuine in its expression, but it is also sometimes lip service and the result of looking back to older, bygone days. America in actual practice stands for the mass and much conformity, and the stress is increasingly — wholly well-meant in general — on the individual fitting harmoniously into the larger social whole: that is the way to achieve happiness. Failure to fit is not yet a sin, but it is increasingly looked upon as calling for remedial action.

But at this point it may be relevant to quote Galileo when confronted with all the weight of evidence that blind conservative tradition could muster: *Eppur si muove!* For good or ill, with purpose unrevealed — if any purpose — the world does move. It was pointed out in the opening pages of this essay that as important as any single characteristic of the modern age has been the rising of the mass. What shape the mass will give to things — whether at last the millennium of freedom with nature fully subjugated to man, or a new form of slavery — we do not know. But on the new phenomenon, mass man and mass production, there is no going back short of annihilation. Whatever hope there is, if any, that man may still be master of his fate and captain of his soul, lies not in any case in looking back. In the acceptance of irrevocable trends lies the only hope of survival; intelligent adaptation to them may make it possible to salvage and retain some at least of those values and qualities rooted in the long past, the disappearance of which would be unquestionable loss; else life — so long as there is life — will proceed unmindful of resistance which, either abruptly and brutally, or with possible gradualness, but no less effectively in the end, it will crush and destroy. The whole wide world is the stage of that struggle, but the sharpness of it is unusually marked on the French battleground which, whether in terms of physical position or in terms of the contending forces of the spirit, lies at the very center of it.

The history of France is long and rich. Her own Great Revolution, if it did not wholly initiate the struggle for the Rights of Man, the course of which has led us to our present quandary, certainly gave that trend one of its major impulses. France may of course repeat the record of eighteenth century Spanish decline, but France is at the moment still too important a factor in European, not to say world, affairs, merely to withdraw from the scene. She is inevitably caught in the changes taking place in Europe, of which economic resurgence is not the least significant. The circumstances of the present day lend special interest to the development of the French scene on which one may expect to witness Triumph or Tragedy.

BIBLIOGRAPHY

Given the scope of the work and the nature of the treatment, an exhaustive bibliography would reach immense proportions, including documentary sources, periodical literature, the press, and a host of individual works, memoirs and studies. No attempt has been made to cover the field with such thoroughness, and the works listed below constitute therefore no more than a sampling of the relevant material.

Of particular value for following developments as they unfolded are the two publications of the Royal Institute of International Affairs, *Survey of International Affairs* and its companion *Documents on International Affairs*. The American quarterly *Foreign Affairs*, besides important articles, contains useful annotated bibliographies of current publications, which, in addition, have been conveniently gathered in the three volumes, *Foreign Affairs Bibliography*, that cover respectively the periods 1922-1932, 1932-1942, and 1942-1952. The French weekly *Europe Nouvelle* and the weekly digests of the press published by the French Ministry of Foreign Affairs, *Bulletin périodique de la presse*, have also been found very valuable. So has the weekly publication *Relazioni internazionali* of the Milanese *Istituto per gli Studi di Politica Internazionale*. Among documentary publications those of the United States government have relatively little bearing on the events covered in this work, while those of German source are still in the main not available for the period under consideration.

Abernon, Edgar Vincent Viscount d', *An Ambassador of Peace,* 3 vols. (London, 1929-1930).

Abetz, Otto, *Histoire d'une politique franco-allemande, 1930-1940. Mémoires d'un ambassadeur* (Paris, 1953).

Ackerman, Martin, *Quelques aspects de l'opinion publique en France sur le problème allemand 1920-1940* (Paris, 1940).

Albord, Tony, *Pourquoi cela est-il arrivé ou les responsabilités d'une génération militaire 1919-1939* (Nantes, 1946).

Albrecht-Carrié, René, *Italy at the Paris Peace Conference* (New York, 1938).

Angell, Norman, *The Great Illusion* (London and New York, 1910).

Bailey, Thomas A., *Woodrow Wilson and the Lost Peace* (New York, 1944).

Baker, Ray Stannard, *Woodrow Wilson and the World Settlement,* 3 vols. (New York, 1923).

Benoist-Méchin, Jacques, *Histoire de l'armée allemande,* 2 vols. (Paris, 1938). vol. II: *De la Reichswehr à l'armée nationale 1919-1936.*

Bergmann, Carl, *The History of Reparations* (London and Boston, 1927).

Bernanos, Georges, *La grande peur des bien pensants* (Paris, 1931).

Beuve-Méry, Hubert, *Réflexions politiques 1932-1952* (Paris, 1952).

Birdsall, Paul, *Versailles Twenty Years After* (New York, 1941).

Bloch, Georges, *La crise économique actuelle en France* (Dijon, 1933).

Blum, Léon, *A l'échelle humaine* (Paris, 1945).

— *Problèmes de la paix* (Paris, 1931).

Brasillach, Robert, *Notre avant-guerre* (Paris, 1941).

Bréal, Auguste, *Philippe Berthelot* (Paris, 1937).

Bresciani-Turoni, Costantino, *The Economics of Inflation; A study of Currency Depreciation in Post-war Germany* (London, 1937).

Carré, Jean-Marie, *Les écrivains français et le mirage allemand* (Paris, 1947).

Castellan, Georges, *Le réarmement clandestin du Reich 1930-1935* (Paris, 1954).

Chamberlain, Austen, *Down the Years* (London, 1935).

Chastenet, Jacques, *Raymond Poincaré* (Paris, 1948).

Chateaubriant, Alphonse de, *La gerbe des forces* (Paris, 1937).

Christopoulos, Georges, *La politique extérieure de l'Italie* (Paris, 1936).

Churchill, Winston S., *The Second World War*, 6 vols. (London, 1948-1954). vol. I: *The Gathering Storm*.

Ciasca, Raffaele, *Storia coloniale dell' Italia contemporanea* (Milan, 1940).

Clemenceau, Georges, *Grandeurs et misères d'une victoire* (Paris, 1930).

Daniel-Rops, Henry, *Les années tournantes* (Paris, 1932).

Déak, Francis, *Hungary at the Paris Peace Conference: The Diplomatic History of the Treaty of Trianon* (New York, 1942).

Delaisi, Francis, *La bataille de l'or* (Paris, 1933).

Drieu La Rochelle, Pierre, *Chronique politique 1934-1942* (Paris, 1943).

Droz, Jacques, *Histoire de l'Allemagne* (Paris, 1945).

Drucker, Peter, *The End of Economic Man; a Study of the New Totalitarianism* (New York, 1939).

Duhamel, Georges, *Positions françaises* (Paris, 1940).

Duroselle, J.-B., *Histoire diplomatique de 1919 à nos jours* (Paris, 1953).

Fabre-Luce, Alfred, *Locarno sans rêves* (Paris, 1927).

Fabry, Jean, *De la Place de la Concorde au Cours de l'Intendance* (Paris, 1942).

Feis, Herbert, *Europe the World's Banker, 1870-1914* (New Haven and London, 1930).

Flandin, Pierre-Etienne, *Politique française, 1919-1940* (Paris, 1947).

Fleming, D.F., *The United States and the League of Nations* (New York, 1932).

Florinsky, Michael T., *World Revolution and the U.S.S.R.* (New York, 1933).

Foerster, F.W., *Europe and the German Question* (New York, 1940).

France, Assemblée Nationale, Première Législature. Session de 1947. *Les événements survenus en France de 1933 à 1945*, 11 vols. (Paris, n.d.).

France, Ministère des Affaires Etrangères, *Documents diplomatiques: Conférence de Washington, juillet 1921 - février 1922* (Paris, 1923).

François-Poncet, André, *Souvenirs d'une ambassade à Berlin, septembre 1931- octobre 1938* (Paris, 1946).

Gatzke, Hans W., *Stresemann and the Rearmement of Germany* (Baltimore, 1946).

Giraudoux, Jean, *Pleins pouvoirs* (Paris, 1939).

Goguel, François, *La politique des partis sous la troisième république* (Paris, 1946).

Great Britain, *Documents on British Foreign Policy, 1919-1939,* edited by E. L. Woodward and Rohan Butler (London, 1947—).
  Series I: 1919-1929; Series II: 1929-1938; Series III: 1938-1939.

Gulick, Charles A., *Austria from Habsburg to Hitler,* 2 vols. (Berkeley and Los Angeles, 1948).

Herriot, Edouard, *Jadis, d'une guerre à l'autre 1914-1936* (Paris, 1952).

Holborn, Hajo, *The Political Collapse of Europe* (New York, 1951).

House, Edward M., *The Intimate Papers of Colonel House,* arranged as a narrative by Charles Seymour, 4 vols., (Boston, 1926-1928).

Howe, Quincy, *The World Between the Wars* (New York, 1953).

Italy, Ministero degli Affari Esteri, *I Documenti Diplomatici Italiani* (Rome, 1952—).
  Serie V: 3 agosto 1914 - 4 novembre 1918
  Serie VI: 5 novembre 1918 - 30 ottobre 1922
  Serie VII: 31 ottobre 1922 - 14 aprile 1935
  Serie VIII: 15 aprile 1935 - 3 settembre 1939

Jordan, W.M., *Great Britain, France and the German Problem, A Study of Anglo-French Relations in the Making and Maintenance of the Versailles Settlement* (London, 1944).

Jouvenel, Bertrand de, *D'une guerre à l'autre,* 2 vols. (Paris, 1940-1941).

Kérillis, Henri de, *Français, voici la guerre* (Paris, 1936).

Keynes, John Maynard, *The Economic Consequences of the Peace* (London and New York, 1920).

Lafue, Pierre, *Gaston Doumergue* (Paris, 1933).

La Pradelle, A. Geouffre de, *La paix moderne 1899-1945* (Paris, 1947).

Laroche, Jules, *La Pologne de Pilsudski, souvenirs d'une ambassade, 1926-1935* (Paris, 1953).

Lloyd George, David, *The Truth About the Peace Treaty,* 2 vols. (London, 1938).

Mandelstam, André, *Le conflit italo-éthiopien devant la Société des Nations* (Paris, 1937).

Mantoux, Etienne, *The Carthaginian Peace, or The Economic Consequences of Mr. Keynes* (New York, 1952).

Mantoux, Paul, *Les délibérations du Conseil des Quatre,* 2 vols. (Paris, 1955).

Marston, F. S., *The Peace Conference of 1919, Organization and Procedure* (London and New York, 1944).

Martel, René, *La France et la Pologne, réalités de l'Est européen* (Paris, 1931).

Massis, Henri, *L'honneur de servir* (Paris, 1937).

— *La guerre de trente ans* (Paris, 1940).

Maurice, Frederick, *The Armistices of 1918* (London and New York, 1943).

Mermeix (pseud., Gabriel Terrail), *Le combat des Trois* (Paris, 1922).

Micaud, Charles, *The French Right and Nazi Germany, 1933-1939; A Study of Public Opinion* (Durham, N.C., 1943).

Milhaud, Albert, *Histoire du Radicalisme* (Paris, 1951).

Miller, David Hunter, *The Drafting of the Covenant*, 2 vols. (New York, 1928).

Monzie, Anatole de, *La saison des juges* (Paris, 1943).

Myers, D. P., *The Reparation Settlement, 1930* (Boston, 1930).

— *World Disarmament, Its Problems and Prospects* (Boston, 1932).

Namier, Lewis B., *Europe in Decay* (London, 1950).

Nicolson, Harold, *Peacemaking, 1919* (London and Boston, 1933).

Nouvelle Revue Française, September 1952, "Hommage à Alain" (Paris, 1952).

Ormesson, Wladimir d', *Confiance en l'Allemagne?* (Paris, 1928).

Pascal, Roy, *The Growth of Modern Germany* (London, 1946).

Paul-Boncour, Joseph, *Entre deux guerres: souvenirs sur la III* République*, 3 vols. (Paris, 1946). Vols. II and III.

Perticone, Giacomo, *La politica italiana nell'ultimo trentennio*, 3 vols. (Rome, 1945-1947).

Pertinax (pseud., André Géraud), *Les fossoyeurs* (New York, 1943).

Pingaud, Albert, *Histoire diplomatique de la France pendant la Grande Guerre*, 2 vols., (Paris, 1938).

Renouvin, Pierre, *Histoire des relations internationales*. Vols. VII, VIII: *Les crises du XX* siècle* (Paris, 1957-1958).

Reynaud, Paul, *Le problème militaire français* (Paris, 1937).

— *Jeunesse, quelle France veux-tu?* (Paris, 1936).

Ronde, Hans, *Von Versailles bis Lausanne* (Stuttgart, 1950).

Rossi, A., *Physiologie du parti communiste français* (Paris, 1948).

Rougemont, Denis de, *Journal d'Allemagne* (Paris, 1938).

Royal Institute of International Affairs, *International Sanctions* (London, 1938).

Rudin, Harry R., *Armistice 1918* (New Haven, 1944).

Salata, Francesco, *Il nodo di Gibuti* (Milan, 1939).

Salvemini, Gaetano, *Prelude to World War II* (New York, 1954).

Sauvy, Alfred, *Le pouvoir et l'opinion* (Paris, 1949).

Schmidt, Paul, *Statist auf diplomatischer Bühne, 1923-1945* (Bonn, 1949).

Schriftgiesser, Karl, *The Gentleman from Massachusetts, Henry Cabot Lodge* (Boston, 1944).

Sédillot, René, *Le Franc; histoire d'une monnaie des origines à nos jours* (Paris, 1953).

Sforza, Carlo, *Makers of Modern Europe* (Indianapolis, 1930).

Siegfried, André, *France, A Study in Nationality* (New Haven and London, 1930).

Sieburg, Friedrich, *Dieu est-il français?* (Paris, 1930).

Spengler, Oswald, *The Decline of the West*, 2 vols. (New York, 1927).

Stresemann, Gustav, *Gustav Stresemann: His Diaries, Letters and Papers*, 3 vols. (London, 1935-1940).

Suarez, Georges, *Briand, sa vie, son œuvre*, 6 vols. (Paris, 1938-1952).

Szembeck, Comte Jean, *Journal 1933-1939* (Paris, 1952).

Tabouis, Geneviève, *They Called Me Cassandra* (New York, 1942).

Tardieu, André, *La paix* (Paris, 1920).

—   *Devant l'obstacle, l'Amérique et nous* (Paris, 1927).

—   *L'heure de la décision* (Paris, 1934).

Temperley, Harold W. V., *A History of the Peace Conference of Paris* 6 vols. (London, 1920-1924).

Templewood, Samuel Hoare Viscount, *Nine Troubled Years* (London, 1954).

Thibaudet, Albert, *Les idées politiques de la France; la république des professeurs* (Paris, 1932).

Times, The [London], *The History of The Times*, vol. IV, *The 150th Anniversary and Beyond*, 1912-1948, Part I (1912-1920); Part II (1921-1948) (London, 1952).

Tirard, Paul, *La France sur le Rhin. Douze années d'occupation rhénane* (Paris, 1930).

Toynbee, Arnold J., *The World After the Peace Conference* (London and New York, 1925).

Trotter, Wilfred, *Instincts of the Herd in Peace and War, 1916-1919* (London, 1953).

United States, *Department of State, Foreign Relations of the United States, The Paris Peace Conference, 1919*, 13 vols. (Washington, 1942-1947).

Vaucher, P. and P.H. Siriex, *L'opinion britannique, la Société des Nations et la guerre italo-éthiopienne* (Paris, 1936).

Wambaugh, Sarah, *The Saar Plebiscite* (Cambridge, Mass., 1940).

Weill-Reynal, Etienne, *Les réparations allemandes et la France*, 3 vols. (Paris, 1948).

Wentzcke, Paul, *Ruhrkampf, Einbruch und Abwehr im rheinisch-westfälischen Industriegebiet*, 2 vols. (Berlin, 1930).

Werth, Alexander, *The Destiny of France* (London, 1937).

—   *France in Ferment* (London, 1934).

—   *The Twilight of France, 1933-1940* (New York, 1942).

Wheeler-Bennett, John W., *The Nemesis of Power: The German Army in Politics, 1918-1945* (New York, 1953).

—   *The Wreck of Reparations* (London, 1933).

—   *Disarmament and Security Since Locarno, 1925-1931* (New York, 1932).

—   *The Pipe Dream of Peace: The Story of the Collapse of Disarmament* (New York, 1935).

—   and Hugh Latimer, *Information on the Reparation Settlement* (London, 1930).

Wolfers, Arnold, *Britain and France Between Two Wars: Conflicting Strategies of Peace Since Versailles* (New York, 1940).

Zoli, Corrado, *La conquista dell' Impero* (Bologna, 1937).

INDEX